modern video production

modern video production
tools, techniques, applications

Carl Hausman
The Center for Media in the
Public Interest

with

Philip J. Palombo
Rhode Island College

HarperCollins*CollegePublishers*

Acquisitions Editor: Daniel F. Pipp
Developmental Editor: Michael Buchman
Project Editor: Katharine Glynn
Design Supervisor: Molly Heron
Text Design: Edward Smith Design, Inc.
Cover Design: Kay Petronio
Cover Photos: Elizabeth Cruise/Image Works (right); Bob Daemmrich/Image Works
(middle); Bill Bachmann/Image Works (left)
Text Art: Edward Smith Design, Inc.
Photo Researcher (interior): Rosemary Hunter
Photo Researcher (cover): Mira Schachne
Production Administrator: Valerie A. Sawyer
Director of Production/Manufacturing: Kewal K. Sharma
Compositor: Waldman Graphics, Inc.
Printer and Binder: R. R. Donnelley & Sons Company
Cover Printer: The Lehigh Press, Inc.

MODERN VIDEO PRODUCTION: TOOLS, TECHNIQUES, APPLICATIONS

Library of Congress Cataloging-in-Publication Data
Hausman, Carl, 1953–
    Modern video production: tools, techniques, applications / Carl
Hausman with Philip J. Palombo.
      p.   cm.
    Includes bibliographical references and index.
    ISBN 0-06-500045-5
    1. Video recordings—Production and direction.   2. Television—
Production and direction.   I. Palombo, Philip J.   II. Title.
PN1992.94.H38   1993
791.45′0232—dc20   92-38525
                                          CIP

95 96   9 8 7 6 5 4 3

contents

Chapter 7   The Switcher and Edit Control Unit   96

Part 2   The Techniques   109

Chapter 8   Camera Operation   110

Chapter 9   Lighting Techniques   122

Chapter 10   Operating the Switcher   138

Modern Video Production is about using video to communicate ideas. It covers all major aspects of equipment, operation, production, and direction. Even so, it does not pretend that operating video equipment is an end in itself. Video is a means to an end, and that end is *communication*.

This book has been designed as a *teaching* tool. Although the chapters cover equipment structure and use, the information is presented on a need-to-know basis. No one can absorb all the details of a new subject at once. Anyone who has taught video production knows how frustrating—indeed, paralyzing—it is to attempt to force-feed a chapter on every permutation of camera operations to students in the same week they first lay hands on the camera. *Modern Video Production* is organized to cycle students through the production process several times. The bare necessities are taught first, the basic rules of operation come later, and the ways one might creatively break those rules come next.

ORGANIZED TO FOCUS ON COMMUNICATION

The text is divided into 4 parts with a total of 22 chapters. Part 1, "The Tools," gets students up to speed as quickly as possible so that they can quickly, effectively, and safely operate (and understand) the video equipment at the most basic level. In Chapters 1 to 7 we discuss the field of video production (including off-air and broadcast video). We also introduce readers to the studio facility, the camera, lighting instruments, microphones and audio equipment, video units, the switcher, and the edit control unit.

Part 2, "The Techniques," builds on fundamental skills and knowledge. Now that readers can handle the basic controls and find the right switches, they're guided through the ways equipment is used to produce quality pictures and evocative concepts and ideas. Chapters 8 to 14 deal with camera operations, lighting techniques, switcher operations, and operation of the edit control unit. These chapters also discuss audio production techniques and scripting for video and graphics.

Part 3, "The Applications," is where the use of tools and techniques come together in the types of projects students are likely to produce in the second half of the course. In Chapters 15 to 20 we show readers, *by explicit description and example*, how to direct, how to edit, how to manage out-of-studio shoots. We also give specifics on how to produce and direct talk shows, news programs, documentaries, dramas, sports broadcasts, and other formats.

Part 4, "Specialized Operations," deals with the new equipment and techniques that make video such an exciting, ever-evolving field. Chapter 21 is a primer on engineering—a necessity now that so many so-called engineering functions have migrated to the realm of the operator. Chapter 22, an absolute requisite for modern production, addresses the role of computers in desktop video. Chapter 22 also looks toward the future and presents readers with some basic forward-looking information that will supply a framework for evaluating the galloping advances of video technology.

WRITTEN TO PROVIDE PRACTICAL LEARNING AND TEACHING TOOLS

- To direct study, chapters begin with a set of *objectives* and end with a *summary* of main points.
- Technical terms are printed in bold and defined upon first use. These terms are defined in the Glossary for easy reference.
- Chapters include *exercises* that require students to apply the principles discussed.
- *Procedural walk-throughs* using "hypothetical" equipment prepare students for labs.
- *Safety tips and checklists* offer clear, sound advice on equipment use.
- *Labeled illustrations* make points quickly. Photos show a realistic view of what the camera operator will see because in many cases illustrations of video shots have been produced by digitizing the actual output of the camera.
- *Boxed feature stories* offer interesting sidebars to technical subjects.

WRITTEN IN PLAIN ENGLISH

Our aim is to communicate a technical subject in a simple and lively style. Because video producers are frequently responsible for the full range of production duties, we have included a great deal of technical information. But we have made a deliberate effort to communicate that information clearly, and without overwhelming detail.

Modern Video Production is an alternative to equipment-based, encyclopedic texts that may overwhelm video novices. Students want to get up and running as quickly as possible, and you, the instructor, probably share that goal. This book was written with all of you in mind.

SUPPLEMENTARY MATERIALS

The *Instructor's Manual*, which supplements *Modern Video Production*, includes three essay questions, five multiple-choice questions, and five fill-in-the-blank questions for each chapter. Activities for each chapter are also included, along with transparency masters.

Carl Hausman
Philip J. Palombo

acknowledgments

First, our thanks to Carol Ranson Palombo who lent her artistic direction to the creation of many of the illustrations. We would also like to express our appreciation to the many reviewers who gave generously of their time and knowledge and who offered valuable suggestions and direction throughout the many drafts of the manuscript. For their thoughtful critiques and insightful comments, we thank the following:

Lewis Barlow
Boston University

David Black
University of Tennessee, Knoxville

Steve Buss
California State University,
Sacramento

Sanjeev Chatterjee
Emerson College

Robert Eubanks
Sam Houston State University

Alan Foucault
Northern Essex Community College

Dana Hawkes
Palomar College

Mike Hilt
University of Nebraska, Omaha

Bob Hunter
Ferris State University

Vincent Ialenti
Mount Wachusett Community
College

Dennis Lynch
University of Akron

Robert MacLauchlin
Colorado State University

Ron Osgood
Indiana University

John Pennybacker
Loyola University

George Rogers
California State University, Chico

Gay Russell
Grossmont College

Michael Silbergleid
University of Alabama

Richard H. Simpson
University of North Carolina

Kalman Socolof
Herkimer County Community
College

Donald Wylie
San Diego State University

Fred Wyman
Ferris State University

credits

TEXT CREDITS

Box 1.1 MTV Meets Big Business. From "MTV at 10: The Beat Goes On," in *TV Guide*, August 3, 1991, pp. 4–5. Reprinted with permission from TV Guide® Magazine. Copyright © 1991 by News America Publications Inc.

Box 1.2 Electric Trains for Grown-Ups. From Midgley, Leslie, *How Many Words Do You Want? An Insider's Stories of Print and Television Journalism*, 1989, Birch Lane Press, New York, page 265.

Box 7.2 The Reaction Shot: Is Editing Ethical? From McCabe, Bruce, "A Hollywood Version of TV News and the Industry's Reaction to It," *Boston Globe*, January 3, 1988, p B3.

Box 17.2 Bulletproof Vests for Videographers? From Premack, John, "Straight from the Shoulder," in *The Communicator*, June 1990; p. 20.

Box 18.2 . . . It's an Infomercial. From "Honey, Cover the Kids' Eyes! It's an Infomercial!" *People Weekly*, April 29, 1991, pp. 44–51, © 1991 Time Inc.

Box 19.1 In the *60 Minutes* Mailbox. From *Minute by Minute* by Don Hewitt. Copyright © 1985 by Don Hewitt and CBS, Inc. Reprinted by permission of Random House, Inc.

Box 19.2 The Viewer as Anchor. From Ellerbee, Linda, "The Viewer as Anchor," in *The Newsday Magazine*, December 9, 1990, p. 11.

Figure 19.2 Courtesy of Carl Ginsburg, CBS Evening News.

Figure 19.3 Courtesy of Carl Ginsburg, CBS Evening News.

Box 22.1 Electronic Paint Systems Tell the Story Pictorially. From Schmerler, David, "Electronic Paint Systems Tell the Story Pictorially," in *RTNDA Communicator*, October 1989, pp. 10–11.

PHOTO CREDITS

Chapter 1   Figures 1.1, 1.2, 1.3, 1.6 Photos by Philip J. Palombo.

Chapter 2   Figures 2.1, 2.3, 2.4, 2.5, 2.6, 2.7, 2.11, 2.12, 2.14, 2.18, 2.19, 2.20, 2.21, 2.22, 2.25, 2.26 Photos by Philip J. Palombo. Figure 2.13 by Carl Hausman.

Chapter 3   Figures 3.5, 3.6, 3.7, 3.8, 3.11. 3.12, 3.13, 3.14, 3.15, 3.16. 3.18 Photos by Philip J. Palombo. Fig-

ure 3.17 Courtesy of Panasonic Broadcast & Television Systems.

Chapter 4   Figures 4.1, 4.2, 4.12, 4.14, 4.16, 4.18, 4.19, 4.23, 4.26 Photos by Philip J. Palombo. Figures 4.5, 4.6, 4.7 Photos by Philip J. Palombo and Gary Bellerose. Figure 4.13, 4.24 Photos by John Hyde.

Chapter 5   Figures 5.8, 5.11, 5.14 Photos by John Hyde. Figures 5.17, 5.19, 5.20, 5.22, 5.23 Photos by Philip J. Palombo. Figure 5.12 Courtesy of Audio Technica US Inc.

Chapter 6   Figure 6.1, 6.4, 6.7, 6.12, 6.16, 6.17, 6.23 Photos by Philip J. Palombo. Figure 6.13, 6.15, 6.18, 6.19, 6.20, 6.21, 6.22 Photos by John Hyde.

Chapter 7   Figure 7.6, 7.10 Photos by Philip J. Palombo. Figure 7.11 Courtesy of Sony Corporation of America.

Chapter 8   Figures 8.2, 8.3, 8.9, 8.10, 8.12 Photos by Philip J. Palombo. Figure 8.5(*b*) *Mona Lisa* by Leonardo da Vinci. The Louvre. Scala/Art Resource, NY. Figure 8.7(*b*) *American Gothic* by Grant Wood. Courtesy of The Art Institute of Chicago. Friends of American Art Collections, 1930.934.

Chapter 9   Figures 9.1, 9.2 Photos by Philip J. Palombo & Gary Bellerose. Figures 9.6, 9.7, 9.9, 9.10, 9.18, 9.22 Photos by Philip J. Palombo.

Chapter 10   Figures 10.5, 10.8, 10.11 Photos by Philip J. Palombo.

Chapter 11   Figure 11.2 Photo by Philip J. Palombo. Figure 11.7 Photo by Carl Hausman.

Chapter 12   Figure 12.2 Courtesy of Shure Brothers, Inc. Figure 12.5 Photo by Carl Hausman.

Chapter 13   Figure 13.5(*a*) Robert Amft.

Chapter 14   Figure 14.2 Used with permission, Prevue Networks, Inc. Figure 14.4 Courtesy of Quanta Corporation.

Chapter 15   Figure 15.1 Photo by John Hyde. Figures 15.2, 15.3, 15.4 Photos by Philip J. Palombo.

Chapter 16   Figures 16.2, 16.3 Photos by Philip J. Palombo. Figure 16.7 Courtesy of Avid Technology, Inc.

Chapter 17   Figure 17.2 Courtesy of Shure Brothers, Inc. Figures 17.1, 17.3(*a*), 17.5, 17.7 Photos by Philip Palombo. Figure 17.4, Photo by John Hyde. Figure 17.10 Photo by Philip Benoit.

Chapter 18   Figures 18.1, 18.2, 18.6 Photos by Philip J. Palombo.

Chapter 19   Figures 19.2, 19.6 Photos by Philip J. Palombo. Figure 19.4 Everett Collection.

Chapter 20   Figure 20.1 Courtesy CBS. Figure 20.5 Courtesy of K & H Products, Ltd.—Porta-brace® is a registered trademark. Figure 20.12 Photo by Philip J. Palombo.

Chapter 21   Figure 21.1, 21.7 Courtesy of Tektronic, Inc. Figure 21.2, 21.3, 21.4, 21.5, 21.6, 21.9 Photos by Philip J. Palombo.

Chapter 22   Figure 22.1, 22.3, 22.5, 22.7, 22.9, 22.10, 22.11, 22.12, 22.13, 22.14 Photos by Philip J. Palombo.

PART I

the tools

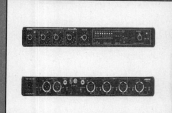

production in today's video marketplace

OBJECTIVES

After completing Chapter 1, you will be able to:

1. Describe, in basic terms, what equipment does what in the studio.
2. Describe the differences between studio and remote operations.
3. Recognize the duties of various TV production personnel.
4. Describe the nature of video: what it can and cannot do.
5. Identify a variety of careers in video and video operations.

Jim, who works at a major metropolitan television station, sits before an enormous bank of monitors (Figure 1.1) and adjusts the intercom that connects him to the camera operators in the studio. "Five seconds to air," he tells the crew. "Roll theme and come up on camera one."

Jim is the director of a popular talk show. The **director** is in charge of the video crew; the director also chooses what camera and audio source are used in a live or taped program and oversees the activity of the performance. For the next half hour, Jim will work with his crew and

- Choose which camera will go on the air with which shot.

- Instruct the control room crew when to open the right microphones and play the theme music and when to put the title of the program on the screen.

- Cue the hostess at the open and close of the show and at each commercial break.

- Coordinate the playback of several videotape inserts during the program.

In other words, Jim coordinates the operation of the entire show. And that's only part of his job—he's heavily involved in preshow planning, too, and has the responsibility of setting the lights, picking the crew, and making sure that everything that is supposed to work during the show actually does work.

Figure 1.1 The director. The director of a talk show will orchestrate the program by choosing shots, cuing talent, and coordinating taped segments for the program.

The type of video production that Jim is involved with is often called **live** or **live-on-tape switching**. With **live-on-tape switching**, the director is able to switch between shots of a program that will be transmitted live or be recorded on tape, in sequence, as it happens. Those shots, of course, are the outputs of several studio cameras or prerecorded video segments.

Lisa is a television reporter for a station in a medium-sized city. Today, she has been covering the aftermath of a fire. She and the technician who operates the editing equipment must now take a mass of videotape and handwritten notes and from them produce a concise, compelling 90-second report.

It's 4 o'clock. Between now and the start of the 6 o'clock news, Lisa and her crew must

- View the videotape that was recorded and select the best shots. All the videotape was recorded on one camera—a portable camera held on the operator's shoulder.

- Using videotape editing equipment, assemble the tape segments in the proper order to tell the story (Figure 1.2). The **editing equipment** allows Lisa to select parts of the tape and rearrange them in any order she wants, regardless of the order in which they were recorded. For example, Lisa's closing remarks—the "standup tag"—was done *first*, before the interviews were conducted. But the flexibility of the editing equipment allows for shooting out of sequence and later assembling the final product in the editing suite.

- Record her narration to coincide with the appropriate pictures used in telling the story. Thus, the editing equipment also allows Lisa to mix her voice with the roar of the flames, and to narrate

Figure 1.2 News editing. A reporter and technician assemble a video news story under deadline pressure.

the scene while the picture shows the fire and the resulting damage.

Lisa uses her production skills in what's known as **single-camera video**, often abbreviated SCV, which is a method of production in which one camera takes all the shots; later the shots are appropriately sequenced with the use of editing equipment. Unlike a talk show done in the studio, Lisa's program requires the use of only one camera. But both types of presentations—the talk show and the news feature—accomplish the same thing: They use a series of meaningful television shots to communicate with an audience. Jim selects the shots live, as they are being recorded by two or more cameras; Lisa selects the shots recorded by only one camera and electronically "cuts and pastes" them together in the editing suite. No physical cutting is actually done, however; all the edits are made electronically by re-recording segments of the original tape onto another tape. Editing equipment then allows the operator to arrange the material in any order.

When single-camera video is used in news production, the process of recording all the shots with one camera and editing the material back at the studio is usually referred to as **electronic news gathering**, or ENG. For non-news programs, such as commercials and feature programs, the process is frequently referred to as **electronic field production**, or EFP, although EFP sometimes refers to multi-camera switching done in the field by means of a remote van or truck.

Max, who works for a large corporation, is the producer of a videotape that will include the company president demonstrating the firm's new product, a desktop computer system. The **producer** is in charge of the overall program and dictates the main theme of the show. The tape that Max is producing will be shown to the company's sales representatives in order to help them better understand the system and share in the president's enthusiasm for it.

Shooting on location—a corporate office that uses the computer network—Max uses two portable video cameras, each recording a separate part of the program. Max and his colleagues will

- Tape the demonstration from several angles, using close-ups for detail and wide shots for overall perspective. The close-ups will provide a perfectly clear and unobstructed view of the demonstration—which is not always possible when a product demonstration is done in person, with crowds of salespeople vying for the best view.

- Return to the editing suite and assemble the final product (Figure 1.3). Max's production is a bit more sophisticated than Lisa's, essentially because it's a longer, more ambitious show with slick

Figure 1.3 Editing corporate video. A corporate video specialist edits a program in an in-house facility.

special effects and background music. For example, a personal computer hooked into the editing system allows the company logo to spin back and forth and fill the screen—all thanks to the magic of a digital effects program that is stored in the memory of the computer.

Max and his associates are involved in what's often called **multiple VTR** (videotape recorder) production. The use of two portable cameras greatly enhances the flexibility of the editing process. The tapes can be edited together using a system that reads electronic synchronizing pulses on the tape. Those pulses are used to control the speed at which the tape moves through the videotape recorder, in much the same way as the sprocket holes on film govern the speed at which the film moves through the projector.

On the tape, the two differing camera angles can be edited together, taking the wide shot when appropriate and cutting to the close-up when the demonstrator is performing a close-up operation. The pulses, which are detected by an electronic scanner in the editing gear, provide a reference point to keep the two tapes in exact synchronization.

Multiple VTR is used in ENG and EFP. Although multiple VTR is not very common in ENG, major interviews for high-budget news programs are frequently shot on location using multiple VTRs. This way, one camera can shoot the newsperson asking questions and responding to the interviewee, while the other camera can tape the interviewee. Then, the two tapes can be edited together to simulate live on-air switching.

It is common practice to use one camera to achieve the same effect. The newsperson simply asks the questions again, after the interview, in what's called a **reverse shot**. To accomplish the reverse shot, the cameraperson switches angles (this time focusing on the reporter), and

the reporter (with the cooperation of the interviewee, who must stay in position) asks the interviewee the same questions.

Live or live-on-tape switching, SCV, and multiple VTR video are used in a variety of production tasks. Although the techniques and the equipment vary, the goal is always the same: To communicate a message to a viewer via video.

The word *video*, incidentally, is used in a variety of ways. Its most basic usage is in reference to the picture portion of a television signal. However, the word has evolved to mean nonbroadcast applications of what we typically call **television**, the programs that are broadcast and transmitted to the home over the air waves or by cable. Today, **video** typically encompasses TV *and* almost all applications of moving picture and sound on the screen, such as home videos, rock videos, educational videotapes, and tapes from the video store. This book will use the term *video* except in specific references to broadcast television or cable operations.

WHO USES VIDEO—AND WHY?

The changeover to the use of the term *video* reflects the fundamental idea that the medium has more applications today than in the early days of commercial television. The medium has changed dramatically in the past generation, and has become more accessible to individuals and institutions.

When video cameras were used almost exclusively for commercial television, they were enormously bulky, complex, and delicate instruments; using them outside the studio required a virtual moving van and a number of technicians to keep them tuned up. Likewise, the videotape recorder of two or three decades ago was impractical for use by all but the most wealthy and ambitious producers. It was typically the size of two office desks and cost about as much as a nice suburban home.

Much of the same technology that miniaturized the personal computer—the power of the computer you can carry in your briefcase dwarfs that of a 20-year-old room-size mainframe—has also brought "television" down to size. No longer is video the sole domain of TV stations and large studios. Today, businesses, schools, hospitals, and enterprising hobbyists employ small, user-friendly equipment to produce their own **video**, often called **institutional video**, which is a program made in-house by institutions for viewing by their employees or for the promotion of public relations. For instance,

- *Video training programs* used by businesses to train or motivate their employees.
- *Videoconferences* beamed by satellite from coast to coast or even from continent to continent.

BOX 1.1   MTV MEETS BIG BUSINESS

MTV celebrated its tenth birthday in 1991, and according to *TV Guide* writer Howard Polskin, MTV had to overcome some initial skepticism to create a new visual language. (After all, just what *was* a rock video?)

That new visual language has crossed over into some unlikely territory, by the way. Alan Bloom, who teaches video production at California State University in Los Angeles, noted that music videos are now wearing pinstripes.

When MTV debuted, sales of rock-and-roll albums were at rock bottom. "We were looking for a savior," recalls Virgin Records boss Jeff Ayeroff, "and it came in the form of MTV." Almost overnight, bands no one had heard of—Duran Duran being a prime example—were selling like gangbusters, thanks to extensive MTV airplay . . .

The "MTV look" began cropping up everywhere. Its effect on TV advertising is almost mythic. "Take Ray Charles' Diet Pepsi commercial," says ad-agency president Fred Siebert, citing a highly visible recent example. "It wouldn't exist without the MTV style. It's a direct descendant of MTV."

Countless Hollywood movies and TV shows have adopted the quick-cut editing and slick, flashy imagery associated with the music videos on MTV.

Source: "MTV at 10: The Beat Goes On,"
TV Guide (August 3, 1991): 4–5.

What do rock star Jon Anderson, lead singer for the group Yes, and Westinghouse Furniture Systems in Grand Rapids, Michigan, have in common? Both have new rock videos directed by Peter Lippman. Lippman, a rock video producer and director with almost 100 major videos to his credit, is one of a growing number of rock video and industrial video professionals across the country who have recently found themselves making salespeople, bankers, and executives into rock video stars.

. . . The industrial rock video phenomenon came to light [in 1985] at the Sony Institute of Applied Video Technology . . . in Hollywood. After returning from some of the many workshops they hold around the country, Institute instructors Tim Broderick and Tom Krug approached me with similar stories about rock videos they had seen made exclusively for corporate in-house use. Tim showed a video called *Future Space*, done by Citibank in New York, to correct a morale problem created by an impending major office move. . . .

Why industrial rock videos? "Everybody's into it and they can understand the concepts and enjoy them," says Rick Possum, whose Indianapolis-based company Telematrix has produced six rock videos for clients ranging from Hardee's Restaurants and Cummins Diesel, to Delta Faucet and Handle and Miller Advertising. "It's not like if you did this fifteen years ago," he says.

Source: "Music Video Puts on Pinstripes,"
Videography (March 1986): 43–44.

- **Interactive videos,** which are programs that allow viewers to watch a presentation and choose which "branch" they would like to follow. Interactive video programming might, for example, allow pilots-in-training to make decisions under simulated conditions and see the simulated results of their actions—without having to crash planes in the process.

In sum, what we've seen in recent years is not only a change in programming, or a change in the types of organizations that use video, but the application of video techniques to different fields. Today, we're likely to see the documentary format applied in its traditional form—long programs generally related to news and public affairs—as well as to a company's "video magazine." The same techniques of television drama used in the staple daytime soap operas are often used in the production of training tapes. Even the relatively new genre of rock video has stretched across traditional boundaries (Box 1.1).

The growing use of video for such varied applications, along with the continued popularity of commercial television and cable, make video production a field with a variety of opportunities for those who understand the principles of video communication. Employment in video, while often hard, is fascinating and exhilarating.

There are many users of video, including broadcast and cable outlets, as well as producers of institutional video. Those institutions include corporations, schools, and nonprofit organizations. In each type of organization, video is produced by people who understand the "language" of video, grasping the medium's strengths and weaknesses in order to produce the most effective program.

Broadcast and Cable

Traditional TV stations, and the networks that supply some of their programming, are facing competition from their counterparts in the cable industry. Nevertheless, broadcasters (who send signals over the airwaves to home television receivers) and cablecasters (who send those broadcast signals *and* some original programming to home receivers over wires) have much in common:

• They generally seek a mass audience. That is, except for certain cable stations and cable networks, broadcast and cable outlets usually produce and show programs that will be of interest to the general public. In the case of cable, the target audience (Spanish-speaking people in the United States, for example) may be considerably narrower than for television. Still, cable programming is more generalized than institutional programs.

• They use a variety of television production formats. A typical day of broadcasting or cablecasting will include entertainment programs, such as dramas and comedies, commercials, news, sports, and talk shows.

Institutional Video

Business, industry, and educational institutions are growing producers and consumers of video. Institutional video (also called private video, corporate video, and professional video) offers extraordinary advantages for training, public relations, and internal dissemination of information.

These producers and consumers of video don't necessarily need or want a wide audience for their programs. While applications vary, most organizations using video seek to:

• Take advantage of video as a training tool. A videotape or videodisc (which, as you can see in Figure 1.4, looks like a large compact disc) is an excellent teacher. It does not tire of repeating the same information, and provides consistent information and delivery.

• Utilize the "user friendliness" of video. Most people like to watch video and are receptive to

Figure 1.5 Videoconferencing. Videoconferencing enables two or more locations to establish video contact with the use of a telephone system or a satellite distribution service. (*Courtesy of PictureTel®*)

video programs (although it is important for the designers of institutional video to remember that watching is not always the same thing as learning).

• Exploit the capability of video to bring people "face to face" without the expense of travel. Videoconferences (Figure 1.5) can vastly diminish the problems and expense associated with coordinating travel plans for a group.

STRENGTHS AND WEAKNESSES OF THE MEDIUM

What we've been discussing so far is a selective sampling of the attributes of video. As a producer, you'll also be interested in the relative strengths and weaknesses of the medium. With the increasing availability of video in many different settings, part of the producer's role is to determine what subjects, ideas, and themes lend themselves to video, and which do not.

Figure 1.4 Interactive videodisc. The videodiscs hold information directly with a videodisc player, or under the control of a computer program designed for interactive self-instruction. (*Courtesy of Pioneer Communications of America.*)

Strengths of the Medium

In general, video is a strong communications tool when it is used to engage attention, show compelling pictures, or motivate the viewer.

A talk show engages our attention because it mimics a lively conversation and, in general, features interesting guests. When talk show directors sit before the bank of monitors, they are looking for the most interesting shots and cutting to cameras to catch the spontaneous reactions and comments of the host and guests.

The strength of an unusual or compelling picture makes video a powerful communications tool. When Lisa, the TV reporter, covered the fire, she was doing what video does best: telling a story by using moving images.

Video is also a dynamic motivator. Max, the institutional video producer, not only had to demonstrate the equipment to his audience, but he also had to convince them that the product was desirable. In effect, the message of Max's training tape was, "This is a great product, salespeople, and here's how you can sell a lot of them." That's why theme music and compelling graphics are an important part of this particular type of presentation.

Weaknesses of the Medium

But video is not all things to all people. It is not a particularly effective medium for presenting dense textual information. Video simply does not do a very good job of providing long or complex lists of items or instructions. Note how grocery stores tend to favor print advertising over video when listing sale items. Viewers simply cannot remember long sequences, nor is it realistic to expect them to maintain their attention through an extended listing of items or actions.

In many cases, video is also not particularly handy as a reference. Should you need reference material that must be consulted or repeatedly referred to, video may not be the most convenient medium. Material on a television newscast, for all intents and purposes, disappears once it is aired—not a good medium on which to advertise your month-long calendar of events.

Although videotape and videodiscs can store information and access it relatively quickly, the user still needs some setup time, access to the equipment, and a method to easily locate the desired portion of the program. So, while first aid instruction can be demonstrated very well on video, video is not really the appropriate medium for an emergency first-aid *manual*. The denser, more tightly packed information of the printed page, combined with an easily accessible index, would be more suitable for this application.

This weakness is closely related to the concept that it is difficult to communicate a great deal of information via video. To use a familiar example, *The CBS Evening News* can do many things *The New York Times* cannot, which includes providing live coverage and moving pictures. But if you were to make a comparison at random, you might find that all the words spoken on *The CBS Evening News* cover only two-thirds of page 1 of *The New York Times*. Sixteen stories may air on a typical evening news report, but *The New York Times* may carry more than 260 stories.

The purpose of this discussion is to illustrate that a television producer—a professional skilled in *communicating* with the medium—learns what works well on video and what doesn't. That is step one in the process of learning production, and it supercedes all the technical and aesthetic factors, which will be discussed in this text. So, in this book, we will always start from the assumption that any concept must be examined in terms of whether or not it is *good video*. As one veteran producer notes (Box 1.2), it is imperative that anyone interested in producing a good program remember that video is about people and ideas, not buttons and knobs.

A CAREER IN VIDEO PRODUCTION

To this point, our discussion of who uses video has only dealt with general categories: television/cable and institutional. But who, specifically, *makes* the programs that are consumed by these users? And where do they work?

The Video Producer

To answer that question, it's probably best to begin by reviewing two of the terms used so far: *producer* and *director*. (A more complete listing of all production personnel follows in Chapter 2.)

Essentially, the producer is the person in overall charge of the program, whether that program is a newscast, a talk show, or a documentary. The producer dictates the main theme of the show, handles budgeting, and in general is the final decision maker.

The *director*, in the most common usage of the term, is the person in charge of the crew and the performers while the program is being broadcast or taped. The director instructs the camera operator(s) as to the composition of the desired shot in SCV, multiple VTR video, and live or live-on-tape switching. In the case of live or live-on-tape switching, the director chooses which camera goes on the air as the show unfolds. The director will select appropriate shots and sequences of shots, as well as supervise the music and narration, in the editing suite if the program has been shot on SCV or multiple VTRs.

The two positions of producer and director are sometimes combined, especially in small operations such as a video documentary. A documentary might involve only a producer/director, a camera operator, and a sound technician.

BOX 1.2   "ELECTRIC TRAINS FOR GROWN-UPS"— A NETWORK PRODUCER TELLS WHAT HAPPENS WHEN YOU REMEMBER THE GADGETS BUT FORGET THE SHOW

Leslie Midgley, who came to exemplify the term *producer*, was in charge of many notable programs during his career at CBS and NBC, including *The CBS Evening News*. Midgley notes that the role of a producer is to communicate the ideas in a program, not simply to operate equipment. Sometimes the pursuit of technical perfection can get out of hand. For instance, during the taping of a news program, Dan Rather and Roger Mudd, whom Midgley says never particularly cared for each other, were kept waiting while the production staff was preoccupied with their gadgets. The show, called "Congress versus the President," was supposed to open with the presidential seals turning while images were placed inside the seals at each turn. But here's what happened.

This was before the days of a lot of electronic trickery, and the seals which were about three feet in diameter, were physically turned by electric motors.

When we got set up in Studio 41, the biggest in the production center, the stars were on their stools, the cameras warmed up and ready, the control room and tape machines manned and up to speed—and the director, Joel Banow, couldn't get pictures to appear as the seals turned around.

One of the problems with television technicians is that they love to play with their gadgets. It's a game

of electric trains for grown-ups. Banow became totally absorbed in the problem of the turning disks and simply didn't pay attention to what was going on out on the studio floor.

Paddy Chayevsky portrayed this phenomenon brilliantly in his great movie *Network*. When the crazy anchor man announces that he is going to kill himself on television, the director and his assistants are chatting up a girl in the control room, totally oblivious to what is going out over the air. It does, believe me, really happen.

As Joel continued to fiddle and a 15 minute delay became an hour, Mudd and Rather were getting very restless and unhappy, their mutual dislike, perhaps rooted in competitive aspirations, began to surface more and more clearly.

I simply had to overrule a director in his own control room, insist that the delays be ended, and tell everyone that the taping would start in five minutes whether or not the turning seals worked. I warned Banow that he was leaving his show on the studio floor, but he didn't understand what I was talking about.

Source: How Many Words Do You Want? An Insider's Stories of Print and Television Journalism: New York: Birch Lane Press, 1989, p. 265.

Regardless of the size of the operation, the producer, director, and producer/director are part artist and part technician who know the requirements of good video, who are able to utilize video equipment to produce the best possible technical image, and who have the capability to construct a program that is visually exciting and logically ordered.

In fact, everyone involved in video needs a working knowledge of the art and the science of production. The producer, of course, must know every aspect of the television process *and* must deal with the tricky problems of staffing, managing creative people, and completing a project by the deadline and under budget (Figure 1.6).

Directors may not always handle budgets, but their need for an overall understanding of video communications is the same as the producer's.

In later chapters, we'll examine the work of various video specialists, but it's worth noting here that video professionals such as camera operators, scriptwriters, and even on-camera performers also benefit from a well-rounded understanding of the production process. Camera operators

need to know, at least in general terms, what a director does and how the director does it in order to fully understand how to follow the director's orders. Scriptwriters need a firm grasp of the mechanics of video in order to

Figure 1.6 The producer. The producer utilizes artistic, technical, and management skills.

specify logical and eye-pleasing sequences of shots. On-camera performers must learn the signals used by certain members of the studio crew; they must also know how to "play to the camera" during a close-up and a long shot.

Work Environments: Who Hires Video Professionals?

Producers, directors, and other video professionals use their skills in a variety of settings, including network and local television/cable, independent production studios and production houses, and in-house institutional production facilities. Some work as free-lancers.

Network and Local Television/Cable. Just a few years ago, most of us had a pretty clear idea of what *network television* meant: CBS, NBC, ABC, and PBS. But today, cable and satellite hookups have created additional permanent networks, as well as temporary networks, designed for a particular one-time event. These are sometimes called ad hoc networks. ESPN, the Entertainment and Sports Programming Network, is an example of a permanent cable network that relies on satellite transmission to gather programming literally from across the globe.

An ad hoc network might be created by a group of TV news departments who decide, for example, to pool their coverage of a storm ravaging various portions of the state. All they need to do is reserve time on a satellite transmission service, beam their individual reports up (uplink) and receive (downlink) the programming from the other stations.

Businesses such as General Motors and Eastman Kodak Company have their own "networks." These and many other firms have an interlinked system of satellite and ground-based microwave transmission that allows them to share programming with their affiliates across the country.

But in the most common usage of the word, *network television* is usually taken to mean the top rung of the TV ladder, the central location where high-quality programming is disseminated to affiliated stations, and certain programs—such as national news—are produced.

Many local TV stations receive most of their programming from networks, as do local cable companies. But TV and cable stations often have extensive production staffs for news and commercials. Newscasts, typically a local station's biggest money-making, locally produced program, must be planned and executed by a surprisingly large number (sometimes dozens) of video professionals. Local talk shows and public affairs programming demand a healthy supply of production personnel too. Advertising is produced by local television and cable stations, although many commercials are crafted by independent houses.

Independent Production Studios and Houses. There is no universally accepted distinction between a "studio"

and a "house," although in common usage a production studio (meaning a type of business, not the physical location—there are "studios" in most TV stations) is thought of as a large firm that produces major programs. The concept of an independent TV studio is not unlike a film company.

Most but not all entertainment programs seen on network TV are produced by major studios not directly affiliated with the networks. MTM, the studio founded by Mary Tyler Moore and Grant Tinker, is one example of an independent firm that produces a number of shows for networks. MTM produced *Lou Grant* and *Hill Street Blues*.

But independent TV production is not confined to the major studios. Smaller firms, often called "houses," produce commercials, institutional tapes, and documentaries. They're not major operations of the same category as a film studio. That is, they typically do not have large staging areas, audience seating arrangements, and other resources necessary for a network-style program. (As a reminder, the labels "studio" and "house" are informal definitions and are used here primarily for the sake of discussion.)

Independent houses may have just a handful of employees and often specialize in one type of production. Some houses, for example, do only high-tech graphics. Sometimes, though, independent houses are quite large and can handle almost any task short of a major TV series.

In-House Video Facilities. One industry analyst predicted that by 1995, 50,000 nonbroadcast businesses, such as commercial firms, schools, and nonprofit organizations, would be producing video in-house.[1] Those figures are among many indicators that nonbroadcast video, what we call institutional video in this text, provides a healthy and burgeoning job market for those educated in video communications. While recessionary times have dimmed the job outlook at the time of this writing, it's worth remembering that institutional video has weathered a series of economic slowdowns in the past.

The in-house video department may be a one-person operation, or it may be staffed by dozens of specialists. Increasingly, there is a tendency for in-house video departments to augment their personnel needs by contracting with independent houses and/or hiring free-lancers to fill in the gaps when demand for video outstrips supply of in-house personnel.

Free-lancers. Free-lancers are self-employed specialists who hire themselves out to organizations. To a degree, almost every type of production agency uses free-lancers. Self-employed scriptwriters, for example, often furnish the raw material for network series. Network news organizations hire free-lance camera operators and stringers (free-lance news correspondents). Independent houses typically engage the services of free-lance camera operators, scriptwriters, and actors.

Broadcast versus Institutional: The Surprising Facts and Figures

Institutional, nonbroadcast video offers some little-known advantages over what we customarily think of as "traditional" TV production (broadcast and cable TV for general audiences and reasonably large audiences with a specific interest). Those pluses include better pay and benefits than broadcast and a wider choice of career settings.

A comprehensive study[2] by Linda Lee Davis of the University of Kansas indicated that starting salaries for institutional video, in general, are higher than in broadcast and cable. While institutional video staffers may work long and odd hours, their working days are typically shorter and more regular than for those in broadcast.

Institutional video usually offers a wider choice of geographic locations than does broadcast work. For the most part, commercial broadcasting is a business in which you progress by starting in small markets and working your way up through larger markets. It is extremely difficult to launch a career in commercial television by starting in large cities.

This is not meant to demean small-town or small-city life or the people who work in small markets. But the pay is generally abysmal in smaller markets, and those who like big-city life often feel as though they are in exile for the first few years of their commercial television career. Also, frequent moves—a virtual necessity in a broadcaster's professional life—do nothing to enhance one's family and social life.

Institutional video, because it is not dependent on market size for revenue, offers a variety of entry-level jobs in big cities *and* small towns.

VIDEO: ITS APPLICATION IN OTHER PROFESSIONS

Although video's role in television and cable is obvious, and most of us are reasonably familiar with the concept that video is an increasingly popular tool in business, it's also worth noting that the medium is increasingly utilized in other fields as well. To add to some information presented earlier, let's take a closer look at video's role in education and public relations.

Video and Education

New technologies enable video users to learn at their own pace; an interactive program, where users see a demonstration and are then quizzed to ascertain whether they understand the concept, can be done in privacy. Moreover, the lesson can be repeated endlessly until the viewer understands the concept. Interactive video is nonjudgmental and infinitely patient.

Until recently, the technology of video was rather daunting to the nonexpert user—limiting the medium's effectiveness as an individual teaching tool. Today, however, interactive technology allows an easy alliance between the video gear and the trainee. Touchscreens (Figure 1.7) simplify the process enormously. A **touchscreen** allows the user to point to or select an answer on a monitor rather than accessing a computerized system via a keyboard or mouse. A **mouse** is a sliding table-top device used to move a pointer or cursor across a computer screen.

Education via video includes the previously mentioned concept of training tapes. Video is often the medium of choice for imparting information, especially when the process being demonstrated cannot be repeated at will. For example, a tape demonstrating the disassembly of an important piece of machinery is far more practicable than an in-person demonstration involving the shutdown of the mechanism.

Also, video shows things that people cannot easily see or grasp. Hospitals find video an increasingly useful tool for demonstrating surgical procedures. A camera, mounted on the surgeon's headband, can record for physicians-in-training a much better view than could be achieved by peering over the surgeon's shoulder or, worse, looking down from the observation deck of the operating theatre.

Animation, now easily accomplished via modern computer technology, also bolsters video's ability to educate. Consider the problems inherent in attempting to demonstrate the workings of an internal combustion engine. How do you show the workings inside a cylinder in a car engine? Saw it in half? Okay, but how, then, can you demonstrate the intake of fuel and the exhaust of burned gases? It's a challenge with traditional in-person demonstrations, and even with traditional video, but it's a relatively simple matter for a creative video producer armed with animation tools and software.

Figure 1.7 High tech/high touch. Touch-sensitive screens provide easy, intuitive control of interactive video equipment. (Courtesy of MicroTouch Systems, Inc.)

Video and Public Relations

The exact definition of *public relations* is somewhat elusive, so we won't attempt to come up with a conclusive description here. But almost all public relations efforts include the attempt to garner favorable publicity for an organization, cause, or individual.

One increasingly popular method of gaining public exposure is the video news release, often abbreviated as VNR. A news release is a document prepared by a public relations practitioner and sent to news organizations in the hope that the information will be printed or aired. The **video news release** is a news release on videotape, provided by public relations practitioners in a package that is ready for use by local TV stations. Most stations, however, prefer to edit the tape to suit their particular needs. Medical and pharmaceutical firms, colleges and universities, and a variety of other businesses and organizations furnish stations with VNRs, sometimes on videotape through the mail, or, increasingly, beamed down from a satellite.

If you watch TV news, you've almost certainly seen a VNR. One survey indicated that more than three-quarters of news directors use at least one edited VNR in their newscasts on a weekly basis.[3] And if you've been to a store recently, you've certainly observed another PR-related use of video: point-of-sale presentations designed to attract customers' interest. Neiman-Marcus, for example, has used a point-of-sale video in its jewelry department, a program featuring celebrities including Angie Dickinson and John Forsythe.

Clearly, video is not *only* used for mass-audience television production. While TV and cable are still flourishing, producers skilled in the language of video can apply their skills to an enormous range of tasks, including training, conferencing, public relations, and advertising.

But the fact that video has become more accessible does not mean that the skills required for communicating through the medium are any less exacting. Indeed, just the opposite is true. A few years ago, the producer/director could count on the services of numerous crew members. Today, the sophistication of the hardware allows small crews to handle big jobs—meaning that you'll need to know more about the entire process of video production to get your message across to the viewer. And that, of course, is exactly what this book is designed to do. Chapter 2 describes the first few links in the chain of video communications, as well as the people and the positions that make up a video crew.

SUMMARY

1. There are three basic ways that television is produced. First is *live* or *live-on-tape switching*, where the director chooses shots from various cameras as the program is happening. The program runs in sequence, as it happens. It may be directly broadcast or cablecast, or it can be taped for later use.

2. The second common method is *edited single-camera video* (SCV). Here, one camera is used to shoot all the shots, and then the order of the program is rearranged in the editing room, where electronic equipment figuratively "cuts and pastes" the program segments in the order that they'll run.

3. A third, less common method of video production is sometimes called *multiple videotape recorder* (VTR) *video*. Here, two or more cameras record the same event but from different angles and perspectives. The shots are then edited together. Sophisticated electronic equipment allows the tapes to be played back in exact synchronization, and the editor can choose the shots that are most effective and appropriate, and mix and match them. This process is almost like live or live-on-tape switching, except that the bulky and complex editing equipment needed to do the switching does not need to be taken on location. The switching can be done later, in the editing suite.

4. The use of one camera and VTR, and sometimes two separate cameras and VTRs, is usually referred to as *electronic news gathering*, or ENG, when the content is news related, and as *electronic field production*, or EFP, for other types of programming.

5. The word *television* usually refers to the mass-audience programs we're used to seeing on commercial and public television and cable. But the term *video* is more inclusive and applies to many other uses of the medium.

6. The uses of video include news and entertainment, training, sales promotion, conferencing, and public relations.

7. Nonbroadcast video is increasingly referred to as *institutional video*. Corporations and institutions often have in-house video departments—and many contract additional personnel, equipment, and expertise from outside production agencies, as well as free-lancers (independent consultants)—that produce videos which will be viewed by employees or used as part of a public relations effort. Nonbroadcast video is an increasingly attractive career field.

8. Video is an outstanding medium for inspiring the viewer and, of course, for showing compelling pictures. Video is not the best medium for every application, however. It is not a particularly good tool for presenting dense textual information or for serving as a reference. If a large amount of material must be communicated in a short time, print is probably a superior medium to video.

9. Several types or facilities produce video, including commercial and public television and cable stations, as well as TV and cable networks. Independent studios produce much of the entertainment programming seen on commercial TV, whereas production "houses," our term for smaller production facilities, produce programs such as commercials and instructional fare.

NOTES

1. Judith Stokes, quoted in "It's Showtime for Business," *Nation's Business* (April 1989): 54.

2. Linda Lee Davis, "Corporate Television: The Lure of a Non-Broadcast Career," *Feedback* (Fall 1987): 37–42.

3. From a survey by Neilsen Media Research, reported in "Making Use of Syndicated Inserts," *The Communicator* (May 1990): 12.

TECHNICAL TERMS

director	institutional video	reverse shot	video
editing equipment	interactive video	single-camera video (SCV)	videocassette recorder (VCR)
electronic field production (EFP)	live-on-tape switching	television	video news release (VNR)
electronic news gathering (ENG)	mouse	touchscreen	videotape recorder (VTR)
	producer		

the studio and crew: a guided tour

OBJECTIVES

After completing Chapter 2, you will be able to:

1. Sketch the basic layout of the studio and control room.
2. Sketch the basic layout of the editing suite.
3. Describe basic camera movements.
4. Describe how the camera handles light, and why video lighting has to be different from conventional room lighting.
5. Set up a simple three-point lighting pattern.
6. Describe the basic workings of microphones.
7. Give examples of the importance of teamwork in both studio and field work.

Despite the seeming complexity of video equipment and operations, video production is a fairly simple and straightforward process.

That statement might not sit well with those who like an air of mystery attached to their jobs—and there certainly are many cryptic displays and controls involved in TV production—but operation of video equipment is much less complicated than it might at first appear to the newcomer.

This chapter will introduce you to both the equipment and the people involved in video production, first by touring the studio, control room, and other parts of the physical plant. Then, we'll examine the basic pieces of equipment found in a video production facility. Finally, we'll meet some of the people involved in the production process and show how their jobs relate to both the operation of equipment and the production process.

THE VIDEO PRODUCTION FACILITY

A studio is designed as a quiet, climate-controlled facility that houses the equipment involved in TV production as well as provides logically arranged working areas for crewpeople. In common usage, the word *studio* is sometimes taken to mean the entire facility. However, in discussing the layout of a typical TV production facility, *studio* generally refers to the area where the cameras, announcers, and performers are located. The control room is a physically separate area where the director and other crew members operate the video switcher, the audio board (which controls the microphone signals), the electronic character generator (which produces letters and illustrations), and other equipment. Master control is an area where engineering functions, including fine-tuning of the camera's signal, are accomplished. Sometimes the videotape recorders (VTRs) are located in master control, although they are often placed in the control room. In many TV production facilities, an area known as the editing suite, houses the equipment used for editing (rearranging) elements on the videotape and adding new elements such as special effects and new parts of the sound track.

The Studio and the Control Room

In the example of the talk show (at the beginning of Chapter 1), we saw the director poised before a bank of monitors, selecting the proper shot to go over the air. In any live or live-on-tape switching operation, there will be people other than the director involved in the process, including an audio operator, an operator for the **character generator**, which is a device that produces letters or some type of graphic or animation on the video screen. And in many cases a technical director who operates the video switcher. Many directors operate their own switcher, but it is difficult to direct a show and run the equipment, hence the frequent use of a technical director to do the actual button pushing.

All this activity takes place in the control room, an area physically separate from the studio. The studio is where the host, performers, and camera operators do their respective jobs.

It makes intuitive sense for the studio and control room to be separate because staffers in the control room must talk to each other. The director, for example, will be issuing instructions to the control room staff, instructions that are obviously not meant to be heard by the viewer at home.

Also, the control room crew must hear what is going on in the studio. Usually, the speakers are turned up quite high so that the director can hear the conversation (and cut to the correct shots at the correct time) and the person in charge of audio can hear clearly and gauge the quality of that audio. If the two rooms were not separate, the sound of the program emanating from the speakers would be picked up by the studio mics and fed back into the audio system. The amplified sound would again be played through the speakers, picked up again by the mics, and so on—amplified and reamplified until all the viewer would hear is the familiar sound of feedback, the high-pitched squeal often heard at concerts when the performer holds the mic too close to the loudspeaker.

Because the control room and the studio remain physically and acoustically separate, communication between the control room and the studio is accomplished by means of wires and headsets. This is known as the intercom system. The director speaks into an intercom or wears a headset. The people operating the cameras as well as most other crew members on the studio floor wear headsets. The headsets are sealed reasonably tightly around the crew member's ears (Figure 2.1), so that when the director says, "Camera one, move in for a close-up of the prop," the sound won't be picked up by studio mics.

Camera operators can also talk back to the director through their headset mic. During camera rehearsals for the show, they can ask questions about upcoming shots, movements, and so forth. However, it is generally considered good studio etiquette to ask questions or offer advice only when absolutely necessary. Because there may be four or five crew members on headsets, the line can become clogged quickly if there is too much irrelevant chatter.

During a show, it is better for a crew member in the studio to talk back to the director—in a very soft voice— only in an emergency or when some pressing situation occurs, such as a mechanical breakdown on the camera controls. Whispered communications generally are not picked up by the studio mics, but the performers can hear them, and they—already nervous enough as it is—are frequently very distracted by headset chatter.

Figure 2.1 Crew member wearing a headset. During production the crew can communicate with the director by means of an intercom headset.

So that is the operative theory of why the studio and the control room are in separate rooms. Figure 2.2 illustrates a typical studio and control room arrangement. Note that there's another room indicated on the diagram: the master control.

Master Control

Master control is the central location where specialists monitor the technical quality of the program and perform other technical operations involved in recording the program or transmitting it over the air. In some cases the main VTR (the unit recording a program for later airplay) is located in master control, although VTRs are often placed in the control room. In addition, staffers in master control generally set the electronic operating parameters of the

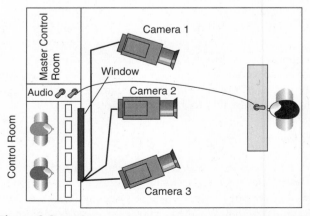

Figure 2.2 The studio, control room, and master control room. In the studio, camera and mics are connected via jacks and cables to the control room. The control room contains the video switcher and monitors, and often audio control equipment as well. Technical adjustments of audio and video signals are handled in the master control room.

EDITING WORK FLOW AND FUNCTIONS

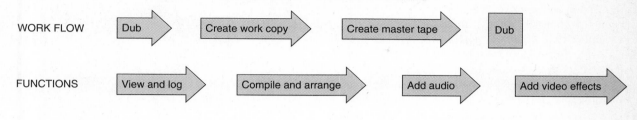

(a)

camera, making fine adjustments to ensure picture quality. Finally, master control is where you will usually find the equipment for converting film and slides to video; this equipment is often grouped in one area; the equipment is called the **film chain** or **telecine** (pronounced "tella-SIN-ee").

Master control is often some distance away from the studio and control room. In fact, to momentarily return to the discussion of the control room and studio, note that the studio and control room themselves are sometimes physically separated. Although it is usually the case that the studio and control room are located side-by-side, with a soundproof window separating the two areas, some control rooms have no direct view of the studio and, in fact, are sometimes located on separate floors of the building. When remote control rooms are used to televise live events, such as football games or concerts, these remote control rooms are generally housed in trucks or vans parked outside the arena and linked to the inside by cables.

It is a convenience to be able to look through the glass and keep an eye on studio operations, but some directors actually feel the window is a *distraction*. After all, the most important thing a director wants to see is what's coming through the monitors—not the events on the studio floor. That's why some instructors choose to keep a closed curtain over the soundproof window, blocking off the beginning director's view of the studio. Indeed, although it is arguable as to whether the view into the studio is a help or a distraction, it is wise for the director *not to habitually depend on looking into the studio because in many cases that simply will not be an option.*

The Editing Suite

When electronic news gathering (ENG) and electronic field production (EFP) tapes are used as raw material for the final program, that program is generally pieced together in a room or series of rooms usually called the editing room or editing suite. Figure 2.3 depicts the editing process; (*a*) illustrates a flow diagram of the editing system and (*b*) shows a multiple VTR editing suite.

The process of editing video usually involves four distinct functions: viewing and logging, compiling and arranging, adding sound, and adding video.

Figure 2.3   (*a*) Editing workflow and functions. To protect raw footage and to save time on expensive equipment, editors generally work from a copy or *dub* and create a rough *work copy*. When the producer is satisfied with the work copy, the editor creates a *master tape* using the original footage. The master tape is then dubbed and stored.

When creating a work copy or a master tape an editor performs four basic functions: (1) view and log the raw footage to get an overview of material available; (2) compile and arrange selected segments of video onto a new tape; (3) add audio; and (4) add video effects.

(*b*) In the editing suite. The editor uses audio and video components to create a program. Serviceable older equipment is commonly used in colleges and in smaller professional facilities.

Viewing and logging. The viewing and logging function involves screening the tape that has been shot, usually called raw footage, and determining which shots will be the most useful and effective. Editors keep a written log of the "locations" of the best shots. Those locations are determined by the electronic counting and timing devices on the VTRs and other equipment such as the editing control unit, which we'll learn about in the next section.

Compiling and arranging. The compiling and arranging function involves sequencing the raw footage, generally using a script, into a logical sequence.

Adding sound. In most cases, adding sound refers to recording a narration, and sometimes music and sound effects.

Adding video. The process of adding video involves adding titles, graphics, and sometimes animation.

The basic method of operation in an editing suite is simple: You play back the raw tape on one VTR, use the edit control unit to select the exact segment of the tape you want to use, and re-record that segment onto another tape—the tape that will become the final program.

Remember that when you are editing ENG or EFP, you are rearranging raw footage—footage shot single-camera video (SCV) style—into a final program. No attempt is made to shoot the program in sequence out in the field, using remote cameras. A reporter doing ENG, for example, might have the closing of her report recorded first, then the interview, then the opening. It makes no difference: The editing control unit allows the raw footage to be used at will.

In either case—live switching or ENG/EFP editing—the program is constructed from the output of standard tools of the trade that produce sound and picture.

TOOLS USED IN THE PRODUCTION PROCESS

There is a variety of equipment used in TV production. First we'll examine the cameras, lighting instruments, and microphones and audio controls. Then we'll see how shots are selected using the switcher or are recorded and structured into a program using editing equipment.

Cameras

Video cameras fall into two basic categories: studio cameras and portable (sometimes called "hand-held") cameras. The **studio camera** (Figure 2.4) is a large camera, usually of very high quality, used exclusively in the studio. The **portable camera** is designed for hand-held work.

Because studio cameras are often significantly larger than the portable variety, they are not suited or used for hand-held work. Aside from sheer dimensions, there are some other differences between studio and hand-held cameras:

Figure 2.4 The studio camera. The studio camera is mounted on a sturdy base and typically has high-quality components, a large viewfinder, and a long zoom lens.

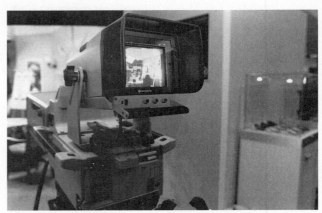

Figure 2.5 A studio camera's viewfinder. The studio camera's viewfinder measures 5 to 7 inches and gives the camera operator a full view of the action.

- Most studio cameras are mounted on sturdy bases that allow smooth raising and lowering of the camera, as well as shake-free movements forward, backward, and sideways.

- Studio cameras can be equipped with **prompting devices**, which are half-silvered mirrors that fit over the lens and reflect a printed or electronic copy of the script back toward the person speaking to the camera without making the script visible to the viewer.

- In general, the larger size of the studio camera allows for more sophisticated and higher-quality components—hence, a better picture and better control over the picture. The viewfinder of a studio camera (Figure 2.5) is larger than the viewfinder in the hand-held camera (Figure 2.6).

Figure 2.6 A portable camera's viewfinder. The portable camera's viewfinder is small at 1½ inches when compared to the studio viewfinder, but it too offers a high resolution image. The eyepiece confines the user to one eye and guards from distractions and reflections with its rubber eyepiece, which shapes to the eye and forehead.

The **viewfinder** is the device that shows the operator what the camera is "seeing." The camera operator using the studio model sees an image comparable to that of a small home black-and-white television, whereas the hand-held operator sees a tiny image through only one eye, so the operator of a studio camera has an easier time focusing and recognizing detail in the shot.

This discussion of the differences between studio and portable cameras is not meant to imply that portable cameras produce a low-quality picture. Indeed, a high-quality portable unit can sometimes produce a superior picture to a low-grade studio camera. But in general, the studio camera does offer better video, wider versatility for in-studio operations, and easier repair and maintenance.

Many studios compromise and use convertible cameras. **Convertible cameras** can be utilized as portable units for ENG and EFP and can also be equipped with a viewfinder and high-quality mount for studio work.

Any camera, portable or studio, has a **lens**, which gathers the light and focuses the picture; an **iris**, which is a variable opening that governs the amount of light entering the lens; a viewfinder so that the operators can see what they are shooting; and some type of **imaging device**, which is an electronic component that produces the raw material of the video signal.

The imaging device includes either a tube or several tubes, or, as is the case with the newest generation of cameras, one or more charge-coupled devices. A **charge-coupled device**, known as a CCD, is a microchip that has special properties which allow it to translate the light focused through the lens into a video signal. CCD cameras are commonly called **chip cameras**.

If you've just been introduced to the video camera, there are some pointers you need to know right away. It's essential to protect the pickup element and prevent physical damage to the camera itself.

Protection of the Pickup Element. Although a camera does not have to be handled like fine china, it can be damaged by careless use. As a general rule, protect the **pickup element** (which transduces light into a video signal) by *never* pointing the camera toward a lighting instrument, the sun, or anything that gives off a strong reflection, such as a shiny auto on a sunlit street. Camera tubes can be ruined by this. Although a chip camera can withstand strong light, it's not always possible to instantly identify whether a camera is a chip or a tube model, so don't take any chances.

Protection Against Accidental Movement or Tipping. Camera mounts have controls (Figure 2.7) that govern the amount of friction applied when the camera head is moved up and down, called **tilting**, or moved from side

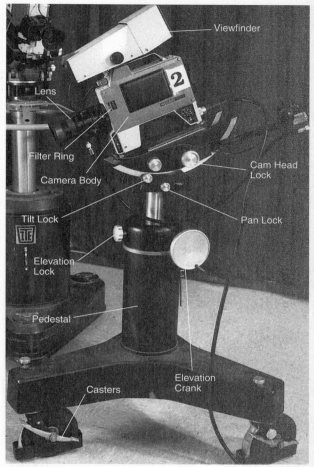

Figure 2.7 Convertible (used for both portable and studio) camera and mount. With the added weight of a studio viewfinder and mechanical lens controls, the studio camera mounts on a sturdy but adjustable pedestal. The pedestal controls provide essential flexibility. Casters provide mobility.

to side, known as **panning**. When the camera is left unattended, it's important to set these controls so that the camera is locked into position. Otherwise, the camera head can be accidentally jarred and pointed toward a lighting instrument. If the camera is severely unbalanced on the mounting device, it can actually pitch forward and fall to the floor.

The device that prevents side-to-side sweeping of the camera is called the **pan lock**; the **tilt lock** prevents tilting of the camera. On many camera mounts, friction controls can be fine-tuned so that you can make a smooth on-air move. More details about the camera will be presented in Chapter 3. But for now, it's enough to know that a camera operator should adjust these controls to a comfortable setting—a setting where camera movements are easy and smooth but there is still enough friction to keep the camera still when you are holding it stationary. As a general rule, do not lock your camera into place during a program. You may be called on to make a sudden move if, for example, the guest unexpectedly changes position.

Lighting Instruments

Without light, there would be no picture for the camera to see. But the *way* the camera perceives light is not so readily apparent because the process is significantly different from the workings of your eye.

For one thing, in order to "see" well, television cameras need more light than does the human eye. Moreover, cameras cannot handle a wide *range* of light. Although you can easily make out details in a room containing brightly lighted and dimly lighted areas, the camera cannot.

Suppose, for example, you were looking at a woman wearing a dark blue dress and sitting on a black couch. In her hands, she holds a silver platter engraved with a fancy design. Your eyes will have no trouble handling the wide range of light that is reflected back at you.

The silver platter will obviously reflect a great deal of light. It has a mirrorlike finish. The black couch, though, absorbs light and reflects very little of it toward your eyes. That is, in physical terms, what *causes* a dark color to be dark is that it does not reflect much light. Most of the light we see—the light that gives shape, color, and texture—is *reflected* light.

And although your eyes will have no trouble with the high contrast between the brightness (the amount of reflected light) of the silver platter and the black couch, the camera will be absolutely bewildered. It cannot handle such a high *ratio* of contrasting light. When the camera sees this scene, one of two things will happen. Either the plate will appear at its proper level of brightness, but the detail of the dress and couch will be lost, or the couch and dress will look fine but the plate will cause a hot, scalding image on the screen.

Another difference between your eyes and the camera is that your binocular vision offers a much better perception of depth. If you were to direct a light at, let's say, a person seated in front of a curtain, you would have no difficulty perceiving that the person and the curtain are not the same distance from the camera, and you could make a reasonable guess as to how far in front of the curtain the person is seated. But the primitive (in comparison to your eyes and optical brain centers which process visual information) video camera cannot interpret this depth, so we must use special lighting techniques to accentuate depth and separation of the subject from the background.

Distinguishing between levels of light and accentuating depth and separation of the subject from the background are the main goals of lighting for video. Specialized lighting instruments are used to illuminate the object pictured. Keeping the lighting from being very intense and very dark is known as maintaining a correct contrast ratio.

Three separate sources of light are used to accentuate the shape of the subject shown on-camera and to create the illusion of depth on the screen; this is known as three-point lighting.

Types of Lighting Instruments. Different types of lighting instruments produce "hard" focused light and "soft" diffused light (see also Chapter 9). The variety of lighting instruments allows you to control (a) the intensity of the light and (b) where the light falls.

Contrast Ratio. Maintaining a correct contrast ratio is important. The **contrast ratio** is the difference between very light and very dark parts of the picture. Television lighting should not have a high *contrast ratio*. The brightest object in the picture should, ideally, be no more than 30 times as bright as the darkest area. In other words, the maximum contrast ratio is 30:1. (This is not the case for all cameras, but it is a generally accepted figure that can be used with confidence in most situations.) We'll learn exactly how to measure light in Chapter 9.

Three-Point Lighting. The camera produces a flat, two-dimensional image that appears, under light which seems "normal" to the human eye, to lack depth and dimension. That's why video lighting is completely different in form and function from normal room lighting. Video lights, called lighting instruments in the trade, are designed to provide shape and depth to the object pictured. In a studio, the object (or person) is often lighted from an angle to the left, with a fairly harsh light, from the right with a softer light, and from the rear with a fairly harsh, intense light. This arrangement is depicted in Figure 2.8. Because the lighting comes from three points, it is logically called *three-point* lighting. Sometimes, this arrangement is referred to as the lighting triangle.

The three sources of video light, as shown in Figure 2.9, are called key, fill, and back. The **key** is the principal source of illumination; it comes in at an angle (usually between 35 and 45 degrees from the camera) and casts shadows that add dimension to the object. The **fill**, a softer light shining from the other direction, fills in some of the harsher shadows but does not wipe out the "modeling" created by the key. *Modeling* means the way light highlights shape and texture. The **back** light, shining on top of an object or a performer's head and shoulders, visually separates the object or person from the background.

We'll demonstrate and illustrate the three-point lighting principle in Chapter 4.

Microphones and Audio Control Equipment

Sound is often the make-or-break factor in a video program—as well as the most frequently slighted aspect of the production process. Think about it: When you see a really poor, obviously cheaply made program, what's the first negative factor you notice? Chances are, it's the hollow,

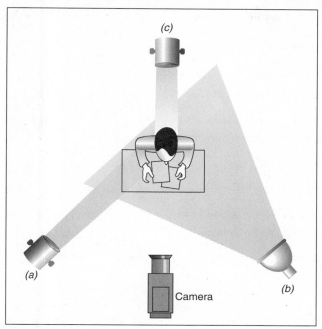

Figure 2.8 Three-point lighting. The harsh "key" light (*a*) casts shadows to model the performer's features. The "fill" light (*b*) is less intense and softens those shadows. The "back" light (*c*) illuminates the performer's head and shoulders and separates him or her from the background.

flat sound of improperly placed mics and/or the mismatching of sound levels that become apparent as two or more on-camera performers talk. Or, you might notice obvious blunders, such as a mic's not being "open" when the person on camera is talking, or worse, the mic's being open when it's not supposed to be.

The use of microphones can become complex, but at a basic video production level a few pointers will serve to get you started. At this point, remember that there are several physical types of microphones and that microphones have varying **pickup patterns**, that is, patterns of directionality in which they pick up or reject sound. The output of the microphone, known as audio, is then transmitted to the **audio console**, which governs the loudness of audio signals and allows the operator to mix them together.

Physical Types of Microphones. The two most frequently used mics (the abbreviation for microphone is usually spelled "mic" but pronounced "mike") in the television studio are lavalieres and shotguns. The **lavaliere** (Figure 2.10) is named after the French word for pendant, because this type of mic was originally worn like a necklace. Newer lavalieres are so small and light that they need not be hung around the neck. Instead, they are clipped to clothing on the upper chest, usually a tie, jacket, shirt, or

Figure 2.9 Positioning three-point lighting. The key light and fill light are usually placed at a maximum angle of about 45 degrees, or a minimum of about 35 degrees to the subject (as measured from the subject-camera line). The back light is usually directly behind or a little to the side of the subject. Lighting instruments are generally hung from the ceiling 10 feet or higher from the floor.

Figure 2.10 A lavaliere microphone. Lavaliere microphones are small enough to clip to the talents' shirt, blouse, jacket lapel, or tie. A "lav" is a sensitive electric mic that requires a battery. (*Courtesy of Telex Communications, Inc.*)

blouse. The lavaliere is the type of mic typically worn by a news anchor.

A **shotgun** mic (Figure 2.11) is often suspended from a long pole (sometimes called a **boom**) and is used to pick up sounds at a fairly long distance, when it is not appropriate or feasible to clip on a lavaliere. For example, on *The Tonight Show*, the guests walk out on stage, greet the host, and then immediately sit down and begin chatting. It would be awkward, to say the least, to have Jay Leno clip a mic to his guests' lapels as they sit. Equally inappropriate would be the image of a lavaliere mic clipped to a performer's lapel during a dramatic series, unless that performer were playing a TV anchor.

Most mics mounted on booms are designed not only to pick up sound from a relatively long distance, but also to have a narrow "focus" so that extraneous sounds do not distract the viewer/listener. A variation on this theme is the mic commonly mounted on a remote camera. It points straight forward and picks up a fairly narrow "cone" of sound; this may produce acceptable sound, but it is not always the best-quality sound. Most remote cameras have a receptacle into which a higher-quality mic, such as a hand-held mic, can be plugged.

The adjective *hand-held* pretty much describes the instrument in question. The hand-held mic is commonly used by news reporters in the field, although some interviews and stand-up reports are done wearing a lavaliere.

Microphone Pickup Patterns. The preceding discussion described mics only in terms of their typical uses—hung from the neck or clipped to the persons clothing, mounted on a boom, or hand-held. But there are many other properties of mics of which you should be aware, and those will be discussed thoroughly in Chapter 5. For now,

one of the more important points to remember is that some mics pick up sound equally well from all sides, but other mics are directional.

Any mic mounted on a boom, for example, will usually be highly directional. That is, it will pick up sound in front very well but reject most sound from the sides and almost all sound from the back. You can intuitively see why this is an advantage when "miking" a talk show guest: You want clear sound from in front of the mic—where the guest sits—but you want as little sound as possible coming from behind the mic, where you'll find the shuffling, mumbling audience.

The Audio Console. Another important concept relating to mics involves what happens to the sound after it is picked up by the mic.

Let's digress for a moment and more clearly define our terminology. Technically, the output of a mic is no longer sound, but audio. **Audio** is the electronic signal that represents sound. Think of audio in this way: Sound is a vibration of molecules in the air or other medium. As such, sound itself cannot travel through electronic wiring. The microphone changes the physical energy of sound, the vibration of molecules, into the electronic energy of audio. At the other end of the wire or transmission, a loudspeaker changes the audio back into sound by creating vibration in the air.

The process of changing one form of energy to another is known as **transduction**. A microphone is a transducer because it changes the physical energy of sound into the electronic energy of audio. A video camera is also a transducer. It changes the electromagnetic energy of light waves into the electronic energy of video.

The audio signal from the mic is fed into the control room where the audio console (Figure 2.12) governs the loudness of the signal; it also controls mic levels to compensate for people speaking at various intensities. The console operator can turn the signal on and off, and using knobs known as potentiometers ("pots") can govern the

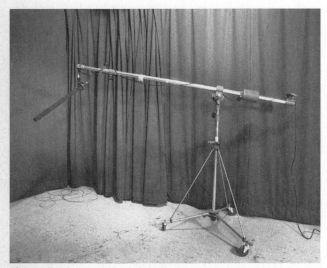

Figure 2.11 A mic boom. A giraffe or tripod boom can move freely and support a shotgun mic easily to capture audio when you simply can not clip a mic onto a lapel.

Figure 2.12 An audio mix console. The audio mixing console enables a number of microphones and various audio sources to be combined.

volume. Instead of knobs, many consoles, especially newer models, use vertical slide faders ("sliders") that are pushed upward to raise the volume and downward to lower it.

The Video Switcher

A video switcher is similar to the audio console. Whereas the audio console allows the operator to choose among audio sources, the **switcher** allows the director to choose among several video signals. The switcher is a device for choosing which shots from a camera or combination of cameras goes over the air or to the tape. It also creates a variety of special effects, such as a dissolve. A **dissolve** is an effect where one picture gradually replaces another.

Some video switchers are quite simple (Figure 2.13). Others are much more complex (Figure 2.14). But regardless of their level of complexity, both switchers do basically the same job. The bigger, more complex switcher can handle a wider array of effects and operations, but the underlying principle is still the same.

Figure 2.15 shows a diagram of a simplified video switcher that allows you to cut, dissolve, and fade and wipe. With these actions, you can direct a simple program.

The diagram in Figure 2.15 represents only a part of the video switcher, a part called the mix bus. A **mix bus** (sometimes spelled "buss") is a collection of circuits or a bank of buttons that activates the circuits controlling a video source.

Cut. A **cut** is an instantaneous change from one picture to another. Cuts are used to indicate an immediate change in perspective taking place in real time, such as cutting back and forth between two people during a conversation.

You would perform the cuts by pressing the corresponding buttons on the top row of the video switcher in Figure 2.15. Why the top row? Because that's the row that has been activated by the "fader bar," a lever that smoothly

Figure 2.14 A complex video switcher. With many more options, this switcher is more complex, but its purpose is the same as the simple switcher—to provide the means of switching between cameras and a combination of video sources to output one video signal.

moves up and down and chooses which bank of buttons is going to be used to select the on-air picture. If the bar is left halfway between, you'll see a mixture of the picture punched up on the top row and the picture punched up on the bottom row—a sort of superimposition of two images. The picture on the monitor instantly changes from the image produced by the previously selected camera to the newly selected camera.

Dissolve. A dissolve, as you remember, is the gradual replacement of one picture with another. A dissolve is generally used to indicate a transition in time or place; it is also used when we want a gentle change between pictures, such as a change from a medium shot to a close-up in a televised ballet.

The fader bar, as pictured in Figure 2.15, is in the top

Figure 2.13 A simple video switcher. Like the audio mixer, the video switcher allows a number of cameras and video sources to be mixed into one signal for transmission or recording.

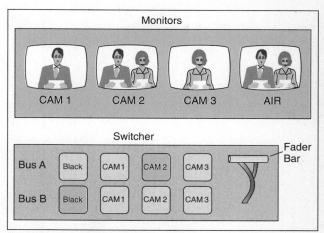

Figure 2.15 Selecting the shots. In the control room the monitors (top) display the shots available from studio cameras one, two, and three (see Figure 2.16). A fourth "AIR" monitor displays the shot selected (from camera two), which goes over the air or to tape.

On the switcher (bottom) "CAM 2" is active in Bus (row) A, and selected by the position of the fader bar. The two-shot appears on both the CAM 2 and AIR monitors.

To cut to camera one for a close-up of the host, the operator punches "CAM 1" in Bus A. To fade to black (or to dissolve to another camera), the operator slides the fader bar down to Bus B. The active signal in Bus B then goes over the air.

position. Should you have camera one "punched up" on the top row of buttons—the row activated by the fader bar—and camera two punched up on the lower row, you will be able to dissolve from camera one to camera two by moving the fader bar downward.

Fade. A **fade** is going to black from a picture or coming into a picture from black and is used to start and end a show or to start and end distinct segments within a program. This is the only correct usage of the word *fade*: You "fade to black" or, as some people phrase the opposite action, "fade in (or up) from black." You do not fade between pictures; you dissolve between pictures. (Remember: *fade* to black . . . *dissolve* to another camera.)

"Black" is an option on either row of buttons on the video switcher. You could, therefore, punch up black and fade to it using the fader bar. The bar allows you to choose which row of buttons controls the image going over the air.

Wipe. A **wipe** is the replacement of one picture with another by having a distinct border from one picture move across, down, or in some other direction—replacing the original picture. The familiar split screen is really a wipe paused half-way between the process of wiping one picture over another. Wipes are not used as frequently as cuts, dissolves, and fades.

Using Cuts, Dissolves, and Fades to Direct a Simple Program. Figure 2.16 demonstrates how you can produce

a simple live or live-on-tape program using the simple functions we discussed. You can:

1. Punch up black on the bottom bus, and fade up from black by punching up camera two on the top bus and moving the fade bar to the top bus.

2. Open the show with a shot of a host and guest on camera two.

3. Cut to a close-up of the host on camera one by pushing the appropriate button on the top bus of the video switcher.

4. Cut to a close-up of the guest as he or she answers the question by pressing the button that selects camera three.

5. Keep cutting back and forth between shots of the host and guest as appropriate.

6. Cut back to the shot on camera two as the host wraps up the interview.

7. Fade to black by moving the fader bar down to the bottom bus, where the button for "black" is still selected.

Most interview programs use cuts, but if you want to dissolve between shots you simply choose the appropriate camera from the bus that is *not* on the air—in other words, choose your next shot—and then move the fader bar slowly from the bus that *is* on air, lowering it until it ac-

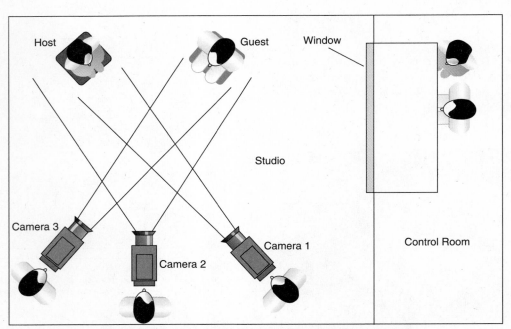

Figure 2.16 A simple talk show setup. Camera one shoots the host, camera two shoots the guest, and camera three shoots both. This standard "two-shot" will open the program. In the control room, the director can select shots that best communicate the interview as it unfolds (see also Figure 2.15). A technical director may operate the switcher, thereby freeing the director to instruct the camera operators and to call the shots.

tivates the lower bus and mixes the pictures. One picture will gradually replace the other.

Editing Equipment

Videotape doesn't have sprocket holes like film, but it does have a system of "electronic sprocket holes" that keeps tape speed constant and provides a very accurate way to measure tape time. There are two primary ways of laying down electronic "sprockets," and we'll explore them in Chapter 6.

For now, keep in mind that the equipment on which you will edit consists, at the most basic level, of two videotape machines and one device that controls and synchronizes both machines. This device, which governs the equipment used in editing, is usually called the **editing control unit**, although it is also known as the edit interface.

Figure 2.17 shows a simplified version of an editing setup. The **source unit**—the VTR on the left—is where you play back the "raw" tape, the tape you've gathered in the field. The **record unit**—the VTR on the right—holds the videotape onto which you are placing the final program. (By the way, the vocabulary used to describe editing is perhaps more confusing than the actual process. See Box 2.1 for a primer.)

Here is how you might use editing equipment to produce a simple ENG piece.

* You return from your assignment with a videocassette on which you have recorded your reporter doing two takes of the introduction to a news report (the first take is not usable), a brief interview segment with the mayor, and three takes of the closing (they're all OK, but the first take is the best).

* Since the reporter ruined the first take of the introduction, you find the second take on the source unit. Using your edit control unit, you "cue up" the tape to the point where you want to

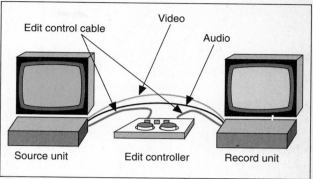

Figure 2.17 A simplified editing setup. Videotapes shot in the field are played on the source unit (left). An editor programs the editing control unit to assemble and insert segments onto the tape in the record (or edit) unit (right).

begin the introduction and the point where you want to stop it.

* Using the computerized controls of the edit control unit, you rerecord (copy) take two of the introduction from the source unit to the record unit. The editing control unit does this for you; it even automatically backs up both tapes for five seconds in order to get them "rolling" at the same speed. Now, you've got the introduction laid down on the tape that will eventually go on air.

* You use the same process to rerecord, or in video terminology "dub," the interview from the tape in the source unit to the tape in the record unit. Note that the interview can be on a different cassette than the one with the reporter's introductions and closings. It doesn't really matter. The editing suite gives you the capability of using any number of tape sources as your raw material.

* The edit control unit allows you to make a smooth joining, or edit, of the reporter's introduction and the mayor's interview.

BOX 2.1   VIDEO EDITING JARGON

The vocabulary of video production is rather murky when it comes to the units in an editing setup. I have chosen *source unit* for the VTR on which the raw tape is played, *editing control unit* as the device that synchronizes the VTRs, and *record unit* as the VTR that records the final program because the names are descriptive and not easily confused.

Many people call the source unit the "slave deck" and

the record unit the "master deck" or "edit deck," but I have observed those terms being used more or less interchangeably at certain facilities in various parts of the country.

Use whatever nomenclature is employed at your studio, but remember that while the functions of the equipment are universal, the names are not.

• Now you find the best take (it was take one) of the reporter's closing. During the closing, the reporter stands before city hall and sums up the interview. You dub take one of the closing from the source unit to the record unit. Again, the editing control unit makes a smooth edit—and you've got your final piece, ready for air.

Whether a program is created live or live-on-tape or edited from SCV, video production is a *communication-oriented* process. Learning what is appropriate, how to communicate the proper message, and how to utilize special effects to enhance communication is what producing and directing video is all about. Learning the operations of a particular piece of equipment, while undoubtedly important, *is not the core of good video.*

In fact, it is a fundamental mistake to regard the operation of equipment as an end in itself—to be content with knowing that "If I push this button, this happens." Concentrate on learning the *principles* of video. By all means learn how to use the equipment, but don't convince yourself that technical proficiency in operating the hardware automatically translates into good production skills. If you learn the basic production skills, you can always pick up the details of operating specific equipment.

For example, many beginning video directors will tell you that their first concern is running the switcher. But after a few months, they find that operating the switcher is one of the simplest parts of the job. And when they change jobs, they find that learning the layout of the new switcher only takes an afternoon.

The same applies to cameras, VTRs, audio consoles, and virtually any other piece of equipment used in video. Although the location of the buttons and switches may differ, and the equipment will vary in complexity, it all performs roughly the same function regardless of its design or complexity.

To deliberately belabor this point, let's note that some people who become enamored of button pushing never learn the principles of good video and—worse—are therefore unable to adapt to new positions and equipment. A director who learns the switcher by rote, who doesn't know the *basic principles*, probably won't be able to pick up another model's operations as easily as the person with a firm grasp of the fundamentals.

Having said that—several times, but it's a point worth repeating—let's now take a look at the people involved in the production process. Specifically, we'll examine the duties of various crew members and show how those *people* working with *equipment* communicate using the video medium. This series of snapshots will add to what we've discussed so far, lending a more detailed perspective of the production process. As you gain experience and read more

detailed chapters, you'll be able to layer additional knowledge onto this overview.

PEOPLE AND THE PRODUCTION PROCESS

All the elaborate equipment demonstrated up to this point is useless without competent, creative people to run it. Those people comprise the video crew—an organization which, depending on the circumstances and the people involved, might seem like an extended family, a paramilitary organization, or a bizarre combination of the two (Figure 2.18). We'll first examine the crew and its duties and then briefly discuss the importance of teamwork among crew members in managing the production process.

The Crew and Its Duties

What follows are brief descriptions of the job duties of a typical video production crew. When examining this overview, keep in mind that all crews do not necessarily utilize all these positions. In small organizations, for example, one person may handle the lighting and the audio. And as already mentioned, the jobs of producer and director are frequently melded into one.

In large crews, though, the jobs may be highly specialized. A lighting director may have several layers of assistants, and various people high in the corporate hierarchy may have vague but impressive "executive producer" status, even though they may never actually set foot in the studio.

The descriptions incorporate the positions you are most likely to encounter in the realm of typical video production—a realm which lies somewhere between the one-person band and the network studio production team. We'll quickly examine the roles of the producer, director, technical director, tape editor, chief engineer, lighting director, audio director, camera operator(s), floor director, assistant director, character generator operator, talent, and scriptwriter. Then, under a broad miscellaneous category, we'll explore some other positions that may or may not be part of the typical crew.

Producer. The producer, as mentioned earlier, is in charge of the program. However, the term *producer* has developed various new meanings as the scope of video has expanded. For example, the person in charge of operations for an ENG shoot is often called a *field producer*. Although the field producer is more or less in charge of operations for that particular shoot, he or she does not have final say on the contents of the report. That responsibility rests with the *news director*, the executive in charge of the department.

Director. The director is in charge of the video crew. The director in modern video is also an *interpreter* of sorts.

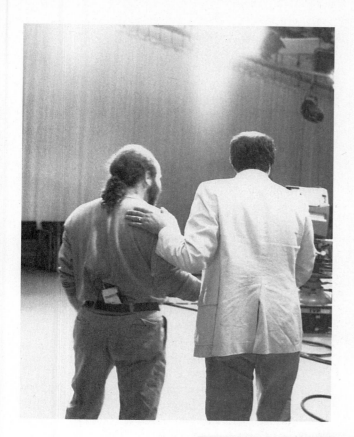

Figure 2.18 The production team. An experienced production team makes television come alive. Every member is a vital link in the chain required to produce high-quality material.

That is, he or she takes the technological options available and makes them into modes of communication. During production, the director is responsible not only for choosing what shot is used, but also for using the shot that conveys the right message. For example, whether a scene is to be shot with the camera representing the point of view of the person about to be murdered is a directorial decision. Does stark, harsh lighting convey the right idea, or is soft illumination better-suited? That, too, is within the domain of the director.

Technical Director. Faced with so many decisions, the director generally needs the help of another crew person to operate the controls of the video switcher. The **technical director**, commonly referred to as the TD, sits before the bank of switches and levers at the video switcher and "punches up" the shots called by the director

(Figure 2.19). This way, the director can keep his or her attention focused on the unfolding program and not the control room operations.

Tape Editor. The tape editor operates the editing equipment while ENG and EFP footage are assembled into a final program. Some producers, directors, and producer-directors in smaller operations operate the editing gear, but in larger organizations, and in companies where union restrictions prohibit anyone but specialized personnel from handling the editing equipment, the tape editor performs all the mechanical operations.

In general, though, the tape editor's job involves more than just machines. He or she usually develops a finely tuned feel for the pace of a program, and helps the producer and director execute the most effective sequence of shots. An editor, for instance, might tell the director, "This scene is building up the tension for the final crisis point . . . I think we should speed up the cuts, make the next four shots much shorter." A good director might not always agree—but he or she will always listen.

Chief Engineer. The "chief" is a highly trained technician who keeps things running. In addition to supervising the repair and maintenance of the video equipment, the **chief engineer** supervises the setup of the proper electrical levels for the output of the camera signals, and is in charge of the master control room.

In large video operations, several technical specialists report to the chief. Some of these specialists' jobs may be limited strictly to repair of equipment, which is usually called "bench work" in the trade. Others may take a direct role in operations.

In broadcast television, chief engineers (if they are also in charge of the transmitter, which is usually the case) must have a license issued by the Federal Communications Commission; the license is granted only after a chief passes a test proving that he or she is capable of keeping the station operating and transmitting within tightly drawn parameters.

Lighting Director. **Lighting directors** have one of the most difficult and underappreciated jobs in video. There is a tendency (even among those who should know better) to assume that the lighting director simply aims some instruments, throws a switch, and drinks coffee until it's time to go home.

That's hardly the case. First of all, the "LD" must create an overall **base light**, which is the light filling all areas of the set, leaving no unintentionally dark areas and, conversely, no hot spots that will create too high a contrast ratio. Second, the LD must arrange three-point lighting for every person (and sometimes several objects) on the set). The setups for such lighting vary enormously. For instance, the lighting arrangement for an actor with a shiny bald head must be radically different than for an actor with a full head of dark curls. Third, the LD may be responsible for changing the lighting scheme *during* the show.

These tasks are accomplished using two basic pieces of apparatus in addition to the lighting instruments themselves: a lighting grid and a lighting control panel. The LD hangs the instruments from a lighting grid, which is a set of tracks high above the studio floor (Figure 2.20). Instruments are then aimed and focused. The LD turns instruments on and off by operating a **lighting control panel**, a device that features controls for raising or lowering the amount of current being fed to a particular lighting instrument or an entire setup of lighting instruments. The lighting director can also control the intensity of the instruments through the panel, and sometimes makes small adjustments. Because lowering current to a lighting instrument affects its apparent color, this is often the last option.

Audio Director. A close second for underapprecia-

Figure 2.20 The lighting grid. The lighting grid is generally suspended 12 to 18 feet above the floor, hanging 2 feet below the ceiling. The grid is often erected from a heavy pipe and is commonly used for suspending other production equipment besides lighting fixtures such as, fans and seamless paper for backdrops.

Figure 2.19 The technical editor. Using the many switches and levers at the video switcher, the technical director (TD) "punches" up the shots called by the director.

tion must go to the **audio director** (AD), who sets up the microphones before the show and operates the audio console (Figure 2.21) during the program. The AD uses the audio console to choose which mic to air or tape, as well as to control mic levels to compensate for people speaking at varying intensities. In addition, the AD uses the console to control the volume of other audio inputs, such as various types of audio playback units including cartridge machines (a cartridge is an endless loop of tape) and reel-to-reel machines, as well as compact disc players. The AD also utilizes broadcast-quality phonograph machines, called "turntables" in the industry. (Please . . . don't ever call them "record players.")

Camera Operator(s). Because there is almost always more than one camera on a studio floor, the names of the camera operators are melded into the numerical designation of the camera they operate. In other words, the camerapeople are no longer "Bob," "Ted," and "Alice" when they assume the controls of their cameras: they're known as "Camera One," "Camera Two," and "Camera Three." Make it a habit to address camera operators this way when they are at their station. Although this practice is a bit dehumanizing, it prevents confusion caused by forgetting or mixing up names of camera operators—not to mention the problems that arise when more than one cameraperson has the same name. (When the camera is hand-held for ENG and EFP, the operator is usually referred to as the *photographer*, or increasingly the *videographer*.)

Camera operators are responsible for producing a shot that is in proper focus and properly composed. The camera operator, in essence, must give the director two things in order to ensure proper composition:

- The right *size* shot.
- A shot with proper *headroom* and *noseroom*.

As you've certainly surmised, the size of the shot refers to how much of the person (or an object) fills the screen.

There are many other types of shots, but a director will often call for a long shot, medium shot, or close-up (Figure 2.22). The shots shown in Figure 2.2 are representative of shots you might take for a documentary; studio shots will be illustrated later. See Figure 2.25 for one example of a studio CU. (These terms, which are largely self-explanatory, will be defined in Chapter 8.) Sometimes, the camera operator will be responsible for taking a two-shot (Figure 2.23) or an over-the-shoulder shot (Figure 2.24).

Figure 2.21 The audio director. The audio director uses an audio mixing console to raise, lower, and shape mic and line level volume to achieve a well-balanced program.

Figure 2.22 The basic shots. The long shot (LS), medium shot (MS), and close-up (CU) represent the subjective distance of the viewer to the subject. The more the subject fills the screen, the closer the shot.

Figure 2.23 A common two-shot.

Headroom is the distance from the top of the person's head to the top of the screen. Generally speaking, you want a comfortable amount of space—but not too much. A simpler way of thinking about this is to remember that the eyes of the subject should be about a third of the way down the screen (Figure 2.25).

Noseroom, sometimes called *lead room* or *looking space*, is determined when the subject's head is turned to the side. The shot appears much more natural if the person on-air has some space in the frame *into which* he or she can look (Figure 2.26).

We've only scratched the surface of the camera operator's duties, but the information presented so far offers a basic guide. If you are working hands-on in the studio at this point, you'll need to know some terms relating to camera movement. See Box 2.2.

Floor Director. The **floor director**, sometimes called the *floor manager*, is the director's link between the control room and the people in the studio. The floor director is in charge of all operations on the studio floor. In addition,

the floor director is usually responsible for cuing on-air talent—using hand signals to tell them when to start, stop, speed up, slow down, or change the camera to which they are speaking. "Cue talent" is the director's command to the floor director, advising the floor director to motion to talent that it's time to start speaking. The floor director also lets the talent and crew know how much time remains in the program.

Assistant Director. Many operations include a crewperson who helps the director keep track of program elements. **Assistant directors** are often used in newscast productions to keep track of time cues and other details because it is very difficult for one person to keep track of the time remaining in various tape inserts.

Character Generator Operator. At the most basic

Figure 2.25 Headroom and balance. Adequate headroom can frame a close-up. On a closeup, the talent's eyes will usually be one-third from the top.

Figure 2.24 An over-the-shoulder shot.

Figure 2.26 Noseroom or looking space. When shot from the side, talent needs space to look into. One quick way to calculate the noseroom, or looking space, is to divide the screen in half and align the tip of the talent's nose with the imaginary line that bisects the screen.

BOX 2.2 CAMERA MOVEMENTS

If you have reached the point where you are now using a camera, there is one other aspect of the operator's job you should understand to perform the most basic operations: movement.

Quite simply, a camera can move forward or backward, up or down, or from side to side. There are some industry-standard terms applied to these movements: *dolly, truck, pan, tilt,* and *pedestal.* A relatively self-evident term relating to a change in the lens' perspective, rather than moving the camera, is *zoom.*

When the camera physically moves forward or backward—when you're actually pulling it or pushing it across the studio floor, you are performing what's called a *dolly.* The word is used as a verb too: you *dolly in* (toward the subject) or *dolly out.*

When you physically move the camera from side to side, you are performing a *truck.* You can *truck left* or *truck right.*

Sweeping the lens from side to side, rotating the camera on its mount but keeping the mount in the same position, is known as *panning.*

Pointing the lens up or down, but not changing the actual height of the camera, is called *tilting.*

Raising or lowering the height of the camera is referred to as performing a *pedestal.*

Zooming means using the lens to magnify the object pictured without moving the camera; you can *zoom in* or *zoom out.* The visual effect of a zoom is different from a dolly, as will be explained in coming chapters.

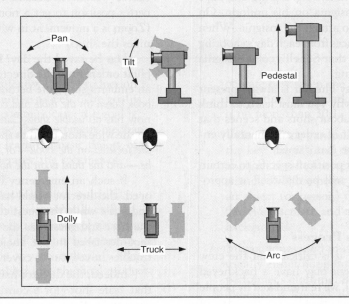

level, the operator of a character generator (CG) may be responsible only for typing in the names of people pictured on screen. But modern CG technology often allows the operator to create sophisticated visuals. First-class operators using the latest generation of equipment can accomplish seemingly miraculous tasks on short notice. For example, during one *CBS Evening News* telecast, a late-breaking story involved a tornado. The director instructed the CG operator (who in this case was also an accomplished video artist) to create a tornado graphic—within five minutes. The tornado graphic—a swirling diagram that actually moved on the screen—was inserted over Dan Rather's left shoulder.

Talent. In video, **talent** refers to any on-air performer. As with many video terms, the exact meaning of *talent* is not universally agreed upon. Although some production personnel use *talent* to refer to anyone on camera, some use *talent* to refer only to professional performers, and a word such as *guest* to indicate an interviewee.

Scriptwriter. Writing for video requires a specialized knowledge of the equipment and techniques *and* a thorough understanding of how to effectively communicate

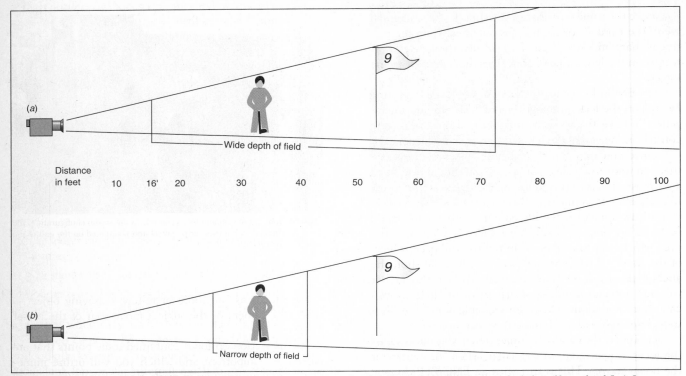

Figure 3.9 Depth of field. In a wide depth of field (*a*), objects from 16 to 70 feet from the camera will be in focus (both the golfer *and* and flag). In a narrow depth of field (*b*), only objects from 25 to 40 feet from the camera are in focus. (The golfer will be in focus, but the pin and flag will not.)

Here is a fuller explanation of the three factors cited earlier that influence depth of field.

- *The magnification of the lens*. A long lens gives you a very narrow depth of field. The longer the lens, the shallower the depth of field.

- *The distance from your camera to the subject*. The farther away you are from the subject, the greater the depth of field. If you're very close to the subject, a slight movement will throw the scene out of focus. But if the subject is farther away, it can move through a much greater depth of field. Don't confuse this with a telescopic magnification of the scene; the magnification properties of the lens are a different effect altogether. What "the distance from your camera to the subject" refers to can be shown in a practical example: Given the same focal length lens, a person standing 300 feet away from the camera who walks 10 feet toward you is likely to stay in focus. But a person standing 11 feet away who walks 10 feet toward you will not stay in focus.

- *The opening of the iris, which varies according to a number of factors, most notably for the amount of light falling on the subject*. The iris must open wide when there is very little light in the scene. When the iris is wide open, the depth of field is

narrow. When the iris is closed to a pin hole, a large depth of field is created. So you can get a larger depth of field in bright light.

Iris and f-Stop. An iris, also called an aperture, is a device that creates an expanded or contracted opening. It performs this function with overlapping leaflike structures which, when retracted, form a wide circle; when extended, they create a small circle (Figure 3.10). The iris opening

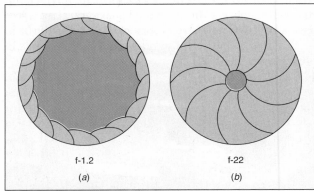

Figure 3.10 Iris openings. The iris controls the exposure, the amount of light entering the camera. With the iris leaves drawn back to an f-1.2 setting, this aperture is wide open (*a*). Extending the iris leaves to an f-22 setting narrows the aperture (*b*). Larger f-numbers mean smaller apertures and less light.

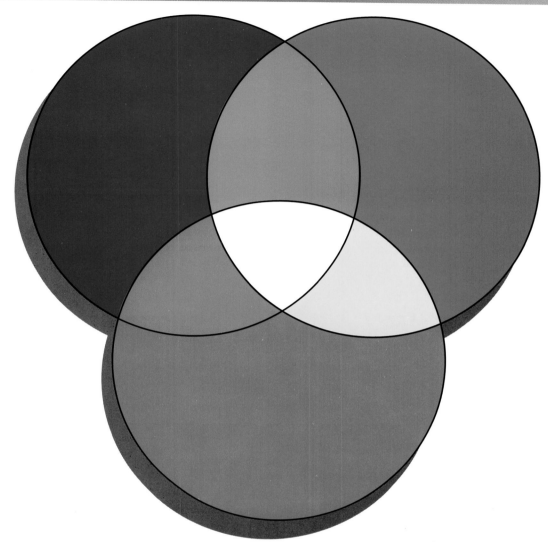

Additive light properties. The pure, primary light colors (red, green, and blue) are blended to produce the secondary light colors (magenta, yellow, and cyan). Combining different intensities of the primary colors can create all possible colors. White light is a balance of all three primary colors.

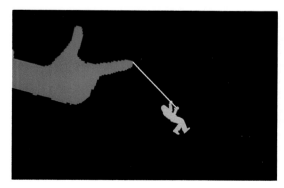

Hanging by a thread. The Videoplace participant's image dangles from a graphic string suspended from the Videodesk participant's finger. By moving from side to side, Videoplace participants can cause their images to swing. Since the two people can be a distance apart, this two-way interaction is really a playful teleconference.

Photo courtesy of Myron Krueger of Artificial Reality.

Plate 1

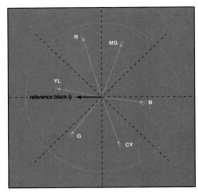

Correct adjustment. To be sure that both the monitor and camera are adjusted correctly, a technician or engineer uses a Color Checker Chart and a vectorscope. Color on the monitor should match the chart (left). The vectorscope (right) displays light vectors in a pattern representing color value. When the video image is correctly adjusted, each vector points toward a labeled color box. Reference black is represented by a 180 degree vector.

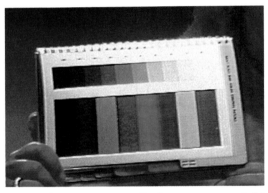
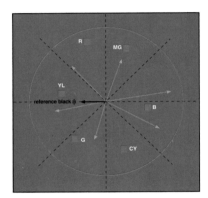

Ninety degrees out of phase toward blue. The monitor image has a blue cast, and the yellow bar of the Checker Chart appears magneta (left). The vectorscope pattern seems to be rotated to the right: the line that once pointed to yellow now points to magenta, and the other vectors are similarly out of phase.

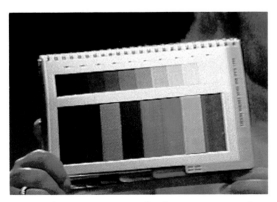
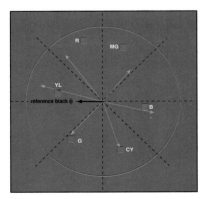

Ninety degrees out of phase toward green. The yellow bar on the Checker Chart appears blue (left). Flesh tones have a green cast. The vectorscope reading shows the line that once pointed to yellow now points to cyan. When the camera is out of phase, only one vector can point to a color box.

Plate 2

color temperature

Outdoor lighting. The color temperature of outdoor lighting is higher than typical indoor lighting. The camera needs to be white-balanced and filtered to accommodate these conditions. The image at the top was shot correctly. Notice the blue cast to the image at the bottom, which was shot with indoor adjustments.

Plate 3

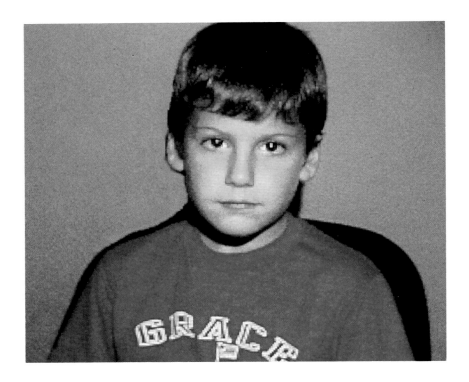

Indoor lighting. Before you shoot an indoor scene, white-balance your camera. The image at the top was shot correctly, but the image at the bottom was shot with outdoor adjustments. Notice the red overtones.

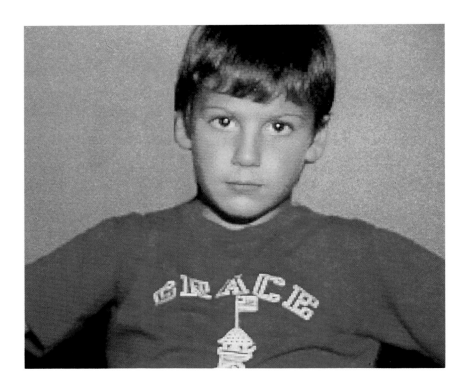

Plate 4

regulates the exposure, the amount of light allowed into the camera. The larger opening obviously lets in more light, to accommodate dimly lit locations. In bright sunshine, the iris will be contracted, letting in less light.

Iris control is an automatic function of most cameras, although cameras do have controls allowing the operator to manually override the iris. This might be necessary, if, for example, you are taping an interview with a person who is sitting in front of a bright window. The camera sees the window and sets its exposure (sets the opening of the iris) accordingly; it has no way of knowing that you want to set your exposure on the person and not on the window. So in this case, you would override the automatic iris control and widen the iris opening, letting in more light and exposing the person's face properly.

There are other instances when you might choose to change the iris setting to achieve an effect. As mentioned earlier, a large iris opening causes the depth of field to be more shallow than a small opening. This is desirable when, for example, you intentionally want to blur a distracting background.

You probably will not set the iris manually very often, except in advanced portable camera work where you must compensate for bright backgrounds. In studio conditions, the light and environment are so constant that the engineering staff will usually preselect the iris setting so that no on-air adjustment, automatic or manual, is necessary.

When the iris is adjusted, either by the operator or by the automatic control, the f-stop is changed. The **f-stop**, sometimes called the f-number, is a number determined by a mathematical formula, indicating the amount of light transmitted through the lens. (Why "f"? See Box 3.1 for this and other camera trivia.) F-stops are indicated on the aperture ring on the camera lens assembly (Figure 3.11).

It is not necessary to go into the derivation of the formula, but it is important to remember that *a smaller f-stop indicates a larger iris opening*. For example, a video camera lens might have f-stops ranging from f-1.2 (very wide, admitting a great deal of light), to f-22 (very small, admitting only a little light).

The f-numbers used on the aperture ring vary from camera to camera, because the formula for calculating them takes into account a number of physical factors specific to an individual lens. The actual numbers do not provide you with any specific information necessary for operating the camera. You won't, for example, be told to take an "f-5.6 shot," although there may be occasions when you are instructed to get a wide or shallow depth of field. But the numbers do have meaning when viewed in relation to each other.

We can sum up what you *do* need to know about f-stops by reviewing information that has already been presented and by adding material that will now make the concept of f-stop less obscure.

- The larger the f-number, the greater the depth of field. A smaller f-number creates a smaller depth of field.

- The bigger the f-number, the smaller the iris opening.

BOX 3.1   SOME CAMERA TRIVIA

Here are some facts about video cameras which may or may not be particularly useful, but they are interesting:

- The first type of camera tube was called an *Image-Orthicon*. The tube was colloquially called an "immy." The term *immy* was modified somewhat into a name, "Emmy," which, of course, became the name of the awards honoring members of the television industry.

- Early black-and-white television cameras could distinguish some colors better than others. The primitive systems required performers, in some cases, to wear green makeup on their faces and to paint their lips black.

- The *f* in *f-stop* stands for the Latin word *fenestra*, which means "window." When you adjust the f-stop, you are changing the size of the window that lets in light.

- Successful politicians use mass media to their advantage, and television journalists too often accommodate them to get good footage. Before cameras became readily portable, news footage from the field was recorded on motion picture film and then shown over the air. The problem with film was the limited amount of running time available—only a few minutes per spool. Senator Joseph McCarthy, who was notorious for his role in instigating anticommunist hysteria, was a master at manipulating the press. He'd instruct camera operators that, during his news conferences, they should start their cameras rolling only when he banged the side of the lectern. This was his signal that he was about to say something that would make for good film.

Figure 3.11 Iris control. The f-stops, or f-numbers, on the aperture ring determine the amount of light allowed to pass through the lens.

Aperture Ring   Filter Wheel

- Some new information clarifies why this is the case: *the f-number is a ratio.* That is, f-4 really means f ¼, and f-8 means f-⅛. One-quarter (¼) is larger than one-eighth (⅛). Therefore, f-4 indicates a larger opening than f-8.

- Each f-stop marked on the aperture ring on the lens indicates a doubling or halving of the light allowed to pass through the lens. If you "open up one stop" from f-22 to f-16, you've doubled the amount of light coming in through the lens. What you actually have done—and what the f-number expresses in mathematical terms—is to double the area of the iris that is opened.

- Some lenses do not allow you to operate with a very small opening. This is particularly true of long telephoto lenses. Why? A telephoto lens has a great deal of glass in the lens mechanism because it needs more and thicker lenses to accomplish the magnification. Glass, even high-quality optical glass, absorbs light. So, the more glass, the less light that can pass through the lens. (A lens needing a lot of light is often referred to as a "slow" lens.)

A TYPICAL STUDIO CAMERA

You now know enough camera fundamentals to perform most basic camera operations, even though we have not gone into great depth about the intricacies of camera controls. We've just seen how video cameras collect images and translate them into electrical signals. Now let's examine the parts and controls of a typical camera.

Because cameras differ from brand to brand, you should compare our "generic" functional descriptions with the equipment available to you. (You may want to examine the manuals that came with your equipment for

more detail about precise information. These manuals are often stored in the engineer's filing cabinet.)

The Viewfinder, Tally Light, and Lens

While reading the following descriptions, refer to Figure 3.12, which shows a studio camera with its anatomy labeled for quick reference.

You are already familiar with the viewfinder, which is a device that shows what the camera is seeing.

- It usually has controls that allow the operator to adjust for brightness and contrast, the same as for a black-and-white television set. These controls adjust only the viewfinder's picture, not the video signal being sent from the camera.

- The viewfinder does not always show exactly what is seen by the director in the control room or the viewer watching the program at home. The viewfinder system often does not show the same image as the monitor, so there may be times when you, as a camera operator, will have to mentally adjust for this factor. For example, the director

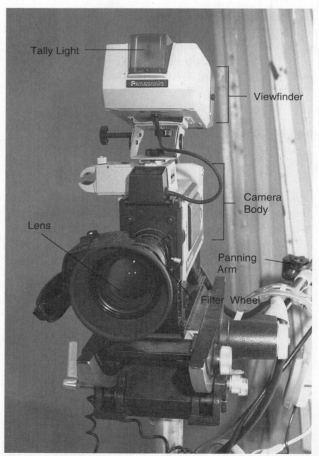

Tally Light

Viewfinder

Camera Body

Lens

Panning Arm

Filter Wheel

Figure 3.12 Parts of the studio camera.

may tell you that you have not allowed enough headroom when your viewfinder shows plenty of headroom. Should this happen, remember that the director is probably seeing an accurate representation of the picture and you are not. Camera operators sometimes compensate by comparing their viewfinder to a studio monitor and drawing erasable crayon marks on the viewfinder to indicate the true framing.

- There is usually a tally light visible to the operator. The **tally light** lets the camera operator know when the camera is on the air. It is automatically activated when the director "punches up" the camera in the control room. A separate tally light is also visible to the talent. The tally light is mounted either on the top of the viewfinder or on the camera body.

You are already familiar with the lens, which has a variable focal length and thus can be zoomed in and out. The zoom control is usually run by a switch that activates a smoothly functioning zoom mechanism. The iris generally takes care of itself with no input from the operator. Both automatic controls can be overridden should the need arise. Focus is usually controlled by a manual adjustment.

- Cameras often have a filter wheel located behind the lens. The **filter wheel** allows you to choose filters that will help the camera adapt to varied lighting conditions. Although the exact function of the wheel is not the same for every camera, the wheels generally contain filters that adjust the camera to process outdoor light. The white balance mechanism then allows the operator to make finer adjustments to the color temperature of the incoming light. Filters are also important in situations where there's little control over lighting: If you're shooting in lighting conditions with a huge contrast ratio, for example—if there is very bright light in the same picture and you simply cannot do anything to correct the lighting—then you may be forced to move the "neutral density" filter into position. This particular filter reduces the intensity of light without varying its color. Check the manufacturer's manual for further details.

The Camera Body

The camera body contains the internal workings of the camera and, of course, has connections for the lens and viewfinder.

The Bars Switch. The studio camera has a variety of controls that can be accessed by lifting a side panel; some of these controls may not be covered, depending on the

camera model. Generally speaking, when you are operating a studio camera it is wise not to change these control settings unless you are instructed to do so by the director or engineer. However, it would be a good idea to ask about the controls for your particular studio unit because you can then troubleshoot certain situations.

For example, most cameras have either an external or internal switch marked "bars." This switch produces the familiar color bar pattern that engineers can use to make calibrations (Figure 3.13). Should your camera not be producing a normal picture, check the "bars" switch (or button) before requesting help from the engineer. But don't take the camera setting off the bars until you are told to do so or request permission because you may interrupt the calibration process.

Note that some controls for the studio camera are located on the camera control unit in a remote area in master control.

Connecting Jacks and Cables. The studio camera body has connecting jacks for the cable that carries the video information and for the intercom that allows the director and camera operator to communicate. Be very careful of these jacks; they are delicate and can be easily damaged if the cable is suddenly yanked.

Incidentally, be careful of the cable too. Don't step on cables; they can be damaged easily. Also, be careful not to trip over cables because most studio floors are made of a concrete base, which means that *you* can be damaged easily should you trip or fall.

The Panning Arms

The camera has handles on both sides, normally called panning arms, although they can be used to tilt the camera too. On most studio cameras, the zoom control is on the

Figure 3.13 The color bars switch. The color bars switch selects between a video picture and color bars. Selecting "color bars" overrides any picture and sends the color bars signal back to the control room for proper monitor calibration.

right handle (the handle you hold with your right hand), and the focus is on the left.

On sophisticated studio cameras, a shot box is often mounted on the right-hand panning handle (Figure 3.14). The **shot box** allows the operator to preset several shots—say a close-up of the news anchor—and select them by pressing a button. The camera "remembers" and recreates the shot by adjusting the position and focus of the camera.

Controls mounted on the panning handles are often called servo controls. **Servo** indicates any device that governs a function via remote control.

The Camera Mount and Pedestal

Studio cameras are mounted on sturdy and mobile bases, usually called **studio pedestals** (Figure 3.15). Studio pedestals allow you to move the camera across the floor, dollying or trucking, smoothly enough so that the shot can be used on-air. Studio pedestals are also designed so that the camera can be raised or lowered ("pedestaled") smoothly enough for an on-air shot.

The ability to glide across the studio floor is possible because of the studio pedestal's high-quality casters, which are highly lubricated wheels that allow for easy changes of direction. The **steering ring** is a ring on the studio pedestal that lets you change the direction of the casters and point the camera pedestal in the direction that you want to move before you push or pull it. (The effect is something like having a shopping cart with a control allowing you to set the direction of the wheels before you start pushing the cart.) As a result, there's no jolt or jiggle when the wheels change direction at the beginning of your movement.

In order to allow smooth movement up and down (the act of physically raising and lowering the height of the whole camera body), studio pedestals use either counterbalanced or pneumatic controls. The counterweight pedestal has a built-in system of weights and pulleys that compensate for the weight of the camera—exerting a

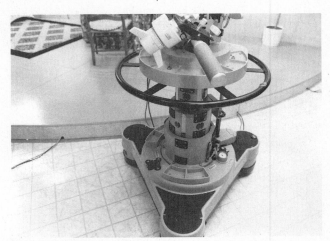

Figure 3.15 The pedestal. The pedestal, which often maintains a pneumatic base, is sturdy and mobile. Firmly positioned on high-quality casters, the pedestal provides the camera smooth movements across the studio's floor.

comparable amount of pressure upward to compensate for the camera weight's downward pressure. (By the way, you raise and lower the height of the camera body by using the steering ring. On some pedestals, there is another ring, located closer to the base, that is used to lock the pedestal in place.)

Pneumatic studio pedestals overcome the camera's weight with a column of air. These pneumatic pedestals are lighter than counterweight pedestals and, because the base does not have to be filled with the counterweight mechanism, they allow for a greater range of up-and-down motion.

Some studios use a tripod with wheels and a manual crank for raising and lowering the camera body. This is only an option when using lightweight cameras, such as ENG/EFP portable cameras that can be converted to studio use. The tripod/hand crank mechanism usually does not operate smoothly enough to allow good quality dollying, trucking, or pedestaling.

The Camera Head

The head (Figure 3.16) is the device that actually attaches the camera to the pedestal. The head governs the smoothness of the pan (side to side motion) and the tilt (pointing the lens up or down).

Most studio cameras are mounted on either cradle heads or cam heads. A **cradle head** is a large platform that "cradles" the camera body and creates a fulcrum on which the cradle can be balanced. Ideally, the camera will be perfectly balanced on the fulcrum and will, therefore, allow the operator to smoothly "rock the cradle." It is difficult, however, to get a large camera precisely in balance on a cradle head.

Figure 3.14 The shot box. The shot box allows the choice of several predetermined zoom settings with the touch of a button.

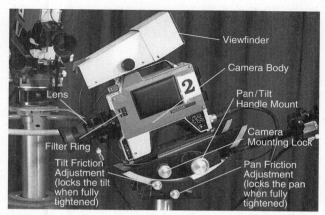

Figure 3.16 The camera head. The cradle or cam head mounts the camera firmly on the pedestal. Locks provide stability.

A better, but more expensive, option is the **cam head**, which uses the friction of lubricated cams to allow smooth movement of the camera.

All studio camera heads have adjustments for the amount of resistance the head will offer to a pan or a tilt. All heads also allow you to lock the camera firmly into place.

The Camera Control Unit

The studio camera is only a part of the chain that produces a video signal. Cameras are connected, via cable, to a camera control unit, which is usually located in master control. The **camera control unit (CCU)** governs the fine adjustment of contrast, brightness, and the trueness of colors. In studio operations, the CCU is under the supervision of an engineer. We'll address the role of CCUs and other related aspects of the video signal in Chapter 20.

A TYPICAL PORTABLE CAMERA

By "portable" camera, we mean a camera designed for ENG/EFP work, and so far we have used the descriptions interchangeably. It should be noted, though, that a remote broadcast *can* be accomplished using studio cameras. Any camera is "portable" as long as you have plenty of muscle and trucks.

But what we'll call the portable camera, the type of camera that can be comfortably used in EFP/ENG work, has some significant differences from its studio counterpart. Aside from the obvious fact that it is smaller, it has more controls and functions that must be operated by the videographer.

Structure and Functions of the Portable Camera

The portable camera can be held on the shoulder, mounted on a tripod, or, as is the case with newer, excep-

tionally small models, held in the hands like a still film camera. A typical portable camera is shown in Figure 3.17.

The basic aspects of the portable camera, how those features differ from those found on studio cameras, will be described in the following paragraphs.

The Portable Camera Viewfinder. Your portable camera's viewfinder is much smaller than a studio camera's. Usually, you view the picture on a portable camera through your right eye, although some viewfinders can be tipped upward so that the operator can look down into the viewfinder. This way, the camera can be held at chest or waist level—a valuable option under certain circumstances.

The VCR Connection. The portable camera, in ENG/EFP operations, is connected to a videocassette recorder. (In some cases, a portable camera is used for a live or live-on-tape production—for example, when covering a sports event.) The newest generation of portable cameras combine the recorder and the camera in one unit and are called **camcorders**.

Zoom Control. Instead of having the controls located on the pan handles, the operator of a portable camera operates the automatic zoom by a rocker switch located on the lens assembly (Figure 3.18), which is held by the right hand. A strap on the lens assembly serves to secure the operator's grip. The focus is controlled by a ring on the end of the lens assembly; you operate the focus ring with your left hand.

Trigger Control. Also on the right-hand control is the "trigger" control for starting the videocassette recorder. The trigger control is a button that is activated, depending on the model of the camera, by your thumb or finger. A light or other indicator inside the viewfinder will inform you that you are in the record mode.

Power Supply. Portable cameras run on batteries, but if a supply of electricity is available, a portable power sup-

Figure 3.17 Parts of the portable field camera.

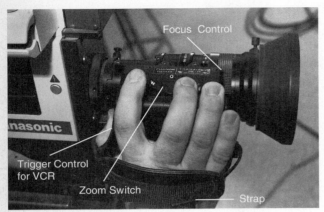

Figure 3.18 Portable camera—right-hand controls. A trigger control starts the VCR. The zoom switch is located on the lens assembly where the right hand is supported through a strap. The focus is adjusted with the operator's left hand (not shown).

ply can be used to convert household current to the required 12 volts of direct current (DC). Battery life varies from model to model, but improvements in technology continue to expand the capability of the battery-powered camera.

Warning Lights. Portable cameras have a "low battery" warning light or indicator visible in the viewfinder. Other warning lights may include "end of tape" or "insufficient light" indicators.

Portable Camera Mounts. Portable cameras are generally mounted on tripods with mounting plates. Good quality tripods have fluid heads—a head containing a viscous oil that allows for relatively smooth movement when panning or tilting. Less expensive heads have simple metal-to-metal friction devices that do not allow for very smooth pans and tilts.

Adjusting the Portable Camera for Varied Lighting Conditions

Because portable cameras are used in the field, there are several functions usually handled by the studio engineer that fall, by default, to the ENG/EFP photographer.

White Balance. One adjustment with which you must become familiar is known as white balance. As mentioned earlier, the camera's eye is not as accurate as yours when it attempts to distinguish colors under various lighting conditions. In particular, it needs to be "shown" what white—the mixture of all colors—actually looks like under the existing source of light so that it can adjust the range of all other colors accordingly.

Color Temperature. **Color temperature** is a measure of light that, for practical purposes, indicates the relative redness or blueness of the light. Red light is cool; that is, the color temperature is low. Blue light is hot; that is, the color temperature is high.

Don't be confused by the typical observation that reddish light, such as from a fireplace, gives off a "warm" glow, or that fluorescent lights give off a "cold blue" hue. These are *aesthetic* impressions of "warmth" and "coolness" and do not correlate—in fact, they're exactly opposite to—with the scientific measurement of color temperature.

Color temperature is important and rather confusing, so an extended definition is in order. We'll cover the basics in this chapter and add some additional detail in Chapter 4, which deals with light and lighting instruments. Again, remember that for the purposes of video production:

Low color temperature light = reddish light

High color temperature light = bluish light

The **Kelvin scale** is a scale used to measure color temperature. It is similar to the centigrade scale except that 0 K is not the freezing temperature of water (0°C); 0 K is absolute zero—the lowest temperature to which any substance can be cooled. (Absolute zero is −273°C.) A scientist named Kelvin devised not only the scale which measures color temperature but the concept itself; he measured the heat given off by a dark surface that absorbed various colors and codified the system to measure color temperature.

A television camera expects pure white to be 3200 K—the level at which video engineers have preset camera tubes to perceive white as pure white under indoor lighting conditions. Outdoor lighting is "hotter." When a camera is set up for outdoor shooting, it wants to see a color temperature of 5600 K as its pure white.

Note that these are basically arbitrary standards and reflect not only the physical makeup of pure white light, but a standardization of cameras and lighting instruments. Indoor television lights are designed to burn at 3200 K. Lights used to highlight outdoor shots (which is quite often necessary to fill in shadows caused by the sun) are designed to burn at 5600 K. For more information about colors and color temperatures, refer to the color plates in this chapter.

Operating under Varying Color Temperatures. Unfortunately we do not live in a perfect world—especially in ENG/EFP situations. Room light from standard incandescent bulbs gives off a reddish hue because the incandescent lights burn at a temperature lower than 3200 K. Fluorescent lights, on the other hand, burn at a higher color temperature than 3200 K.

Outdoor light is variable too. Although mid-afternoon sunshine might produce a color temperature of 5600 K, the light will become progressively more reddish as the sun sets. You can observe this with the naked eye.

That's why the camera has a control to "balance" the color temperatures. In practical terms, here's what would happen if you were not able to adjust for color temperature: In a room with dim incandescent lights, the faces of the

BOX 3.2 CAMERA DOS AND DON'TS

Things to Do When Operating a Camera

1. **Let it warm up.** The circuitry of some cameras needs some time to "cook." (This is true of older cameras but you will probably encounter older cameras, so ask the studio supervisor about the need for warm-up time.) You'll confuse the camera's fine adjustment if you turn it on and immediately shoot with it. If you're worried about conserving battery power when shooting ENG or EFP, use the portable camera's "standby" setting. This allows you to keep the camera cooking but doesn't route full power to the unit.

2. **Follow your engineer's directions.** The video engineer is often involved in delicate camera setup routines in master control, where you cannot see him or her. So, if the engineer asks you not to move the cameras, change their focus, or change the room lighting, *don't*.

3. **In the studio, ask permission to uncap the camera**, for reasons relating to point 2.

4. **Check your camera** well before you go on-air in the studio or before you take a portable unit out into the field. Make a checklist pertaining to your particular situation and run down that list each time. Do all the servo controls work? Is the viewfinder functioning properly? Have any of the controls been set, either accidentally or on purpose, to positions where they are not normally set? If you're going out into the field, do you have enough spare batteries? Is your battery charged?

Things *Not* to Do When Operating a Camera

1. **Don't point a camera toward any bright light source** like a lighting instrument or the sun unless you have been instructed that the camera is equipped with a CCD. There are occasions when you can point a camera toward a bright light, but only when using proper filters under the supervision of an engineer.

2. **Don't *ever* walk away from a mounted camera without locking the pan and tilt controls.** You're asking for major trouble if you do. The camera, for instance, could be nudged so that it points toward a lighting instrument. Studio cameras are very heavy and despite the fact that they are supposed to be balanced on their cradle or cam heads, and firmly attached to those heads, they may not be firmly secured. A severely unbalanced and poorly mounted camera can actually tip forward so violently (if left unattended) that the camera body may slide off the head. This is an extremely rare occurrence, but it has been known to happen. The moral: Don't take any chances on creating $15,000 worth of broken glass and sheet metal.

3. **Don't use the intercom for casual conversation.** This is extremely annoying to directors, who have other things to worry about than where you went to eat last night. In all seriousness, directors need to keep track of many threads in the production process, and any idle chatter on the intercom distracts them and prevents meaningful conversation. If there's a problem, or if you are responding to a question from the director, do respond. Otherwise, don't clog the lines of communication.

---

people you interview would have a decidedly reddish cast. In a room with hot fluorescent lights, the faces of your talent would have an unhealthy bluish hue.

But the "white balance" control lets you tell the camera what white is supposed to look like under prevailing light conditions in your shooting environment. You usually accomplish this by holding a white card in front of the lens and pressing the white balance control for a second or two. The white balance mechanism senses if there's too much blue (high temperature) or red (cool temperature) light and adjusts the camera accordingly. Now, you'll not only have an accurate white, but flesh tones will appear natural too. Because flesh tones are your primary concern

when white balancing, it's a good idea to hold the white card at the level of the performer's face.

In many large operations, studio cameras are generally white balanced by the engineering staff, but portable cameras are white balanced by the operator. It's important to white balance whenever you have a change in scene, location, or lighting.

BEYOND THE BASICS

Chapter 8, "Camera Operation," will examine the principles and aesthetics of camera work. In that chapter, you'll learn more about shot composition, movement, effect of the zoom lens on the camera image, and how shoots communicate a certain image or message.

One important concept to remember from this chapter is that basic camera operation, while not extremely complex, does require some careful attention on the part of the operator. If you are careless, you can ruin a shot or possibly even the camera. (See Box 3.2 for a quick review.)

Also, keep in mind the notion that camera operation involves more than pointing and shooting. Getting the shot is the first consideration, but getting a *good* shot is the overriding goal—and you cannot obtain a usable shot unless you combine good technical quality with a shot that communicates appropriately in the language of video.

SUMMARY

1. The video camera is a tool; understanding its functions allows you to use it more effectively and troubleshoot common problems.

2. A modern video camera can accomplish many tasks, but it is nowhere near as sophisticated as the information-gathering equipment located in your eyes and brain. The camera cannot focus as quickly as your eye, it has trouble perceiving colors accurately, and it does not have the same depth of field as your eyes. Also, because the camera has only one "eye," and you have two, the camera has trouble with depth perception. It needs special lighting to create the illusion of depth on the video screen.

3. The imaging device in a camera is either a tube or a charge-coupled device (CCD). High-quality models have three tubes or three CCDs, each processing one of the primary colors after the colors have been separated. The primary colors are mixed together again when the image is transduced by the monitor.

4. An electron gun scans the target on the imaging device; the target is light sensitive and allows different levels of the electron beam to penetrate, depending on how much light is focused on the target. The electron beam scans 525 lines—odd lines first, even lines next—to produce a complete picture. The scan is completed 60 times a second. Because it takes two scans to produce a complete picture, the video scanning process creates 30 frames per second.

5. The same process is repeated in reverse when the picture is recreated. Scanning guns shoot a beam that scans the back of the picture tube to illuminate colored dots that create the picture.

6. Lenses with a long focal length are telescopic; that is, they magnify. Shorter focal-length lenses produce a wider field of vision. A long focal length decreases depth of field. A short focal length enlarges the depth of field.

7. Almost all video cameras have variable focal-length lenses, customarily known as zoom lenses.

8. To set your focus with a zoom lens, you usually zoom in on the object and then focus. Under normal conditions, everything between that object and the camera will be in good focus.

9. The iris opening is expressed in terms of an f-stop or f-number. The larger the f-stop, the smaller the opening.

10. Studio cameras are mounted on large, sturdy studio pedestals that are counterweighted or pneumatically controlled; studio pedestals let you perform smooth on-air moves. Small convertible cameras and ENG/EFP cameras are mounted on tripods that usually have a crank handle to physically raise or lower the body of the camera. Although you can pan and tilt a camera on such a tripod smoothly enough for on-air motion, it is very difficult to do a smooth on-air truck, dolly, or pedestal.

11. The part of the mount onto which the camera body is physically connected is called the head. On studio pedestals, cradle heads or cam heads are usually the devices of choice. Good ENG/EFP tripods have fluid heads.

12. It's good practice to let your camera warm up before use, if you are instructed to do so by the studio supervisor. Don't uncap or move the camera without permission, and never engage in idle chatter over the intercom.

TECHNICAL TERMS

additive color mixtures	cam head	f-stop	frame
burn	color temperature	field	iris
camcorder	cradle head	filter wheel	Kelvin scale
camera control unit (CCU)	depth of field	focal length	persistence of vision

pickup element	servo	tally light	white balance
Plumbicon	shot box	target	zoom ratio
primary color	steering ring	tube	
Saticon	studio pedestal	vidicon	

EXERCISES

1. Photograph the screen of a standard television set using a 35mm film camera. It is almost certain that one member or your class or group of co-workers will have a standard 35mm single-lens-reflex (SLR) camera. Shoot the screen using the highest shutter speed on your film camera. (Most 35mm SLRs have a shutter setting of one-thousandth of a second.) Take several shots. When the film is developed, you will have a clear—and surprising—illustration of the television scanning process.

2. Videotape a demonstration of depth of field. Either in studio or at a remote location, set up a series of objects or people at varying distances from the camera and create a situation in which all (or almost all) are in focus and a situation in which only some are in focus. Accomplish this by:

   a. Using different focal lengths for each demonstration.

   b. Using a wide-open iris and a closed-down iris. You don't need to manually adjust the iris. Instead, with the help of your instructor, tape the demonstration under bright light and under dim light. The iris will adjust itself.

3. Dim the lights in your studio or, if you are using a portable camera, in whatever room you happen to be using. (But don't dim them so low that you cannot produce a decent picture.) Use incandescent lights instead of fluorescent lights. Now, set your camera's white balance.

   Next, turn the lights up full, or better yet, move outdoors or to a room illuminated by fluorescent lights. *Do not white balance the camera again*. Tape a quick interview or take another shot of a co-worker or classmate. Play back the tape and note whether or not the coloration, particularly the flesh tone, seems appropriate. If not, explain exactly what seems wrong with the picture.

   This exercise can also be done in reverse of the described sequence. Try taping indoors with a camera that you have just white balanced outside. Observe and describe the effect.

principles of lighting and lighting instruments

OBJECTIVES

After completing Chapter 4, you will be able to:

1. Identify all varieties of lighting instruments.
2. Take measurements.
3. Explain the balance of the lighting triangle.
4. Explain how color temperature relates to the lighting setup, and that color temperature involves more than pressing a button on the camera.
5. Replicate the example of setting three-point lighting.
6. Operate precise controls of lighting instruments.
7. Operate the controls of the lighting panel (and understand the patching system), and realize that the controls cannot be dimmed excessively because doing so alters color temperature.
8. Operate all the lighting instruments in a safe manner.

As pointed out in Chapters 2 and 3, video lighting involves more than simply throwing a switch a minute before the cameras are uncapped. Because the camera is such a poor imitation of the human eye, it can operate well only within a limited range of light intensity and coloration.

Although lighting requires knowledge and skill, the subject of lighting for video is sometimes overcomplicated. You need not be part physicist and part electrician to light a decent video picture. For basic video, you really need a working knowledge of only five primary factors:

1. You need to understand the use of three-point lighting to illuminate the subject and give it shape, lend texture, fill in harsh shadows, and separate it from the background.

2. You must remember that there should not be too large a contrast ratio between the brightest parts of the picture and the darkest parts.

3. You need to know how to create an even, overall *base light* so that there are no "black holes" in the scene and, conversely, no overly bright spots.

4. You must have a rudimentary understanding of the two physical types of lighting instruments: the *spot*, which throws a focused, directional beam, and the *fill*, which produces a broad, diffused area of light.

5. Finally, you should have a reasonable understanding of color temperature, and, to the best of your ability, you must use light of the appropriate color temperature. Quite simply, this means that the light should not cast a bluish hue or a reddish hue *as seen by the camera*. In practical terms, this translates to not mixing light of differing color temperatures and, of course, white balancing your camera when lighting conditions change.

Those are the basics. Now, all we need to do is fill in the details about what types of equipment accomplish these goals. This chapter is a primer on the equipment itself. Chapter 9, in the section of the book devoted to techniques (Part 2), will explain more fully how to utilize the equipment to achieve an aesthetically pleasing effect. Although this chapter and Chapter 10 will address remote lighting applications, Chapter 17 will devote more extensive detail to producing a well-lighted picture on location. If your classwork calls for you to immediately take to the field, you can, at the conclusion of this chapter, skip ahead to pages 221–232 in Chapter 17. Before you do *anything* with video lighting instruments, please read this entire chapter and the concluding suggestions on safe handling of lighting instruments.

Now, we'll cover the fundamental method of measuring light, adjusting of the light so that it forms a proper three-point lighting arrangement, and the physical types of lighting instruments used in setting up your lighting arrangement.

LET THERE BE LIGHT

What, exactly, are we dealing with in this chapter? Essentially, we'll discuss light itself, the mechanics of three-point lighting, the instruments used to cast the light, and the consoles that control those instruments. After the vocabulary and concepts have been defined, we'll conclude with some remarks about safety.

Measuring Light and Correcting Lighting Problems

The most perceptible function of light is the way that it provides information about shape and texture when it bounces back to the eye or camera lens. **Reflected light** is light that bounces off an object. Thus, it is reflected light that paints visual images.

But as you remember, cameras have a problem with reflected light: If one object in the picture is highly reflective and another very dull, the camera won't be able to handle the contrast. That's why we take a reflected light measurement (which we'll discuss in the next section).

There's also another kind of light we need to be aware of, and, of course, know how to measure: the light that shines directly on the source. This type of light—light making a direct path from the lighting instrument to the subject—is known as incident light. **Incident light** is light that emanates directly from a lighting instrument. If there is not enough incident light spread across the scene or set, there will be a "black hole," a dark, muddy area in deep shadow. In order to prevent this effect, the lighting director also takes a measurement of incident light.

A measurement of incident light is the most common type of measurement made in video. Two types of meters (shown in Figure 4.1) are used to measure reflected and incident light. They are called, as you might expect, reflected light meters and incident light meters, respectively. In order to ensure that the contrast ratio is not too high, we measure reflected light. In order to ensure that the set is evenly lit, we measure incident light. And here is how it's done.

Measuring Reflected Light. We perceive shapes and colors because an object absorbs certain frequencies and amounts of light, and the light not absorbed is reflected back to the eyes or lens. The color is determined by the frequency of the light wave, a topic beyond the scope of

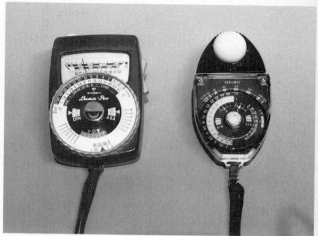

Figure 4.1 Light meters. Two types of light meters are the reflected light meter (left) and the incident light meter (right).

this chapter. But in brief: Light wave frequency is something akin to sound wave frequency. If we directed a mixture of all pitches at an object and that object absorbed all of them except for one musical note, we would hear that one musical note echoed back. In a very broad sense, the same happens with light.

In addition to color, reflected light tells us about the shape and texture of objects. A bright wall painted with light, high-gloss paint (shown by the meter on the left in Figure 4.1) reflects a pattern of light that is decoded by our eyes and brain; that decoding process tells us that the surface is indeed a flat plane and that it is reflecting a great deal of light.

A rumpled herringbone jacket, on the other hand, reflects less light from those crevices deep in the folds—showing us that it's rumpled—and does not reflect light in a regular, planelike pattern, proving to our eyes that the jacket is not flat. Also, because the surface of the jacket is irregular, composed of minute threads interwoven with each other, it does not present a smooth, polished texture. Therefore, it is not likely to reflect back much light. If it's a dark jacket, it will reflect even less light because, as a general rule, darker colors reflect back less light than do lighter colors.

So what does this have to do with video production? As you remember from Chapters 2 and 3, cameras are limited in their ability to handle a wide range of reflected light. So a shot of a man wearing a dark, rumpled herringbone jacket seated before a wall painted with white glossy paint is probably going to cause trouble. You might have the engineer "boost the blacks" so that you can see the jacket clearly, but then the wall will be badly, glaringly overexposed.

How do you know if the lighting setup is going to cause contrast problems? And more to the point, what can you do to fix the situation?

Step 1 is to take a reflected light measurement of the items that will be in the picture. You might start with the man's jacket. A reflected light measurement is as simple as pointing a light-meter *toward* the subject.

Light meters vary in design, but they all perform essentially the same task: They measure the intensity of light in footcandles (abbreviated "ftc"). As you might imagine, a **footcandle** is a unit of measurement of the intensity of light. It originally was calculated as the total amount of light that would be collected on an object one foot away from a "standard" candle. The candle is no longer regarded as a particularly uniform source of light, so the term today is pegged to what is now known as an "international" candle, which is a theoretical source of light of a given intensity (to come full circle, the theoretical "international" candle level is about the intensity of an average-sized candle on a restaurant table.)

If a great deal of light is falling on an *extremely* shiny wall (as in Figure 4.1a), the reflected light reading on your meter might be 700 ftc. The reflected light from the jacket (Figure 4.2) could be as low as 15 ftc; this might happen if the man's key light doesn't fall on his jacket brightly enough to illuminate it properly. (Note that we're using an extreme example here for the sake of easy illustration.)

Using basic arithmetic, you'll find that you have a contrast ratio of about 46:1 (700 ÷ 15), meaning you have contrast problems. More than likely, the man will appear

Figure 4.2 Measuring reflected light. To take a reflected light measurement, point the meter toward the subject.

as nothing more than a silhouette. The details of his jacket will be lost, as will the features of his face.

There are two ways to solve the problem (Figure 4.3). One of the most obvious is to do something about the bright wall. Can the amount of light falling on it be reduced? If so, then do it. If you move the man away from the wall, you will diminish the intensity of the reflected light from the wall, and do so with surprising effectiveness.

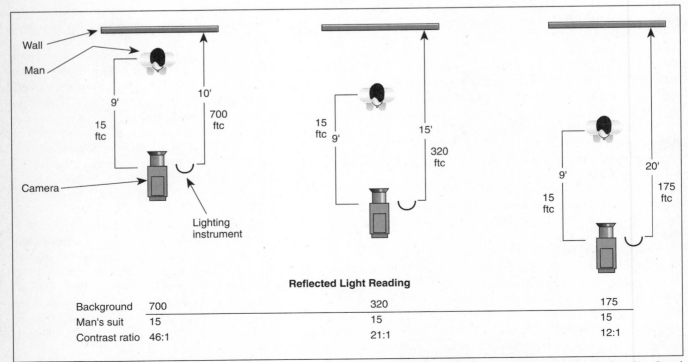

Reflected Light Reading		
Background	700	320	175
Man's suit	15	15	15
Contrast ratio	46:1	21:1	12:1

Figure 4.3 Adjusting background distance to change contrast ratio. By moving the subject and light source away from the white wall, we reduce the reflected light reading from the background. The subject's distance to the light source remains the same.
    As seen by the camera, the contrast ratio of the subject and background decreases from 46:1 (700/15) to 12:1 (175/15).

Now that you've cut down on the light from the wall, let's boost the intensity of the key and fill that are falling on your subject. A more powerful lighting instrument, which is better aimed, might bring the reflected illumination from the jacket to 45 ftc. If the intensity of reflected light from the wall has been reduced to 450 ftc, you will have a comfortable contrast ratio of 10:1.

Now that you've got the general idea, here are some pointers on measuring reflected light:

1. You don't have to measure each part of the subject and background every time you light the scene. The type of scenario just outlined is usually played out after a problem has been spotted on the control room monitor. ("Hey, I can't even see that guy's face . . . what's the problem?") Remember, contrast problems are usually spotted on the monitor—not by the eye—because our eyes are so accommodating to varying light conditions. Only an experienced producer would know by naked eye evaluation that the wall and the herringbone jacket won't mix, and even he or she might be fooled from time to time. (Actually, the trickiest scenarios usually involve a small reflective object, such as a plaque.) That's why we use the light meter to locate trouble spots and fine-tune the setup.

2. When you take a reflected light measurement, don't stand between the subject and the lighting source or your shadow will distort the reading.

3. If at all possible, reduce the bright spots rather than throw more light on the dim areas. Although it seems like an easier option to crank up the light falling on the man with the herringbone jacket and leave the background alone, you'll just be creating more problems. Anyone or anything else introduced into the too-bright set will appear in silhouette too, and you'll have to throw additional light to compensate. The camera won't be happy, and your performer will invariably begin to blink and perspire when you start shining more lights in his face.

Measuring Incident Light. A footcandle meter is used to measure incident light too. But when measuring incident light, you want to measure the intensity of the individual lighting instruments. This is done primarily to establish reference levels for the instruments. For example, if you do a news show from the same set every day, you'll want to calibrate the lighting instrument by aiming the meter toward it and adjusting the dimmer until the amount of light falling on the anchor today is the same as it was yesterday. A **dimmer** is a variable control switch that adjusts power levels to lighting instruments.

But why bother checking incident light levels if you are using the same lighting instrument in the same position? First of all, as mystifying as it may seem, lights put out different intensities from day to day. Part of this has

to do with slight changes in position of other lighting instruments and the resulting addition or subtraction of their light to the instrument you're measuring. Sometimes your instruments will be moved a bit, or the set will be moved, so you'll want a hard number as a reference point. Although television lighting elements typically do not go dim with age (they just blow out at the end of their lives) sometimes mechanical malfunctions—and even a buildup of dust on the instrument's lens—can contribute to a slight dimming of the incident light level. Also, there are occasional variations in local or building electrical power, which account for changes in a light's intensity. (Brown-outs during high energy-consumption periods, such as mid-summer air-conditioning seasons, can sometimes account for this.)

You can also take an incident light reading by pointing the meter toward the *camera* and walking across the set. This will check for falloff points, indicating a dark spot that might not be visible to you, but apparent to the camera.

Base light, the light spread over the set, often takes care of itself. We'll deal with this at greater length in Chapter 9, but be aware that from a technical standpoint you often will produce perfectly usable base light simply by properly establishing your three-point lighting. Sometimes, widely spread three-point lighting arrangements may leave holes, but those dark spots can be filled with lighting instruments that cast a wide beam. There's no great trick to that. So worry about good three-point lighting on *the subject* first, and then take care of the base light, if you actually need to.

Base Light Level. What's the proper base light level? That's a good question, and one best directed toward your video engineer because equipment requirements vary enormously. *In general*, many good-quality cameras want to see a base light level of about 180 to 200 ftc, but the newest generation of chip cameras can operate with much less base light. Check with your engineering staff about the ideal base light level for your particular equipment. I recommend such a consultation because certain technical adjustments rely on the appropriate level of base light for the camera, and this is one case where a nontechnical operator may not be able to accurately "eyeball" the situation. Also, the engineers will appreciate your concern.

Portable cameras are quite adaptable to base light variations, and most can produce a reasonable picture in standard room light—but the more base light they have the better. In addition to having a cleaner overall picture, your depth of field will be increased in strong base light because the iris will not have to open as wide as it would in dim light. When you use additional light in ENG/EFP operations, often that light is nothing more than an instrument clipped onto the camera. This may not seem to be a very enticing picture, but at least the camera is able to see. A better option is to bring along a portable lighting kit. With some imagination, you can set up a three-point lighting system.

The Basics of Color Temperature

Handling different color temperatures is a common dilemma in remote work, but the problem can be simplified by merely understanding what color temperature is and why light is of varying temperatures. Once that is accomplished, you can avoid mixing the two.

We've covered color temperature pretty thoroughly in Chapter 3, but it's such a confusing topic—and a cause of much concern to people who work with remote cameras—so a little more discussion is in order.

A Review of Color Temperature. When substances are heated, they produce light of varying color. As an example, when a blacksmith heats an iron horseshoe, the horseshoe will first emit a dull reddish glow; the hotter the horseshoe gets, the redder the glow becomes—and soon the horseshoe is "red hot." But iron, when heated to an even higher temperature, turns "white hot." If the blacksmith's forge has the capability to heat the iron past the white-hot state, the metal would eventually give off a bluish glow.

The elements in lighting instruments operate in much the same way. Instead of iron, lamps typically use substances such as tungsten to produce light. That light will be of a different color depending on the extent to which the element is heated *and* on the physical properties of the element itself. Video producers rarely use a meter designed to measure color temperature. Rather, they simply adjust for the differences between outdoor and indoor light by using the camera's filter wheel, and then white balance to make the fine adjustment.

Color temperature is a different phenomenon from thermal (heat) temperature, and it is measured with a different temperature scale, known as the *Kelvin* scale. The British scientist Lord Kelvin derived a method of accurately measuring color temperature. To oversimplify, it involved measuring the way in which a black substance emitted various colors and at what temperatures those colors were produced. The Kelvin scale begins at absolute zero (-273° Celsius, the lowest temperature to which any substance can be cooled).

The physical principle underlying color temperature is that as the element is heated to a higher temperature, it emits a different color (frequency) of light. As mentioned in Chapter 3, video cameras expect to see indoor white light at 3200 K and outdoor light at 5600 K. These are *arbitrary* figures that were chosen by the television industry to standardize cameras and lighting instruments.

Production Problems Associated with Color Temperature. Color temperature usually causes difficulty only under certain circumstances (Figure 4.4):

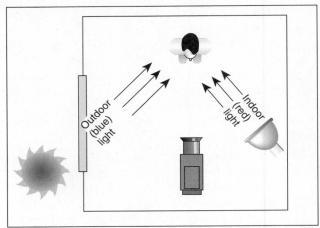

Figure 4.4 The risks of mixing color temperatures. Daylight (from the left) mixes with light from an indoor incandescent source (from the right). If the camera is white balanced for the indoor light, the subject's left side may appear with a bluish tint.

Possible solutions: (1) Block the outdoor light, (2) use a lighting instrument that matches the outdoor light, or (3) check the actual effect on a properly adjusted monitor. Your camera may be able to accommodate the differences in color temperature.

- *When you move from location to location and forget to re-white balance the camera.* That's an easy problem to solve: Simply remember to white balance whenever you change location. Now, you've told the camera what "white" is supposed to look like so that it can readjust for all the other colors including (and most importantly) flesh tones.

- *When you cut the amount of power to a lighting instrument.* We'll discuss this issue in the last section of the chapter.

- *When you are in a location in which outdoor and indoor lights are mixed.* This situation is examined at greater length in Chapter 17. For now, though, suffice it to say that the more you can avoid mixing light of different temperatures, the better. For example, fluorescent lights burn hotter than normal incandescent lights, thereby producing a blue-green cast. If you are shooting a remote location using portable lighting instruments rated to produce a normal indoor light, you should turn off the fluorescent lights whenever possible. If an open window lets in hot (bluish) outdoor light and causes the same problem, you should close the blinds.

You may run into temperature problems in remote locations where there are fluorescent lights. Fluorescents usually burn at about 4500 K. Often, your best bet is to turn the fluorescent lights off and use portable lighting equipment. If you have trouble with outdoor (5600 K) lighting from a window, shutting the window (or taping at night) might be the best alternative.

BOX 4.1   LIGHTING AND THE INVERSE-SQUARE LAW: SOME EXAMPLES

Here's an example of how the inverse square law might work in practice. Assume that at 100 feet, the intensity of the light reads 100 ftc on your light meter; at 200 feet, the intensity of the light reads 25 ftc; and at 400 feet, the intensity of the light reads 6.25 ftc. In chart form, you can visualize the fraction of intensity this way: N stands for any arbitrary measurement. If N equals 100 foot, 2N equals 200 feet. Or if N equals one foot, 2 N equals 2 feet.

Distance	Fraction of Intensity	Percentage of Intensity	Example
1N	1	100%	100 ftc
2N	1/4	25%	45 ftc
3N	1/9	11.11%	20 ftc
4N	1/16	6.25%	11.25 ftc

Now, remember the example in the text about the person standing near the shiny wall? We mentioned that moving him away from the background would cut the intensity of the reflected light more than you would expect. According to the inverse-square law, a distance of 10 feet from the camera to the wall could produce 700 ftc of illumination. But moving the man 20 feet away from the wall would produce only 175 ftc.

Assuming the amount of light on the man remained constant, you have solved a contrast ratio problem and a silhouetting problem (a bright background making the man's features difficult to discern) at the same time.

In sum, try not to mix color temperatures in remote operations. The best indicator of whether you are adjusting properly for color temperature is to bring a high-quality portable monitor on your shoot. If the flesh tones appear natural, you've properly adjusted the lighting and equipment.

Light and the Inverse-Square Law

The reason why moving the man in the herringbone jacket away from the wall would produce such a surprisingly fast falloff is that unfocused light falls in intensity according to this formula:

$$\text{Light intensity} = \frac{\text{strength of source}}{\text{distance from the source squared}}$$

Although the formula is not that complicated, it's much easier to think of it this way: As the distance from the light source is doubled, the intensity of the light is cut to one-quarter, not one-half. This rule is known as the **inverse-square law**. If you're interested in seeing how the figures work out in practice, you might read through Box 4.1.

The important point is not so much in understanding the mathematical ramifications of the inverse-square law, but in remembering that light intensity falls off at a rate much higher than you would expect it to if it were simply a regular, even multiple of distance.

Note that inverse-square law applies only to light traveling in all directions from a single source. Focused light, such as that from a spotlight, won't behave in the same way. In truth, the reflection off the wall will not fall off exactly in synch with the inverse-square law either, but because it is not highly focused light, the general scenario is close enough so that you can use inverse-square falloff as a rough guide.

SETTING AND BALANCING THREE-POINT LIGHTING

As discussed in Chapter 3, three-point lighting allows the video camera to perceive shape and depth. Three-point lighting is the normal method of setting studio illumination, and is often used in remote applications as well.

Three-Point versus Flat and Cameo Light

Sometimes, other types of lighting are used, either because there is no other option or for effect. For example, *flat* light is just that: a light from one source that provides no real three-dimensional look to the picture (Figure 4.5).

Figure 4.5   Flat lighting. Lighting with one instrument directed straight onto the talent will result in harsh shadows without any real sense of dimension.

Figure 4.6 Cameo lighting. Cameo lighting is considered a special effect that can be achieved by using barn doors (see Figure 4.13) to direct a spotlight onto the talent without casting any illumination onto the background. This stark effect can be softened by adding fill and back light as shown in Figure 4.7.

A setup called *cameo* lighting (Figure 4.6) illuminates the subject only from one direction with strong light, giving a harsh effect and imparting a sense of dimension to the picture. Cameo lighting is sometimes used for special effect.

You can observe the limitations of flat and cameo lighting for normal video operations, which is why three-point lighting is used to *overcome* apparent lack of dimension. We have already described three-point lighting, so now we'll discuss the technical means whereby the three components—key, back, and fill—are balanced, and how the background is sometimes lighted to enhance the illusion of dimension and space. Incidentally, the key, back, and fill are usually aimed and measured in that order.

Setting the Key

The key light is produced with a focused beam of light. Because it is the primary source of light falling on the subject, you need a beam of reasonably strong intensity. Let's say you use the light meter to set intensity and discover that the key light throws about 170 ftc. That's a fairly typical intensity in a studio situation.

Setting the Back Light

The intensity of the back light is usually set between 100 to 150 percent of the key light. So if the key light produces 170 ftc, the back light might be set between 170 and 255 ftc. This setting depends on the specifics of the particular situation. A blond-haired person, for example, needs less back light to separate him or her from the background than a dark-haired talent.

Setting the Fill

How strong should the fill be? Usually, the standard practice is to keep the fill level at about one-half that of the key. So 80 to 85 ftc would do nicely to balance a 170 ftc key light.

The fill will usually be supplied by an instrument that projects a softer, less-focused light than the instruments used for key and back.

(a)

(b)

(c)

Figure 4.7 (*a*) Key light. A single key light source will model the subject and create harsh shadows such as on the subject's right side. Notice the right earring is obscured.

(*b*) Key with fill. Adding the fill light will fill in the stark shadows, but it will not eliminate the modeling entirely.

(*c*) Key, fill, and back light. Completing the lighting triangle with the addition of the back light separates the subject from the background with contrast. The added dimension makes the picture appear more lifelike.

Setting the Background

You may also wish to light the background. Sometimes, the light from a three-point arrangement will adequately spill over and illuminate the set, but sometimes it won't. If you have a light-absorbing background, such as a bookcase filled with dark, cloth-bound volumes, you'll probably want to illuminate it with a separate lighting instrument.

There's no hard-and-fast rule on exactly how much light to use, because backgrounds vary in their reflectance, but any light you shine at the background will usually be at about the same level as (or a little below) the fill light used on the subject.

Incidentally, if you try these settings, using the readings we've calculated so far, you'll probably wind up with a base light level of about 180 ftc, just about right for many modern cameras. But check it out; sweep the area with your light meter pointed toward the principal cameras. Notice any holes? If so, position a fill light to brighten the dark spots.

Figure 4.7 on page 56 shows how the key light models the subject with harsh shadow, how the addition of the fill light fills in the stark shadows but still maintains the modeling, how the back light separates the subject from the background, and how the background light illuminates the set and makes the entire picture seem more real and lifelike.

STRUCTURE OF LIGHTING INSTRUMENTS, ELEMENTS, AND LIGHTING CONTROL FIXTURES AND APPARATUS

It's time for an explanation of the tools that provide the light: the physical types of instruments; the *elements* used to create light; the grids, clamps, and stands that hold the instruments; and the control panel that governs the power to the instruments. Note that from now on we will use the word *element* to describe the substance that actually burns. The term *lamp* will be used to describe the transparent housing for the element—we won't call it a "bulb" because lighting elements are not always bulb shaped. And the entire unit will be referred to as a lighting instrument.

Irrespective of the variations in design and nomenclature, video lighting instruments fall into two categories: spot and flood. The **spot** light (or **hard light**), sometimes called a *directional* light, projects a narrow, focused beam. The **flood** light, sometimes called a *soft* light, produces a broader, more diffused pattern of light than a hard light.

Spot lights are used for key light and back light. Flood lights are used for fill. Both types have other uses, so don't mix up the terms that describe the physical properties of the instruments (spot, flood) with the words that describe lighting functions (key, back, fill).

Spot Instruments

The spot light is based on a simple principle: The farther the light source is moved back from the focusing lens, the narrower the shaft of light will be.

Figure 4.8a shows a spot light with its element lamp far forward in the instrument, very near the lens. This produces a relatively wide beam. (Remember, we're using the word *element*, rather than *bulb*, to describe the part of the instrument that actually heats up and produces the light.) In Figure 4.8b, the lamp is pulled to the back of the instrument—"pinned," in video jargon. To **pin** a light is to make the beam narrowly focused.

Basically, this effect is purely a function of geometry. As the lighting element is pulled back, the angle at which the beam can spread is limited. (Note that some lighting instruments don't move the element and its reflective

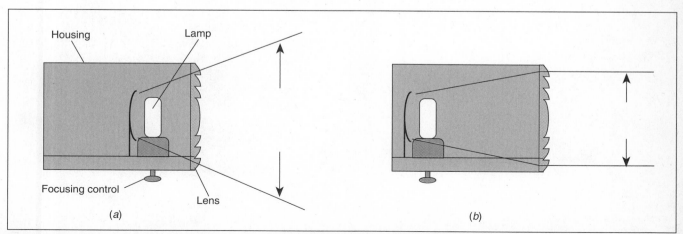

Figure 4.8 Geometry at work. With the lighting element and reflector far forward (*a*), the instrument produces a wide beam. When the lens and reflector are far to the rear (*b*), a narrow beam is produced.

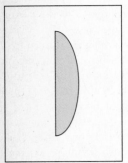

Figure 4.9 Convex lens. The light can be further focused by a convex lens.

housing but, instead, move the lens; the effect is exactly the same.)

In addition to geometrical constraints, the spread of the beam is also limited by the focusing power of the lens. What a lens does when it focuses light is to force the light waves into a column. Its optical properties bend the light rays into alignment—into a column that will travel at a much narrower angle than light simply released in all directions.

Lenses such as the type shown in Figure 4.9 are used in video, but the variety pictured in Figure 4.10 is more common. It's called a Fresnel lens (pronounced freh-NEHL).

The **Fresnel lens**, which has the distinctive pattern you've probably seen in old lighthouse lenses, is a lighting instrument that uses a lens having concentric rings to focus the beam of light. It was designed to produce the focusing power of a curved lens while using much less glass. The "steps" of the lens take the place of the curves in the solid glass, but, because the stepped design can be pressed out of relatively thin glass, the Fresnel lens produces much less heat buildup. More heat can radiate out of the unit through the thin glass.

The Fresnel is the workhorse video spotlight—by far

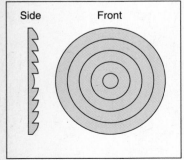

Figure 4.10 The Fresnel lens. The familiar convex lens is heavy and traps heat. The concentric rings of the Fresnel lens perform the same focusing function with much less glass (and less heat).

the most popular key and back in TV studio operations. Fresnels come in different sizes; the larger the size, the larger the wattage. (Wattage is a unit of measure for power consumption. It stands to reason that larger-wattage instruments will use more power, produce higher intensity light, and hence be larger in order to accommodate the bigger element and lens.) Figure 4.11 shows a Fresnel spotlight.

Each Fresnel has some mechanism to change the focus of the beam (Figure 4.12). Figure 4.12 also displays the degree of focus on the side of the instrument. Some instruments have a focusing ring that can be adjusted from the floor using a long pole. The grid mounting system allows you to attach and aim the light.

The Fresnel spot is usually equipped with a set of folding flaps called barn doors (Figure 4.13). Some instruments have two barn doors; some have four. The **barn door** is a mechanical device to prevent light from spilling into areas where you don't want it. Each door can be adjusted from the floor using a pole. Barn doors can also be moved by hand, but be sure to wear gloves if you do; the doors become extremely hot and can stay hot long after the instrument is turned off.

Figure 4.11 Fresnel spotlight. (Courtesy of Strand Lighting.)

Figure 4.12 The light focusing knob. The focusing knob adjusts the width of the light beam ranging from a broad flood (F) to a narrow spot (S).

The same principle which underlies the focusing power of the Fresnel is used in the external reflector spotlight (Figure 4.14). The **external reflector** has no lens, so the beam is less columnated than the light from a Fresnel. Nevertheless, the beam can be focused by moving the element and reflector forward or backward. Because it is smaller and lighter than a Fresnel, the external reflector is a good spot for remote use.

A special type of spot less commonly used is called an ellipsoidal spot (Figure 4.15). The **ellipsoidal spot**, or **leko**, has internally mounted shutters to shape the light pattern. The beam from a leko is extremely focusable because of the instrument's complex lens system. As a result, the beam can be sharply defined. Whereas a spotted Fresnel will throw a rough circle, a spotted leko will form a *precise* circle—or whatever shape you can concoct using the shutters.

The razor-sharp focus of a leko (and the ability to throw the beam out of focus) is primarily useful for producing special effects. One such effect is achieved by inserting a patterned metal wafer called a cucalorus—almost always called a "cookie"—into a slot on the leko. The

Figure 4.14 External reflector spot. This small, lightweight instrument is a good candidate for remote use.

Figure 4.13 Barn doors. These folding flaps are known as barn doors. They keep light from spilling into areas where you do not want it.

Figure 4.15 Ellipsoidal spot or leko. (Courtesy of Strand Lighting.)

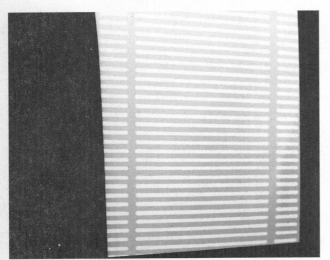

Figure 4.16 Shadow cast by a "cookie." This backdrop effect of a window was produced by inserting a cucalorus into the leko (ellipsoidal) spotlight.

resulting pattern (Figure 4.16) forms an interesting special effect, a pattern commonly used as a backdrop. There are dozens of patterns available. Some, as in Figure 4.16, mimic venetian blinds or prison bars.

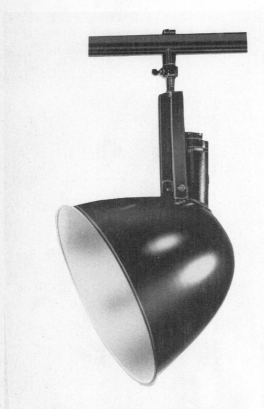

Figure 4.17 The scoop. Scoops in television typically measure 14 or 16 inches in diameter and cannot be focused. (Courtesy of Strand Lighting.)

Figure 4.18 Lighting scrims. This wire scrim is positioned in front of a scoop for protection.

Flood Instruments

An instrument called a **scoop** (Figure 4.17) is the most common flood light; it's so named because of the scooplike shape of the instrument.

A scoop cannot be focused. Indeed, focusing would destroy the whole point of using a scoop, which is to provide diffused fill light. But you can "defocus" a scoop, softening the light even more, by use of a scrim. A **scrim** is a sheet of spun-fiber material, often held by a metal frame that slides into slots on the front of the scoop. Scrims also can be used on a variety of instruments other than scoops. In addition to softening the light, the scrim provides a measure of protection to people working on the studio floor in the event the lighting element bursts (Figure 4.18). This doesn't happen often, but it *can* happen, and the idea of white-hot pieces of metal and glass falling on one's head

Figure 4.19 The broad light. The broad is popular on location for providing a widely diffused light.

Figure 4.20 The softlight. (Courtesy of Strand Lighting.)

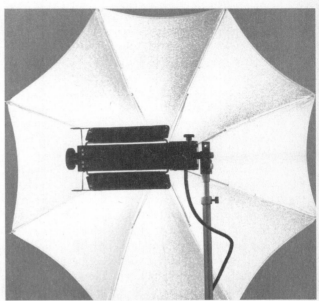

Figure 4.21 Lighting umbrella. The umbrella is an ideal means for softening a light in the field. (Courtesy of Lowel-Light Manufacturing, Inc.)

case, they are lightweight and can be mounted using a clip device.

Lighting Elements

You generally won't need an extensive knowledge of the particular substances that produce light when heated by electricity, but a couple of items pertaining to lighting el-

contributes to the popularity of scrims in most video studios.

Another type of flood light is the broad (Figure 4.19). The **broad** is a large instrument with several illuminating lamps inside; it produces widely diffused light and is often used on remote. Many broads have some provision (such as barn doors) for directing the light as well. A variation of the broad is a similarly shaped instrument called a *soft light* (Figure 4.20). The softlight usually has a flat diffusing cover to produce an extremely unfocused field of light. Softlights are sometimes used on remotes, but they're bulky. A good alternative for producing fill light is to use a specially designed umbrella (Figure 4.21) attached to a portable spot. This simple diffuser-reflector instantly transforms your spot to a flood, making it a versatile addition to your portable lighting kit.

And an even easier option is to use a so-called **internal reflector**, which is a lighting instrument with the reflecting element built inside (Figure 4.22).

The internal reflector can be purchased in spot or flood varieties, by the way. Although it is commonly used as an instrument to fill a small area, the spot varieties are useful for providing directional light on remotes. In either

Figure 4.22 Internal reflector light. The reflector light is very handy for lighting small areas. (Courtesy of Lowel-Light Manufacturing, Inc.)

ements are useful. First, remember that most instruments use quartz elements rather than tungsten elements.

Tungsten elements are typically found in household light bulbs, the type of bulbs that are known as "incandescent." **Quartz elements** are lighting instruments that use tungsten as part of the lighting element, but they utilize a quartz tube that may hold a highly reactive halogen gas. This combination of elements allows the quartz lamp to burn much more brightly than a standard tungsten lamp; the element itself is also much smaller and uses less power. But there's a price to be paid for this efficiency: The quartz lamp produces intense heat in a small space and has a fairly limited lifespan. Quartz elements designed for video work burn at 3200 K, the standard for indoor video white light.

There is another type of element that you may encounter. It's known as an HMI lamp. The **HMI** (halogen-metal-iodine) **element** burns at *outdoor* color temperature (5600 K), making it very desirable when you must contend with a bright window. If you have an HMI element, you can forget about mixed-temperature worries. The HMI will bathe the whole scene in bluish outdoor-colored light. And should you need a lighting instrument to use outdoors in the sunlight—not uncommon because you frequently need to fill in shadows caused by direct sunlight—the HMI is perfect.

Many organizations don't have HMI lights because they're expensive and somewhat cumbersome. To use them you need a special unit called a ballast, which serves the same purpose as the "starter" in home fluorescent light fixtures. But do keep the HMI in mind in case you encounter special color temperature problems. HMI lights are available at most video equipment rental agencies.

Lighting Grids and Clamps

Lighting instruments are usually hung from a grid on the ceiling (Figure 4.23). Most grids are made out of pipe, although some are constructed of beam-shaped metal. Grids

Figure 4.23 A lighting grid. A grid of pipes supports lighting instruments above the studio floor.

Figure 4.24 The C-clamp. A C-clamp can attach a lighting instrument to a batten or pipe grid.

are generally stationary. Some are counterweighted so that a crew member can simply lower a batten, adjust the instrument with a pole, and use the pole to return the batten into place. A **batten** is an individual beam that makes up part of the grid. This eliminates the need to climb a ladder to hang a lighting instrument.

Fresnels and other instruments are usually connected to the grid by means of a C-clamp (Figure 4.24). In order to get power to the instrument, the cord hanging from the instrument is attached, using a special three-prong twist device, to a cord hanging from the lighting grid. The cord hanging from the lighting grid is sometimes called a pigtail.

Lighting instruments can also be mounted on floor stands (Figure 4.25). Studios have pigtails available at floor level, to accommodate floor stand-mounted lighting instruments.

Irrespective of whether it's located on a grid or on the floor, each pigtail is numbered so that it can be "patched," meaning connected, at the control panel.

The Lighting Control Panel

Lighting instruments in the studio are "patched" into a control panel, often called a dimmer board, which governs the power supply to the instrument. Now, we'll present some specifics on exactly how—and why—the control panel does what it does.

Attached to or above several of the battens, the pipes or beams that are part of the lighting grid, is a power cord.

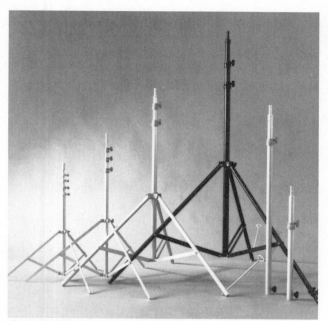

Figure 4.25 Floor stands. Floor stands are commonly used for lighting in the field but are also found on the studio floor. (Courtesy of Lowel-Light Manufacturing, Inc.)

patch the appropriate lighting instruments into one dimmer and accomplish the task by moving one lever.

You also want the flexibility of setting up your lighting instruments ahead of time, turning them off, and turning them back on again at *exactly the same levels*. Modern lighting control panels have a memory control that allows you to fine-tune the setups using various dimmers (more on the fine-tuning process in a moment), shut them all off, and turn them all on at the press of a button.

Why bother turning lighting setups on and off? There are two reasons:

1. One lighting setup may interfere with another. If, for example, you are shooting a dimly lighted living room scene on the left-hand side of the studio but later need to move to a scene set 15 feet to the right, which ostensibly takes place in a starkly lit hospital operating room, you probably won't want the operating room lights on while you are taping the living room scene. There would certainly be some spillover, and you wouldn't want all that light coming from the right-hand side of the screen.

The cord is numbered. The number of the cord corresponds to a plug on the lighting control panel. Note that it is the *electrical outlet* and not the lighting instrument that is numbered. (Lighting instruments are numbered, but not for this purpose; the numbers are usually for inventory purposes.) Lighting instruments are moved all over the grid, so using their numbers as a reference would be hopelessly confusing.

That plug is inserted into a panel containing many receptacles. Several receptacles can be assigned to a single dimmer, so the operator can control the lighting levels of a number of instruments at once. A dimmer, as mentioned earlier in the chapter, is a device for raising or lowering power, just like the rheostat that dims or raises the household lights in a dining room or living room.

The concept of having several lighting instruments plugged into one bank of receptacles that is controlled by one dimmer level is known as patching (Figure 4.26). A **patch bay** is a bank of receptacles into which plugs are inserted. The patch bay is used to connect certain lighting instruments to various controls.

The theory behind the patch bay is simple: It allows you to control several lighting instruments with one dimmer. For example, you may wish to have the entire news set go dark at the end of the show, but you want to keep the background lighted. This puts the newscasters in silhouette. Think how cumbersome it would be if you were forced to lower the power level on each individual lighting instrument. But with the lighting control panel, you can

Figure 4.26 Lighting strategies and the control panel. Plan your lighting setup for convenient execution. Using the lighting control panel, or "dimmer board," you can patch together and control a number of lighting instruments with a single switch. Here, five instruments are wired into circuit 3 (*a*) and controlled by one lever (*b*).

2. You want to keep lighting instruments turned off as much as possible. All video lamps have a limited lifetime, much shorter than a standard household light bulb, so you would usually elect to conserve the lamps (and the electricity needed to power them). Also, keeping all the lighting instruments burning makes for a very hot studio.

As already mentioned, the dimmer board allows you to adjust the level of light conveniently. It's much easier to lower the dimmer to fine-tune the light level than to reposition the lighting instrument. And that, of course, is one reason why dimmer boards were invented.

But you can't excessively lower the power supply to lighting instruments because if you dim them beyond normal operating limits *you will lower their color temperature*. Studio lights are designed to burn at standard white *when receiving full power*. But when you begin lowering the power supply through the dimmer—as the temperature of the light falls below 3200 K—you make the light falling on the subject more reddish.

Usually this doesn't present a problem; reasonable lowering of power won't create a color temperature problem. But if you have a gigantic lighting instrument too close to a performer—for example, casting a key that's not in accord with the rest of the lighting scheme—you cannot solve the problem by cranking down the dimmer. Instead, use a smaller lighting instrument or move the too powerful instrument back. It's more work initially, but it will save work in the long run.

Automated Lighting Control Panels

The dimmer board has come a long way from the days when it resembled an old-fashioned telephone switchboard. Many modern units accomplish the patch electronically rather than mechanically and can retain many setups in their microchip memory. But one of the basic rules of business, "if it's not broken, don't fix it," applies quite nicely to dimmer boards. The early versions were reliable, accomplished the work (perhaps without the ease of modern units, but they still got the job done), and functioned for years virtually unnoticed. That's why you'll still find many older-generation dimmer boards tucked into the corner of the studio or control room.

There is an enormous variety of dimmer boards, and presenting a catalog of them would confuse rather than enlighten. And it is unnecessary to know the controls of each and every unit. Simply remember the basic concepts of patching and grouping and you'll be able to pick up the operation of any unit within a few hours.

This chapter, in an attempt to clearly present what you need to know in order to get started with studio and remote lighting, has covered only the basics. There are several other types of lighting instruments and an entire range of lighting techniques yet to be explored. We will examine those items in Chapter 9.

But one issue that must be addressed at this time deals with the possibility of injury to yourself and coworkers when working with lighting instruments. Please read the following section carefully. It is presented at the end of the chapter not because it is less important than the other material, but because it makes more sense here than before the fundamental concepts and vocabulary were explained and defined.

SAFETY

With the exception of news videography in civil disturbances and combat zones, video production is not a particularly dangerous occupation. But people *do* suffer injuries during studio and remote productions—and the culprit is usually the lighting equipment. Please follow the rules outlined in Box 4.2 when working with lighting instruments and related hardware.

Sometimes the hazards can be a result of someone else's sloppiness. For example, if a crew member routinely installs lamps without wearing gloves (or uses the paper sleeve that often comes with new lamps, which is removed before the instrument is turned on) the buildup of finger oil will cause a change in the way the lamp conducts heat and will weaken it, causing the strength of the lamp to erode and possibly burst—perhaps in your face.

Or someone could leave a wrench or other tool on top of a ladder, and the tool could fall when the ladder is moved. A wrench dropping 15 feet could leave a very large dent in your head, so be careful and help your crew to work as a team to avoid mistakes that may harm others.

BOX 4.2   SAFETY REMINDERS

1. Don't move a ladder when a crew member is on it. Yes, you *will* see this being done, even in professional studios, but there's always an element of danger, so *please* don't take any chances. It's best to have the crew member climb completely off the ladder before moving it.

2. Turn off the power at the dimmer board before you plug or unplug lighting instruments into the pigtails. This is only common sense; you don't want to be handling two outlets carrying live current. They can arc (form a sustained discharge of electricity).

3. Look away from lighting instruments. When you turn on a lighting instrument, keep your face averted. Occasionally, a lighting element will burst when it's turned on. Be particularly careful of external reflector lighting instruments because there's usually nothing to stop the fragments from striking you. Such mishaps are very rare, but it's still not worth taking a chance.

4. Use some sort of security device to double-lock studio lighting instruments in place. Some studios use a special chain in case the C-clamp fails to hold to the batten. Another practice is to loop the power cord around the batten so that it forms a "safety line" should the instrument come loose. Although it's not as effective as the chain or some other separate locking device, this practice could help keep the instrument from crashing to the floor and possibly (a) hitting people or (b) showering them with hot glass.

5. Wear gloves. Lighting instruments are *hot*. Even the outside of an instrument that has been turned off for several minutes can burn you.

6. *Never* touch a lamp that is burning. The heat is so intense that you can suffer a serious burn even with gloves on. You might also cause the element to burst.

7. Never put a lighting instrument close to anything flammable.

8. Never touch a cold lamp with bare fingers. You only need to touch a lamp to change it when it burns out. Be sure the old element has cooled, and wear gloves during the process of changing lamps. Wear gloves even when handling the *new* lamp. Acid and oil from your fingers will cause an erosion of the lamp's exterior surface, shortening its life and increasing the chance that it may burst.

9. Secure wires. When you place lighting instruments on floor stands, tape down the wires, string the wires from the ceiling grid, or do anything and everything to prevent someone from tripping over them. If anyone trips over a lighting instrument wire, you've got a dual problem. First, he or she will probably fall down on the hard studio floor. Second, the instrument will probably be tipped over, possibly striking someone, burning someone, and/or bursting when it hits the floor.

10. Don't look directly into lighting instruments from close range. You can certainly look at a Fresnel light from the studio floor when you are measuring its incident intensity, but don't look into it from a few feet away. In addition to the possible danger to your eyes, you'll be momentarily blinded—not a condition in which you want to find yourself while atop a studio ladder. Make it a point not to look directly into the lenses of inactive lighting instruments while you're working on the ladder; someone at the dimmer board could unexpectedly turn them on.

11. Announce that you will be turning on a lighting instrument. To avoid the problem referred to in number 10, it is a good practice for the crew member operating the dimmer board to announce what he or she is doing ("I'm going to power up number six and eleven now.") . This adds an extra measure of safety for the crew working on the instruments.

12. Use scrims on scoops that are positioned directly over talent. In the unlikely event that the lamp bursts, the scrim will keep the superheated fragments from falling on crew members and talent. (This really is not a joking matter, but I do want to illustrate that this *can* happen. I have been showered with hot glass from a scoop lamp twice. Once, while I was reading a live newscast, the fragments set my script afire. So be forewarned.)

SUMMARY

1. Lighting for video involves more than simply throwing a switch, but it is generally less complex than some people might have you believe.

2. Your basic task is to produce three-point lighting, which adds dimension to the picture; at the same time, you want an even base light that does not produce "black holes." Finally, you must be aware of the contrast ratio. Don't let it exceed 30:1.

3. Reflected light is what bounces back off the subject. Incident light is the light that makes a direct path from a lighting instrument to the subject. You need to measure both types of light using a light meter.

4. Although there are many different types of measurements, the most important are those done to ensure that there is even base light and to find hot spots that may affect the contrast ratio.

5. Indoor light is more reddish than outdoor light. Most studio lighting instruments are set to burn at what we consider the standard for indoor white light: 3200 K. The arbitrary standard for outdoor white is 5600 K. The essential point is that you do not want to mix color temperatures, but in practice, you'll find that modern cameras can often be white balanced to accommodate a reasonable mixture of indoor and outdoor light.

6. Light radiating in all directions drops in intensity according to the inverse-square law. Although you don't have to calculate the falloff of light intensity according to the inverse square every time you set up your lighting instruments, it is important to remember that the intensity of light does not decrease in equal proportion to distance; instensity decreases much more quickly. When you double the distance, you cut intensity by three-fourths, not by half.

7. The light levels of the key and back light are usually about the same, but the back light is generally a bit higher. Sometimes, if the subject blends into the background, the back light has to be considerably higher than the key. Fill and background are generally about one-half the intensity of the key.

8. There are two basic categories of lighting instruments: spot lights and flood lights.

9. The Fresnel is the most commonly used spot in the studio. The scoop is the most commonly used flood.

10. Most video lighting instruments use quartz elements. These elements burn hotter and brighter than standard incandescent bulbs.

11. The lighting control panel, often called the dimmer board, allows you to patch several lighting instruments into one dimmer. This gives you flexibility in adjusting power levels to instruments or groups of instruments and allows you to preset groups of instruments so that you can turn them on and off when needed.

12. Lighting instruments can be dangerous. Observe the cautions listed in Box 4.2 when working with them.

TECHNICAL TERMS

barn door	external reflector	incident light	pin
base light	flood	internal reflector	quartz elements
batten	footcandle	inverse-square law	reflected light
broad	Fresnel lens	leko	scoop
dimmer	hard light	light meter	scrim
ellipsoidal spot (leko)	HMI element	patch bay	spot

EXERCISES

1. As noted in this chapter, prescriptions for lighting don't always work for everyone under all situations. For this exercise, set up a basic three-point lighting arrangement for a seated person, preferably someone with long, dark hair and wearing a dark jacket, using the following ratios:

   a. Your key = 1 (in other words, whatever the intensity of your key light, a level you'll have to decide yourself but based on recommendations of your engineer, it equals an arbitrary figure of 1).

   b. Fill = ½ key.

   c. Back = 1½ key.

   Does the picture look right? Is there separation of the person from the background? Are facial features well defined but not stark? Does the picture seem three dimensional? If not, make adjustments; measure incident light and note the readings.

2. Use the same lighting setup on a blond wearing light clothing. Does it work? If not, why? What has to be changed? Make the appropriate adjustments and note the incident intensities.

3. As the third part of this experiment, place the dark-haired person wearing the dark clothing about 10 feet away from the blond with the light clothes. Have both face forward into separate cameras. Set up three-point lighting arrangements for each person (as illustrated by Figure 4.27). But set up the lighting instruments levels *without having the people on the set.* Do it entirely by light meter and your previous notes. Now, have the people take their appropriate seats. Check and adjust the lighting as necessary.

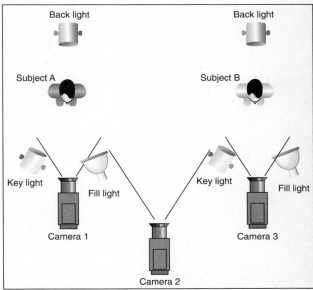

Figure 4.27 Lighting setup for Exercise 3.

a. Do individual close-ups of the people look right?

b. On a two-shot, is there a black hole between the two people? If so, attempt to fix it by adding fill light.

c. Then check the individual close-ups to make sure the fill (if you needed to add it) hasn't fouled-up your lighting scheme. If suddenly the close-ups don't look right, experiment with your fill until you have resolved the problem.

audio principles and equipment

OBJECTIVES

After completing Chapter 5, you will be able to:

1. Use the correct microphone in the correct situation.
2. Describe sound and audio principles related to the operation of audio equipment.
3. Run an audio console, the device that routes and mixes audio sources.

Audio is every bit as important as the picture component in the production process. Audio quality is an essential aspect of a quality program. And at the other extreme, poor-quality audio can ruin a show as much as a botched call by the director or an out-of-focus camera shot.

This chapter, because it resides in the "tools" section of the book, deals with the principles and hardware involved in audio production. Chapter 12 will expand on the *techniques* of audio production.

Audio is often used synonymously with *sound*, but the terms are not identical. Audio is the electrical representation of sound after that sound has been transduced. The microphone is the instrument that transduces the physical energy of sound—motion—into the electrical energy of audio. And here's how it happens.

SOUND

First, some information about sound. Sound is simply a vibration of molecules in the air or other medium. The sound "wave" is produced by a series of compressions and rarefactions in the air. To put it much more simply, a sound vibration produces ripples similar to those created when you throw a stone into a pond. **Compressions** are those parts of a sound wave in which the air molecules are packed tightly together. **Rarefactions** are those parts of a sound wave where air molecules are pulled apart.

Physical Principles of Sound

The "ripples" produced by sound waves are a series of areas where the air molecules have been pushed together (the *compressions*) and pulled apart (the *rarefactions*). Figure 5.1 illustrates this concept. If you were to measure the degree to which the molecules were condensed or pulled apart,

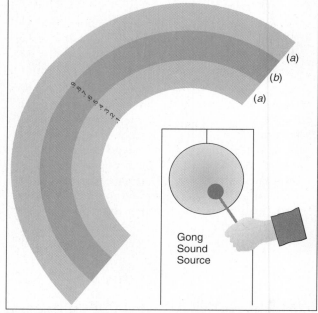

Figure 5.1 The physical nature of sound. A sound source—the gong—produces waves in which there are (*a*) compressions and (*b*) rarefactions. (See also Figure 5.2 for a graph of the air pressure at points 1–9.)

taking that measurement at regular intervals, you would find that the molecule density increases gradually until it reaches the area of greatest density, the positive peak, and then recedes back to a normal air pressure level. Then, during the rarefactions, the molecule density is lessened until it reaches a negative peak.

Continued measurements, of course, would show that the density returns to normal and then starts the cycle all over again.

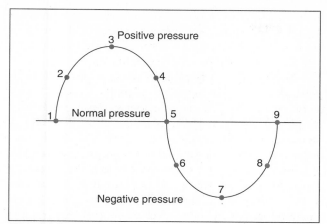

Figure 5.2 Sound as a sine wave. Continuous measurement of pressure changes would produce a sine wave, like this one. (See also Figure 5.1.) 1. Normal pressure. 2. Higher pressure. 3. Center of compression—highest pressure. 4. Lowering pressure. 5. Normal pressure again. 6. Beginning of lowering pressure in rarefaction. 7. Center of rarefaction—lowest pressure. 8. Rising pressure. 9. Normal pressure.

The cycle we've just measured is represented by a sine wave (Figure 5.2). A **sine wave** is a graphic depiction of a sound wave cycle. (A sine wave can also depict cycles other than those produced by sound.) Remember that the sine wave is a *representation*, a graphic readout of the pressure changes. It is not meant to depict what a sound wave "looks" like. The sound wave more closely resembles a series of pulses, rather than a rising and falling sine wave.

Measuring Sound

There are two important measures of sound waves about which you should be aware: frequency and amplitude. **Frequency** is the number of times the wave goes through a complete cycle in one second. **Amplitude** is the height of the wave, a measure that indicates the power of the highs and lows (high and low *intensity*, not pitch) and, by extension, the loudness of the sound.

Frequency. Frequency is measured in cycles per second, or **hertz** (abbreviated Hz). What we perceive as the "pitch" of a sound is a measure of frequency. The higher the frequency, the higher the perceived pitch; the lower the frequency, the lower the perceived pitch. We're using the terms "frequency" and "pitch" synonymously, although they really don't mean quite the same thing. "Pitch" is the ear's and mind's interpretation of a sound frequency. A frequency is a scientific, numerical measurement of the number of times the sound wave repeats in a second.

If you've ever heard a symphony orchestra tune up before a concert, you've noticed that each orchestra member tunes his or her instrument to a musical note played by the oboe. That particular note vibrates at precisely 440 cycles per second, or 440 Hz. (And it does vibrate *precisely*;

in these days of miniaturized technology, the oboe player almost always has an electronic tuning meter on his or her stand, and that tuner gives a readout indicating when the oboist hits 440 Hz exactly.)

Human ears can hear sound ranging from about 16 to 16,000 Hz, although this figure is approximate and varies widely according to the age and condition of the listener. Young people with good hearing can perceive sounds up to about 20,000 Hz.

Sound frequencies are divided into octaves. An **octave** is a doubling or halving of an existing frequency. When an instrument plays the concert note A at 440 Hz, the octave can be doubled by playing a high A at 880 Hz or a low A at 220 Hz. That's how the musical scale works. Our musical scale is a series of notes grouped around the tones labeled A, B, C, D, E, F, and G. When A returns again, we've arrived at a note one octave higher. The same note in a different octave sounds similar to us. We know, via the sound-processing function in our brain and ears, that it's somehow a closely related tone, even though it is higher or lower than the original tone.

Humans can hear about ten octaves. If you are so inclined, you can start with 16 Hz as a base and keep doubling the number until you reach 16,384 Hz. Should you be that ambitious, you'll see that you have calculated the ten octaves for yourself.[1]

The lowest octaves provide the "power" in a sound; the octaves in the middle usually provide the basic "fundamental" pitch of the sound; the upper octaves—from 2048 Hz up to the topic limits of human hearing—provide much of the information that gives sound brilliance and clarity.[2] Sound components around 3000 Hz contain many of the fairly high pitches that lend intelligibility to speech.

By *sound components* I refer to the various waves that make up a sound. The "pure" wave pictured in Figure 5.3 would be produced only by a special electronic instrument designed to produce a simple, pure tone. Almost all other sounds we perceive are known as **complex waveforms,**

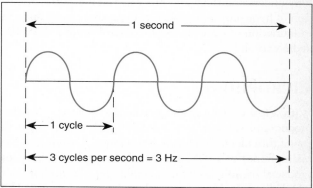

Figure 5.3 Cycles per second. This sine wave completes 3 cycles per second; its frequency is 3 Hz. Humans can hear sounds in the range of about 16 Hz to 16,000 Hz. The higher the frequency, the higher the pitch.

the incoming sound, moving the coil through a magnetic field to produce an audio signal.

or sometimes crackling sound.

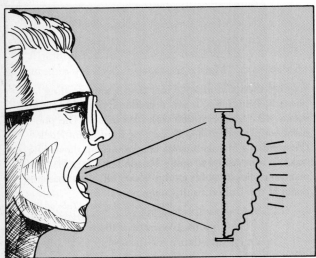

Figure 5.6   Limitations of ribbon mics. As seen from the side, the ribbon is very thin, limiting its performance in two ways. (1) A strong gust of air would overpower and possibly damage it. (2) Too strong an air current will simply press it back, not allowing it to vibrate.

Condenser.   *Condenser* is an old-fashioned word for capacitor. Both terms refer to a unit that stores an electrical charge. A **condenser mic** uses this phenomenon to release an electrical signal, which corresponds to the vibration of the diaphragm.

The primary advantage of a condenser mic is that the sophisticated electronic components are highly sensitive and versatile. In particular, condenser mics typically have very good response to high-frequency sounds. Also, the frequency responses and the pattern in which the mic picks up sound can be adjusted on most models.

The disadvantages of a condenser mic directly parallel its advantages. Sometimes you don't want extremely sensitive pickup of high-frequency sound. Certain announcers, for example, tend to produce highly noticeable mouth noises and wheezes (which are high-frequency sounds). The condenser mic will faithfully pick up these distractions. Moreover, condenser mics need a separate power supply, such as a battery, to power up the capacitor. Condenser mics also tend to be fragile.

For quick reference, the pluses and minuses of microphone types are summarized in Table 5.1.

Pickup Patterns

Microphone electronics also determine the directions from which microphones pick up sound. The representations of these patterns are typically called **pickup patterns** or, sometimes, **polar patterns**. Understanding pickup patterns, as well as the pluses and minuses of their pickup elements, will allow you to choose the mic that's best suited for the job at hand. Incidentally, you are probably wondering whether or not there is a direct correlation between pickup elements and polar patterns. The answer is yes and no; there is *some* relationship, and we'll explain it at the relevant time.

The basic pickup patterns—omnidirectional, bidirectional, and cardioid—are shown in Figure 5.7. (Note that all pickup patterns are graphic depictions of what you would see if you were standing above the mic, looking directly down on it.)

Omnidirectional.   As you might guess from the prefix *omni-*, mics that are **omnidirectional** pick up sound equally well from all directions.

At first consideration, an omnidirectional pickup pattern doesn't seem possible. How could a mic pick up sound as well from the back as from the front? The answer is that the diaphragm of the mic is pushed and pulled by compressions and rarefactions. The diaphragm senses the changes in air molecule density and movement irrespective of which way the mic is pointed. (To be strictly accurate, there *is* a slight drop in the pickup pattern directly behind the mic. It is caused by the mass of the mic interfering with the sound wave.)

You would use an omnidirectional mic (also called an "omni") in situations where it would be inconvenient to keep reaiming a mic that picks up sound only from the front. For example, television news reporters frequently use omnidirectional mics for interviews. Omnis, because of their simplicity of design, are also quite rugged.

Bidirectional.   The prefix *bi-* indicates that a **bidirectional** mic picks up sound in two directions, namely, from

Table 5.1
Microphone Pros and Cons

Microphone Type	Advantages	Disadvantages
Moving coil	Sturdy Reliable	Fairly poor frequency response
Ribbon	Warm sound Good response	Delicate
Condenser	Excellent response Adjustable pickup patterns	Sometimes *too* sensitive Expensive Needs external power supply

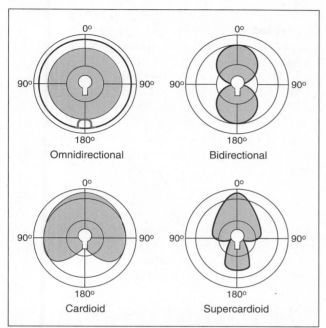

Figure 5.7 Microphone pickup patterns. Specialized microphones are designed to pick up sound in different patterns (see shaded regions in these polar diagrams). Of course, their areas of audio sensitivity are three-dimensional: omnidirectional = sphere; bidirectional = double-sphere; cardioid = heart-shaped; supercardioid = spade-shaped.

the front and from the back. A bidirectional mic rejects sound from the side.

Here is a case where the element and the pickup pattern are linked in form and function. The bidirectional pattern is common to ribbon mics; the ribbon, in many mics, will be struck by air from both sides, but for obvious reasons won't be sensitive to sound waves that strike it on the edge. You can demonstrate this for yourself: Hold a standard-sized sheet of typing paper stretched out flat in front of your mouth and speak directly at the flat surface. You'll feel the paper vibrate. Turn the paper sideways and speak at the edge; you won't feel any vibration. A bidirectional pattern is usually produced by a ribbon mic, but occasionally, condenser mics have adjustable patterns that allow you to create a bidirectional pattern should the need arise.

The bidirectional pattern is handy for conducting an in-studio interview where you sit opposite your guest, but there are few other advantages to the bidirectional pattern. It is largely a consequence of the construction of the ribbon mic and usually not a pattern manufactured to serve a particular purpose.

Cardioid. *Cardioid* means "heart-shaped," and the term has the same root as the word *cardiac*, which is an easy way to remember the pattern.

In essence, the **cardioid** pattern indicates that the mic picks up from the front but rejects noise from the rear. In other words, it is directional.

The advantage of a cardioid mic is simple and obvious: It rejects sound you don't want to hear. It is an excellent choice when you want to mic a guest on set and reject noises from the audience *in back* of the mic.

Some mics have longer range and highly directional pickup patterns, such as the supercardioid microphone. However, such highly directional instruments are also sensitive to sound from a small region behind the mic.

Physical Types of Microphones

"Physical type" describes the mic in terms of its shape, size, and intended use. For example, one physical type of mic is the hand-held microphone. Hand-held mics can have any variety of pickup element or pickup pattern, but that's not what we're defining. We're simply describing the physical form of the mic (small enough to hold in the hand) and the task for which it is intended.

Common physical types of microphones used in video production are hand-held, shotgun, lavaliere, studio, wireless, and a catch-all category we'll label miscellaneous.

Hand-Held. Mics meant for hand-held use are generally not very sensitive to handling noise and are reasonably rugged.

An example of a hand-held mic is the Electro-Voice 635A (Figure 5.8). This mic uses a moving coil element and is omnidirectional. The 635A is incredibly rugged and is a favorite of roving news reporters.

Shotgun. The shotgun mic is named for its physical shape. It has a very narrow cardioid pickup pattern. The reason why highly directional mics are long and pointed is because the mechanism that produces directionality involves ports, or holes, in the side of the mic. The sound admitted from the side, through the ports, is altered so that it cancels itself out. (Technically, it is "out of phase," a concept we'll explain in Chapter 12.) That's why a long,

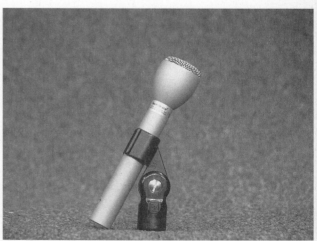

Figure 5.8 The Electro-Voice 635A. This rugged all-purpose mic has an omnidirectional pickup pattern.

Figure 5.9 The Sennheiser 816. This universal long-reach microphone for remotes has a supercardioid pickup pattern. (Courtesy of Sennheiser.)

thin mic is almost always directional. These mics are typically mounted on booms, long polelike devices, and therefore are sometimes called boom mics. The two categories don't precisely coincide, though, because some shotguns are meant to be hand-held and not mounted on a boom. But in either event, the goal of the shotgun mic is to pick up sound from a distance within a very narrow pattern.

The Sennheiser 816 (Figure 5.9) is a popular shotgun mic; it has a condenser element and a very narrow cardioid pickup pattern.

Lavaliere. The lavaliere is usually clipped to some piece of a performer's clothing, and the wire is hidden by the shirt, jacket, or blouse. Using lavalieres for a studio shoot, such as a talk show, is generally much easier than using a shotgun or boom mic. For one thing, the mic doesn't have to be pointed. Second, lavaliere mics are reasonably inexpensive; two good lavalieres will cost you much less than a high-quality shotgun. Third, their proximity to the performer (about 6 inches below his or her chin) usually produces surprisingly good sound quality.

The Sony ECM-55 (Figure 5.10) is a very popular lavaliere mic. It has a condenser pickup element and an omnidirectional pickup pattern.

Studio. Studio mics come in many shapes and varieties. What they have in common is that they are meant to be more or less permanently installed and not carried around. As such, video producers will sometimes use them for voice-over narrations, where an announcer records a narration that goes "over" the video. In other cases, you'll use studio mics to record musical groups.

The Neumann U-87 (Figure 5.11) is a popular and versatile studio mic. It picks up a wide range of frequencies, and has an adjustable pattern. It can be made to pick up sound in omnidirectional, bidirectional, and cardioid patterns. This mic uses a condenser as its pickup element.

Wireless Mics. Wireless mics are hand-held or lavaliere mics with built-in transmitters or attached transmitters. They send a weak signal to an amplifier, which boosts the signal to a usable audio level. Wireless mics are useful when, for example, a performer ventures into the audience and does not wish to contend with a cord.

Miscellaneous. You'll encounter some other types of mics and mic apparatus in video production. For example, should you cover sporting events, your announcers will likely wear headset mics (Figure 5.12), which leave the sportscasters' hands free to shuffle papers and keep notes, and also cover their ears so that they can hear themselves (and the director) under noisy conditions.

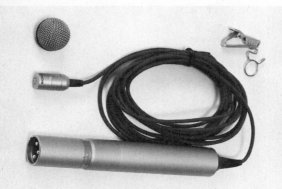

Figure 5.10 The Sony ECM-55. This condenser lavaliere mic has an omnidirectional pickup pattern. (Courtesy of Audio Service Corp.)

Figure 5.11 The Neumann U-87 studio mic. This sensitive, very good quality condenser microphone has an adjustable pickup pattern from omni to cardioid.

Figure 5.12 A headset microphone. The cardioid microphone in this headset is aimed at the wearer's mouth. Most sound from other directions will not be picked up.

An alternative to the shotgun mic is using a hand-held mic in a parabolic reflector (Figure 5.13). The **parabolic reflector** is a disk-shaped reflector that collects sounds and bounces them back toward a microphone mounted inside. It is a good choice for rugged-use situations, such as along a football sideline, because it picks up sound from a distance and provides reasonable directionality, but is not as delicate or expensive as the shotgun mic.

Cables, Connectors, and Booms

Microphone cables are generally "balanced," which means they have two conducting elements and a grounding shield to prevent interference.

Cable Cautions. The most important things to remember about audio cable are:

1. Have enough cable on hand. If you're going on remote, take about twice as much as you think you'll need.

2. Never step on a cable or crimp it. Although audio cable looks sturdy—and it is, to some extent—you can damage the cable with rough handling. The damage itself is bothersome, but what's really troubling is the time you will probably waste trying to track down the problem.

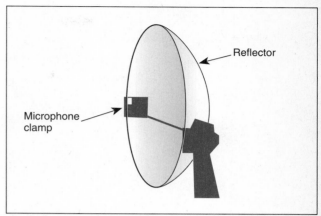

Figure 5.13 A parabolic reflector. An omnidirectional mic would face inward and attach to this parabolic reflector. A mic with a parabolic reflector is often used in sporting coverage. Although it picks up well from a distance, it is not as sensitive as the shotgun mic.

3. Coil and store cable carefully without kinks. This will save you much time when organizing the next job.

Connectors. Cables are usually connected to microphones and to a box in the studio wall (and thereby into the control room) with XLR connectors (Figure 5.14). The female end of the cable (Figure 5.15) connects to the male pins on the microphone base, and the male end of the connector fits into the locking female wall unit in the studio (Figure 5.16).

Sometimes, you'll need adapters to change a female connector into a male connector—a device quaintly called a gender changer. It's a short cable with identical connectors on each end. Take an adequate supply of gender changers with you on remote, as well as adapters that have XLRs on one end and different connectors on the other.

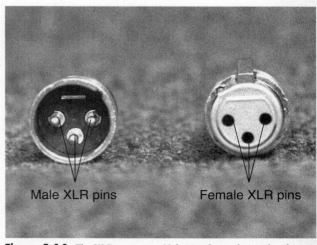

Male XLR pins   Female XLR pins

Figure 5.14 The XLR connector. Male pins fit snugly into female connectors.

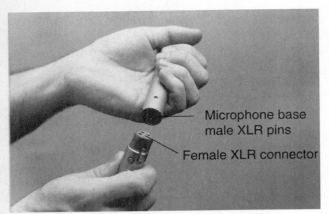

Figure 5.15 An XLR mic connection. The female cable connector plugs into the male connector at the base of a microphone.

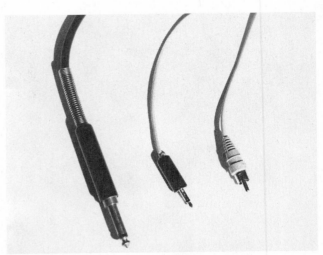

Figure 5.17 Common connectors. A ¼-inch phone connector, miniphone connector, and RCA connector.

A variety of connectors are used in remote work and some studio operations. The most common are the phone connector, the miniphone connector, and the RCA connector (Figure 5.17). One adaptor you'll be sure to need at some point is a female XLR, which terminates in a male miniphone; this cable is frequently used for plugging a mic into a camcorder.

Booms. Booms come in many varieties. Some booms are elaborate; they are equipped with an operator control so that the shotgun (boom) mic can be swiveled. Other devices are nothing more than "fishpoles" held by a crewperson. A **fishpole** is a hand-held pole onto which a microphone is attached.

The most elaborate booms have sound-absorbing shock mounts to ensure that movement of the mic is not transmitted.

THE AUDIO CONSOLE

The audio console (often called "the board") looks more complicated than it really is (Figures 5.18 and 5.19). A console really only performs two main functions: It determines the volume and the path of the audio signal. (Another function, not directly performed by the operator, is amplifying the audio signal to a higher level usable by the recording unit or transmitter.)

Here's how the audio console works: The microphone is plugged into the studio wall, and internal wiring brings the signal into the console. If, for example, you plug the mic cable into the studio XLR wall connector labeled MIC 1, the signal will be governed by the knob on the console marked MIC 1.

Audio Console Potentiometers

That knob on the console is known as a potentiometer, or, in video parlance, a pot. The **pot** is a rheostatlike device that turns the volume up and down. Increasingly, circular pots are being replaced by vertical slide faders (Figure 5.19). But whether the "knob" is round or vertical, it's still usually called a pot.

Using the Console to Control Volume

The pot governs the volume of the signal—it's a handy tool, for instance, if you have a loud, booming person hooked onto the MIC 1 pot and a soft-spoken person whose mic is being fed into the MIC 2 pot. You would keep the pot for MIC 1 at a low level and crank up the pot for MIC 2. We'll diagram a console having two mic pots in a moment.

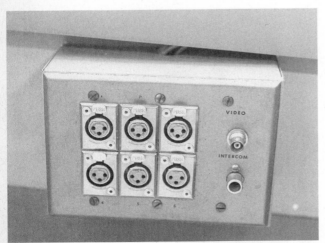

Figure 5.16 Female wall unit. The studio wall unit has locking female XLRs to accept microphone plugs.

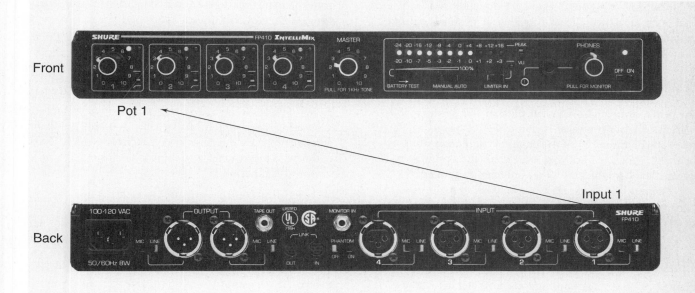

Figure 5.18   Audio mixer. The audio sources plugged into inputs 1, 2, 3, and 4 are controlled by pots 1, 2, 3, and 4, respectively. The mixer, a small audio console, controls input and output volume and the path of the audio signal. (Courtesy of Shure Brothers Incorporated.)

But how do you know what volume is the correct volume? The **volume unit (VU) meter** (Figure 5.20) provides an arbitrary standard that gives an objective, visual readout of the audio level. On many volume units the bottom scale is registered in decibels and the top scale is registered in percentage of modulation.

The decibel scale indicates how many decibels above or below the ideal audio level the audio source reads. If you're 2 decibels high, you're running "in the red" (that part of the meter that is drawn in red, hence the term). If you're 5 or so decibels too low from the arbitrary 0 standard, you're "in the mud."

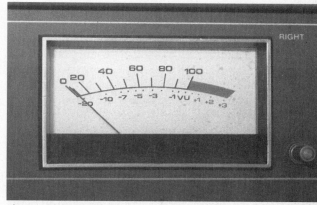

Figure 5.20   The VU meter. The volume unit (VU) meter is a visual readout of the audio level, a volume meter. Typically, the bottom scale is in decibels and the top is the percentage of modulation.

When you run in the red, the signal is distorted; when you run in the mud there's too little sound signal and too much noise, which produces an unacceptable signal-to-noise ratio (the comparison of how much signal there is to extraneous interference or noise) and generally poor-quality audio. The reason that running in the mud produces too much noise is that both the program material and background electrical noise are boosted by the amplifier. The noise will be boosted to a distracting level if it is not overwhelmed by the program material.

The upper scale indicates the ideal as 100 percent, meaning 100 percent modulation. **Modulation** is the elec-

Figure 5.19   Audio console with vertical slide potentiometers. This audio board controls the volume of each source with a vertical slider bar. Notice how easily volume levels can be compared.

trical imprint of a sound signal on the audio wave. The goal, of course, is to have the loudest portions of your program 100 percent modulated. If you have only 80 percent modulation, you have eight-tenths modulated signal—in this case, the output of the mic—and two-tenths random electrical noise put out by the system.

That's the long explanation of why you want to keep the peaks of the audio signal at 0 dB or 100 percent modulation. The short answer is that 0 dB/100 percent is the level at which the rest of the chain of equipment wants to hear the signal; it's nothing more than the optimum operating level at which all other units are calibrated.

Keeping the peaks as close as possible to 0 dB/100 percent is not nearly as difficult as it seems, because the needle is damped and tends to float, making it relatively simple to adjust the levels.

Console Channels

Figure 5.21 is a diagram of a console that might be used in a very simple audio operation. You'll notice that above each pot is a "key." The **key** is a switch that can either direct a signal into one of two separate channels, or turn the signal off. The program channel is to the right; the audition channel is to the left; the "off" position is in the middle.

The **audition channel**, as you might suspect, is a separate channel for listening to a source off-air. The audition channel is routed through the studio speaker and is useful when you have to listen through a full-size speaker.

There is also a cue channel, which is activated by lowering the pot all the way to the counterclockwise position, or, with a slide fader, all the way down. Cue performs the same function as audition—listening to a source off-air—but cue only routes the sound through a small speaker, and you can't perform any other production duties through cue.

Cue is used to hear a sound without putting it over the air. It allows the audio console operator to search for the proper starting point of a tape while the show is on the air. The audio operator can also cue up an LP record by spinning the turntable until the first sound is heard and then backing up the turntable a quarter-turn or so. (Don't try this with a consumer-grade turntable; it's not meant to perform this function.)

Using the Console for Mixing Sources

Now that we've explored the fundamental workings of the console, you can understand what is really its more important function: It allows mixing of sound sources. For example, if you want to open a program with theme music, you would start the turntable and bring up the level on the corresponding pot (TT1). Then, as the host introduced the program, you would lower the music and raise the host's pot (MIC 1), mixing the voice and music at a comfortable level. Then you could fade out the music entirely.

The console in Figure 5.21 has pots for three mics, a turntable, an audiocassette player, and a cartridge machine. A **cartridge (cart) machine** (Figure 5.22) is a device that plays back an endless loop of tape which automatically recues itself to the beginning. It does not rewind; it plays forward until it reaches a special tone that causes the tape to stop at the desired beginning point.

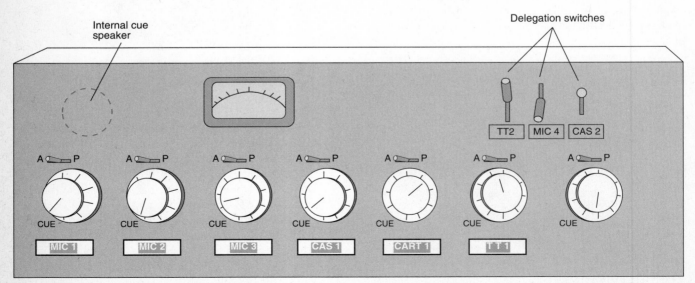

Figure 5.21 A simplified audio board. This audio console controls and directs signals from three mics, a cassette player, a cartridge machine, and a turntable. In addition, the right-most pot is wired into "delegation" switches, allowing the operator to select one of the three sources available—turntable 2, mic 4, or cassette 2. (Sources wired through delegation switches to a single pot cannot be used simultaneously.)

Figure 5.22 The cartridge machine. "Cart" starts instantaneously and then cues itself to the next programmed spot on the tape. Carts often are used to provide theme music and sound effects at the touch of a button.

Audio sources also include standard reel-to-reel tape, the format in which tape from one reel is drawn over the heads and spooled onto another reel. Turntables are being replaced at the consumer and professional level by compact disc players, although we're not likely to see turntables disappear soon because much production music is on standard vinyl disc, and compact discs are difficult media with which to do production. (Finding a section of a song on a CD is more difficult than simply dropping the stylus on a vinyl disc.)

You'll notice in Figure 5.22 that one of the pots on the board has a "delegation switch," which chooses between several sources. The delegation switch allows one pot to control several sources that are not used at the same time. With a delegation switch, you can only choose one source for the particular pot.

Patching around the Console

Sometimes you may need to reroute the sources going to particular pots. For example, if you need to use two of the sources on the delegation switch at the same time, you can use the audio patch bay to connect, let's say, CART 3 to TT1's pot. The patch bay (Figure 5.23) lets you interrupt

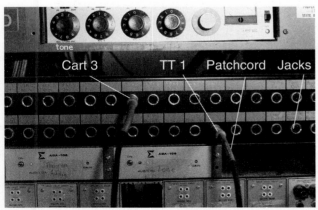

Figure 5.23 The patch bay. The jacks (holes) in the patch bay let you connect audio sources to different controls on the audio console using patch cords (wires). For instance, you might want to patch the input from CART 3 into the pot that once controlled TT1.

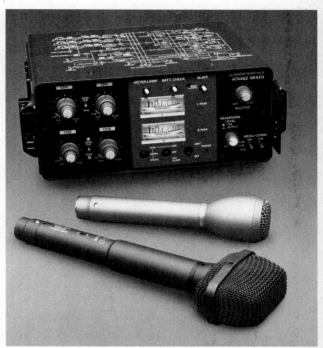

Figure 5.24 The field audio mixer. In remote operations, a field mixer is often used to mix input from several mics and to match their levels. (Courtesy of Audio-Technica.)

the normal signal flow by using a special cable called a patch cord. The patch cord allows you to bypass the normal wiring by inserting the cord in the female jacks governing the source and into the jacks feeding the receiving unit. As another example, should you want to record a program coming off the network line onto tape recorder 2, you need not pot up the network on the board and record the board's output on tape 2. You can patch NET OUT (the labeling will vary, but it will probably be something like this) to ATR (audiotape recorder) IN.

Mixers

It used to be that you only used a mixing console during studio operations or, perhaps, in a remote van. Now the state of the art is small enough to fit into your portable VCR case (Figure 5.24). The primary use of a mixer in remote operations is to mix several mics to match their levels and tonal qualities.

Professional Audio Mixing Consoles

Professional audio mixing studio consoles operate in a slightly different manner than has already been described. There are, in actuality, two different types of consoles. The variety discussed so far is the standard broadcast console—the type typically used in radio and, in many cases, in television audio control rooms. But some operations use what are commonly called multichannel consoles. A

multichannel console, sometimes, but not always, has two "sides" or "sections." On one side, usually the left, are input modules that route signals from mics and other sound sources through various sound-shaping controls. The input modules also have delegation buses, meaning banks of switches, which allow the operator to delegate the destination of a signal, thereby sending the signal to specific output buses.

The output buses, usually on the right (although some modern units have the output buses located in the middle) correspond to the functions of the standard audio console: They mix and route signals over the air or to the master tape recording unit.

The advantage of using a multichannel console is that the signal can undergo a great deal of processing—for example, adding echo or filtering out unwanted high-frequency hiss—before being delegated to an output bus. Although exceptionally useful for complex operations such as recording music, these boards are somewhat more complicated than basic broadcast consoles.

Operating a console—indeed, any audio component—is part science and part art. Chapter 12 picks up where this chapter ends and explains some of the fine points of using mics and audio production equipment as aesthetic tools.

SUMMARY

1. *Audio* is the word we use to indicate the electrical signal that reproduces sound. Sound is transduced into audio by the microphone; audio is transduced back into sound waves by a loudspeaker.

2. Sound is a vibration of molecules in the air or other medium. Compressions and rarefactions produce the sound wave. Most sounds we hear are complex combinations of sound waves.

3. Sound pitch is measured in frequency. Remember that we are using the word *pitch* colloquially. Loudness, the amplitude of the sound wave, is measured in decibels.

4. A microphone uses what's called a pickup element to transduce sound into audio. The most common pickup elements for microphones used in video production work are the moving coil, the ribbon, and the condenser.

5. Microphones operate with three primary pickup patterns: omnidirectional, bidirectional, and cardioid.

6. Another way to categorize microphones is by their physical appearance and/or intended use. Common physical types of mics include hand-held, shotgun, lavaliere, studio, and wireless.

7. Cable carries the audio signal. Be careful, because you can damage a cable by stepping on it or crimping it. Most cable for studio use terminates in an XLR connector. Cables for remote applications often terminate in a miniphone plug except on pro gear where it is an XLR.

8. The audio console, often called "the board," determines the path a signal takes and how loud that signal is. The primary features of the board are pots, keys, delegation switches, and VU meters.

9. You can interrupt the normal signal flow by patching. Because patching procedures are highly specific, it is best to ask for a demonstration of patching on your particular equipment.

NOTES

1. For an explanation of sound, octaves, and just about any other aspect of audio as it applies to the mass media, refer to Stanley Alten's definitive volume *Audio in Media*, 3rd ed. (Belmont, CA: Wadsworth, 1990).

2. See Alten, pp. 4–8.

3. For more extensive information on decibel level, see Lewis O'Donnell, Philip Benoit, and Carl Hausman, *Modern Radio Production*, 2nd ed. (Belmont, CA: Wadsworth, 1990), pp. 78–80.

TECHNICAL TERMS

amplitude	condenser mic	modulation	polar patterns
audition channel	decibel (dB)	moving coil mic	pot
bidirectional	diaphragm	multichannel console	program channel
cardioid	fishpole	octave	rarefactions
cartridge (cart) machine	frequency	omnidirectional	ribbon mic
complex waveforms	hertz (Hz)	parabolic reflector	sine wave
compressions	key	pickup patterns	volume unit (VU) meter

EXERCISES

1. Using a hand-held mic and portable tape deck, record some narration (reading a newspaper article aloud will do) under these conditions:

   a. In a tiled room, such as a large kitchen or bathroom
   b. Outdoors
   c. In your living room with the mic 6 inches away from your mouth
   d. In your living room with the mic 6 feet away from your mouth
   e. With the mic 6 inches from your mouth as you face a bare wall
   f. With the mic 6 inches from your mouth as you face heavy curtains

   Notice the difference for yourself, and, in a group comparison, among the sound samples collected by others.

2. Set up a variety of microphones from your studio. While one person talks or reads into the mic, bring it up onto the board. Notice the difference in sound quality.

   Now, prepare a demonstration of pickup patterns. Have the person walk around the mic while continuing to speak; this will illustrate the ways in which the mic rejects sound and *how much* sound it rejects.

3. In a brief written paper, compare the mics set up during exercise 2. (Your instructor will furnish you with the names and model numbers of the mics so you'll know how to refer to them.)

   Specifically, list each mic and—for each mic—explain:

   a. What application you believe it would perform well.
   b. What application you believe it would perform poorly.
   c. The "character" of each mic. Granted, this is an abstract concept, but you'll find it surprisingly easy to describe the character with concrete words. (*Hint:* You'll probably find yourself using words such as *warm*, *flat*, *hissy*, and so on.)

videotape and recording units

OBJECTIVES

After completing Chapter 6, you will be able to:

1. Identify the most common formats of videotape.
2. Describe the ways a signal is laid down on videotape—the relationship between recording and editing procedures.
3. Operate standard videotape recorders.

Chapters 6 and 7 conclude the "tools" section, so we thought it appropriate to remind you at this point that the first seven chapters of this book are "quick takes." Just enough information is provided to:

- Get you up and running on the equipment.
- Offer some basic understanding of the *principles* that underlie the equipment and its operation.

In keeping with that strategy, Chapter 6 offers some reasonably detailed information about running the videotape recorder—enough to get you up and running and to acquaint you with the various workings of VTRs. (Note that we use the abbreviation VTR when referring to all videotape recorders, some of which are open-reel. A videocassette recorder, or VCR, is a type of VTR.)

The goal of modern videotape recording machines is to create an environment where you can simply pop in the tape and shoot. In some cases, that's really all you have to do. But integrating VTRs with other video production functions calls for a deeper understanding of the process. You will find in-depth information, that will be useful in understanding some other aspects of production in Parts 2 and 3. With that in mind, let's examine what videotape is and how it works, the most common types of videotape recorders and playback units, and standard operational principles.

VIDEOTAPE: WHAT IT IS AND HOW IT'S USED

Now that most American households have a videocassette recorder, much of the mystery is gone from the discussion of videotape. Nobody (well, almost nobody) will hold videotape up to the light looking for little pictures and sprocket holes. In general, we all realize that videotape is a medium that stores a signal that can be translated back into video. But recently manufacturers have put some of the mystery back into videotape by marketing new formats, most of which are incompatible with each other.

Videotape is much like audiotape: It is thin tape made of plastic base that is coated with particles, often **iron oxide** (a fancy name for rust). Some newer videotapes use other metal particles instead of iron oxide. In either case, the videotape recorder transduces the video signal into a magnetic pulse, which rearranges the oxide or metal particles into a pattern. That pattern can be "read" by the playback head of the VCR and transduced back into a video signal.

Videotape Formats

Most videotape in use today is 1 inch, ¾ inch, ½ inch, or 8mm (about a quarter inch) wide. One-inch videotape is spooled on an open reel (Figure 6.1) and is used in high-quality recording, generally within the confines of the studio. Videotapes that are ¾ inch, ½ inch, or 8mm are each housed in cassettes. A **cassette** is a closed reel of tape that allows for easier handling and transport, and makes each an ideal medium for remote shooting. Furthermore, the technical quality of newer types of tapes and VCRs rivals that of open-reel 1-inch tapes.

You may occasionally encounter 2-inch videotape. The 2-inch system was the first to offer a convenient and practicable way to store video signals, but like all first-generation equipment, the 2-inch system was bigger, bulkier, and more expensive than its descendants. Although you will encounter a 2-inch machine from time to time, the days of this format are numbered because smaller and much less complicated devices can do the job better and more cheaply.

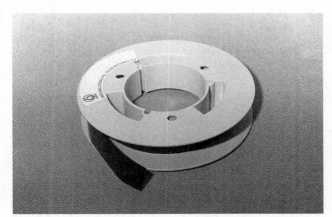

Figure 6.1 One-inch open-reel videotape. One-inch videotape is spooled on an open reel and is used mostly in the studio. It provides a high-quality recording.

How and Where the Signals Are Placed on Videotape

One reason why 2-inch tape is on its way to obsolescence is the fact that it uses a cumbersome and space-wasting (by today's standards) method of laying a signal down on tape. The 2-inch **quad** machine, so called because of its four heads, uses those four spinning heads to lay video infor-

mation vertically on the tape as it moves past. But advances in miniaturization and a clever approach to laying down the signal (Box 6.1) have enabled modern slant-track machines, which lay down the signal in a slanting pattern across the tape, to store more information on less tape.

Today, almost all formats use the slant-track method of encoding the video signal on tape. Often, this method is called a **helical scan**, because in order to produce the slant track, the tape is wrapped around a drum inside the VCR, and the tape forms the shape of a helix (*helix* is a synonym for *spiral*). Wrapping the tape in a spiral causes it to slant past the moving heads, as illustrated in Figure 6.2.

A typical ¾-inch broadcast-quality tape will contain the following information: the video track, located in the middle; the audio channels, located at the bottom; and the control track, located at the top (Figure 6.3).

The video information has been placed on the tape by two rotating heads. Each slash represents the magnetic path made by the head as it lays down *one field* of video. On the control track a synchronization (sync) pulse marks every video frame (every second field).

The audio channels are laid down by stationary heads in the same manner as a standard audio-cassette records

BOX 6.1 EVOLUTION OF THE MODERN VTR: AN HISTORICAL OVERVIEW

The development of modern VTRs is more than an historical footnote: It's an illustrative example of the innovation that has made recording possible and—in recent years—eminently practical.

To start with the quad machine . . . Until the system of four moving heads was devised, video engineers could find no practical way to lay down video information on tape. In order to record all elements of the complex video signal by moving the tape over a static head (the way audio is recorded), it would be necessary to move the tape at an impossibly high speed. But engineers at a company named Ampex devised a solution. Instead of moving the tape at lighting speed, they decided to move the head, the device that produces the tiny magnetic field which arranges the particles on the tape. And because it was not technically feasible to rotate one head quickly enough, they decided to use four.

As described in the text, the quad system is outmoded—replaced by spinning heads that slant *across* the tape. But what's probably most interesting about the historical development of the VTR stems from the origination of recording tape itself. (The practical use of audiotape preceded videotape only by a few years.) As broadcast historians Kitross and Sterling note in *Stay Tuned*:

If necessity is the mother of invention, then laziness may be the mother of necessity. The broadcast networks long had prohibited recordings because of their generally inferior quality, even refusing to bend the rules for on-the-scene news coverage during the war [World War II]. Popular radio singer Bing Crosby wanted to record his program rather than follow the usual network practice of doing two live shows in one night to cover different time zones. NBC's ban on recordings kept him from pursuing other interests, including golf. Crosby had seen tape recorders in use in Europe when he was entertaining troops during the war, and his Crosby Research Foundation, which eventually amassed many patents on magnetic tape recording, developed recording techniques and equipment of high quality.[1]

Crosby's research company began experientation with videotape recording in late 1951 (again, according to Kitross and Sterling, to free himself up for other pursuits). By the late 1950s, companies such as Ampex had built on Crosby's concept and had used the principle of moving head to perfect a practical means of video recording.

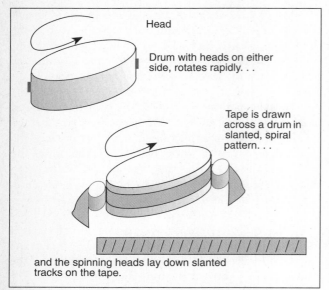

Figure 6.2 Helical scanning. Helical scan recording is also referred to as "slant-track." Wrapping the videotape around the drum in a spiral causes it to slant past the moving heads.

transduced sound. However, the sound quality available on videotape does not have the same fidelity as standard audio recording, primarily because the area allocated for the audio portion of the signal is very small; hence, the VTR is able to record only a limited amount of audio signal.

There are usually two audio tracks on a videotape. Having two tracks allows you to perform a number of functions, including, for example, mixing narration with "wild" sound: You might put your narration on track 1 and the sound of a fire scene on track 2. Some equipment may use one of the audio tracks to record time code information.

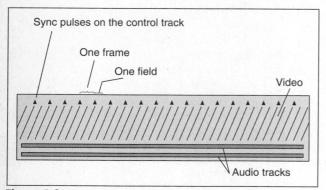

Figure 6.3 Information stored on videotape. The control track (top) contains sync pulses marking every video field (two frames). The video track is stored in a diagonal pattern in the middle of the tape. Audio tracks are stored at the bottom.

Sync Pulses and Control Track Timing

All recorded videotapes have some sort of control track. Synchronization pulses on the **control track** are like magnetic "sprocket holes" that tell the videotape unit the rate at which to play back the tape. A device in the VTR reads the control track and uses that information to instruct the tape capstan to pull the tape at a specific speed.

Control track information can also be used to locate certain points in the tape for editing. However, editing systems that rely on control track information are not usually accurate to the frame. That is, they tend to miscount and gain or lose a frame in the editing process. Moreover, the control track readout varies according to where you start and stop the tape. It does not indicate a specific point in the tape; it only gives a readout of how long the tape has been playing since you last inserted and started it.

Time Codes

Time codes[2] were introduced to make editing more efficient. The standard for time codes most common in North America was established by the Society of Motion Picture and Television Engineers (SMPTE). The time code identifies each frame on the tape by number and by **birthmark**, the original time of recording.

The time code is produced by a time code generator, a device now commonly built into the videotape recorder (or the recording section of the camcorder). In certain video formats there is a separate track for the time code; in others, the time code is embedded in certain synchronization information contained in the video signal.

Not all recorded videotapes have a time code. Older equipment and less expensive units use the control track for editing. However, even many of these units can be fed a time code with an external time code generator.

The time code appears on a window in the editing monitors (Figure 6.4). A time code allows you to automate the editing process. A computer can keep track of your edit points and generate an **edit decision list (EDL)**, to keep track of edit points. In addition to the convenience of having edit points electronically stored, a time code editing system allows you to make changes in the edited program much more easily than if you were limited to control track editing. Should you wish to make a change in the middle of the program, for example, the computerized edit control unit will not only allow you to make the change by entering a few keystrokes on the computer, but will also automatically redo ("recut") the entire editing process automatically.

This is a tremendous advantage to organizations that cut and recut material on deadline. Network news editors, for example, may often be instructed to make changes an hour before deadline. They typically approach this task

Figure 6.4 Time code on editing monitor. A time code identifies each video frame in the upper right of the editing monitor screen. Counting from the start of the tape, the code displays hour: minute: second: frame number. ("Hi8" identifies the equipment used in recording this example.)

with glacial calm because the automated editing system will take care of redoing all the other edits. The tape editor (meaning the person) need only worry about making the one change dictated by the news executives, who typically view the tapes shortly before airtime. Then, the automated editing system, which "remembers" all the other edits, will recut the piece automatically.

THE VIDEO RECORD AND PLAYBACK UNIT

Now that we've established some of the rudimentary points about what videotape is and how it stores a signal, let's examine some specifics that are relevant to video production.

First, the mechanics: A reel-to-reel or cassette video recording unit drags the tape past moving heads. As you record, the machine lays down the audio and video information by means of heads on either side of that spinning drum. Most VCRs have two heads, although some use four. No matter: The function of the heads on the drum is to lay down a track of video information *across* the tape spiraled around the head drum.

Time Base

As discussed earlier, each swipe of the head lays down one field. Two swipes equal one frame. And, as you remember, a sync pulse is created for each frame. There is some other synchronization information on the tape too—information relating to the number of times the horizontal scan occurs and the number of times the vertical scan occurs. This is important because it has a direct bearing on the

technical quality of the picture related to its stability. A jittery picture can often result.

The error can occur this way: Each field consists of either the odd- or even-numbered lines of the scanning pattern. Because there are 525 lines total, the sum for each field is exactly half of that total: 262.5. If each horizontal scanning line is not created precisely on time, cumulative errors will cause the picture to be technically unstable, and it will be difficult for the picture to be processed by other equipment.

The way in which the picture recreates itself on this precise time schedule is known as the **time base** of the signal. A jittery tape can often be the result of a time base error. In other words, if the horizontal or vertical synchronization information is not exact—and it often isn't when the signal comes from a portable VCR—the signal's time base will be incorrect. When there is a time base error, other picture processing equipment will usually perceive this as a jiggle or wobble. Sometimes time base errors show up as an expansion or contraction of the picture, what's called a "breathing" motion.

A device known as a **time base corrector (TBC)** (Figure 6.5) is used to counteract this problem. The TBC uses computer circuitry to store each frame in memory (a "buffer") and then release the frame at the *precise* instant it is to be played back or broadcast. Many new-generation VCRs have the time base corrector built right in. Others must have their signals fed into a separate unit in order to be time-base corrected.

Time base correction causes a great deal of confusion among newcomers to the production facility, so let's take another moment to further define the concept. Every video signal has sync information embedded into it in order to create the scanning pattern. This sync information is not the same as the control track. The control track is *created* from sync information, but it does not comprise the entirety of sync information.

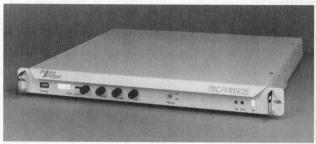

Figure 6.5 The time base corrector. A time base corrector (TBC) is connected between the output of a VTR and the video switcher. The TBC corrects any time base error introduced by the videotape recorder by providing it a new and more stable sync signal. The TBC can also process the video signal's chroma, luminance, and hue. (Courtesy of Prime Image, Inc.)

If you were to view a video signal through a device designed to electronically display the electronic waves of the picture (it's called a waveform monitor, and is explained in Chapter 21), you would see that there are sync pulses at the beginning of every horizontal scan and every vertical scan. (By vertical scan, we mean the time period as the signal works its way down the screen). The sync pulses that "fire" each horizontal scan come in incredibly rapid succession (one every 0.0000635 second, to be exact[2]). The pulses that signal the scanning line to return to the top of the frame don't occur quite as rapidly (one each 0.0167 second), but in quick succession nonetheless. The point is that if any of these pulses is out of sync with the other equipment, the picture will jitter, roll, or have some problem in picture quality. And as you can imagine, when dealing with such tiny periods of time, errors can and do occur.

Genlock

When you integrate the picture from one VCR with another video source—say, dissolving from one VCR to another, or from a VCR to a live camera—those units must be in perfect sync (this point will be discussed at greater length in other sections of the book). In order to accomplish overall integration, sophisticated video systems lock all the sync patterns from each source together. This is called **genlocking** (*lock*ing the sync *gen*erators together).

Why do we need a time base corrector if we have the sync signals locked together? Because all the mechanical contortions a VCR must go through in order to produce a picture make it more prone to time base errors than any other video source. There is some measure of time base error in almost all video equipment, but the problem is much greater in the VCR.

We need a stable signal to begin with before we can lock the sync with other video equipment. That's the purpose behind the TBC: to make the VCR signal stable enough so that it can be locked with the sync of other video inputs. You *can* play back a VCR that has not been run through a TBC and get a near-perfect picture on the VCR monitor, but as soon as you start to mix the signal with other sources of electronic information, the signal instability becomes apparent. (Signal instability is more likely when a tape is played back on a different VTR than the one from which it was recorded.)

The Most Common Videotape Recorder Formats

Competition has lead many firms to design innovative video recording formats. A format is an organizational form, and in video it means the size, shape, and design of a videotape unit. Each format has its own advantages and disadvantages, but one disadvantage shared by all formats is that, generally speaking, they are not compatible with one another.

This is proving to be a real problem at television stations and other video facilities that are attempting to upgrade their current equipment. News departments, for example, obviously want the lightest and most portable gear available, but the format of that new gear is, in many cases, incompatible with the VCRs they use for editing. Those who control the purse strings in video production are often not inclined to scrap several hundred thousand dollars' worth of existing equipment in order to accommodate the latest technical advances in videotape recording (which we will describe presently), so one or more of the following actions are taking place at video facilities across the country.

- Producers using the latest, most innovative formats are standing in line to use the editing equipment that can accommodate the new tape.
- They are copying (*dubbing* is the word used in the business) the tape onto another format before editing. This causes some degradation of the video signal because in most cases each generation (copy) of a videotape is less crisp and clear than the original. (Think of making a photocopy of a photocopy and you'll immediately understand generation loss.)
- They are beguiling station engineers into designing editing suites that can accommodate several different formats.

This last option seems to be gaining in popularity. Although it is not as simple a process as it might seem, engineering staffs have designed innovative editing suites to mate new and old formats.

What exactly are these formats? Following is a description of the ones you are likely to encounter. Figure 6.6 shows a collection of the various tape formats grouped to show differences in size.

One-Inch Reel-to-Reel. Currently the broadcast standard (meaning the best quality tape available for airing a program), the 1-inch reel-to-reel videotape system (Figure 6.7) is far less complex than its ancestor, the 2-inch quad. But 1-inch reel-to-reel is facing a serious challenge to its broadcast standard title by Betacam and M-II cassette tapes.

Three-Quarter-Inch Cassette. This format (Figure 6.8), known as "U-Matic," has been the workhorse of the industry for almost two decades. Unfortunately, it's beginning to show its age. Newer formats offer higher quality and greater portability.

However, there is so much ¾-inch equipment still in use that the demise of this format does not seem likely. In order to extend the life of this venerable format, manufacturers have introduced upgraded versions. The ¾-inch

Figure 6.6 Videotape cassette formats. A wide range of videotape cassette formats are available. (Courtesy of Sony Corporation of America.)

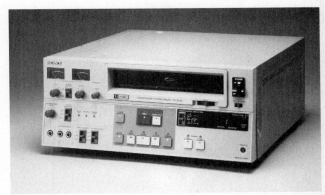

Figure 6.8 Sony ¾-inch U-Matic. (Courtesy of Sony Corporation of America.)

U-Matic SP (superior performance) system introduced in 1986 allows for better picture and audio quality than the older ¾-inch U-Matic system. U-Matic SP requires a special tape for the technical improvements to be fully exploited, but SP units can still use the older-style U-Matic tapes.

S-VHS. The **S-VHS** format (Figure 6.9) is a higher quality version of the ½-inch cassette format typically found in home VCRs. Standard VHS (video home system) cassettes are *upwardly compatible* with S-VHS, meaning that you can record and play back a standard VHS cassette (the kind you can buy in the drugstore) on the S-VHS gear (the upwardly higher model in terms of sophistication), but not vice-versa.

The *S* stands for *separate*. The term stems from the fact that the color and brightness components on the S-VHS tape are separated out and processed more cleanly than they are in regular VHS.

S-VHS is relatively inexpensive—about 30 percent cheaper than ¾-inch.[4] It is used by many institutional production facilities, and local newsrooms across the coun-

try find that the inexpensive format allows them to field more camera crews. The picture quality of S-VHS is not as high as the other formats we'll examine, but it's attractive because of the price and the fact that if a news crew on assignment runs out of tape they can pick up a compatible cassette at most department, drug, or grocery stores. (Many observers feel S-VHS produces a picture of about the same quality as U-Matic.)

Betacam SP. The Betacam (not to be confused with the ill-fated consumer Betamax format) uses a compact half-inch tape (Figure 6.10). As you might have guessed, **Betacam SP** is an improved version of a professional format known as Betacam, and the two formats are compatible, upwardly and downwardly, with each other. (Although you can play back a Betacam SP on a Betacam machine, you won't get the enhanced quality offered by the SP unit.)

Betacam SP is popular with networks (CBS uses Betacam SP) and many medium and major market TV stations, as well as large institutional producers. The system is quite compact, yet it produces a brilliant picture.

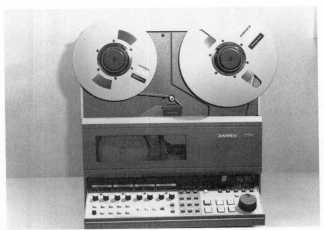

Figure 6.7 A reel-to-reel system. An Ampex one-inch, Type C.

Figure 6.9 Panasonic S-VHS camcorder. (Courtesy of Panasonic Communications & Systems.)

Figure 6.10 Sony betacam camcorder. (Courtesy of Sony Corporation of America.)

Figure 6.12 Sony Hi8 camcorder and cassette.

One reason for the enhanced picture quality of Betacam SP is that it treats the video signal differently than, for example, ¾-inch U-Matic. Betacam SP separates the portion of the signal that carries light intensity information (luminance) from the portion that carries color information (chrominance). Instead of mixing them into the same *composite signal*, Betacam SP treats luminance and chrominance separately, recording them as *component signals*. The components of luminance and chrominance are laid down on different tape tracks, not mixed together. Technical jargon aside, the Betacam SP component recording system can record a wider spectrum of the video signal—meaning a better picture. (S-VHS does this too, but the picture quality is not as high as Betacam SP.)

Betacam SP can use an exceptionally high-quality metal-particle tape as well as conventional oxide tape.

M-II. M-II (Figure 6.11) is a format developed by the Matsushita firm, which owns Panasonic and is affiliated with JVC Corporation of America. Like Betacam SP, M-II (pronounced "em-two") is a component system. Unlike Betacam and Betacam SP, M-II and its ancestor M-I are not compatible with each other. While both measure ½ inch, Betacam and M-II are not compatible either.

Figure 6.11 Panasonic M-II camcorder. (Courtesy of Panasonic Communications & Systems.)

The primary difference between Betacam and M-II is that M-II cannot operate with an oxide base; it requires the use of higher quality (and higher cost) metal-particle tape.

8mm. An 8mm tape and camcorder unit is extremely small and portable (Figure 6.12). The newest generation of 8mm, known as Hi8, incorporates time code capability and produces a startlingly good picture, given the unit's diminutive size.

Although not yet universally accepted as a broadcast medium, Hi8 is gaining acceptance for acquisition in many news and institutional applications. The camcorder units can be ideal for certain news applications; they are small and require little light.

Digital Formats. A digital signal is a signal that has been changed to the binary on-off codes of computer language. Digital recording and playback is something we'll examine in greater depth in Chapters 21 and 22 because it promises to revolutionize the entire field of video.

At this point, let's simply note that digital videotape recording is in its infancy, although digital special effects creation is widely used. Digital audio—the format used on a compact disc (CD) and digital audio tape (DAT)—is quite common, of course.

D1, D2, and D3 are the names of currently available digital videotape formats. It's doubtful you'll encounter them soon, and by the time you do deal with digital video recording, the recording formats may have changed considerably. In fact, the video storage medium of the future may more closely resemble a computer disc than a cassette or reel-to-reel tape.

STANDARD CONTROLS AND OPERATING PRINCIPLES

The individual controls of a VTR vary from model to model. Most, though, are probably familiar to you because the basic functions of a VTR are fairly standard. Let's run through the basic system. Because you are much more likely to find yourself operating a cassette unit than an open-reel VTR, we'll concentrate on the "typical" VCR.

That "typical" unit has tape transport mechanism controls, several input and output connections, and an array of warnings and indicators.

Tape Transport Mechanism Controls

When you insert a cassette into the unit, the housing that holds the tape either automatically or manually (meaning you push it shut) brings the tape into the machine. As the tape is inserted, a small arm is depressed, enabling the recording process. A button on the cassette (Figure 6.13) or a removable tab actually pushes the control in; by removing the button or breaking out the tab you can prevent the cassette from engaging the recording mechanism, thus protecting a cassette that contains irreplaceable footage.

The "play" button causes the tape to be moved across the heads, and—as is certainly obvious—be played back. In some cases, you must press "play" in addition to "record" in order for the machine to record a signal. Fast forward and reverse are self-explanatory, although on most models pressing the "fast forward" while the machine is in "play" puts the device in the "search" mode. Whether activated this way or by a separate control, "search" allows you to see a fast-motion picture. On many modern VTRs, fast forward and rewind will always show you the fast-forwarding or rewinding picture, usually at up to 40 times normal play speed, without disengaging the tape from the head drum.

"Pause" keeps the picture frozen on the frame. "Stop" halts tape motion altogether and on some units unwinds the tape from the head drum. On other VTRs the tape won't be unwound.

Note that "search" and "pause" functions are tough on tape and heads. "Search" drags tape over the moving heads at a high rate and causes a great deal of friction; in "pause" the rotating heads scan—continually—one frame of the tape. That's why most VCRs will automatically disengage "pause" after a certain amount of time.

The "eject" button mechanically disengages the carriage mechanism and removes the videocassette from the internal housing (in most cases, "spits it out" of the housing).

Input and Output Connections

A VTR has a variety of connections that bring signals in and out of the machinery. The most important is the camera cable connector (Figure 6.14). This connector has several pins, each of which is connected to wires bundled inside the cable. Each wire carries a different portion of the signal, such as Audio 1 and Audio 2, video, and sync information. Power is also channeled through the camera cable connector. In addition, one pin connects the camera remote control to the VCR, allowing you to turn the tape machine on and off by using the trigger on the camera. (There is, of course, no camera cable or connector needed in a camcorder unit because both camera and recorder are connected inside a single housing.)

A VCR commonly has separate inputs and outputs for video and audio, *as well as an output that carries both video and audio.* The separate audio and video outputs and inputs are used to feed the signals to another VCR (you would use these connections to hook editing systems together or to dub from one machine to another) and/or to feed a monitor. The exact configuration of audio and video inputs and outputs varies from machine to machine.

Separate versus RF Inputs and Outputs

Separate audio and video inputs and outputs provide a higher quality signal than does the output that carries both

Figure 6.13 Erasure protection button. When removed, the red button on the rear side of the video cassette will prevent the videotape from being recorded over.

Figure 6.14 The camera cable connector. The camera cable carries the video, audio, and tally information to the VTR or CCU.

audio and video. This is known as the radio frequency, or RF, output. The RF line feeds what is known as a *modulated* signal; that is, the RF line sends an electromagnetic carrier wave that is imprinted with the audio and video signals, the type of signal used in airing a TV signal or propagating a closed-circuit signal. Radio frequency is what is used to feed a standard television set.

An audio input on the VCR and/or the camera overrides the input of the shotgun mic mounted on the camera. Using this input allows you to connect an external mic.

A VCR may also have an audio input for the output of another device like another VCR or audio recorder. Since this input requires a different signal level than a microphone, it is called a line input. Don't confuse the two because they won't match and you'll get lots of hum and buzzing in your audio.

Connectors

The question of "what connects with what" is usually one of the more baffling aspects of hooking up a camera to a VCR or a VCR to another video unit. Fortunately, the connectors themselves will sometimes give you a hint. If the male end fits into the female end, you've probably made the right connection. If not, don't try to force a connection because this strategy will *never* work. There is no occasion when two plugs that don't quite fit will work when jammed together.

The camera cable connector (shown in Figure 6.14) is a good illustration of the intuitive nature of connecting video equipment. Once you know that the only reason for a cable with so many pins is to carry the complex components of a video signal, it becomes obvious that it must be the connection between the camera and the VTR. When you make the connection, you'll also notice that there is only one way that the pin will fit into the receptacle. It won't work upside down or sideways, and it cannot be inserted that way; the pin alignment and a rectangular spacer on the plug assure that the fit will be correct.

It's important to note that all camera cable connectors are not compatible. You will typically be handed the right camera, cable, and VCR, but mistakes will happen, so you should always check that the camera cable connectors are correct before venturing into the field.

So the question of "what connects with what" can sometimes be solved by using Yogi Berra's noted maxim: "You can observe a lot just by looking." Let's look at a few of the more common connectors so that you will be able to recognize them and, more importantly, recognize their function.

RF Connector. The **RF connector**, or F-connector (Figure 6.15), is used to link a VCR to a standard television set. A coaxial cable carries the video and audio signal.

Figure 6.15 The RF connector. The RF (radio frequency) connector carries the audio and video signal from a VTR to a standard television set.

The **F-plug** has a thin wire that protrudes from the center of the male unit. The female F-plug has a receptacle for the center wire; the plugs are threaded and are screwed together.

The standard television set often has a receptacle for the F-connector. If not, you would use the twin-lead adaptor, known as a matching transformer, to allow you to attach the output to the twin screws that normally connect to the "rabbit ear" antenna leads on the back of the TV. The twin-lead adapter (Figure 6.16) screws into the F-plug.

BNC Connector. The **BNC connector** (Figure 6.17), also known as a **bayonet connector**, terminates a cable used to carry video only. The video in and video out connectors on most industrial and professional equipment use the BNC. BNC connectors are joined by a short twisting motion, and lock into place.

UHF Connector. While less in use today, sometimes the **UHF connector** (Figure 6.18) is used to carry the

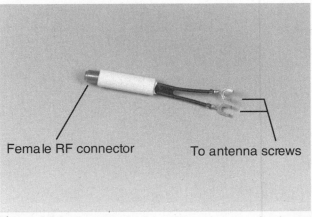

Female RF connector   To antenna screws

Figure 6.16 The twin-lead adapter. This connector attaches from an RF output connector to the television's antenna leads.

Figure 6.17 BNC video connector. This video-only connector is secured with a locking slot.

Figure 6.19 The RCA connector. Sometimes called the phono connector, the RCA connector is used for line-level audio in professional equipment. Consumer video equipment manufacturers use it for *both* audio and video, however.

video signal. This connector is larger than the F-connector, but is similar in that it has a center pin and a screw-type collar.

RCA Connector. The RCA connector (Figure 6.19) encases a rigid metal prong in a segmented metal sheath. When you see an RCA connector, you can usually assume that the cable in question is carrying line-level audio; line-level audio is audio that has been amplified to a level usable by record and playback units. The output of the mic, commonly called mic-level audio, is so weak that it is difficult to process before being amplified. Note, though, that some cables carrying video also terminate in an RCA connector; you will often find such cables on consumer VCRs.

XLR Connector. Mic-level and line-level audio is carried by a special cable that often terminates in the **XLR**

connector (Figure 6.20), a three-pronged plug that inserts into most professional microphones and into the audio patch panel at the studio wall. Whenever you see an XLR connector on a VTR, you know that you are dealing with audio.

Phone Connector and Miniphone Plugs. The **phone connector** (Figure 6.21a) and its smaller relative, the **miniphone plug** (Figure 6.21b), generally terminate a line that carries either line- or mic-level audio. If you look carefully, you can see that the phone connector and miniphone plug each has two connectors built onto one protruding prong, separated by a shield that segments the top and barrel of the plug. The miniphone is very common and is typically used as the terminus on cables that carry audio on a VCR, such as the microphone input and the headphones output.

Figure 6.18 The UHF connector. This video-only connector is secured with a screw collar. The UHF connector is larger than the RF connector it resembles.

Figure 6.20 XLR connectors. Professional microphones use XLR connectors, which use three leads, two for signal and one for a ground shield, to provide a balanced audio signal.

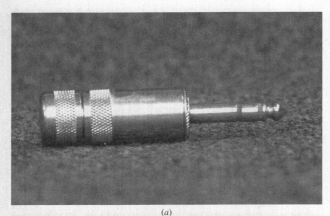

(a)

(b)

Figure 6.21 Phone plugs. The ¼-inch phone plug (a) and the ⅛-inch miniphone, or miniplug (b), generally terminate a cable carrying line- or mic-level audio.

Adapters. The miniphone is the most common connector used for the input of the mic. But because most broadcast-quality mics have an XLR connector, you'll need a cable that has an XLR at one end and a miniphone on the other. In fact, there will be times when you need various adapters: One piece of equipment, for example, may feed audio out through an RCA plug but must be mated to another that accepts only miniphone. Sometimes, you'll need a "y" connector of some type to feed two sources instead of one. That's why it's a good idea to survey your needs for connectors and adapters before a shoot.

A Basic Strategy for Connecting Equipment. There are some nuances involved in making connections that are really more of an engineering function than a production function, so when in doubt consult your facility's engineering staff. Making a connection is not always an intuitive matter and may involve consulting the schematics and soldering together the proper wires and connectors. But, in general, it is likely that the equipment you'll use will have connections that do make sense if you remember:

- When you see a round, multipin connector, you're usually looking at the cable that carries informa-

tion and control data from the camera to the recorder.

- This isn't the only multipin setup you'll encounter; monitors sometimes use a multipin connector too. (Usually this has only 6 or 8 pins and is a square plug; a camera cable usually has 10 or 12 pins on a round plug.)

- When you're looking for a place to hook up the mic on portable equipment, search for a miniphone input. The audio in receptacle may be on the camera or the VCR. It doesn't really matter which you plug into, although the camera is usually more convenient. One thing you'll need to check out is to what audio channel the mic input directs the mic audio. Generally, you'll record the mic's audio only on one channel, saving the other channel (track on the videotape) for other uses. There's no mystery to this: Many VCRs (and all VCRs used for editing purposes) have VU meters that indicate the output of each audio channel, and you'll *see* the location of the audio when you play back the tape.

- When you're looking to connect a monitor, search for the RF-connector if you're connecting to a standard TV. If you are connecting to a studio monitor, you may use a multipin connector.

- For other connections, some thought about the purpose of the signal and the reason for its flow will help you mate the right cables and pins. Are you setting up a system to dub from one VCR to another? Obviously, you will want to check the side and back of the VCRs for the audio and video outs of the source unit and the audio and video ins of the record unit. That's where your connections will be made, probably with a BNC connector for the video and an RCA or miniphone connector for the audio. Looking for a place to plug in the mic? Try the camera or VCR; you know that mic-level audio is most often carried on a cable terminating in a miniphone, and that will aid you in your search—as will, of course, the labels on the inputs and outputs.

Power Connections. A final note on connectors: The most fundamental connector of all—power—is made with a variety of connectors, depending on the particular brand of equipment. For portable gear, all power comes either from the battery or from a power source known as an AC adapter (Figure 6.22). Portable video gear is set to run on 12 volt direct current (DC), and you must have an AC (alternating current) adaptor (also known as a power supply) to change the alternating current from a household

Figure 6.22 The AC adapter. Portable video equipment operates on direct current and requires an adapter to plug into standard AC house current. The adapter often doubles as a battery charger.

to charge VCR or camcorder batteries. (Box 6.2 explains the difference between alternating current and direct current.)

Warnings and Indicators

VTRs, cameras, and camcorders have a variety of controls designed to keep the operator informed of the status of the equipment and the recording. Most VTRs have a VU meter, which functions as described in Chapter 5. The only difference is that the VU meter of a VTR frequently is used to calibrate the *video level* too. (Sometimes one meter is assigned solely to video; in other cases, a meter may be assigned double duty—video and audio—according to the setting of a switch.) To regulate the level of incoming video, you will invoke an **automatic gain control (AGC)**, which is a control that adjusts the incoming signal, limiting its power or boosting it as needed.

All VCRs have a counter of some sort. The most primitive type of counter keeps track of the revolutions of the take-up reel. Such counters are not particularly accurate. Other units utilize an hours, minutes, seconds, and frames display. Remember, though, that neither counter will be of much use to you unless you *reset* the counter (usually with a push-in button) to some zero point. The location is arbitrary, but the beginning of the tape is a logical place to start.

Inside the eyepiece of the camera you will typically find a variety of indicators, ranging from a light which warns you that the battery is low to a warning unit which informs you that you're about to run out of tape. All units feature some indication of when you are in the record mode.

BOX 6.2   ALTERNATING AND DIRECT CURRENT

Alternating current (AC) is the type of electricity that comes from a standard household outlet. What "alternates" is the polarity of the current: The wave switches from positive to negative. Direct current (DC) now usually comes from a battery. You can't substitute one for another without a device to convert the current to the proper type.

It's interesting to note that alternating current was not always the standard for household current. When cities were first being wired for power, Thomas Edison's system called for use of direct current. But direct current does not travel over wires as efficiently as alternating current; it loses power and, under Edison's first setups, had to be boosted at power stations every few blocks.

Edison's competitors wanted to wire cities using alternating current, and a marketing battle began. Alternating current was portrayed as the "death current" because a person shocked by AC would be held in the grip of the current. But DC generally throws back the person who touches a live wire. (The fact that AC was used in the newly developed electric chair played into this propaganda war quite well.)

But it soon became evident that AC was far more practical for household use, and it's what you'll get at a standard outlet in the United States.

Operating Hints

We'll be examining the operation of VTRs in Chapters 11, 15, and 16. But the goal of Part 1 of this book is to get you up and running quickly by supplying the information you immediately need to know, we'll conclude with a discussion of common procedures, problems, and solutions to those problems relating to operation of the VTR.

Adjustment of Tracking. **Tracking** is the path of the tape through the VTR. Sometimes the tape will not track properly in the machine. If the picture has a distorted "band" on it (Figure 6.23), look for the tracking control and twist it until the picture looks best.

Adjustment of Skew. Some machines have a control that lets you adjust "skew." **Skew** relates to the tension of the tape. Tape will stretch: If it's stretched too far during playback, the sync pulses will be too far apart and the cumulative time base errors will cause "flagging." **Flags** are **bends** in the edge of the picture. Note that the sync pulses can also be too close together during playback if the tape was stretched on the original machine on which it was recorded. If the bend goes to the right, the pulses are too close together; if the bend is to the left, they are too far apart.

In any event, you don't want a skewed picture playing back during an editing session. The skew itself will make it more difficult for the editing decks to seize on the correct portions of the tape. If the machine has a skew control, you may be able to fix the problem. But if this is a continual malfunction, your VCR needs to be professionally serviced. Note that since tracking and skewing are videotape related adjustments, we won't require them in all digital formats.

Care of Videotapes. Videotapes are not indestructible. In addition to being subject to breakage if treated roughly, the tape itself will wear out sooner or later. Although the figure varies according to the type of tape composition, you'll definitely see signal degradation after 150 or 200 passes. You won't get a good picture after many uses of the tape because the particles will eventually be worn off and the tape itself may be stretched.

You can guard against physical damage to the tape by taking up slack in the cassette before inserting it into the VCR. Use your thumb or finger to turn the hub of the take-up reel until you feel tension and see the supply reel turning.

Condensation will cause a videotape to malfunction. Avoid taking cassettes and or the VCR from a cold place to a warm place and firing the unit up immediately.

Figure 6.23   Adjustment of tracking. A tracking error causes the picture to break up at the bottom of the screen.

Also, don't leave the videocassette in the machine for storage. Take it out and put it back in its protective cover. When you store tapes, it's best to line them up on edge, library-style, rather than laying one on top of another. The reason: Pressure downward on the videocassette can cause it to bow slightly, and this can cause friction against the edges of the tape as the tape moves through the bent housing of the cassette.

Streaks or snowy areas of the tape may indicate that the tape has been damaged and/or that the heads of the VTR are clogged with debris. The heads do make contact with the tape, but if that contact is too intimate they will scratch the tape and wear off some of the coating. When that happens, the coating may adhere to the heads (or a part of the head) and cause distortion. You can often solve this problem by cleaning the heads. Head cleaning is not particularly complex, but it is best to have engineering personnel show you how to do it, and ask their permission before attempting it.

Incidentally, never touch the tape inside the cassette, or, for that matter, open-reel videotape.

Learning about Equipment. The most important action you can take to ensure good recording quality is to *read the manual* that the manufacturer of the VTR provides. Those manuals often wind up shoved in a drawer or filing cabinet, but with some diligent searching you can usually track them down.

You'll be better able to operate the equipment and in the process you probably will endear yourself to the engineering staff.

SUMMARY

1. Videotape and videotape recordings come in various sizes, using tape of various formats and widths. The broadcast standard is 1-inch open-reel videotape,

    although the technical quality of that format is being challenged by innovative cassette designs.

2. Modern videotape units use a helical scan, meaning

that the tape is wrapped around the drum in a spiral shape. This causes the track to lay down in such a way that it slants across the tape.

3. The VCR's internal sync generator creates sync pulses that in turn are used to generate a control track. The control track is used to govern the speed of the playback and synchronize VTRs with one another.

4. In addition to the video track and the control track, videotape is typically impregnated with two audio tracks and sometimes a track for time code.

5. The newest generation of videotape recording units process the luminance and chrominance components of the picture separately. This is known as component, as opposed to composite, recording.

6. When the control track is laid down, that forms the time base for the tape. A time base is nothing more

than the rate at which the tape is to be played back. Because of all the mechanical gyrations a VTR produces, the time base is not always accurate to the split second. Therefore, videotapes frequently need to have their time bases corrected before playback.

7. The ¾-inch cassette was, and in some cases remains, the workhorse of electronic news gathering. Although newer formats are technically superior, there are so many ¾-inch decks in use that they are likely to be around for many more years. Other formats include ½-inch VHS, a particular type of which has been adapted for professional use; ½-inch Betacam; and ½-inch M-II. Hi8 is emerging as a viable format for institutional and some broadcast use. Eventually, digital formats may completely dominate the field.

8. All tape machines have some sort of tape transport mechanism, a variety of input and output connectors, and controls.

NOTES

1. Sterling, Christopher and John M. Kitross. *Stay Tuned.* Belmont, CA: Wadsworth Publishing, 1978: 251.

2. There are two basic mechanisms of inserting time code: LTC and VITC. LTC means "longitudinal time code," and refers to time code laid down on a track on the tape. VITC (pronounced "VITS-ee"), is "vertical interval time code," a time code hidden in a certain part of the video signal. Some equipment companies are using their own time code systems in VITC format, meaning that you need their brand of editing

equipment to match their device that laid the time code on the tape.

3. See "Reduce Shake and Roll: TBC and Synchronizers," *Video Manager* (June 1987): 18–29.

4. This varies, of course, and the estimate was made at the time of the introduction of the format as reported in "More Options for Managers: JVC Unveils S-VHS and M-2," *Video Manager* (October 1987): 1.

TECHNICAL TERMS

automatic gain control (AGC)	control track	M-II	skew
bayonet connector	edit decision list (EDL)	miniphone plug	time base
bends	flags (videotape flagging)	phone connector	time base corrector (TBC)
Betacam SP	F-plug	quad	tracking
birthmark	genlocking	RF connector	UHF connector
BNC connector	helical scan	S-VHS	XLR connector
cassette	iron oxide		

EXERCISES

1. Produce a diagram of one of the VTRs available to you at your department. Your instructor may assign different units to various class groups. Label *each* control and *each* connector. In addition to labeling them, describe their basic functions. In the case of

the connectors, identify what kind of connector each is. Don't be reluctant to consult the manual.

2. Under the supervision of your instructor or engineer, actually disconnect and reconnect the cables. Refer to the diagram you made in exercise 1 for reference.

the switcher and edit control unit

OBJECTIVES

After completing Chapter 7, you will be able to:

1. Use the basic types of video switchers.
2. Perform simple edits.
3. Describe the relationship between the switcher and edit control unit in more complex editing setups.

The switcher and edit control unit are mechanisms to route and mix video signals. This chapter is a very brief introduction to the basic principles of the hardware itself. We'll take a quick glance at the relevant hardware, but won't get involved deeply in the technicalities. There are two reasons for this approach:

1. Unlike most other video production equipment, the switcher is a device that comes in so many varieties that hands-on, individualized instruction on the particular model available to you is a necessity. Although we certainly can (and will) outline the basic design principles, examining each and every aspect of switcher design would serve to confuse rather than to enlighten.

2. Video switcher and editing technology is in a state of flux. It is true that most video equipment will stay in use long after new generations of that equipment are introduced, but that probably will not be the case with switching and editing gear. Even as you read this text, new advances in digital and personal computing technology are enabling the construction of highly "intelligent" switchers and editors that in some cases cost *less* than currently existing models.

So, with those points in mind, let's examine the fundamentals. We'll start with a broad overview of:

- The video switcher
- The edit control unit
- The use of the video switcher in editing functions

We might note that in your particular course, editing may not be taught until later in the semester. (On the other hand, some institutions teach editing first.) But because new technologies have so closely linked switchers and edit control units, it is worthwhile to gain an overview of them at this time.

After all, both are devices to control how pictures are chosen and how transactions are made among those pictures. Also, many modern installations integrate the switcher and the editing equipment.

THE VIDEO SWITCHER

First, a definition: The device that originally allowed us to mix video signals, to punch up and dissolve between different cameras and other sources, was called a video switcher or (a term more popular in Europe) a video mixer. As the device grew more technically complex and offered operators the capability of producing effects such as split screens and intricate graphics, it became known as a **special effects generator**, or **SEG**. Sometimes, the designation SEG was applied only to the section of the switcher that produced those effects. In this book we'll call the entire device a switcher and the special effects section the SEG, but do remember that terminology varies.

The Basic Theory of Video Switching

What does a switcher do? Essentially, the switcher is a device that mixes and routes the outputs from a variety of sources, including cameras, videotape players, and even computers. The switcher allows the user to:

- Switch from source to source
- Integrate the sources into one picture
- Preview the upcoming shot before putting it on air or on tape

The first generation of video switchers was designed primarily to mix only camera shots and an occasional graphic (which was usually on a card and shot by a video camera). The switcher permitted a program to be played out live on tape, a process mimicking the multiple film camera technique pioneered by early shows such as *I Love Lucy*.

From the 1950s to the 1970s, video switchers essentially did not change drastically in form or function. Although the switcher of the 1970s was undoubtedly more technically sophisticated than its ancestors, it still utilized the same basic structure: It was designed to mix the composite signals of cameras and some of the growing variety of character generators, devices that could print graphics (usually standard alphabetic characters) on the screen.

But in the mid-1970s, the switcher began to evolve in order to accommodate the new types of inputs available. Today's switcher is equipped to integrate many *layers* of pictures and graphics. By this we mean that the new-generation switcher places several images "on top of" or "underneath" others, so that a complex picture can be built. We can include graphics that might tumble, grow, or shrink; we might place a person in front of computer-generated graphics and place a logo or name identification in front of that person.

Standard Layout of Controls

There are no sharp distinctions between "old" and "new" switchers. The devices did not change overnight, and many features on the switcher that mixed the output of three cameras in *I Love Lucy* remain in the most modern generations of switching equipment.

A typical switcher contains many rows of buttons (Figure 7.1). Each button refers back to a source (a camera, a VTR, a computer, whatever). The rows are arranged so that the operator (usually the technical director, or TD) can move from row to row to set up shots in advance and then put those shots over the air or on tape. In this most basic application of the switcher, we would cut between shots or dissolve between shots.

Using the Switcher to Cut. We've introduced the transition between shots in previous chapters, and in any

Figure 7.2 Key insert of title. The text "Boston Massachusetts" fills the area where the key or "hole" has been cut.

event the term is virtually self-defining: One picture is immediately replaced with another.

Using the Switcher to Dissolve. As you remember, dissolves are created by gradually replacing one picture with another. A dissolve generally is reserved for a shot that indicates a transition in time or location, or for a "soft" transition in a gentle piece, such as the videocast of a ballet.

Using the Switcher to Key. Almost all switchers produce some sort of special effects—taking information from one source and layering over another or mixing camera shots into the same picture, sometimes placing one picture into a box, circle, or other shape. Among the more common effects is the key.

A **key** involves cutting out a certain portion of the video picture and replacing it with another image. Figure 7.2 shows an illustration of a video picture with graphic characters ("Boston Massachusetts") keyed in. The key also can be used to eliminate a background. For example, weathercasters in all but a few markets today do not work in front of an actual map; they stand before a blue or green wall that is keyed out of the picture and replaced with an electronically generated map.

There are many types of keys, but cutting letters into a background is one of the more common. Usually, this is done by a method known as a luminance key. What happens in a **luminance key** is that you use the switcher to instruct the picture processing equipment to cut out any part of the original picture when the *second image*—in this case the lettering—reaches a certain voltage.

Another familiar type of key is the chroma key, which (as the name implies) cuts a certain *color*, typically blue or green, from the picture, allowing insertion of another picture into the area that has been removed. An example of the chroma key has already been mentioned: The

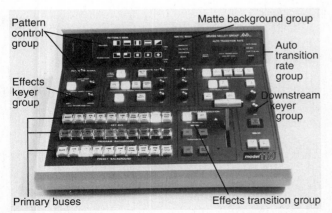

Figure 7.1 The video switcher. Although it looks complex, the video switcher's primary function is to mix the various incoming video signals. (Courtesy of Grass Valley Corporation.)

weathercaster stands in front of a blue or green wall. The key function invoked by the switcher removes the blue or green from the picture and replaces it with the other selected image, the computer-generated weather map.

What happens when the weather reporter is wearing a blue jacket? Well, in the early days of chroma key technology, the jacket would disappear and be replaced, possibly with the image of several midwestern states. (Blue-eyed weathercasters also were subject to some strange "special effects" thanks to primitive chroma key.) But today, chroma key controls are much more selective and there very rarely is a problem with clothing or eyes. (In case you're wondering, blue and green were usually chosen as the chroma key colors because they were the least similar to skin tones.)

Using the Switcher to Wipe. A **wipe** is an effect whereby you take one picture and insert it into a portion of another picture according to a preselected pattern. You can get a split-screen effect by wiping vertically or horizontally (Figure 7.3). A wipe also allows you to choose what sort of shape you want to use to insert one picture into another. Buttons on the switcher allow you to choose circles, diamonds, squares, and many other shapes and to insert those shapes into any portion of the picture.

Insertion of one picture into another can be accomplished in other ways besides a wipe, but for the purposes of our initial discussion we'll use *wipe* as a generic term to describe any sort of picture insertion.

Now that we've defined the most basic special effects, let's "build" a hypothetical switcher that can accomplish basic mixing and the two special effects we've just discussed.

Figure 7.4 shows an effects bank, a basic mix bank,

and a preview bus. The mix bank simply consists of two rows of buttons. For our purposes (remember, terminology varies widely) we'll reserve the word *bank* to indicate any location on the switcher where there are two rows of buttons combined to perform a specific task. And we'll use the word *bus* to refer to an *individual* row of buttons. Thus, a bus can be part of a bank.

Each button on the mix bank represents a video source—in this case, black; cameras 1, 2, and 3; the character generator (CG); a VTR; and the *effects bank* (EFF).

Before explaining the use of the effects bank, let's review the function of our hypothetical switcher.

Executing a Simple Cut

Using the most fundamental function of the switcher, the TD can cut between cameras by pushing the button on the row (bus) that is active. For many switchers, the row that is active is determined by the position of the fader bar. (There are exceptions to this, but for the *sake of discussion and with the understanding that the particulars of each model switcher differ*, we will make that assumption for the sake of illustration.)

Executing a Simple Dissolve

As you remember, if the TD wants to dissolve from camera 1 to camera 2, he or she would punch up camera 1 on the bus activated by the fader bar, in this case the lower bus, and punch up camera 2 on the bus not yet activated by the fader bar, which, in this case, is the upper row of buttons.

Moving the fader bar from one bus to another would cause the gradual mixture of pictures from both banks. If you stop the bar halfway between buses, you'll have both pictures superimposed over one another. Continuing the dissolve, you'll totally replace the picture from the camera activated by the lower bus with the camera punched up on the upper bus.

Quick Review: To dissolve from one camera to another, gradually move the fader bar between the activated bus. On the activated bus, you'll already have punched up the picture to which you want to dissolve.

Selecting a Simple Split Screen Wipe

You're not limited to cuts and dissolves. Suppose the next shot is a split screen between camera 1 and camera 2. There's no provision for creating a wipe on the mix bank. There is, however, an *effects bank* designed to produce this and other effects. We activate the effects bank by pressing the EFF button on the active bus in the mix bank.

Before pressing the EFF button, though, we'd want to make absolutely sure the split screen was set up correctly. That's the purpose of the **preview** monitor, a color monitor that is larger than the black-and-white camera monitors.

Figure 7.3 A horizontal wipe pattern. A horizontal wipe displays two images side-by-side. One image may take up more than half the screen, depending on the pattern you set. (A vertical wipe splits the screen into upper and lower sections.)

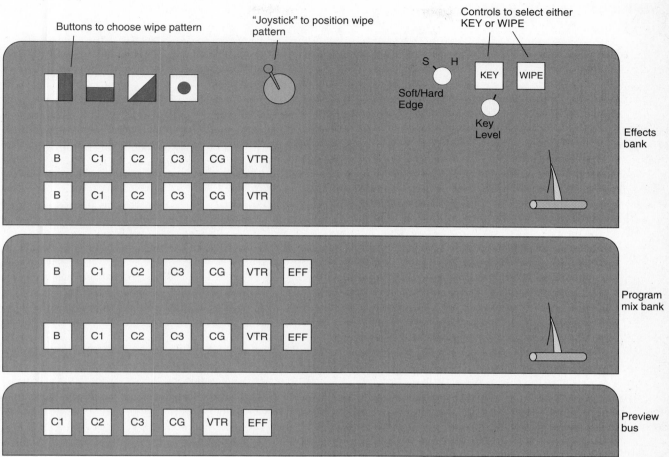

Figure 7.4 Hypothetical switcher. With an effects bank, a program mix bank, and a preview bus, this hypothetical switcher is capable of basic mixing and special effects.

Preview can be punched up to view any source before putting it on the air. The TD may also elect to punch up a camera on the preview monitor to check for color and focus.

To review: The mix bank has buttons on the top and bottom bus that activate the effects bus, in effect, selecting the effects bus for the program. The output of the effects bus can be viewed in advance by punching up EFF on preview bus.

Now, let's set up a hypothetical example to illustrate the steps a TD would use to create and tape a split screen. Box 7.1 contains this step-by-step exercise. You may find the description difficult to follow from one reading, but it's not important for you to memorize this procedure word-for-word and step-by-step. Read and reread the sequence until you understand the basic strategy of what's happening. If possible, recreate the scenario using your own switcher.

Remember that Figure 7.4 is a vastly oversimplified

diagram of a switcher, but it does correctly illustrate how two of the most basic operations in video switching are performed.

- Cutting between and dissolving between cameras on the program bus
- Activating the EFF bus and setting up a wipe and a key

Chapter 10, "Operating the Switcher," examines other methods of setting up and taking shots, and also introduces features of the newer generation of "smart" switchers. Although the operation of a smart switcher is beyond the scope of this chapter, there are some points that are relevant at this time.

Image Priority and Flip-Flopping

"Smart" switchers (like the one shown in Figure 7.6a on page 102) allow more flexibility to the operator. You can create images with several "layers" of video, and you can quickly exchange images at the touch of a button.

BOX 7.1   SETTING UP A SPLIT SCREEN WIPE

The anchor is about to moderate a discussion between an economist in Washington, who is standing in front of the White House, and an economist in New York, who is sitting in front of a window that shows the twin towers of the World Trade Center. The economist in Washington is on camera 1. The economist in New York is on camera 3. (Note that normally these signals would not come in on the studio's internal camera lines, but we're using them for the sake of clarity of the illustration.) Figure 7.5 shows the setting up the split screen. (The lettered controls in Figure 7.5 are referred to in the following discussion.)

Here's the setup:

1. Camera 2 is punched up on the lower bus of the program mix bank (*a*). The fader bar (*b*) is positioned to select that bus. The shot on camera 2 is a close-up of the TV anchor.

2. The TD wants to set up the split screen, so he punches EFF on the preview bus (*c*). Remember, the anchor is still on air and camera 2, the anchor's camera, is still punched up on the bottom row of the program mix bank, the row currently activated by the fader bar.

3. The TD selects WIPE as the function to be accomplished by the effects bank (*d*). He then selects the *kind* of wipe by pushing the selector button that depicts the vertically split screen (*e*).

4. Camera 1 is punched up on the top bus of the effects bank (*f*). Camera 3 is punched up on the bottom bus of the effects bank (*g*). Note that the shots are set up by the camera operators in Washington and New York to accommodate the fact that only the left and right halves, respectively, will appear on the screen. *As has become apparent by now, a split screen is nothing more than a wipe that*

has been stopped about halfway through. The fader bar is used to position the exact placement of the split (*h*). (Moving the fader bar to the top bus, where camera 1 is punched up, will fill the screen entirely with camera 1; moving the fader bar to the bottom bank, where camera 3 is punched up, will fill the picture with camera 3's image. Positioning the fader bar halfway between will split the screen in half.)

5. Now the split screen is set up; the TD and the director have viewed it on the preview monitor and deem it suitable for air.

6. To put the split screen on air, the TD punches the EFF button on the active program bus (*i*), the bus activated by the fader bar. (Alternately, the TD could choose to dissolve the split screen by punching up EFF on the top bank and using the fader bar to dissolve it.)

And that is the basic mechanism by which you would activate the effects bank for a wipe. Should the TD wish to set up a key, such as keying the character generator over the anchor, he would push the KEY button (instead of WIPE) and punch up camera 2 on one bus of the effects bank and CG (character generator) on the other bus. This would instruct the switcher to cut out the appropriate portion of the picture and insert the letters. Some adjustment would probably be necessary in the key level. The **key level** knob, called the "clip," adjusts the level at which one picture cuts into another. Fine adjustment allows for a crisp, distortion-free key.

You'll notice some other adjustments on our hypothetical switcher. One is a joystick that allows us to position a wipe. To the right of the joystick is a knob governing the relative hardness/softness of the edge of the wiped image.

Image Priority. The newer generation of switchers allows you to layer many levels of video information (Figure 7.6*b* on page 102). In effect, you are *prioritizing* information with the switcher, telling it what information comprises the base, what goes over the base, and what information goes over the second layer of video.

Flip-Flopping. Another useful function is called flip-flopping, the process of exchanging—and reexchanging—two video images *and* their control settings at the touch of one button. Flip-flopping is useful, for instance, when you want to cut back and forth quickly between two people having an argument.

Figure 7.7 on page 103 illustrates the steps of flip-flopping with details of a smart switcher. In step 1, camera 2 is selected on the program background bus; its output would be shown on the program monitor. Camera 1 is selected on the preset background bus as the output to be taken "next." (**Preset** refers to the monitor that shows the next shot that will go over the air or onto the final tape.)

In step 2, the operator simply presses the CUT button. Step 3 is accomplished automatically: The program and preset controls are reversed; camera 1 is now shown on the program monitor, and camera 2 is the "next" shot. When the operator presses CUT again, the shots and control set-

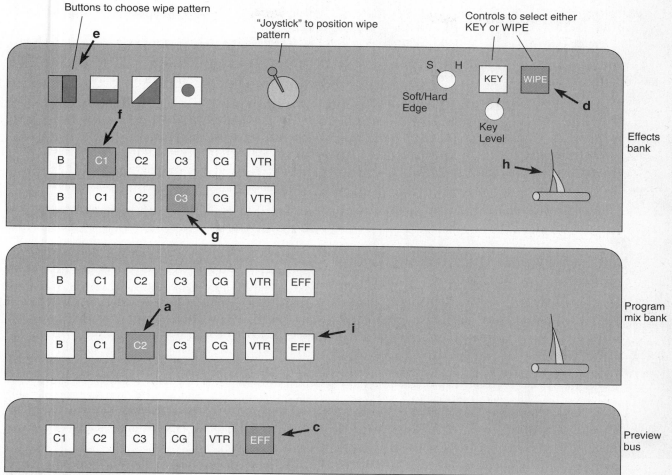

Figure 7.5 Setting up a split screen wipe. The arrows indicate what buttons are pressed. The split screen effect is being set up on PREVIEW, but won't go over the air until "cut" is pressed on the active bus of the program mix bank.

tings will be reversed once more. With flip-flopping, the operator can follow cues in dialog by pressing the same single button.

THE EDIT CONTROL UNIT

The other basic piece of equipment with which you will manipulate images is the edit control unit. The basic anatomy of an edit control unit has been described in Chapter 2, but now that we've learned some of the nuances of video signal flow and video recording formats, we can elaborate on specifics.

To briefly review, the edit control unit provides control of two or more VTRs and allows precision copying of material from the source deck onto the record deck.

What we have not mentioned yet is that editing equipment allows you to copy:

- Video and audio
- Video only
- Audio only—one or both channels

Intuitively designed controls allow you to choose whatever source you want copied. For example, if you want to add a voice over to a taped segment that has video of a fire and audio of the crackling flames (on audio channel 1), you would press the control on the edit control unit labeled "Audio 2 Dub"; this way, you'll put your voice-over script on audio channel 2 but not erase the "wild" sound of the crackling flames from audio channel 1. This is known as an **audio-only edit**. (The exact labeling of the controls, of course, varies from machine to machine.) The VU meter for audio channel 2 will give you an indication of the proper level of the voice-over, and if you replay the tape and find that the levels of voice-over and background audio do not sound right, you can simply redo the edit.

(a)

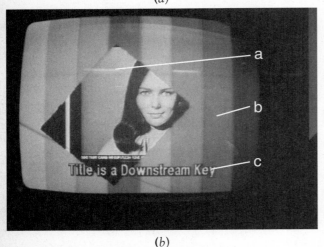

(b)

Figure 7.6 Image layering and prioritization. The Grass Valley 200 switcher (*a*) layered three images to create the display (*b*). 1. The woman's image is assigned to the program background as layer one. 2. Color bars are in the preset background as layer two. 3. The character-generated title is the furthest downstream and is assigned as a "Downstream Key" effect.

The Basic Theory of Videotape Editing

We'll devote a good deal of attention to the art and science of video editing in Chapter 16, but as you begin operation of editing equipment, it's important to understand the function of the hardware. First, let's define the difference between assemble editing and insert editing.

Assemble Editing. **Assemble editing** is adding pieces *sequentially* onto the tape in the record unit. It lays down control track as you add material. To put it another way, it copies *all* the material on the source tape segment, including the control track, the video, and all the audio tracks. Each time you add another piece, the machine matches the control track of the video that comes before the new addition and copies the new material after the old material. The edit control unit accomplishes this by backing up both machines for five seconds' worth of tape and

matching the control tracks during the five-second preroll before the edit is made.

The reason an edit control unit backs up both machines sometimes causes some confusion, so it is worth clarifying here. When you perform an edit (assemble or insert) you are copying information from the source unit to the record unit. But in order to do this, the tapes must be running at exactly the same speed. Backing the tapes up and letting them roll allows the speeds to be matched. It's something like the runner of an anchor leg of a relay race getting up to the same speed as the runner who will hand him or her the baton. If one is moving faster than the other, the handoff will be bobbled. If one *tape* is moving faster than the other, the edit point won't be hit precisely (Figure 7.8, page 104).

Insert Editing. But there's a basic problem with assemble editing: It only works once you lay down audio, video, and control track in sequence. Should you wish to go back and add something in the middle of the piece, you can't—because you'll introduce a new control track and cause the tape to go out of sync at the end of the new assemble edit. The machines simply cannot lay down new control track accurately enough in the middle of a presentation to keep the sync pulses perfectly accurate. Also, the erase head, which erases the entire width of the tape, precedes the record head, so when you stop the assemble edit, there is a piece of tape between the erase and record head that will have no program material on it.

The solution is to lay down, or record, control track first and then perform insert edits. **Insert editing** is copying video and/or audio without the control track. Of course—to repeat an essential point—you need a control track on the tape to begin with before you perform an insert edit.

Most editing personnel will record (lay down) enough black (control track) to accommodate the entire program. This provides the control track and lets you edit and reedit until you have exactly the product you want.

Figure 7.9 on page 104 shows the control panel of a hypothetical edit control unit. You'll notice that it has readouts for both tape units that count the time elapsed on the tape by sensing the sync pulses. Above the readouts are monitors for viewing the tape. (The monitors are physically separate from the edit control deck.) Below the readouts are push buttons for marking entry and exit points. There are two sets of these controls; the left-hand side governs the source deck and the right-hand side governs the record deck.

Usually, you set your entry and exit points on the controls governing the source deck. This means that you find the beginning of the tape segment you want to copy and press ENTER. Then you locate where you want the copying to stop and press EXIT. You've then programmed the edit control unit to copy that section of the tape from the source deck to the record deck.

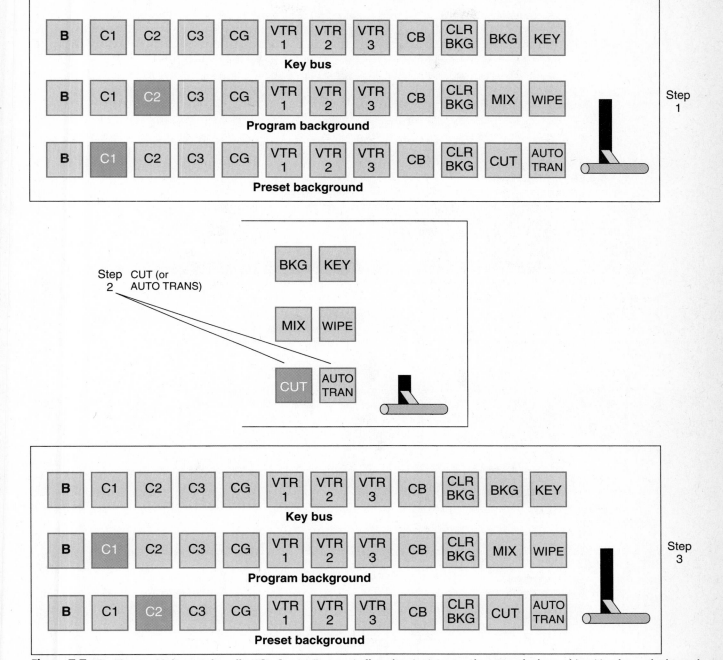

Figure 7.7   Flip-Flopping. Modern switchers allow "flip-flopping," automatically exchanging images on the program background (on air) and preset background at the completion of a transition. In Step 1, camera 2 is selected on the program bus and camera 1 on the preset bus. In Step 2, "cut" (or "auto-trans") is pressed to take the transition and activate the switcher's flip-flop capacity. Step 3 finds the sources reversed automatically: C1 is on the program bus and C2 is on preset bus.

The tape transport controls allow you to move the tape backward and forward in order to locate the entry and exit points. The play, fast forward, rewind, and stop buttons duplicate the controls on the VTR, but there is also a shuttle knob that allows you to jog the tape back and forth at varying speed. The speed varies according to how far to the right (forward) or the left (backward) you twist the knob.

In the middle of the edit control deck are trim controls, which allow you to add or subtract frames from the

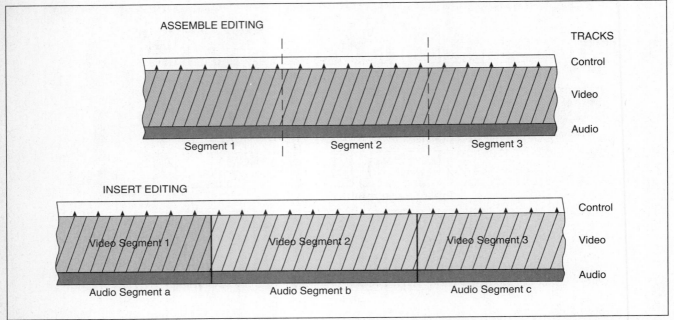

Figure 7.8 Assemble and insert editing. Assemble editing copies all tracks of any tape segment you select. To match the control track of the source tape to the control track of the previous segment on the record tape, the equipment synchronizes both tapes in a five-second preroll period.

Insert editing, by contrast, copies any audio or video segment onto a tape with prerecorded control signals.

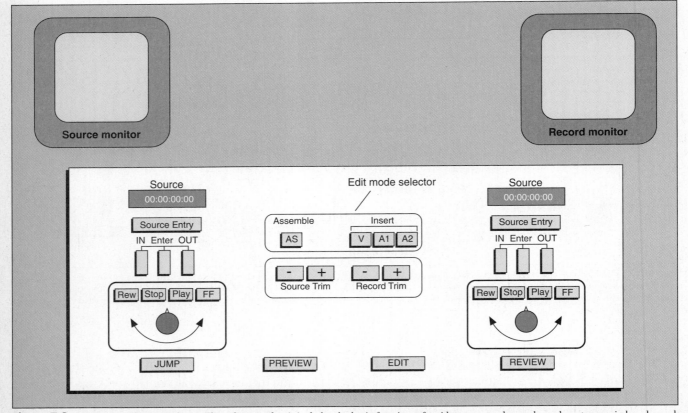

Figure 7.9 Hypothetical edit control unit. This edit control unit includes the basic functions of a videotape recorder, such as play, stop, rewind, and search. The operator can execute both assemble and insert edits. Placement of controls varies among models (compare Figure 7.10).

programmed edit's entry and exit points, and—this is important—the *edit mode selectors*. You must push INSERT in order to perform any insert editing. Many editors, even experienced editors, often forget to punch this button and wonder why their edit does not work.

Once you have pressed the INSERT command, the machine also wants to know exactly what source you want inserted, and you are given a choice of video (V), audio 1 (A1), and audio 2 (A2).

Beneath the edit mode selectors are two buttons: preview and edit. Preview will back up the machines (to allow the appropriate preroll lockup time) and show you what the edit will look like *without actually copying anything*. The edit button tells the unit to go ahead and make the copy.

A Sample Edit

Here's an example of how the edit control deck might be used. Let's assume you want to create a simple insert edit for use in a news program. You have on your source tape:

- A stand-up opening in which your reporter sets the scene: The mayor has declared that a local school building will be demolished.

- A stand-up close, with the reporter wrapping up the story, briefly discussing the implications of the demolition.

- An interview with the mayor.

- Some cover video showing the school building and illustrating its state of deterioration.

Notice that these elements aren't in the order in which you would normally see them in the news report. They must be edited; not only are they not in the correct order, but they probably are on different tapes and the reporter typically has done several takes of his or her opening and closing.

To edit this segment, you would:

1. Lay down enough black (control track) on the record unit tape. Most news stories don't run longer than three minutes, but play it safe and lay down about four minutes of control track.

2. Find the best take of the reporter's introduction. Set your entry and exit points (where you want the introduction to begin and end). Leave some extra time—a couple of seconds, if you have it—at the end point so that you'll have a little breathing room when you make your next exit at that point. Set the controls so that you are dubbing (inserting) video and audio. (For the sake of this simple illustration, we'll dub both audio tracks, but this isn't always the way it's done.)

3. Find the best section of the mayor's interview and repeat the copying procedure. Remember to position the

record unit tape to begin right after the reporter's introduction.

4. Find the best take of the reporter's closing and repeat the copying procedure.

Now, you've got a complete news report: An introduction, an interview, and a closing. But the mayor talks about the deteriorating condition of the school for a full 30 seconds. Isn't there some way to liven up this "talking head" interview?

Yes. Here's the final step.

5. Set the entry and exit times for about 15 seconds of the cover video showing a pan across the deteriorated front of the school building. Perform a **video-only edit** (an edit where you copy only the picture portion of the tape) over the mayor when he talks about damage to the front of the building. You would do this by punching up only the video button on the edit mode controls. Don't copy the audio, because you'll erase the mayor's remarks.

Now, you have a more complete and more visually interesting report. When the mayor is interviewed, the subject of his remarks will be shown over his voice. Be sure you put the cover video in the middle of the mayor's interview spot so that he appears on camera before and after the video-only insert edit. Remember, you must cue up the other unit tape to the proper position too. That's essentially how you would execute a simple edit using a control track editing system, such as the one pictured in Figure 7.10.

A computerized time-code editing system (Figure 7.11) displays the hours, minutes, seconds, and frames on a display inserted into the window of the editing monitors. If you were to edit the preceding story on a computerized time-code system, you would enter the entry and exit points onto a computer screen through a standard key-

Figure 7.10 The control track editor. A control track editor is an editing control unit that uses synchronization pulses to locate information on tape. Control track edits are usually accurate to plus or minus 3 frames.

Figure 7.11 Time-coded editing controller. Time-coded editing uses an accurate frame count to locate material on tape. Edits are accurate to the exact frame specified.

board. This way, you could construct the whole story in advance and play back the entire sequence. If you don't like the preliminary cut, you can retype certain entry and exit points and try again. You don't have to rebuild the story from scratch. All edits after the change would still have to be recorded onto the record unit tape, but the automation will take care of that function for you.

So you can see the advantage of an editing system. It allows you to put visual and audio elements in any order, *regardless of the order in which they actually occurred.* In this hypothetical example, you could shoot the ending of the story first (which is sometimes done). You can finish the interview with the mayor and then tape "reaction shots" of the reporter listening to the mayor and edit them in, using them to cover parts you might want to slice out of the mayor's interview or just for visual variety.

But as we'll discuss in Chapters 15 and 16, you can't take too many liberties when editing because you'll be distorting reality. For example, it would be unfair to re-ask

and edit in a question that implied that you cleverly extracted some information when the interviewee offered it willingly. Some organizations frown on the "reaction shot" itself, feeling that it's a distortion of reality (see Box 7.2).

On-Line and Off-Line Editing

There's another set of terms with which you should be familiar: on-line and off-line editing. **On-line editing** is generally taken to mean editing that is performed using a video switcher, integrated with an edit control unit. **Off-line editing** is done simply with two VTRs and an edit control unit.

The essential difference is that on-line editing can utilize dissolves and special effects, whereas off-line editing involves using cuts only.

SWITCHERS AND EDIT CONTROL UNITS IN A MODERN EDITING SUITE

So far we've discussed switchers and edit control units as parts of a separate operation, but increasingly the switcher has become a tool for editing as well as live-switching.

The Role of the Switcher in Editing

Why? Because the ability of a switcher to synchronize various sources allows you to dissolve from videotape to videotape or from videotape to camera, and to integrate advanced special effects into the presentation.

You'll note that there is no provision for dissolves in the standard edit control unit. But when VTRs are time-base corrected and routed through a switcher, the fader bar can be used to dissolve from one tape to another.

This is called **A-B rolling**, a term held over from film days when filmmakers would send a reel of film marked

---

BOX 7.2   THE REACTION SHOT: IS EDITING ETHICAL? AN HISTORICAL FOOTNOTE

In 1962 [the late] CBS president William Paley complimented correspondent Daniel Schorr on his interview with an East German leader. "What impresses me most," Paley said, "was how coolly you sat looking at him while he talked to you like that."

Schorr laughed. "Mr. Paley," he said, "surely you know that those were reaction shots, which were done later?"

Paley, it seemed, didn't know. "Is that honest?" he asked.

"That's a funny question," said Schorr. "I'm uncomfortable answering it. But no, it's not."

At Paley's instruction, CBS News established a policy prohibiting after-the-fact reaction shots. The policy was soon ignored.

Source: Bruce McCabe, "A Hollywood Version of TV News and the Industry's Reaction to It," *Boston Globe,* 3 January 1988, p. B3.

Figure 7.12 A modern editing suite. Mixing of sophisticated titles and digital effects are commonplace in a modern editing suite. Some of the equipment pictured: (*a*) preview monitor, (*b*) program monitor, (*c*) waveform monitor, (*d*) vectorscope, (*e*) character generator, (*f*) routing switcher, and (*g*) switcher. (Courtesy of Grass Valley Corporation.)

"A" and a reel marked "B" to the lab. The A and B reels were carefully synchronized so that the film processor could print a final film with dissolves—which could not be done if the film were simply cut and pasted.

Video's equivalent of A-B rolling performs the same function—but it cannot be done with an off-line editor, video's equivalent of cut and paste.

Advanced Editing Capabilities

Later in Chapter 16 we'll explore many of the capabilities of the high-tech modern editing suite, such as the suite shown in Figure 7.12. Advanced facilities not only provide the capability of A-B rolling, but they also allow for the use of sophisticated titling. A sophisticated production suite usually has one or more types of computer graphics generators. You can animate your titling, move your logos, or produce translucent "paint box" effects.

With the introduction of computers and digital manipulation of images, new ways of treating the video image have been developed. The introduction of digital circuitry has opened intriguing horizons. In the professional arena, it is becoming more commonplace to "dump" all our video into the equivalent of a video "computer" and assemble the program by use of digitized controls. (This technology is in existence as of this writing, but not in widespread use.) Also, cutting-edge systems allow the editor to point to computer-displayed representations of entry and exit points.

The possibilities are almost limitless, but the most immediate consequence of digital editing is freedom from the "linear" constraints of editing onto a master tape. Even with sophisticated control track editing systems, the program has to be laid down from beginning to end, although the changes can be made automatically and the program laid down on the record tape via computer control. But when editing units are fully digitized and all video information is stored in computer memory (which may be common by the time this rolls off the press), digital editing will allow infinite manipulation of the program from *within*.

For example, if you want to shorten a segment that appears half-way through a 61-minute program (in order to shorten the whole program to exactly 60 minutes) there won't be any need to re-lay the program again onto the final tape. Remember: The final tape has been copied from source tapes piece by piece. With standard equipment you'll have to go back to the middle of the tape and begin the editing process again, eliminating the extra minute in the middle of the tape and then laying down the segments from source unit to record unit as before.

But by using your computer controls, you can excise a minute's worth of material and immediately emerge with a final product. In addition, digital technology allows copying of the material without signal degradation.

SUMMARY

1. A switcher allows the producer to integrate several sources, choose among them, or mix them in various ways.

2. As its most basic function, the switcher integrates all video sources. The TD, the crewperson who usually operates the switcher, can then choose sources at will. Modern developments have allowed the integration of highly sophisticated computerized special effects.

3. On a typical switcher, the program bank allows you to access the effects bank. Among other effects, the effects bank will allow you to produce a wipe or a key.

4. New generations of "smart" switchers enable the TD to layer various levels of video. The controls serve several functions; they are not "locked into" as many set functions as older switchers.

5. The edit control unit allows you to copy from one tape to another, re-ordering the sequence of pictures and copying only audio or only video if you so desire.

6. Assemble editing involves laying down video and audio segments, and control tracks, in sequence. Insert editing is when you lay down a control track first and then insert video and/or audio. (You can use video and audio separately when desired.) The advantage of insert editing is that you do not have to

work from beginning to end; you can add material to the middle of the program or reedit sections of the tape.

7. The typical editing scenario involves programming entry and exit points for the particular segment you want copied. The edit control unit performs the function automatically once you have entered the entry and exit points.

8. On-line editing usually means editing accomplished with a switcher; on-line editing can create dissolves and other effects. Off-line editing usually means using a system without a switcher and producing a product with cuts only. Creating dissolves using videotape is usually referred to as A-B rolling.

TECHNICAL TERMS

A-B roll	key	on-line editing	special effects generator (SEG)
assemble editing	key level	preset	video-only edit
audio-only edit	luminance key	preview	wipe
insert editing	off-line editing		

EXERCISES

1. Make up cards with "camera 1," "camera 2," and "camera 3" printed on them in bold magic marker. Set the cards on studio chairs, focusing the respective cameras on the cards that identify them.

   Now, run through a switcher drill. Have one person (the "director") call out these commands while the TD puts the appropriate shot over the air. In this drill, everyone gets a chance to be TD.

   Here are the commands:

   • "We're in black. Ready to fade up from black to camera 1. Fade to camera 1."

   • "Ready to cut to camera 2. Cut to 2."

   • "Ready to dissolve to camera 3. Dissolve to 3."

   • "OK, we'll leave camera 3 on the air for a few minutes while we set up a split screen between camera 1 and camera 2. Set up the split screen on preview, please. [*When the split screen is set up*] OK, ready to take the split screen on effects. Take effects."

   Try some other combinations and commands if you have the time and equipment.

2. Remember the hypothetical interview with the mayor, the segment used as a demonstration of editing technique? Here's a chance to edit such a story together. Record the following script, having class-mates act the parts of the reporter and mayor. You can use a studio camera recording on one tape, or, if you have access and guidance, a remote camera. (We haven't covered remote shooting yet, so your instructor may have to help if you're using remote gear.)

   The important aspect is not the shooting, per se. That will come later. Simply put this down on tape *exactly* as it's written and you'll have an easy editing exercise.

Intro: Five, four, three, two, [*pause for a second instead of saying "one"*] [REPORTER:] The Kelsey Street school is headed for the wrecking ball, according to mayor Norm Hazlett. He says the building has deteriorated so badly that it's more than an eyesore—it's a safety hazard.

Out: [*Repeat the count*] [REPORTER:] In the long run, what this may mean is an increase in your taxes. The city had been hoping to sell the school to a private developer as a site for a condominium project. But that project—like the school—is going to be scrapped. This is _____ reporting for the News at Ten.

Interview: [REPORTER:] Mayor, why tear this building down?
[MAYOR:] The answer's right in front of us. The city engineer says the edifice of this building is about ready to give way. The whole front wall is decayed. If it goes—and it could go at any minute—somebody could get killed. Kids play here all the time, and people walk in front of the building as a shortcut between Maple and Elm Streets.

Also: Tape a shot of the front of a building— any building. If you're using one studio camera for this exercise, get a photo of a building from a magazine and tape the photo.

As you can see, the goal is to rearrange what you have on tape. Instead of "Reporter in . . . reporter out . . . mayor . . . shot of building," You want "Reporter in . . . mayor . . . a little bit of video only over mayor as he (or she) talks . . . reporter out."

PART 2

the techniques

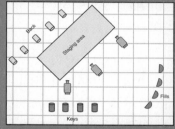

EYEWITNESS NEWS

camera operation

OBJECTIVES

After completing Chapter 8, you will be able to:

1. Select the basic camera shots to express appropriate ideas and moods.
2. Use the video camera to create those shots.
3. Operate a camera and meet the basic requirements for working as a camera operator on a video production crew.

Traditionally, the way the camera has been positioned in the studio has limited the producer/director's methods of capturing the images unfolding before the lens. In the worst cases, the "television image" has become a stereotype: a stagnant, stationary picture, flooded with harsh lighting, and photographed by cameras that, aside from an occasional zoom, don't change perspective very much.

But the mobility of modern cameras, and their ability to adapt to different lighting conditions, allows the modern video producer the opportunity to inject life into the images he or she captures.

This brief chapter deals with the techniques of operating a modern camera. (Chapter 9 will explore lighting techniques that enable the producer to produce those lively, interesting video pictures.) The main thrust here is to present some new ideas and encourage you to experiment with techniques that will make your images come to life.

THE FUNDAMENTAL CAMERA SHOTS

The video medium is maturing aesthetically. Obviously, this is not meant as a pejorative assessment of all video to date. Modern video production, however, places greater emphasis on creative images that are somewhat cinematic in nature. Throughout this chapter, we'll further explain what the "cinematic" comparison means, and we will also discuss the visual *meaning* of shots—how video shots are used to communicate a message. In short, we will focus on the camera as a communications tool, rather than as simply a technical device for reproducing a picture.

A Visual Glossary

The basic camera shots—long shot (LS), medium shot (MS), and close-up (CU)—are illustrated in Figure 8.1. These are relative terms that require little in the way of definition because the concepts have been explained previously and they are reasonably self-evident.

What merits explanation here is the *visual meaning* of those shots. For example, why would we choose a long shot over a close-up? The simple, mechanical answer is that the long shot shows more of the scene. The answer relating to visual meaning is that the long shot gives the viewer a frame of reference. (That is why we use a landscape shot to introduce this concept.) A long shot used as an **establishing shot** lets the viewer become familiar with the environment and more comfortable with the evolving series of shots that follow. For example, a face suddenly appearing in full frame at the beginning of a program is unsettling; it's like introducing yourself to a stranger by thrusting your nose two inches from his or her face. But the visual meaning of a close-up carries important aesthetic information too. A close-up indicates familiarity. We'd *expect* to see a close-up in a talk show during a moment of tension or during a crisis point in a dramatic presentation.

Despite the need for an occasional establishing shot, video is a medium of *detail*. An enormous amount of detail is lost when the picture is too wide. That, indeed, is one of the more common failings of novice camera operators.

Although we will expand on some of the artistic relationships between the video shot and the cinematic shot, remember that there is also an important *physical* difference: The video picture is typically shown on a relatively small screen. Panoramic shots lose much of their impact on video because of the small picture area. Also, much detail is commonly lost on the typical viewer because we

(a)

(b)

(c)

Figure 8.1 Basic camera shots. The three basic shots are (*a*) the long shot, (*b*) the medium shot, and (*c*) the close-up. While we more commonly refer to framing basic shots with people in the picture (see Figure 2.23), these landscapes are more representative of shots from a documentary or narrative.

forget that the viewer won't see the picture as close up as will the producer. Moreover, the viewer is usually much farther away from the monitor than is the camera operator who shoots the scene and the editor or director who views it on the studio monitor. Remember: *Video is a medium of detail—you can begin your shot sequences with establishing shots, but your images must be close enough to convey detail and accurately communicate the message.*

Perspective

In addition to visual meaning is another point that should be an important entry in your visual glossary: perspective. **Perspective**, which essentially means the way the camera views the subject, plays an extremely important role in visual communication. For example, the *height* of the camera in relation to the subject communicates a powerful message. When the camera looks down on a subject, the impression conveyed is greatly different than when the camera looks up at the subject (Figure 8.2). Although portraying height is not always a purely directorial device—for example, sometimes you'll have to point a camera at a certain angle simply because that's where the subject of the shot happens to be—height does communicate a message.

Overall perspective can be categorized under three headings: the exposition mode, the subjective mode, and the observational mode. Box 8.1 presents some very basic details of how each mode communicates.

Shot Composition

The modern video camera can be placed in a variety of perspectives and communicate many messages, but it's important to remember that before the shot can communicate anything it must be composed in a way that reinforces the idea. That does not necessarily mean a shot composed perfectly, "by the numbers." Sometimes, shots are deliberately out of balance, perhaps to communicate confusion and disorientation. But for "typical" shots, such as a close-up of a television anchor, we want a well-composed shot.

What do we mean by "well-composed"? Although it's difficult to present a definitive list of descriptors, we are essentially describing a shot (a shot used in standard situations and not for dramatic effect) that presents accurate detail, fills but not overfills the screen, has a stable horizon, is aligned using the rule of thirds, and provides appropriate visual balance.

Accurate Detail. As one veteran producer noted, the most important aspect of showing an apple to a viewer is to make sure

1. The viewer can tell it's an apple, and

2. It's red

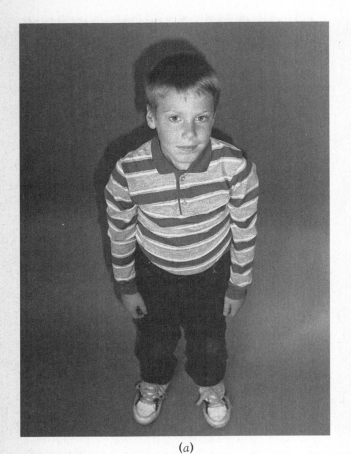

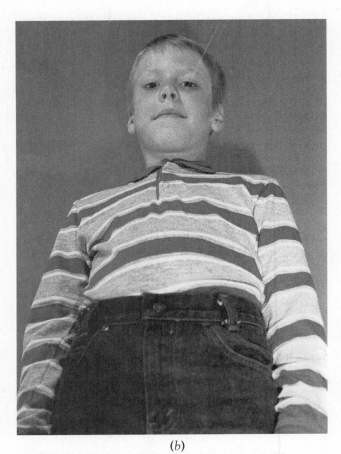

(a)   (b)

Figure 8.2   Perspective and camera angle. Shot from above (a) the subject seems dwarfed. Shot from below (b) the subject seems more powerful.

That may sound simple, but it's not really. Prove the point to yourself by trying an experiment. Put an apple on a table and pull back your camera shot until the apple occupies only an eighth of the screen. Is it still recognizable as an apple? Maybe; maybe not.

Now, try fooling the camera by inaccurately white-balancing the unit or introducing some additional light into a previously well-balanced picture. If, for instance, you shine a fluorescent light on the apple—which, remember, now fills only an eighth of the screen—you might have trouble telling if the object is an apple or a pear. And to pardon the pun, that is an "object" lesson in the need for close-up detail and technical accuracy in video images.

You'll find that this concept holds true in almost all aspects of video production. Always be sure you are close enough to the subject to produce adequate detail *that can be perceived by a viewer who, as you remember, will not be sitting a foot away from a high-quality monitor.* Also, be sure that your camera is accurately color-balanced and registered. (**Registration** is the accurate alignment of the three pickup tube images in the camera to produce a composite color picture.)

Filling the Screen. Whereas it is not necessary to have every shot in tight close-up, it is much more typical for a novice camera operator to shoot too loosely than too tightly. Don't overfill the screen, but always keep in mind that too-distant shots, lacking detail, do not communicate energy and they appear amateurish.

Be careful of zooming in too tightly on subjects such as graphics, where losing a small portion of detail will distort the image. You can lose detail because what you see in the camera's monitor or eyepiece is not always what you get when the picture is transmitted to a home receiver (TV set). Some of the information along the outside edges of the picture is lost during the transmission process. (More discussion about the areas that will and will not be transmitted is presented in Chapter 14.)

Many production texts recommend that the camera operator leave 10 to 15 percent of extra space around the **essential area**—the part of a scene in which the important information must be contained, but that calculation is virtually impossible to make in spatial terms. The only practical way to solve the problem is to experiment; recognize that there will be an area along all edges of the camera

BOX 8.1   VISUAL MODES

Exposition Mode

The **exposition mode** is the perspective in which people present themselves (or sometimes an object) to the camera. For example, in a television newscast, the camera is a substitute eye for the viewer, a conduit for information. There is no pretense that the presentation is anything but a performer speaking to a camera. We don't try to convince the viewer that he or she is on the set with the newscaster. We're simply recording an image and replaying it.

In the exposition mode, the director usually keeps the camera relatively stationary, uses a medium close-up, and keeps the camera at the subject's eye level.

Subjective Mode

In the **subjective mode**, the camera is put in the position of a person—simulating his or her vision under a variety of situations. Whereas the camera is nothing more than a conduit in the exposition mode, it is a tool for presenting a dramatic, personal observation in the subjective mode.

The most familiar example of the subjective mode is the **point-of-view (POV) shot**. A POV shot might, for instance, depict an attack by shooting straight up from the ground as a mugger with a knife slashes down at the camera—which

has taken on the subjective view of the victim. Sometimes a POV is an over-the-shoulder shot, but quite often it is subjective.

Observational Mode

A camera in the **observational mode** is a surrogate person: It is *you* as you accompany the police on a drug bust or "overhear" a fascinating conversation on a talk show. The difference between the exposition mode and the observational mode is that the observing camera is not directly addressed: It is an interloper that captures action as it happens.

Mixing Modes

It's important to remember that although you can occasionally mix perspectives in a program, your perspectives must be reasonably consistent and, more importantly, make sense. When a host introduces a talk show, for example, the camera is correctly in the exposition mode. But when the guests begin chatting with each other, we usually do not expect—or want—the conversants to look and speak into the camera. It is only when the host wants to directly address the viewer that he or she turns to the lens. The guest addressing the camera would spoil our status as observers.

---

viewfinder that won't be transmitted (and that the extra area varies from camera to camera), and experiment accordingly.

On a studio or convertible model, you can view the director's monitor and actually draw lines, using a china marker or grease pencil, onto the camera viewfinder to indicate the "real" area that is fed to the program monitor. With a portable camera you'll have to experiment because drawing lines is not practical on an eyepiece.

Maintaining a Stable Horizon. The **horizon** is the part of a scene, usually a flat graphic, in which the important information must be contained. Unless it's done for effect, a tilted horizon (Figure 8.3) makes the picture appear awkward and amateurish. But sometimes you may want to tilt the horizon for effect. For example, if you were creating a POV shot of a child stepping off a wild amusement-park ride, would you insist on a stable horizon? No, of course not. In fact, the stable horizon would detract from your message.

Assume for the moment that we are composing a normal shot. Because it is disconcertingly easy to have your horizon off kilter, especially with a portable camera, it's important to pay strict attention to keeping the camera level. Just a fraction of an inch in the eyepiece of a portable

camera translates to a wide horizon error when the image is shown on a large receiver.

The Rule of Thirds. A tour of your local art museum will give you some insight into an artist's sense of balance. One of the most important aspects of an aesthetically bal-

Figure 8.3 Titled horizon. Normally when setting up the tripod, use care not to skew the horizon. Note how the horizon line here seems to slant down to the left.

— 2/3

— 1/3

Figure 8.4 Framing a landscape. Typically the horizon should align with one of the trisecting horizontal lines (here with the lower third).

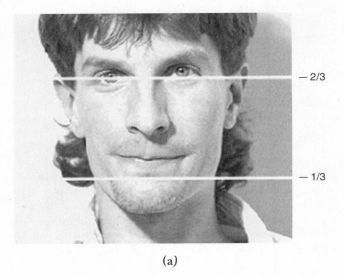

— 2/3

— 1/3

(a)

anced shot is that important details usually appear on the lines that trisect the frame—the **rule of thirds**. For example, the horizon on a landscape is generally one-third or two-thirds of the way up the painting. In a portrait, the eyes of the subject generally fall on a line one-third from the top. You should frame a landscape (Figure 8.4) or portrait in video much the same way.

The eye often finds a picture uninteresting when main elements are located directly on the horizontal center. That's why we frame the TV picture with the subject's eyes about a third of the way from the top (Figure 8.5). Notice how the picture in Figure 8.6 looks awkward—downright silly, in fact—when the eyes fall right in the center.

When two people are in the frame, such as in an over-the-shoulder shot, their heads are typically on vertically trisecting lines (Figure 8.7).

The rule of thirds is not applicable to every circumstance because rules are frequently broken in art, but it does serve as a starting point for good shot composition.

Visual Balance. The straight-ahead shot, which typically uses the rule of thirds by having the talent's eyes along a horizontal line one-third of the way down the screen, is usually centered vertically. That is, the nose of the on-camera performer is in the center of the picture. This mimics normal eyesight, although a pleasing picture can be created using the rule of thirds by keying in a graphic (Figure 8.8) that occupies one side of the screen. The graphic placed over a newscaster's shoulder is, if you examine it, a good example of how a pleasing picture is created using the rule of thirds.

It would appear unnatural for a person looking straight ahead to be off-center, if nothing else were in the picture. Again, this is because the picture mimics the image we normally create with our eyes. But when the talent looks to one side, proper composition requires what is often called looking space, eye room, nose room, or some similar term. When the person on camera is walking or running,

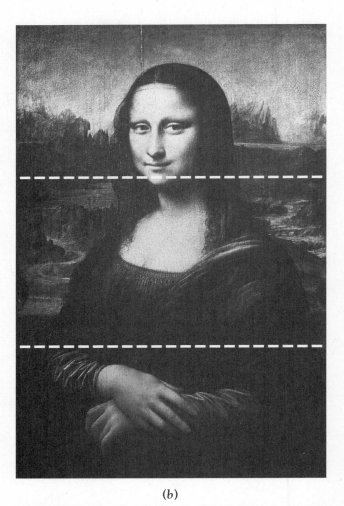

(b)

Figure 8.5 Framing a close-up. (*a*) The viewer's attention is generally focused at the eyes. (*b*) The famous smile of Leonardo's *Mona Lisa* is positioned at the upper third of the portrait.

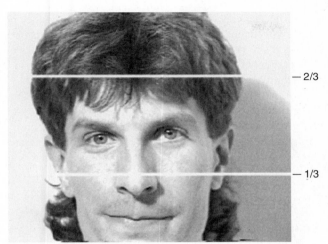

Figure 8.6   Awkward framing. Do *not* position the eyes at the center of the shot.

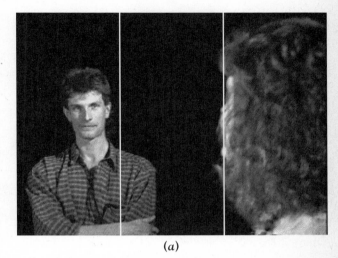

(a)

we provide similar room, usually called **leading space** (Figure 8.9), to show what the performer is moving into. There's a reason for this convention of composition, and *understanding* the reason allows you to automatically create the proper composition without having to think about it. The purpose, again, is to mimic normal eyesight patterns.

For example, when we watch a football player running downfield with the ball, we hardly ever look *behind* him (unless we're specifically watching an approaching tackler). Instead, we instinctively look *ahead*. We want to know the environment into which the runner is heading. Are there tacklers ahead? How close is the goal?

You'll find yourself naturally providing leading room—with your eyes—any time you follow a moving object. When a horse runs across your field of vision, you instinctively look ahead and view the environment into which the horse is running. If you see a fast-moving car careening down the street, you don't look behind it—you look to see what's ahead, what might be hit.

Note that sometimes we deliberately throw a shot out of balance to disconcert the viewer and create an aura of tension or bewilderment. We'll show examples of this in later chapters, including Chapter 14, "Graphics."

FUNDAMENTAL VISUAL ELEMENTS: IMAGE AND MOTION

Earlier, we mentioned that a modern camera is more than just a stationary recording device. As the video medium has matured, the camera has become an integral part of the action.

A classic example of this was the TV show *Hill Street Blues*, which is now widely shown in syndicated reruns. Although the show was filmed, rather than taped, it serves as a good example of how any camera—film or video—

(b)

Figure 8.7   Framing a two-shot. (*a*) The subjects of a two-shot often align with vertically trisecting lines. (*b*) The subjects of Grant Wood's *American Gothic* are positioned to direct the viewer's attention.

can convey action and become part of the drama by entering into the observational mode. Notice the next time you see a *Hill Street Blues* rerun how the camera frequently "steps into" the action; when the actors move forward, the camera does too, making the viewer part of the scene.

Moving the camera is hardly a revolutionary concept, but almost all aesthetic revolutions come in a series of small changes. For example, film did not always use close-ups, but it evolved into a close-up medium.

Figure 8.8 Good balance. The center of the graphic and the anchor's eyes align at the upper third of the screen. Each is also positioned on a vertically trisecting line.

The modern video producer is in the business of building on convention and tradition—but also in the business of experimenting and establishing new practices. As many producers note, the business is in a state of flux, and you'll be entering part of an industry that is evolving day by day.

Overall Image and Lighting

Change has occurred in many aspects of the video production process, but lighting is probably the most immediately apparent aspect. For example, for many years the "typical" video set was lighted with a harsh, flat light that, although a healthy environment for the technical require-

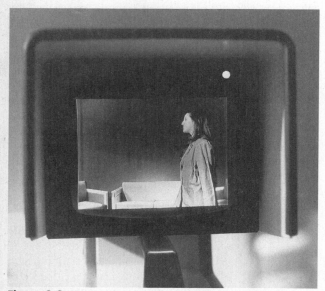

Figure 8.9 Leading space. As the subject moves, the camera operator maintains leading space for her to walk into.

ments of cameras, did nothing to establish the reality of the environment. We'll deal with this in depth in Chapter 9, but it's important to note here that lighting practices reflect one of the more radically changed areas in the composition of the video image.

A typical video set was also very static. The cameras taping a dramatic show, for example, (usually three of them) very rarely changed position. An occasional zoom added some motion to the image, but we basically created a two-dimensional environment—a highly artificial and static milieu.

The Mix of Motion and Composition

But the static picture is no longer the rule. Cameras that are easier to move and more tolerant of changing and/or lower light levels have altered—to an extent—the way we view the process of creating a program.

There are two primary points to be considered when discussing the new motion available to a producer:

1. Motion is a mixed blessing. It creates problems that must be dealt with in advance of shooting.

2. Each moving camera shot conveys a different aspect of *visual communication*. It's crucial that all on-air motion not convey a mixed signal to the viewer.

Problems of Motion

Primarily, the idea of "motion creating problems" relates, first of all, to the fact that when people (or the camera) move, your focus may have to be changed. It's advisable to check your entire field of focus while setting up a shot, anticipating whether you will have to change focus on-air when the subject moves.

Anything involving motion (and focus) requires careful attention, and one way to head off such problems is by careful blocking. **Blocking** is a term borrowed from the theater and it essentially means putting your performers through their on-stage motions so that camera angles, shadows, and other problems can be worked out in advance.

One problem you'll certainly want to avoid via careful blocking is the problem of extraneous objects being juxtaposed into the picture. For example, if a performer moves in front of a potted plant, the compression of a video picture may make her appear to have a plant growing from her head (Figure 8.10).

A moving performer obviously causes problems if he or she walks out of the lighted area, but a more subtle problem is the shadow from a mic boom. If you rehearse the move in advance, you can avoid having the performer walk into an area where there is a boom shadow. Or, if you choose, you can rearrange the lighting so that the shadow is removed or hidden.

Figure 8.10 Jarring juxtapositions. Be aware of the background as your talent moves on a set. The compression in this video image makes the plant appear to be "growing" from the talent's head.

Using Motion to Your Advantage

Sometimes you'll have to change focus to follow movement; this is usually called pulling focus and is a skill that can be perfected only by practice. When **pulling focus**, the camera operator refocuses the lens on a second subject, pulling the initial subject out of focus.

Pulling focus is more than a method for compensating for motion. It is a powerful tool for directing attention. For example, a scene in a dramatic episode may call for one person in the foreground to be surprised by a person entering from the rear; as he or she notices the visitor, we pull focus to direct attention to that person (Figure 8.11).

Camera Movements and What They Communicate

Remember, of course, that cameras move too. In earlier chapters we described the physical components of basic camera moves, but now we'll take a quick look at some of the *reasons* for the zoom, dolly, tilt, pan, and pedestal and what the movements convey.

Zoom. Remember, a zoom is a *magnification* of an image and does not visually translate to moving toward the object. There are many cases when a zoom is appropriate, such as in news footage where we establish an overall perspective and then zoom in on (magnify) the detail.

But also keep in mind that excessive use of the zoom is the mark of an amateur cameraperson. Continual zooming makes a tape look more like the record of a birthday party than a piece of polished video production; it's also quite distracting to the viewer. So use the zoom with discretion: It says, visually, "Let's take a closer look at a detail in this picture." Be sure that what you're zooming into *warrants* a closer look before you press that zoom button.

(a)

(b)

Figure 8.11 Pulling focus and directing attention. In (*a*), the subject closest to the camera is in perfect focus, while the other person is not. In (*b*), the camera has shifted its focus to direct attention to the visitor. A camera move such as this provides a sense of motion and drama.

Dolly. A dolly involves the physical motion of the camera toward or away from the subject. We can illustrate the profound difference between the visual imagery of a zoom and dolly by this simple example: Let's establish a scene of three surly toughs, one—the one in the middle—with a baseball bat. If we start with an establishing shot and *zoom* into a closer shot of the person with the bat (Figure 8.12), we are visually making a closer examination of the person with the bat. That would be the natural visual imagery of someone who turned a corner, spied the thugs, and focused his or her attention on the most menacing part of the image—the person holding the baseball bat.

Now look at the difference created by *dollying* toward the person with the bat (Figure 8.13). Here, the camera

Figure 8.12 Zoom. Notice how in this figure the zoom forces us to more closely examine the person with the bat.

(in the subjective mode) represents a person who actually moves past the two people on either side and toward the person with the bat. This conveys the visual idea that the person is moving toward and confronting the person holding the weapon.

Tilt. Sometimes, the tilt (an up or down movement) serves a purely utilitarian function. If someone stands up, we must tilt up to keep his or her face in the frame. But a tilt also conveys a visual message. For example, in the subjective mode a tilt would be used to mimic our eyes' method of assessing, for example, stature.

What do you do when looking at a statue? Do you start at the top, look down, and look back up again? Do you typically use the same motion when "sizing up" a person? The tilt, in this case, reproduces your natural visual instincts.

Figure 8.13 Dolly. Dollying in on the subject provides a feeling of moving toward the subject without the magnification that occurs when zooming.

Pan. A *pan* is the horizontal movement of a camera head on a stationary pedestal. It can serve a purely utilitarian purpose, but a pan also conveys a message in terms of mental imagery. Often, the pan is used to shift attention from one speaker to another, which is visually more powerful than simply having both speakers in the shot. As another example, a pan can be used to accentuate the breadth of a vista. You can certainly show a panorama in one static shot, but a lingering pan far more accurately conveys the idea of an impressively broad landscape and gives a more detailed view of the scene.

Pedestal. What's communicated by raising or lowering the camera head? Well, from a POV shot, a pedestal up is a good representation of someone standing up from a chair. From an observational or exposition mode, the pedestal often serves to show a new perspective on the subject and add some motion and excitement. A pedestal up is a common way to open a news program.

Other Movements. A camera can be maneuvered in just about any way in which it's possible for the operator to move. If you work for a high-budget operation that uses a camera crane, you may move laterally from your elevated position, a movement known as a **tongue**. Although cranes are more common in studio film operations, some events taped on video, such as symphony orchestra concerts, lend themselves well to the use of a video camera mounted on a crane.

The development of **Steadicam** technology makes hand-held movements virtually as smooth as those made with a studio dolly—but of course the camera operator has much more freedom to move. The Steadicam (Figure 8.14) is becoming an increasingly popular tool for video producers who wish to tilt, pan, pedestal (or make any other move that can be invented) with impunity, and without the constraints of the camera pedestal and mount.

New technology *inside* cameras is also allowing for increased flexibility in hand-held operations. Stabilization circuits within the camera prevent (to an extent) picture jiggle and help smooth camera movements considerably.

OTHER TECHNIQUES TO COMMUNICATE WITH CAMERA WORK

The combination of camera work and other technologies can significantly change the thrust of your message. Increasingly, quality video has taken on more of the characteristics of cinema. In its most basic terms, this means that:

- Greater attention is paid to shot composition.

- Shots are more carefully planned to include meaningful motion.

Figure 8.14 Steadicam Jr. The Steadicam has been scaled down to operate with smaller camcorder. It is now possible for any producer to incorporate the smooth motion of the Steadicam. (Courtesy of Cinema Products.)

The Visual Meaning of Shots: Ideas and Examples

To illustrate, hold a portable camera at knee level and raise it to chest level. Record the shot and consider the difference between the movement when (a) the camera is zoomed in tightly, and (b) the camera is on a wide shot.

Shot (a) will jiggle quite a bit. (Remember, the tighter your zoom, the more apparent the camera motion.) It will probably resemble news footage more than a cinematic effect. Shot (b) will appear smoother because you will not have to hold the camera on a very small, highly magnified area.

Try this experiment and attempt to ascertain what the visual meaning of each shot might be. When we made these movements, we perceived shot (a) as a soldier raising his head out of a foxhole; shot (b) gave the impression of someone awakening and sitting up in bed.

Get the idea? View a variety of programs and notice how camera work and editing techniques combine to reinforce ideas about speed and timing.

Speed and Timing of Shots

Closely scrutinize the camera work and editing in the series *L.A. Law*, especially dramatic action that centers around meetings in the boardroom. How, you might ask, can you make a meeting visually interesting?

The producer's answer was to use a novel technique related both to camera work and editing: Cut to an eye-level shot (the shot you would see if you were sitting at the table) of the person who will speak next *before* he or she begins talking. This adds forward motion to an otherwise static scene, and it imitates the way we would use our eyes in a tense meeting—probing, checking to gauge the reaction of the person being talked about, and so forth.

If you have the opportunity to view the classic western *Shane* (it's available in almost any video rental store), pay close attention to the camera work. Notice how virtually every shot has a purpose, and how every shot includes some relevant motion (see Box 8.2).

And notice how the popular TV show *M*A*S*H* used innovative camera techniques. Sometimes, the shots

BOX 8.2   POINT OF VIEW: GEORGE STEVENS AND *SHANE*

When director George Stevens wanted to focus audience attention in the famous barroom scene in *Shane*, he wasn't content to simply pan or cut. Instead, he perfectly communicated the idea of a lazy day by following a dog as it walked across the barroom floor.

Stevens' mastery of narrative point of view helped make the film a classic. But that artistry was absent from the first test screening, which did not particularly impress the audience. Stevens instinctively knew what was wrong: The film needed to be told from the boy's perspective.

As Tony Randall notes in his book *Now That I Think*

of It, the producer of *Shane* did not take kindly to the idea of reshooting the movie. But Stevens, being a chronic overshooter, already had shots from just about every perspective and was able to re-edit the film into one of the most popular westerns ever made.

Some directors do not shoot a great deal of extra film. In a way, Randall says, this is their way of exercising control: If there is no extra film, the producer cannot demand a recut. But Randall contends that Stevens had so much film he could have re-edited *Shane* even if he decided it should be shot from the *horse's* point of view.

were from the point of view of the patients; in other cases, rapid series of close-ups communicated the near panic of surgery carried out in close quarters under enormous pressure.

Camera operation is primarily an acquired skill. There is little else we can tell you—other than to once again stress the need to

• Show detail
• Pay attention to good composition
• Inject life, energy, and meaning into your shots

Those three suggestions are, for the purposes of a working definition, what we mean by "cinematic" values. Cinematic values are also achieved by modern lighting techniques, which is the subject of Chapter 9.

An interesting aspect about camera work is that, unlike many other professions, you can see demonstrations of top-notch work whenever you choose. Simply view a quality television program, corporate video, or feature film and notice the way the cameraperson and director use their most basic production tool.

SUMMARY

1. The medium of video is changing from an aesthetic standpoint. Modern cameras allow for more creativity in shots because they can move more easily and adapt to widely varying lighting conditions. We are seeing a trend away from harshly lighted, static compositions.

2. In addition to purely picturing the subject, video shots carry a visual meaning. It's important for the producer/director to remember that the video camera is designed to do more than record; it can also express.

3. Video is a medium of detail. One of the more common mistakes of novice camera operators is to stay too wide and not show the detail necessary to communicate information over a television screen.

4. A camera can assume a variety of perspectives. The perspectives described in this chapter include the exposition mode, the objective mode, and the observational mode.

5. It's important for a camera operator to produce a well-composed shot. To an extent, "well-composed" is in the eye of the beholder, but there are some basic conventions that we tend to find pleasing to the eye.

We want to see shots that show accurate detail, fill but not overfill the frame, have a stable horizon, use the rule of thirds in their composition, and provide a measure of visual balance.

6. Moving the camera is hardly a revolutionary concept—it's long been a film technique—but it is gradually working its way into the realm of video production. In fact, the overall image of the "typical" video program has changed. At one time, a video program was often lighted with a harsh, uniform base light, but modern productions allow for a more realistic depiction of lighting conditions and inventive movements of the cameras.

7. Motion is not without its problems: When a camera or performer moves, shadows and juxtapositions of the backgrounds can create unwanted effects. It may be difficult to maintain focus. That's why blocking a shot is so important.

8. The zoom, dolly, pan, tilt, and pedestal—indeed, all camera movements—are often more than utilitarian methods of capturing a picture. Those movements can impart various messages depending on their use.

TECHNICAL TERMS

blocking	horizon	point-of-view (POV) shot	Steadicam
essential area	leading space	pulling focus	subjective mode
establishing shot	observational mode	registration	tongue
exposition mode	perspective	rule of thirds	

EXERCISES

1. Put two performers on chairs, side-by-side but angled toward each other in a typical talk show setup. Using any device you can arrange, dolly the camera in steadily toward the talent. (If possible, don't use a studio dolly; try a hand-held camera on the shoulder of a person sitting in a wheeled office chair. Have two helpers push the cameraperson toward the scene, (*but be careful not to tip the chair!*).

Now, use a stationary camera to zoom in on the performers. Record both and compare the difference.

2. Using your home or studio VCR, record about five minutes of a documentary. Log each camera shot; describe the framing and motion. Also, attempt to determine whether the camera or the on-camera performers are moving.

    As an example, your log may look like this:

    a. Jane and the crime victim walk side-by-side down the sidewalk. We see them from the rear. The camera is following them at walking speed.

    b. Close-up (from the rear/side of the crime victim as she points to the alley where she was attacked). Camera pans across her pointing arm and into the alley.

    Now, using the same strategy, log a dramatic program. Prepare a brief analysis describing the differences and similarities between the use of the camera.

3. Remember the shot described in this chapter in which someone is startled by the arrival of someone entering the room? Attempt to set up such a shot and use a pull focus to direct the viewers' attention.

    The scenario is this: Talent 1 is standing about 10 feet from the camera when Talent 2 enters from a point about 25 feet from the camera; Talent 2 is quite menacing, of course, and Talent 1 is quite surprised by his or her arrival. Remember to block this shot carefully. In addition to rehearsing the pull focus—you'll probably need quite a bit of practice to pull this off smoothly—you'll need to block the head turn of Talent 1 and the movement of Talent 2. Don't leave anything to chance; use masking tape, if necessary, to mark the location of the talent when blocking the shots.

lighting techniques

OBJECTIVES

After completing Chapter 9, you will be able to:

1. Use light as a tool to create mood and image.
2. Apply basic techniques to fine-tune the lighting triangle to produce a high-quality picture.
3. Set up and adjust lights for remote, out-of-studio applications.

Now that you have a basic understanding of the tools of lighting for video, we'll discuss ways of using those lighting tools, not only to make a picture visible but to produce high-quality, expressive pictures.

The modern approach toward video lighting requires a bit of history and explanation. Early generations of television cameras and receivers were far less tolerant than modern equipment of varying gradations of light. But the evolution of video hardware has changed the way producers look at the typical lighting scenario.

First of all, modern cameras are able to produce acceptable pictures in a wide range of lighting conditions. Just a few years ago, a sizable change in base light level would make the camera go virtually haywire. If you're a football fan, and you can remember back ten years or so or have seen tapes of games from that time, you recall that in those days when a runner moved from the shadowed part of the field into the sunlight the picture would immediately be washed out—until the engineer could make a hasty adjustment of the camera control unit to compensate for the varied lighting condition. But in a very short period of time, with advances in video technology, the shadow effect has become hardly noticeable.

Also, new-generation cameras are more sensitive to lower light levels. Although low light still creates problems for the camera (not the least of which is a decreased depth of field), modern units can produce an acceptable picture in surprisingly low levels of light.

The camera isn't the only changing link in the chain. Home receivers are far more tolerant of varied lighting levels. Many years ago, home TV sets did not have a device known as DC restoration. The function of the DC restoration circuit is not important for our discussion, but suffice it to say that a set without DC restoration cannot accurately reproduce scenes shot under wide variations of light level.

You may logically wonder why we're belaboring these historical artifacts. The answer is this: Video equipment has changed, but many video practices have not. Some producer/directors still light a set the old-fashioned way: flood it with light and make the light level as consistent as possible *on every square inch of the set*, producing a bland, old-fashioned effect.

MODERN LIGHTING TECHNIQUES

Why? One reason is that video producer/directors trained in the "old school" method of TV lighting subscribed, first and foremost, to the technical dictates of equipment manuals as interpreted by the engineering staff. Engineers typically would insist that the light levels and contrast ratios meet the parameters prescribed in the specifications that accompanied the camera.

Why Old-Fashioned Lighting *Looks* Old Fashioned

There is nothing wrong with maintaining a 30:1 contrast ratio; in fact, you'll recall that in Chapters 2 and 4 we advised conforming to that ratio. But recognize, at this point, that advice is predicated on two assumptions:

1. You may indeed, at this time, be dealing with older-generation equipment that can handle only limited contrast ratios.
2. Modern video production allows us to break the rules on occasion, but we have to learn the rules before we can break them.

The upshot of this discussion is that intelligent use of light can produce much better-looking pictures. For one thing, modern video equipment can use a wider range of light to produce more cinematically oriented shots—in other words, shots that resemble film rather than video.

There are many technical and aesthetic differences between film and video, but generally we ascribe to video the quality of being more "realistic" but at the same time producing a "flatter," less "lively" picture.

Part of the reason for these subjective and objective impressions deals with the nature of light. A film camera can handle a much greater latitude of light than can a video camera. But modern video units are capable of handling a wider range of lighting conditions, meaning that a video production can create softer, more creative effects than were possible even a few years ago.

Perhaps this discussion seems overly abstract, but a quick example can bring the point home quite pointedly. Consider a set that attempts to recreate a living room. Under the theory of lighting—for lack of a better term, *engineering driven*—we would establish a high level of exquisitely even light across the entire set. The result would look like Figure 9.1. Figure 9.1, you'll notice, looks exactly like what it is: A bunch of furniture dragged into a television set and flooded with light.

"Cinematic" Lighting for Video

But the "cinematic" approach recognizes that a living room is not typically flooded with light levels dictated by engineering manuals. The lighting designer with an artistic bent would, for example, allow corners of the room to be fairly dark—as they are in normal living rooms—and would direct light in from the windows and highlight areas around lamps. The result would look more like the scene pictured in Figure 9.2.

Although we're still working with the basic lighting triangle, modern video producers recognize that every scene need not be lighted like a game show set.

Figure 9.1 Flat lighting. When a set has perfectly even lighting, it is referred to as flat lighting (what we called "game show lighting").

Figure 9.2 Cinemagraphic lighting. Well-shaped lighting requires creative thought and a keen attention to detail. Resetting of lights for each new shot requires more effort, but this level of cinemagraphic expression is well worth the labor.

BALANCING THE LIGHTING TRIANGLE

Let's review the rules of lighting before we experiment with breaking them. In most lighting situations you'll *still* want three-point light if it is at all appropriate and practical. (Three-point lighting is not appropriate if you are attempting to achieve a special effect by harsh cameo lighting, and certainly not practical in fast-breaking news situations.)

How can a producer hope to use three-point lighting when there's such a wide variety of situations? Well, the good news is that lighting scenarios really do not vary all that much. In most instances, you'll be using standard three-point lighting and, when necessary, using lights for special effects (such as shining a light through a window on a set to imitate sunshine). When more people are added to the set, you'll add another lighting triangle. In most cases, it's that simple.

Let's see how this works on a relatively complicated news set. We have three people, three cameras on the floor, a suspended camera that shows the overall news set, and a cyc. A **cyc (cyclorama)** is a curtain behind the set.

In this case, you would probably want to establish your initial lighting plan using a grid. Often, the grid is drawn on standard graph paper. Some grids are directly proportional to actual studio floor footage; others represent consistent increments. The grid is sometimes a representation of the actual lighting battens, and the pigtails are individually numbered.

Your diagram will allow you to plot, in advance, the *probable* location of the lighting instruments. Because lighting almost always involves some trial and error, making your initial mistakes on paper is much easier than hoisting lighting instruments. Granted, you may still have to do some trial and error, even with the most detailed and well-conceived plot, because for a variety of reasons paper plans sometimes just don't work in practice.

Setting Key and Fill

You'll notice from the diagram in Figure 9.3 that keys, fills, and backs have been set for each talent. Although there are many lighting instruments hung—and the diagram looks rather complicated—you'll notice that it is nothing more than three keys, three fills, and three backs . . . the same basic lighting triangle discussed in Chapters 2 and 4, but *reproduced for each person on the set*. Note that sometimes you won't have to use a separate light for each person. Large lights, set far back, are frequently used to light more than one on-camera performer. But for now, *start* with one lighting triangle for each person; then experiment with lighting multiple subjects as you gain proficiency.

You won't always be able to key and fill each person on the set. In the case of our news set, you might be able to get away with keying the newscasters who sit side-by-side with one instrument, if you had to. If there are many performers on the set, you can accomplish a reasonable compromise by crossing several keys and fills to cover the

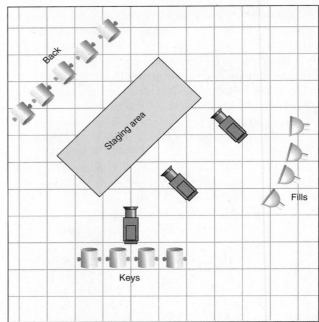

Figure 9.4 Lighting the essential area. Sometimes, a broad area can be lit with a combination of cross-keying, and cross-filling, and broad back lighting.

essential area that must be lighted (Figure 9.4). Also, you might not always have the opportunity to set up three lights for each performer; in many cases you can produce an acceptable picture by using "spillover" from another lighting instrument to serve as fill, or, sometimes, key (Figure 9.5).

We have pretty well covered the basic mechanics of setting key and fill levels in Chapters 2 and 4, but it's useful to briefly explore the fact that light meter readings alone do not determine an acceptable shot. Unacceptable shadows or holes in the base light might not always be apparent to the lighting assistant who reads the meter. (In setting base light, you may want to rely on a device called a waveform monitor; we'll discuss that later in the chapter.)

The aesthetic basis of properly setting key and fill is to ensure that there are no harsh shadows (unless you want them for special effect) or, conversely, that the shadows are not so washed out that the performer's face appears doughy and featureless. Either extreme produces an unacceptable picture. Figure 9.6 shows how a person's face appears with too much key and too much fill. Figure 9.7 demonstrates the effect of too little key and not enough fill.

One other point: You generally don't want the key and fill to shine from too high or too low an angle. In many cases, the height of the lighting instruments is limited by the height of the ceiling. But in any event; you will usually want key and fill to shine from an angle of not

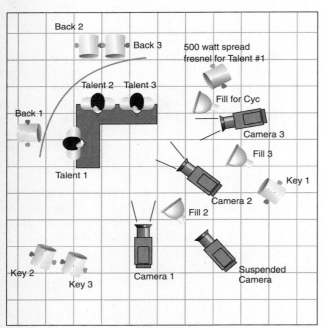

Scale 1/2" = 2.5'

Keys - 1,500 watt fresnels
Backs - 1,500 watt fresnels
Fills - 1,000 watt scoops

Note: Cameras and lighting instruments are not drawn to scale

Figure 9.3 Light plot: news set. Draw your lighting plot on grid paper to show approximate distances. Notice how the key, fill, and back lights create basic triangles.

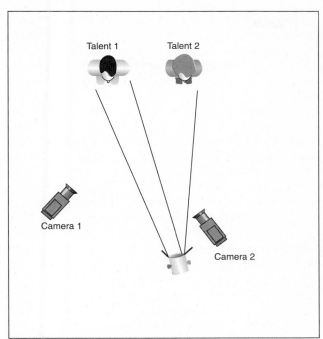

Figure 9.5 Spillover lighting. Sometimes spillover from a key can be used as fill. Here, a fresnel is barn-doored so that it fills one side of the talent's face.

Figure 9.7 Too little key; too little fill. An intentionally low key can establish a mysterious mood, but ordinarily it is not acceptable.

much more than 40 degrees (Figure 9.8 shows how we are measuring that angle). If the lighting instrument is too high, you'll produce some odd-appearing shadows (Figure 9.9*a*), especially if the talent has a prominent brow. But if the lighting instrument is too low, you'll tend to wash out

some of the subject's features, and you'll also invite trouble from reflections created by talent who wear eyeglasses (Figure 9.9*b*).

This lighting angle recommendation, though, is not carved in stone. You may want to change the vertical angle of your lighting instruments for special effect. Many pro-

Figure 9.6 Too much key; too much fill. Too much fill will not eliminate the shadows of too much key. Instead, the subject will appear featureless and unnatural.

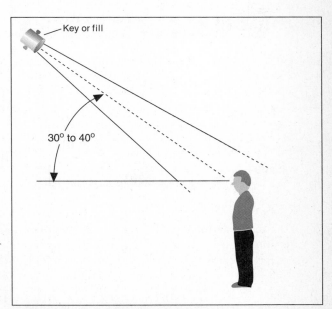

Figure 9.8 Vertical angle of lighting. The vertical angle of key and fill should measure between 30° and 40°, whereas the back light angle should measure 45° to 55°.

Figure 9.9 Key angle. (*a*) Notice how much shadow appears when the key is positioned at *too high* an angle. (*b*) The reflection of the lights in the talent's glasses could have been avoided if the key light were positioned higher.

ducers, for example, believe that putting the fill at a much lower angle—as low as the height of the talent's eyes—produces a more natural-looking shot.

Back Light

There are some important picture design considerations to be taken into account when setting back light. In Chapters 2 and 4, we noted that the back light serves to highlight the talent's head and shoulders and separate talent from the background (Figure 9.10).

There's a little more to it than that. Back light is used to create the illusion of *depth*, an important consideration

in video production. As an example of the need for good, strong back lighting, note that many sets by necessity occupy a small portion of the studio. (Studio space must often accommodate other sets, as well as camera operators and other crewpeople.) If you are attempting to recreate an office environment within the confines of a television studio, you will often be working with a smaller space behind talent than is typically encountered in a real office.

You may need strong back lighting to keep the scene from looking like you have "plastered" the talent against a background wall. (Which, of course, is more or less what you *have* done, but video is a matter of illusion, and our job is to use the illusion of light to create the sensation of depth.) A strong back light will immediately add several feet of apparent depth between the talent and the wall behind him or her. Another way to increase the apparent distance between the talent and the wall is to make sure an intense light isn't on the background; careful focusing of the talent's light can help in this effort.

There may also be occasions when you have *too much* background and *too much* depth, and the talent becomes "lost" in the busy backdrop. This is a common problem in cases where a journalist reports from a newsroom crammed with desks, video editing equipment, and monitors. Although there is plenty of actual depth—perhaps 50 feet to the nearest wall—the talent blends in to the cluttered background. One solution is to use a **side light**—a lighting instrument shining from the side—in conjunction with a back light. This helps separate the top and the edge of the performer from the background.

Figure 9.10 Back lighting. Setting a backlight will highlight the back of a subject's head and shoulders and provide a sense of dimension by separating the talent from the background.

Base Light

As you know, there are two ways of establishing base light. One is to set the base light first, ensuring that it does not have any unwanted holes, and then to set the key and fill, making sure that the highlights do not exceed your contrast ratio (usually between 30:1 and 20:1). The other method is to set the keys, fills, and back lights first and then search for holes in the base light. Remember, in many cases, setting key, fill, and back often takes care of base light all by itself; sometimes no additional base light is required.

Base light is an extremely important consideration when establishing the overall texture of the picture. It is also one of the most frequently ignored aspects of scene composition. As mentioned earlier, in video, we have become accustomed to an overall flat base light. But today, video producers who are advancing the idea of making the screen something more than a dull rectangle are paying close attention to *natural falloff of base light* in the overall lighting design. As producers Harry Mathias and Richard Patterson noted, "Ideally, the mood and style of the production should determine the approach to lighting, and a cinematographer should strive to remain flexible, rather than relying on traditional methods."[1]

What Mathias and Patterson refer to, in the context of their remarks, is the idea that video lighting can be used to create roughly the same "depth" as we perceive in film. Further, they note that video is now being evaluated on an equal footing with film, and with the advent of high definition television (HDTV is discussed in Chapter 22), video will offer increasing competition to film as an artistic medium.

Of course, there is no reason why video cannot approximate the same mood-setting power of film. Good base lighting can make the capabilities of the media reasonably comparable (Box 9.1).

MEASURING AND BALANCING LIGHT LEVELS

Given the opportunity to use a wide range of illumination, let's add a little technique to the mechanics of measuring light.

Using the Waveform Monitor to Measure Light Levels

As you remember, a light meter is used to measure both incident light and reflected light. Incident light is the light

---

BOX 9.1 QUALITY LIGHTING AND QUALITY VIDEO

Video is widely considered inferior to film in terms of contrast, picture quality, and depth of field. Although film cameras are still technically superior to video, much of video's supposed "inferiority" relates to the flat, bright lighting used to accommodate multiple-camera, live, or live-on-tape situations.

But it doesn't *have* to be that way. Two of the best-lighted television series in video history are still in syndicated reruns across the country. And although you obviously cannot see the lighting instruments, you can certainly see the results. *Barney Miller* and *WKRP in Cincinnati* both used many relatively small lighting instruments—as opposed to a few large instruments. The results in both cases were sets that had enormous depth, realism, and clarity.

Watch both shows, if you have the occasion, and note that:

1. The background sets contained indentations that were realistically lighted; this created the illusion of great depth. For example, the doorway and back hallway of the *Barney Miller* set may have extended only a few feet, but they created the illusion of a much larger room.

2. Using a larger number of accurately aimed lighting instruments, rather than flooding the set with a few powerful and vaguely aimed instruments, resulted in the virtual elimination of shadows. You'll very rarely see a shadow cast by an actor or an object on the *WKRP* set.

3. The backgrounds were important to both shows, and the lighting reflected that. Notice how the equipment in the WKRP studio was brightly lighted—but also note that light was allowed to fall off in *naturally dark* areas. The hallway had deep shadows at the ends and corners—as indeed a hallway would.

Today, we can't assume that a modern video camera will automatically be able to handle the same lighting range as film. At their present stage of development, video cameras can handle a range of about five stops (doubling or halving of light five times), whereas a film camera can handle seven stops. But that difference in range continues to decrease—as do the differences in technique between lighting for film and video.

shining from the instrument; reflected light is what bounces back off the subject. Incident light is the reading you'll use to establish the level of a lighting instrument (it's especially valuable to keep a written record if you have to set lighting levels each day) and to check for holes in the base light. Reflected readings gauge the brightness of the highlights and make sure that the contrast ratio is not extreme.

To add to what was said in Chapter 4, there are some other functions that light-sensing instruments provide which cannot be done by eye. One such function is regulating consistency of **skin tones**. Especially in cases when you are out on remote, you need an extremely precise way to measure the amount of light reflected from a subject's face in order to maintain consistent skin tones when scenes are edited together. You simply can't judge this with the naked eye.

Measurement of light can also be accomplished, with great accuracy, via the **waveform monitor**. One function of the monitor (Figure 9.11) is to provide video engineers with a graphic readout of lighting levels. (The waveform monitor performs several other functions, which will be detailed in Chapter 21.)

A waveform monitor measures light levels on a scale of 0 to 100, with 100 generally representing the maximum level of light that the videotape recorder or transmitter will reliably handle, and 0 being the theoretical absence of all light. (In practical terms, the video system cannot operate with levels as low as theoretical zero, so the video version of "black" is set at 7.5. This is explained fully in Chapter 21.) The measurements are in increments of 20, and are expressed in IRE, an arbitrary measurement that was originally established by the Institute of Radio Engineers. The exact derivation of IRE is complex and beyond the scope of this chapter.

In any event, the waveform monitor reading the output of a camera provides you with a superbly sensitive

"light meter." Panning the camera across the scene and monitoring the waveform monitor gives an extremely accurate indication of light level variations, and also provides your engineer with a visual readout of the brightest and dimmest elements of the picture.

The waveform monitor can also be used to measure reflected light, and a portable waveform monitor is well worth carrying in your remote kit.

Using the waveform monitor, you can measure the consistency of flesh tones with pinpoint accuracy *because you make the measurement through the instrument that counts—the camera*. Generally, caucasian skin in the key light is expected to produce a reflectance reading of about 70 percent[2] of the top white level (which is usually, as you remember, 100 IRE), with black and brown skin causing reflective readings proportionately lower. Although the numbers are essentially arbitrary, they help maintain consistency so that the flesh tones do not vary when scenes are edited together.

Don't forget, of course, that you also must white balance the camera when lighting situations change. The light meter and/or waveform monitor measure light intensity. The white balance corrects light coloration. Variations in either intensity or coloration will change the apparent skin tone of the subject.

Contrast Ratios: How They Affect the Lighting Environment

We know that video cameras do not handle high contrast ratios very well, but here's some additional information on contrast ratios you might find useful in lighting operations.

First, be aware that it is often an advantage to have white and black "referenced" in a scene. In most cases, this involves including a small black object and a small white object somewhere in the portion of the shoot illuminated by the key so that the engineer can set the full range of the "gray scale." (**Reference** means that the electronic equipment will be adjusted so that the black will appear appropriately black, the white will appear appropriately white, and all shades of light and dark in between can be adequately reproduced.) Try it on your equipment and judge the results for yourself.

The reason we recommend a *small* black and white object in each scene—perhaps a throw pillow and an envelope—is because when black and white fill the whole screen, the contrast ratio may indeed be too large for the camera to comfortably handle, and shades of gray in between will be compressed. This is why newscasters usually avoid wearing a black suit and a white shirt. A few years ago, color TV cameras could barely handle the high-level reflectance of a white shirt regardless of the color of the jacket, but now white shirts are generally acceptable for TV performance. You'll see network anchors wearing

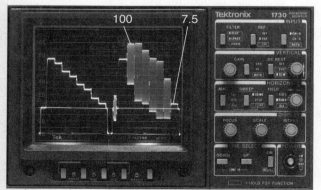

Figure 9.11 Waveform monitor. A waveform monitor provides an excellent representation of the overall contrast ratio by accurately measuring whites and blacks. (Courtesy of Tektronix, Inc.)

white shirts, but remember that your camera might not be as competent at handling white as network-quality equipment. If you notice that white shirts lose their detail or darken the talent's face, recommend pastel-shade shirts or blouses to your performer. (The issue of setting blacks and whites on a waveform monitor deserves more attention, and will be discussed in greater depth in Chapter 20.)

Remember that you do not have to be a slave to arbitrary contrast ratios. Yes, a reflection of a shiny object will cause problems, and a sparkling white shirt against a black suit is not an ideal outfit for a newscaster. But in general, you need not bathe each and every corner of your scene with light of exactly equal intensity. Use your eye and your instinct to establish contrast ratios; after some practice, you'll be able to spot potential trouble-making reflectances while still creating a natural-looking environment.

REMOTE LIGHTING TECHNIQUES

As the camera became more portable, lighting directors found themselves faced with a host of new problems. In the earliest days of remote production, the material gathered was usually news footage—and it was usually flatly lighted material with little depth.

But today, more program content is shot on location. Parts of corporate videos are typically taped in an executive's office; segments of magazine-type shows are produced out of studio; and commercials, too, are often recorded on location.

Typical Problems

The list of examples is long—and so is the list of problems engendered by being in a location where so many of the lighting factors are essentially beyond your control. For example, many directors shooting outdoors have had their entire projects sabotaged by something we know is going to happen but which we frequently ignore: the sun moving across the sky. Just an hour's difference can change the lighting complexion completely (and make two edited shots essentially incompatible).

The seasons change our lighting parameters too. A scene "scouted" in early fall may present an entirely different set of lighting problems two weeks later in the season, when more leaves have fallen and the sun is just that much dimmer.

Moving indoors doesn't solve all our location problems, by the way. Windows are the bane of the location-producer's working life, particularly because people in office environments usually insist on sitting in front of them when being taped.

So how does the location producer create a decent lighting environment? The answer usually involves some specialized (but relatively simple) equipment and a will to experiment.

Improved Lighting on Remote

Actually, lighting on remote is not particularly complex; it merely requires the adequate arsenal of equipment and a willingness to try several approaches until the picture looks right. Sometimes, you'll have to go to extremes: If a window creates insurmountable problems, maybe you'll be better off taping at night—a simple solution but one not commonly considered.

Each remote lighting situation poses a slightly different dilemma, so we'll provide some general guidance on use of portable lighting instruments, lighting accessories, natural light, and outdoor shooting.

Use of Portable Lighting Instruments. Ideally, you would like to duplicate studio lighting on location, a goal that is not, in truth, totally unattainable. Portable lighting kits can and do replicate much of what is in the studio, but on a smaller scale. One of the more useful spot lighting instruments is a 750 watt spot/flood omni light (Figure 9.12). An **omni light** is an instrument that can project narrowly or widely focused light, which makes it versatile and a good choice for remote work.

A permanently focused hard light can be converted to a soft light by use of an umbrella (Figure 9.13). An **umbrella** reflects light backward. The instrument pictured in Figure 9.13 is an 800 watt lighting unit, but you may want to use larger instruments when using them with an

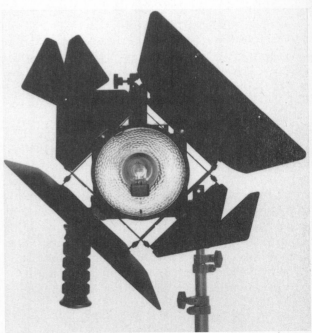

Figure 9.12 The Lowel Omni Light. The Omni is a very versatile instrument for location production. (Courtesy of Lowel Light Manufacturing.)

Figure 9.13   The lighting umbrella. The umbrella, a very useful lighting accessory, reflects soft light when a hard light is shined into it. (Courtesy of Lowel Light Manufacturing.)

umbrella. Some circumstances may call for the use of instruments as large as 2,000 watts (or, as it's often called, 2K; "K" means 1,000).

If the umbrella absorbs too much light, and you don't have a powerful enough instrument to provide adequate reflection, you're probably better off scrimming or bouncing the light off a wall to produce fill.

Portable soft lights (Figure 9.14) provide fine fill and are useful for lighting wide areas. They come in various sizes; large-wattage models (such as 2 K soft lights) produce a fine soft light but need a great deal of power. You may need to use smaller soft lights and a wider camera f-stop if your power supply is limited. Remember that by its very nature, a soft light does not produce an intense beam, and you need wattage to compensate for the spread of the light.

Assuming you have enough power, you're usually better off starting with large lights and then working your way down. A lighting instrument can always be scrimmed, moved back, reflected off a wall, or in some other way diminished in intensity if it's too powerful. If your lighting arsenal is lacking in power, however, there's not much you can do except send back for more equipment. But experience will also demonstrate that lighting instruments can be too big for the situation; if you are overpowered, the lighting instruments may be difficult to control. Experiment, but err on the side of power.

And while we're on the subject, let's mention one other peculiarity of lighting equipment. If you leaf through several catalogs, you'll notice that there is a wide variation in price of instruments. But in all of life, there are few really free lunches. As Emmy Award-winning lighting designer David Clark points out, "You can get twelve lights for the same price as only six of some other lights." His advice? "Take the six! There is good reason why some equipment is expensive. It works better. The light output may be similar, but the durability and flexibility is worth the extra cost."[3]

Lighting Accessories. Even the best lighting kit won't be of much use if you can't place the instruments or control their falloff. Here's where extendable lighting poles and clamps become useful (Figure 9.15). Clamps come in many varieties, but the familiar alligator clamp, sometimes called a **gaffer's clamp**, is one of the more useful tools you can carry; it allows you to mount an instrument virtually anywhere—a tremendous advantage when you are backlighting a subject.

For example, if you are interviewing a woman in her office, you might establish your three-point lighting by:

1. Putting a 1 K spotlight on a pole, as high as you can reasonably extend it, and using that as your key.

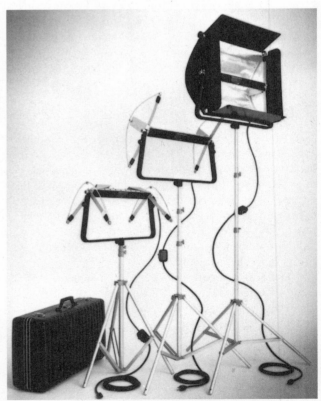

Figure 9.14   Portable soft light. Exceptional for location work, the soft light provides an even quality of light. (Courtesy of Lowel Light Manufacturing.)

Figure 9.15 Extendable lighting pole and clamp. (Courtesy of Lowel Light Manufacturing.)

commercially made flags that can be hooked onto a pole and used to block unwanted light. When flags are attached to camera lenses, they're often referred to as **French flags**; they serve the same purpose.

Location Shooting and Natural Light

Windows often present a problem for the location shoot, but there are several techniques to overcome this obstacle.

Gelling the Lighting Instrument. Gel your lighting instruments with a blue transparency. A frame that fits in front of the lighting instrument, holding a blue **gel** (Figure 9.17), can give your instruments a bluish hue, thus simulating outdoor light. This way, you'll minimize color-balance problems. Gelling your lighting instruments is a good option when there are so many windows—from so many different angles—that you cannot hope to achieve a graceful mix of indoor (3200 K) and outdoor (5600 K) light.

Gelling the Window. Video supply houses sell rolls of virtually transparent material that will bring the outdoor light down to indoor color temperatures. This obviously isn't practical if you're dealing with a huge wall of windows, but it's a surprisingly easy quick fix if the window is small.

Using the Window as Fill. If your camera is of high quality, and indoor and outdoor lights don't shine sharply from widely varying directions, you can sometimes get away with a natural mix of unfiltered indoor and outdoor light. If this is the case, in fact, you can turn the window to your advantage. If possible, use the window as a fill and

2. Throwing a portable soft light, perhaps a 2 K, from the other direction (the other side of the camera), using that as your fill.

3. With a gaffer's clamp, mounting a 1 K or 2 K hard light from the ceiling as your back light. The angle of the back light can be reasonably steep, sometimes exceeding more than 50 degrees, but for most practical purposes almost any back lighting is better than none.

Bear in mind, though, that you have to be extremely careful with back lights because a light clipped to a high object can create a fire hazard. Some people clip the light to the grid on a suspended ceiling. This tactic works but bears a measure of caution. (Common sense will guide you here. One location director clipped his back light to the fire system's heat detector and received an unexpected shower. Don't do things like that.) In fact, all portable lights should be handled with caution. Review Box 4.2 for safety hints.

Now, concerning other accessories you'll need, a variety of barn doors will be most helpful. They will allow you to control lighting spill and reduce hot spots. **Flags,** which are devices similar to barn doors (Figure 9.16) are

Figure 9.16 Flags. Flags, when mounted on a light or camera, block areas of unwanted light. (Courtesy of Lowel Light Manufacturing.)

Figure 9.17 Lighting gel. The lighting gel—a colored plastic transparency—provides color for temperature adjustment or effect, and it lessens the lamp's intensity. (Courtesy of Lowel Light Manufacturing.)

your hard light as a key. The results can sometimes be quite attractive.

Coping with a Window in Back of Talent. The biggest dilemma you'll encounter is people who insist on sitting in front of windows. Some people regard a desk in front of the window as a status symbol—in any event, they are not likely to be responsive to your requests to rearrange the furniture. If the window doesn't have blinds or a curtain, the best you can do is attempt to shoot from the side (hoping the window will work as a fill or, sometimes, a key), or—if you have a large budget, you can gel the whole window to reduce the incoming light level.

When you have no choice but to shoot someone in front of a window, you must "fool" the camera by taking it off auto-iris (which you probably won't be using, anyway, after you gain some experience) and deliberately overexposing the scene. This is necessary because most cameras will read the light from the window and leave your subject in silhouette. Opening up will overexpose the window but will also give reasonable exposure to your subject's features.

Overcoming Extremely Difficult Daytime Window Problems. If you're completely befuddled by too many bright windows, shoot at night. Night shoots are often much easier to manage than day shoots. It's not unusual, for example, for commercial producers to beg car dealers to allow them to shoot indoor shots at night. Car dealer-

ships typically have so many windows (so that passersby can see the cars inside) that effective daytime light control is a nightmarish proposition. If you shoot at night, the window can provide an impressive background. Your only major problem may be the reflection of lighting instruments off the window. Experiment with lighting placement to avoid reflections.

Foam-Core as a Lighting Problem Solver. When you are facing really tricky location problems, it might be advisable to bring along some foam-core sheets; foam-core looks like wallboard but it's very light. You can use it to mask out very large areas when you are faced with abundant light spill and/or reflection.

HMI Lighting Instruments. HMI instruments are, as mentioned in Chapter 4, quite handy but also large and fairly expensive. If you have one or more HMI instruments, they'll be useful on many remote shoots.

Outdoor Shooting

Don't assume that your problems are over if you are shooting outdoors. In point of fact, your problems may just be beginning. Harsh sunlight creates distracting shadows, and hazy sunlight often makes the entire scene seem lifeless.

You can and should use lighting instruments outdoors when necessary. It's best if you can use instruments balanced to outdoor temperatures (like HMI lights) or gelled for outdoor use, but you can sometimes get away with a "highlight" instrument burning at indoor temperature used outdoors.

A better option, though, is to pack a reflector that can use the sun's light to fill in shadows or highlight features. (**Reflectors** are devices that bounce light.) Commercial reflectors are quite useful; crinkled aluminum foil over a piece of cardboard works fine too. You can have a crew member shine the reflection on a talent's face (either holding the reflector or mounting it on a stand) to either counteract shadows caused by harsh sun or model the talent's features, if they're washed out by dim sun. Sometimes just a plain piece of white posterboard, the kind you can buy in any art supply or stationery store, will work almost as well.

One increasingly popular option is to pack so-called space blankets in your camera case. These are high-tech blankets used by mountain climbers and hikers to retain heat; they also are very shiny. A space blanket can fit into a small pouch and be quickly retrieved for use as a reflector. Such blankets are sold in many sporting goods stores and come in silver and gold colorations.

Signal-to-Noise Ratios in Lighting

In the studio, you will usually have a much more complete array of lighting instruments and some technical help to ensure that your pictures are receiving enough light to make them technically acceptable. But on a remote shoot, you must be particularly careful about keeping pictures bright enough so that they don't become "noisy."

Video noise is apparent in a picture when there is an unacceptable **signal-to-noise ratio**—the comparison of how much signal there is to extraneous interference. This exactly parallels the situation we discussed in Chapter 5: If there is too much noise and not enough signal, you'll produce an unacceptable sound.

Video signals have a signal-to-noise ratio too. A good camera, for example, might have a signal-to-noise ratio of 70 to 1 when shooting in good light. That means the video signal is 70 times stronger than the electronic noise produced by the circuitry (measured in decibels).

When you record in low light, you will have a weaker video signal. That situation is comparable to recording, in audio, a person with a soft voice when you are sitting several rows away: There will, obviously, be less signal (the person's voice) and more apparent noise (the general ambient noise of the room).

Even if the tape you record on location looks marginally acceptable when you play it back, remember that you will lose signal strength—and add noise—every time you dub the tape. It's rare that raw tape shot on location will go directly over the air. It will almost always be edited (dubbed), resulting in the injection of more video noise and a lowering of the signal-to-noise ratio.

If lighting on remote is inadequate, you may return with a tape that has a 40:1 signal-to-noise ratio. Your edit will usually subtract about 4 dB, meaning that the final tape has only a 36:1 signal-to-noise ratio. In other words, the video signal will only be 36 times stronger than the noise level, and your picture may be degraded to the point where it appears washed out, snowy, or fuzzy.

It's generally not possible to compute signal-to-noise ratios in the field, and in any event that was not the purpose of this discussion. What we do want to impress on you is that it's always important to have enough light to produce a clear picture because the editing process will degrade the quality of tape made on location shoots.

Hence, we'll repeat the warning stated earlier: It's better to invest some sweat in lugging around many large portable lighting instruments than to try to save effort by using smaller, weaker ones. That's a false economy: Saving a little effort in the beginning may require investing an enormous amount of energy later on to mop up the results. (Note that size does not always relate directly to power, but in *most* cases, physically larger instruments project a higher intensity of light.)

PRODUCING SPECIAL EFFECTS WITH LIGHTING

Whether you're on remote or in the studio, there will be times when you are concerned with more than just producing a good-quality video picture. You'll want to manipulate the light in such a way as to create a special effect or mood.

Background Lighting

One of the simplest special effects is to use the cookie, described in Chapter 4, to throw a pattern on the cyc or other background. The effects are limited only by your imagination: You can create the image of a doorway, a stained-glass window, or a jail cell.

Sometimes the cookie pattern is purely decorative, and we would urge you to consider cookie patterns as backgrounds for programs. The reason is this: Constructed sets do not always look good on television, especially if you're not an expert in set design. One crew, for example, when producing a talk show, sawed off the spines of several hundred books and glued them to a flat in order to produce a "library effect" (the set had to be taken down and reassembled daily, so restacking the books was out of the question). A "window" was built in, and various pictures were nailed to the wall.

And it looked *awful*. It looked exactly like book spines and cheap prints nailed to a flat. Finally, the set was scrapped and a cookie pattern was projected on a blue cyc—an effect that was very appealing and, in fact, reinforced the theme of the show.

Very often, simple sets are the best, and lighting effects may be the best way to create part of your simple set.

In some cases, you'll want to use light to convince the viewer that he or she is seeing a real window. A TV set window will look phony if the structure of the window is not accentuated by incoming light. A very simple enhancement to a window on the set is to aim a lighting instrument through the window (from the outside of the set, of course) and cover the window with a colored gel (or gel the lighting instrument). A pale yellow ("straw") gel indicates midday sun; a reddish gel portrays evening sun. In any event, this creative use of light will add depth and visual interest to your scene.

One of the trickiest special effects is to simulate room lighting from normal household lamps, especially when a dramatic script calls for the lamps to be turned on and off. There is nothing sillier in all of TV lighting lore than the notorious scene where a person is awakened by a telephone call, turns on the lamp next to the bed—and the room is suddenly flooded with light.

Invest some thought into the *natural patterns* of light and how you might invent a lighting scheme to realistically cover the preceding scenario. One possibility is to position a fresnel behind the nightstand and point it straight up at the lamp; you can insert some diffusing material in the lampshade. When the talent turns on the lamp, the lighting console operator kicks in the fresnel. (This has to be done with precision, of course, or else the scene will appear *really* ludicrous, an effect akin to talent's answering the phone before it rings.) You may have to bring up the overall lighting at the same time (to provide a technically acceptable picture), but be judicious. Don't bring them up full. In fact, it might be better to have a separate "nighttime" set of lights set up. Your nighttime lights might be gelled with a dark blue and could include a cookie backdrop indicating moonlight through a window.

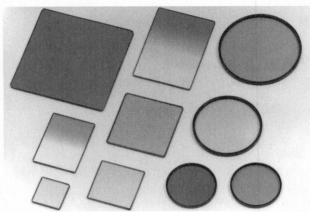

Figure 9.19 External filters. External screw-type filters are used primarily for effect. (Courtesy of Tiffen Manufacturing Corp.)

Mood Lighting

Light coming from an angle can be used to create a variety of effects. When the light strikes an actor's face from below (Figure 9.18), the mood is sinister. If an off-camera assistant crinkles a golden space blanket as a powerful light

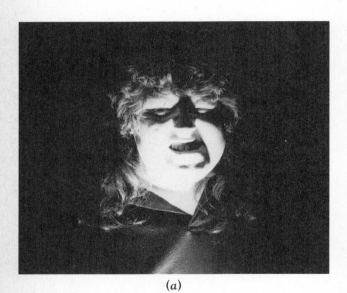

(a)

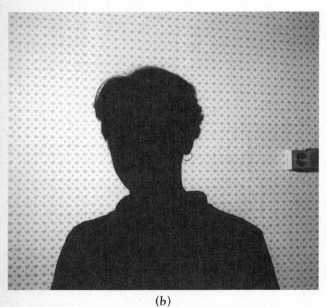

(b)

Figure 9.18 Lighting effects. (*a*) A sinister lighting effect is produced when light is aimed up at a face from below. (*b*) A silhouette lighting effect is achieved with a well-lit background and little or no light on the subject.

Figure 9.20 Effect of Tiffen Soft/FX. Soft filters soften or lower the contrast. This can produce a dreamlike feeling. (Courtesy of Tiffen Manufacturing Corp.)

Figure 9.21   Effect of star filter. The star filter creates a glistening star effect by adding brilliance around reflections from bright sources. (Courtesy of Tiffen Manufacturing Corp.)

reflects off the material, the viewer can be convinced that the sun is shining through the leaves of trees (if the light is aimed downward) or reflecting off water (if the light is aimed upward.)

Filters can also be used to affect the mood of the lighting environment. To backtrack a bit, we should note that a number of different devices are used to filter light. Gels attached to lighting instruments are one previously mentioned example. We also have some familiarity with the internal filters on the camera's filter wheel.

The internal filters generally are used only to help adjust for light temperatures.

But screw-type filters (Figure 9.19), which mount on the end of the lens assembly, *manipulate* light and create texture. **Diffusion filters**, for example, is a screw-type filter that makes a scene appear very soft by lowering the contrast, creating a romantic or sometimes dreamlike atmosphere (Figure 9.20). **Star filters** cause a pointed effect around bright light sources and add brilliance to a scene (Figure 9.21); they are a favorite tool of producers who make commercials for jewelry stores.

SUMMARY

1. Modern cameras still need a considerable amount of light, but we no longer need to flood a scene with harsh light that fills every nook and cranny of the set. Natural falloff of light is more acceptable today, and is, in fact, preferred. Modern cameras are much more adaptable to lower light levels.

2. Although we don't need blinding light, we still use three-point light in many situations, because even the most sophisticated camera will produce a better picture when the subject to be modeled is separated from the background.

3. If you can key, fill, and back light each person on the set, fine. If not, you have to key and fill broad areas. But don't get carried away; there's such a thing as too much light. Remember, you're lighting a TV set, not an operating room.

4. Balancing key and fill is tricky, and the ratios suggested in Chapter 4 won't always work with precision because the actual need for key and fill depends to a large part on your subject. Remember that the ultimate goal is not to achieve a mathematical precision, but to highlight the subject's features without harsh shadows.

5. Back light is often important not only to separate the talent from the background, but to create the illusion of depth. If the scene is not properly lighted from the rear, the talent may appear to be pasted against the wall. Conversely, if there is a great deal of area behind the talent, a side light is often useful to separate talent from a busy and deep background.

6. Base light is one of the most important elements of the video picture. Although the minimal goal of base light is to provide enough light for the camera to see, the aesthetic goal is to realistically create a setting.

7. Measuring reflected light is important because it allows for consistency among shots. If reflected light levels from the performer's face are consistent, it is likely that skin tones will remain consistent too. Consistency is vitally important when collected tape from different locales will be edited together.

8. If you have access to a waveform monitor, it can be used to give very precise readings of reflected light levels.

9. Some producers like to have a "black reference" and a "white reference" in the scene so that the engineers can accurately set an entire range of grays. This is not a universally accepted strategy, but it is worth

experimenting with as you begin to explore the effect of light on your video pictures.

10. For remote shooting, a good portable lighting kit is a necessity. Bring more lighting instruments, cables, and batteries than you think you will need. You can always back off if there's too much light, but you can't create more light if you don't have the tools at hand.

11. Windows are a problem. You can often solve color-temperature differences by either gelling the lighting instruments or gelling the window. The light coming in through the window can also play havoc with your lighting angles. Sometimes it's best to use the window as a fill or key instead of trying to fight it. If you have an HMI instrument, you can solve much of your problem.

12. Lighting can be used to create special effects and enhance a mood. *Don't be afraid to experiment*, but remember that simple lighting schemes are often the best.

NOTES

1. Harry Mathias and Richard Patterson, *Electronic Cinematography* (Belmont, CA: Wadsworth, 1985), 178.

2. We're using 70 percent to indicate 70 percent of the IRE reading. This is not, strictly speaking, 70 percent of the light because the IRE scale is not linear.

3. David Clark, "The Location Lighting Game," *International Television* (March 1984): 40, 41.

TECHNICAL TERMS

cyc (cyclorama)	gaffer's clamp	reference	skin tone
diffusion filter	gel	reflector	star filter
flags	IRE	side light	umbrella
French flags	omni light	signal-to-noise ratio	waveform monitor

EXERCISES

1. Refer back to the exercise in Chapter 8 where you were instructed to pull focus for the scene in which a visitor enters from the rear and surprises our hero. Your assignment in this chapter is to draw up a lighting plot for the scene.

   One important factor is this: The rest of the scene should be relatively dark. Imagine that this is a living room at twilight. (You don't have to create a set; although, if you have the materials on hand it wouldn't hurt.) You want the hero and the visitor *perfectly* lighted because this is the most important shot of the program.

   Use whatever format (as far as graphs and grids) is common at your facility. Your instructor will provide you with specific details.

2. Set your camera on manual iris. (See Figure 9.22 for some basic information on how to do this, and also check with your instructor and/or engineering staff as to the proper procedure.) Tape or shoot live in a situation where you can see the waveform monitor. Be sure the waveform monitor is set to measure light levels. Shoot various objects in the studio, control room, or engineering facility. Note the drop in IRE increments as you shoot; by noticing when and how you create a drop (or an increase) of 20 IREs, you'll be able to judge how you move up and down one f-stop in your light levels. (Remember, a change of one f-stop corresponds to 20 IRE.)

Figure 9.22 Example for exercise 2. Setting the camera to manual iris.

3. Still keeping the camera on manual iris, line up three people. Put person 1 about 10 feet away, person 2 about 20 feet from the camera, and person 3 more than 30 feet away. (For a number of reasons, including availability of space and light, this is best done outdoors with a portable camera.)

Open up one stop and shoot the scene. Now stop down one stop and shoot it again. Lower the stop again. When you play back the tape, note the effect that stopping up and down has on your depth of field.

operating the switcher

OBJECTIVES

After completing Chapter 10, you will be able to:

1. Direct and technical-direct a program using a standard switcher.
2. Use many of the more sophisticated techniques available on modern switchers.
3. Create some special effects with the switcher and understand how the effects are integrated with modern computer technology.

The operations carried out at the switcher coordinate the efforts of most of the crew. The camera operators, the performers, and virtually everyone who produces part of the picture, will have his or her work routed through this device. In Chapter 7, we learned about the basic anatomy of the most simple type of switcher. Here, we'll explore the operations of more complex, modern units and also begin to bridge the gap between operation of the switcher (meaning accurately putting shots on air) and directing a program (meaning using the switcher to communicate effectively in video language).

SMART SWITCHERS

Chapter 7 introduced the rudiments of what might be called, for lack of a standardized term, a simple "matrix" switcher. The matrix switcher allowed us to cut between cameras on one bus and, using the fader bar, dissolve between cameras on different buses. You'll also remember that by activating the effects bank, it was possible to create keys and wipes.

Many switchers still use that basic matrix layout, but the newest generation of equipment is more aptly called a "multilevel source and effects switcher," meaning that it can layer a number of video sources, including composite sources from computer-based graphics inputs. (Some manufacturers call this a parallel architecture switcher.) These high-tech, "smart" switchers also change the position of their activated controls automatically, so you spend less time setting up the configuration of buttons for the next shot.

A tour of a modern switcher and a demonstration of one possible application will give you a clearer idea of:

- The mechanics of switcher operation
- The effects that can be created by a modern switcher

The mechanics and effects won't be identical in every case, of course, but *in general*, you'll find that most of the features discussed will be found—somewhere, and in a similar form—on some switcher. To be accurate, we should preface this tour by noting that we've combined features from many different switchers (some basic, some very high-tech), in order to portray the range of options available in modern video switching hardware. It is a *hypothetical* model, "built" solely for the sake of illustration—but we believe it is far more instructive than a catalog of different switchers.

Another point: Although it is true that in most college facilities you won't be using the very latest generation of equipment, there is a good possibility that many professional studios and some student studios will feature quite advanced switchers. One reason is that the price of the hardware itself is declining, while its technical capabilities are increasing. As a result, many institutions opt to replace cumbersome older equipment—which may be chronically in need of repair—with newer gear that is reliable, compact, versatile, and surprisingly affordable.

Upstream and Downstream Sources

The fundamental function of the switcher is to mix video sources together. Switchers also allow the insertion of other picture elements, some upstream and some downstream. The concept of upstream and downstream is illustrated in Figure 10.1.

Downstream means the source that is the last source added to the video signal. It is figuratively farther down

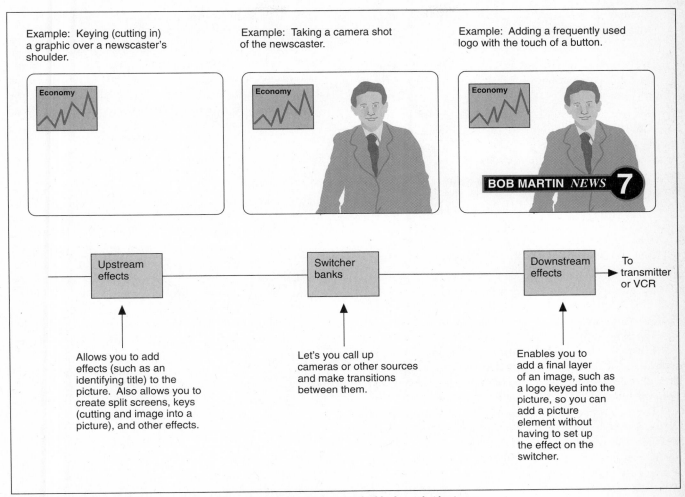

Example: Keying (cutting in) a graphic over a newscaster's shoulder.

Example: Taking a camera shot of the newscaster.

Example: Adding a frequently used logo with the touch of a button.

Economy

Economy

Economy

BOB MARTIN *NEWS* 7

Upstream effects

Switcher banks

Downstream effects

To transmitter or VCR

Allows you to add effects (such as an identifying title) to the picture. Also allows you to create split screens, keys (cutting and image into a picture), and other effects.

Let's you call up cameras or other sources and make transitions between them.

Enables you to add a final layer of an image, such as a logo keyed into the picture, so you can add a picture element without having to set up the effect on the switcher.

Figure 10.1 Upstream and downstream key effects. The switcher allows you to build a layered video image.

the "stream" of events than the program background bus, the preset background bus, and the key bus. As you might have guessed already, if you use the key bus to *create* a key, you would have called that the **upstream** key.

Why do we differentiate between upstream and downstream? The most immediate ramification is that because downstream effects are added last, they can be removed without changing the underlying picture. An image that will be flashed over a newscaster, for example, and then quickly removed is best generated by the downstream effects unit.

Why use a downstream key? One reason is that graphic effects are so common in modern video that you may have more than one key or effect active in a single picture, hence the need for an upstream and downstream key. Another reason is that the downstream key, because it is the final video signal inserted into the picture, usually produces a clearer and sharper effect than the upstream key. The downstream key makes the graphic appear as

though it has been "layered" on top of the whole image. Moreover, a downstream key is available at the touch of a button; you do not have to set the key up on the buses.

If, for example, you were the TD of a newscast and must superimpose the logo "Eyewitness News Weather Watch" many times, you would find it convenient to use the downstream key because it has no other effect on the picture than superimposing the keyed graphic. You might, for instance, have a very complex picture on program, such as a camera shot keyed into a map generated by the upstream key. Adding the logo is quite simple if you have a downstream keyer: Your camera shot and map stay the same—all that changes is the addition of the "Eyewitness News Weather Watch" logo. And all that you need do to insert it is to press an on-off switch.

Video "Layering"

The switcher can layer several video images in one picture with relative ease and little degradation of signal quality.

For example, if you were the TD for a segment on the economy within a newscast, you might use the switcher to:

1. Take a computer-generated graph and route it through the switcher, creating a video signal you can punch up on the switcher.

2. Seat your newscaster beside a blue or green wall, electronically remove the image of the blue wall, and replace it with the graph. This makes the graph appear over the shoulder of the newscaster.

3. Superimpose the newscaster's name and the station's logo, "Bob Martin NEWS 7," over the entire image. Because the logo would typically be added as the last picture element, the element farthest downstream, it would appear to be layered *over* the entire image and would provide an exceptionally clear and crisp image.

This effect would have been much more difficult with the previous generation of switchers. For one thing, old-style switchers could not accept a digitally encoded image from a computer, so introducing the computer graphics would have been impossible.

Secondly, the effect of cutting out a particular color, such as the blue panel in back of the newscaster, was more difficult to achieve before computer chips were integrated into the switcher. Today, this effect, called a "chroma" key, can be performed with a variety of colors and the key predicated on a very precise shade of color. At one time, weathercasters had to shun blue clothing because just about any shade of blue was keyed out of the picture. (In extreme cases, some blue-eyed weathercasters had to wear colored contact lenses to prevent their eyes from being chroma-keyed out of the picture and replaced, for instance, with portions of a map of a high-pressure front over Utah.)

SWITCHER FUNCTIONS

Let's begin a step-by-step tour of a hypothetical switcher; this will not only introduce you to various typical controls, but it will take some of the mystery out of terms such as *chroma key* and *downstream key*. (Note that although this is a hypothetical switcher, certain of the simpler functions are somewhat similar in layout to a model called the Grass Valley 100, a popular educational and institutional unit.)

Preset and Transition Controls

The hypothetical unit pictured in Figure 10.2 offers some advantages over the type of switcher in which all shots must be physically positioned by lever and button settings, the most important of which is the preset function, which allows you to see *the next shot that is going over the air* (see Figure 10.2, cluster 2). Preset is an advanced function typically found in very expensive switchers, but the option

has been working its way down into less expensive models and may someday become an industry standard.

Preset is slightly different from *preview*, in that preset allows you to view and experiment with any combination of shot and effects; preview shows exactly what will go over the air when the next transition is made. The transition on a modern switcher may often be accomplished via an auto transition control. Using this control, a preprogrammed transition can be performed with the push of one button.

In many modern switchers, you do not have to use the fader bar to dissolve from bank to bank (although you may). Many switchers have an automatic "fade to black" control, which lets you fade to black or up from black without using the fader bar (see Figure 10.2, cluster 8). This may not seem like a life-changing innovation, but TDs experienced on older boards know that setting up a sequence of shots that will allow you to fade to black can, under certain circumstances, be quite tricky. If, for example, you had a graphic superimposition over a picture and wanted to fade *both* images to black at the same time, you had a difficult task ahead of you if you were equipped with an antiquated switcher.

Today many boards use a bus called the program background bus that selects the main picture. Everything else is either added to or cut away from that main picture.

Planning, Setting Up, and Taking Shots Using Switcher Controls

We've divided the controls used for planning, setting up, and taking shots into clusters. We'll begin with cluster 1 and proceed sequentially.

Cluster 1 is the program background bus. In cases where there are many controls that deal with similar functions, we've clustered them within an encompassing line and numbered the general area.

Please read through this section in one sitting and then review it. Because switcher functions can be accomplished in a variety of sequences and various controls interact with one another, there is no single method of explaining the complete action and interaction of each control in sequence. It is unavoidable that certain explanations, when they are first offered, may seem incomplete. Indeed, that may be the case because the controls in question might only be understandable when discussed in relation to several other controls on the switcher.

But by the time you complete the *entire* tour, you'll have a much better understanding of the relationships among controls and will have been given a reasonably thorough introduction to the array of capabilities offered by modern video technology.

Cluster 1: Program Background. **Program background** is the bus that is usually on the air (Figure 10.3).

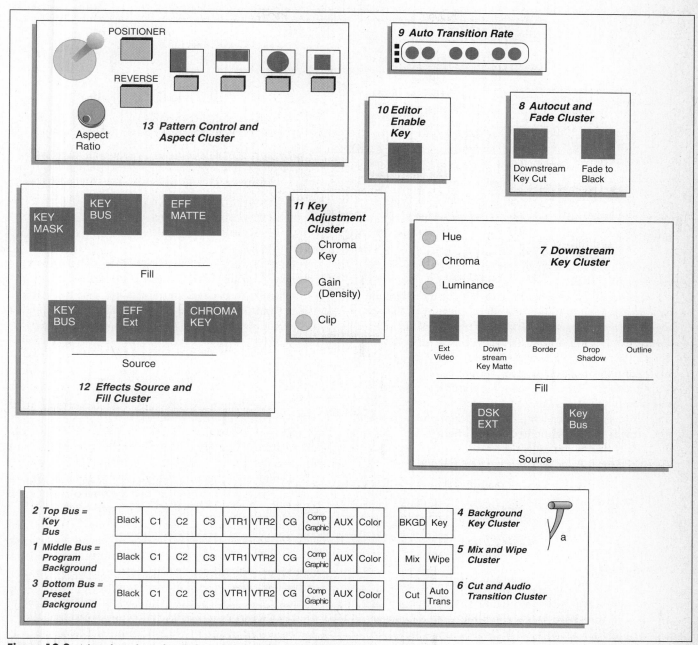

Figure 10.2 A hypothetical switcher. Refer to the numbered control "clusters" as you read the text.

It has a series of buttons for choosing inputs, and those buttons are mirrored on the other buses as well. Program background is the basic image, the main picture before special effects are added. On some switchers the program background bus is pretty much the same thing as a mix bus, because you can put the program background bus or the bus beneath it on the air by means of the standard fader bar (1A).

If the director calls for a shot that simply involves cutting from camera to camera, the TD can perform the entire operation on program background, if he or she so chooses.

Cluster 2: Key Bus. The **key bus** is where you select the picture or graphic that will be keyed into the picture (Figure 10.3). Remember, keying is the process of placing another image into the picture on program background. Although it's really not quite this simple, adding a graphic could be accomplished by having camera 1 punched up on program background and the character generator (CG) punched up on the key bus.

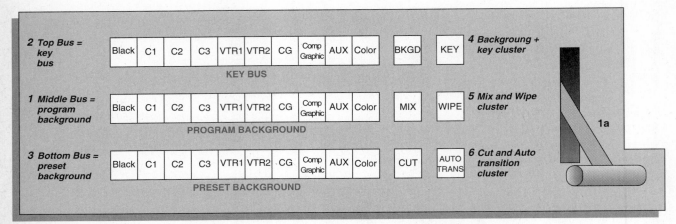

Figure 10.3 Switcher controls, clusters 1 to 6. The main buses, effects transition controls, and the fader bar.

In addition to keys, you can choose wipes and some other effects as well.

Cluster 3: Preset Background. On many switchers, the button you push on this bus selects the *next video to be taken when the next transition is made* (Figure 10.3). In other words, if camera 2 is on the air, and you want camera 1 to be the next shot, you would select camera 1 on the preset background bus.

When you select the source for preset background—in this case, camera 1—it is highlighted with a dim light. The source punched up on program background—in this case, camera 2—is highlighted with a bright light.

Let's continue the example:

- Camera 2 is on the air. It is punched up on the program background bus, the main bus that indicates what goes over the air, and is highlighted with a bright light.

- Camera 1, the *next* camera you want to take, is punched up on the preset background bus. It is highlighted with a dim light. The image from camera 1 appears on your preset monitor.

Now, on some switchers you make transactions by hitting an **auto transition** button that "flip-flops" the images and the highlighted buttons. When you press the device that triggers the automatic transition, the switcher will flip-flop not only the camera shots—putting camera 1 on the air and camera 2 on the preset monitor—but will also flip-flop the switcher settings. Camera 1, now the on-air camera, will *automatically* be highlighted on the program background bus. Camera 2, now relegated to preset background, will be highlighted with a dimmed indicator light on the preset background bus.

The switcher has changed the button settings for you. By pressing AUTO TRANS, the transition is created automatically and the switch is made. In addition, the board *tells* you what you've just done, indicating the new condition by the light intensities of the buttons.

Not all switchers have this **look ahead** capability (swapping the air image and the preset image).

Cluster 4: Background and Key. The background and key buttons allow you to determine what component of the picture will change during the next transition (Figure 10.3). If you press BACKGROUND, the next transition will be between the lower two buses—program background and preset background. If you press KEY, the next transition will be between the key bus and the program background bus. Many switchers allow you to press and activate both buttons simultaneously.

Cluster 5: Mix and Wipe. If you press the mix button, the switcher is set up to make standard transitions (cuts and dissolves). But if you press the wipe button, a wipe (for example, one picture being replaced by another picture that moves horizontally across the screen) will be the transition created by the switcher (Figure 10.3).

Cluster 6: Cut and Auto Transition. The cut and auto transition functions allow you to cut or dissolve (or wipe) between shots by pushing one button (Figure 10.3). Of course, you still can cut by changing cameras on the active bus, and you still can execute a dissolve by using the fader bar. The cut and auto transition buttons, however, make the job easier and allow the board to "follow" you from shot to shot. (The transition is most commonly used to perform a dissolve.)

As already mentioned, there are two light intensities on the buttons: a bright intensity for the source on the air and a lower intensity for the source selected to be next on the air. (Grass Valley calls these "high tally" and "low tally.") When you press CUT, the board will automatically execute a cut between the source punched up on the program background and the source punched up on the preset background. The indicator lights, and their relative brightness, will automatically change.

Hitting the auto transition button will accomplish exactly the same thing, except that you'll dissolve. (Or, you may wipe if you have chosen to do so in the cluster of controls shown in area 5.) You can preprogram the rate of the dissolve. You enter, via a control explained under item 9, the number of frames you'd like in order to complete the dissolve. If you want the dissolve to take a full second, you would program in "30 frames."

Cluster 7: Downstream Key. There are several controls in the downstream key cluster (Figure 10.4). The two source buttons, DSK EXT and KEY BUS, select the source of the key. DSK EXT means downstream key external. Pressing this button selects a device that has been wired to the downstream key (for instance, a separate character generator or other graphics device).

Alternatively, pressing KEY BUS selects the source lighted on the key bus (cluster 2). Selecting KEY BUS effectively makes the key bus your "downstream key," improving the quality of that key because it becomes the last video source added.

The next row up is labeled "Fill." This row allows you to select what you would like the inside of your key to look like. Examining the fill buttons from left to right, we see:

• *External video*. The external video button calls up an outside source wired into the switcher.

• *Downstream key matte*. The **matte** fills a key electronically "punched" in the picture with a shade of gray or a color.

The TD can change color, shade, and brightness of the matte by using the three twist knobs to the left of the square buttons. Those twist knobs are labeled "Hue," "Chroma," and "Luminance." By twisting the **hue** knob, you run through a full circle of the color spectrum. If you want red, for example, just keep twisting until red appears. (What you're really doing is twisting through a "wheel" of primary colors.) The **chroma** control allows you to adjust the amount of red you want—choosing blood red, a bluish red, and so on.

The **luminance** control adjusts the amount of light (white) added to the key; say, brightening a dark red to make it a rose red.

• *Border*. Pushing the border button places a thin black or white line around the character created. You do this to increase contrast.

• *Drop shadow*. The **drop shadow** button places a border along the bottom right edge of the key. A drop shadow effect is shown in Figure 10.5.

• *Outline*. The outline control allows you to change the color, shade, or brightness of the outline (border) of the characters keyed in.

Cluster 8: Auto Cut and Fade. The auto cut and fade controls allow you to quickly remove the entire picture (fade to black) or part of the picture (cutting the key) at the push of a button. FADE TO BLACK automatically does just what you would expect: fading to (or up from) black. Your fade rate is preprogrammed according to the auto transition rate that you set. KEY CUT allows you to conveniently insert and remove the downstream key at will (see Figure 10.2).

Cluster 9: Auto Transition Rate. **Auto transition rate** is a setting on the switcher that allows you to enter the number of frames you want to use to execute your fades, dissolves, and transition to the downstream key (Figure 10.6). You can set each function independently. That is, your fade to black function might be set for 60 frames while your dissolve can be set for 15.

Cluster 10: Editor Enable Key. Activating the **EDITOR ENABLE key** allows the switcher to be controlled by an external source, such as an edit control unit. We'll examine the connection between the switcher and the edit control unit in Chapter 11.

Cluster 11: Key Adjustment. The key adjustment control adjusts the appearance of the key (Figure 10.7).

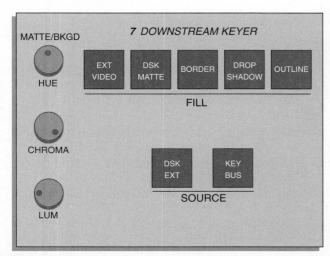

Figure 10.4 Downstream keyer, cluster 7.

Figure 10.5 Drop shadow lettering. The drop shadow effect gives these characters a three-dimensional appearance.

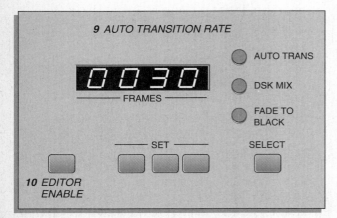

Figure 10.6 Auto transition rate (cluster 9) and editor enable key (cluster 10).

Although we've so far spoken about the key in general terms, this is a good opportunity to further define the key so that we can better understand some of the processes used to control it with the switcher.

A common way of conceptualizing a key is to think of it as one picture inserted into another, such as a newscaster's name keyed in the lower third of the picture, or a graphic of a dollar sign keyed over a newscaster's shoulder as he or she reads a story about the economy.

But to be more technically precise, a key is a *hole electronically cut into the picture*. In order to cut this hole, three video signals are necessary:

1. *A background signal (background scene)*. We must first have a picture to cut into. On our switcher, this is usually the signal that comes from the program background bus.

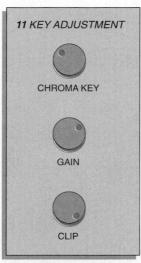

Figure 10.7 Key adjustment, cluster 11.

2. *A key source*. This is what cuts the hole into the background. For example, when a character generator is keyed into the picture, the letters are actually cutting an electronic hole in the background.

3. *A fill signal to put into that hole*. In many cases, the source that cuts the hole also provides the signal to fill the hole (such as the character generator that cuts the holes in the shapes of letters and then fills them in with a CG-generated color). When a fill signal is combined with the signal that cuts the hole in the background, it's called a *self key*.

The three twist knobs shown in cluster 11 control the chroma key, the gain, and the clip. A chroma key removes a certain color from the background picture and allows you to substitute another video signal; the twist knob allows you to spin through an electronic color wheel to determine the color you wish to eradicate. The gain control adjusts the solidity of the key; if you want a semitransparent key, for example, you'd set the gain control at a low level. The **clip** control sets the signal intensity threshold that will trigger the key insertion. Too much key signal can cause the key to **tear**, forming a raggedness at the edge of a key. For example, if you had an art card with white letters, you might have to adjust the key clip control carefully to prevent tearing or distortion of the key effect (Figure 10.8).

Why? Because the key circuitry is searching for a strong, bright white signal to cut out the holes in the video picture. If the clip threshold is set too high, reflections off the dark art card will be perceived as a strong, bright white signal and will cut holes in the picture too.

Cluster 12: The Effects Keyer Control Group. This cluster controls the upstream key (Figure 10.9). The very bottom button in the cluster is labeled "Key Mask." **Key mask** is an advanced function that allows you to "hide" the part of an image that you don't want to use as a key, positioning the part you want to hide with the joystick located in cluster 13.

The three source buttons are frequently used. From left to right, they are KEY BUS, EFF EXT and CHROMA KEY. These controls choose the source of the key. (Again, there are two places in which to insert the key: "upstream," at the key and mix banks, or "downstream," after the signal has left the main buses of the switcher. Also remember that should you want the clarity of a downstream key, you can, under certain circumstances which depend on the exact configuration of your equipment, channel the output of the effects keyer group to the downstream key by pressing the button in cluster 7 marked "Key Bus.") Should you select KEY BUS, you'll activate that bus as the source from which your key—the shape that cuts the hole in the picture—will come. EFF EXT might be the output of a character generator or some sophisticated graphics device wired into the switcher. CHROMA KEY cuts the hole by

(a)

(b)

Figure 10.8 Adjusting the key effect. Too much key signal produces a "tearing" effect (*a*). With the signal properly adjusted, the key is sharp (*b*).

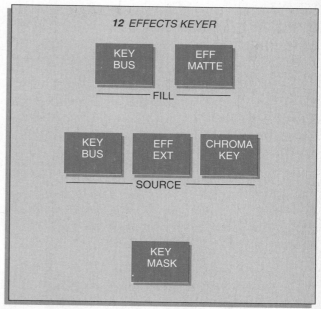

Figure 10.9 Effects keyer control group, cluster 12.

eliminating a specific color and using the area previously occupied by that color as the hole.

Let's return to the example of the weathercaster standing in front of a blue wall. Typically, the blue wall is chroma-keyed out and a computer-generated map is inserted into its place. Although weathercasters appear to be pointing toward the map, they are actually pointing toward a blank wall while gauging their hand movements by viewing the keyed image—themselves and the map—on a monitor.

Recall that this is a key effect, and *the blue wall is actually the hole.* The blue wall is the part of the picture that has been cut out. Anything else in the picture that matches that *precise* shade of blue will also be cut out, but that's rarely a problem nowadays because chroma key adjustments on the switcher are so sensitive that they can be set to an exact shade of blue and, therefore, not cut out most blue blazers, ties, or eyes. This used to be a difficult situation, and problems with chroma key still do arise (see Box 10.1).

Above this bank of buttons there are controls that determine the source you'll use to fill the hole cut by the

---

BOX 10.1 CHROMA KEY PROBLEMS

Not so long ago, chroma key created a problem for people with blue clothes or blue eyes. The earliest chroma key would remove almost any blue, so a weathercaster with blue pants or skirt might find a map of Georgia and Florida crawling down his or her legs.

Some blue-eyed anchors found that their eyes were a perfect "chroma key blue"—and in some cases were forced to wear contact lenses to change their eye color.

Connie Chung once wore a particular shade of blue eye shadow during her *NBC News Digest.* Every time she blinked, her eyes disappeared and were replaced by the chroma key insert.

key. On our hypothetical switcher, you get to choose KEY BUS or EFF EXT. If your weather map is being shot by one of the studio cameras, wired into the key bus, you'd want to choose KEY BUS, with the studio camera punched up. But if the map were coming from an external source, say, a computer wired into the switcher, you would choose external effects. On some switchers, one of the sources on the buses is COLOR. You may, under some circumstances, wish to punch up the color source on the key bus to fill the hole cut by the key.

Cluster 13: Pattern Control and Select. The **pattern control** allows you to select a pattern to use in a wipe. Our hypothetical switcher shows three wipe patterns: horizontal, vertical, and circular (Figure 10.10). On a real switcher there would undoubtedly be many more patterns. The joystick at the far left of cluster 13 allows you to change the location of many of the wipe patterns; you could, for example, use the joystick to position the circle wipe in the lower left-hand corner of the picture (Figure 10.11). Almost all switchers also have various controls that allow you to change the aspect of a wipe—for example, making a circle into an oval, and making the edges of the wipe softer.

Don't forget that you must always take some specific action to invoke the wipe effect. On our console, you would press WIPE in cluster 4; this would allow you to use the two bottom buses to select the video source for the background video and the source you want to "wipe into" the picture. You would make the wipe move or grow by using the fader bar (1A). You can also use the auto transition button to perform the wipe (cluster 6).

Now, you've been exposed to most of the features available on modern switchers. As mentioned earlier, there is no practical way to describe controls in a linear fashion because the controls are utilized differently depending on particular circumstances.

Please take a moment to re-read the descriptions of clusters 1 to 13. Now that many of the actions *and inter-*

Figure 10.11   Circle wipe effect. Here, the wipe pattern is centered in the frame.

actions have been explained, the function of the unit as a whole will make more sense.

CREATING A "NEWSBREAK"

At this point you are familiar with the controls of our hypothetical switcher. Now, we'll use that switcher to produce a short taped "newsbreak."

First the anchor will appear, read a few headlines, and turn the newsbreak over to the meteorologist. The meteorologist will then give a brief forecast standing in front of a computer-generated map. During part of this segment, the weather logo will appear. Finally, we will switch back to the anchor who will sign off and ask viewers to tune in at six.

Here's how to create the newsbreak, referring to control clusters in Figure 10.2.

Sources

The components of our newsbreak come from several video sources:

- The anchor is on camera 1.
- The meteorologist is on camera 2.
- The computerized weather map is wired into the computer graphics button in each of the three buses (in clusters 1, 2, and 3).
- The logo, "Eyewitness News Weather Watch," comes from an external character generator wired into DSK EXT (downstream key, external) in cluster 7.

You can see your source images on a bank of monitors. In addition, you can see the image that is leaving the

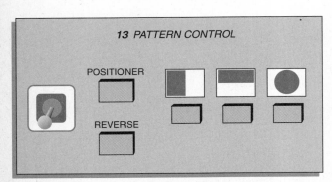

Figure 10.10   Pattern control and select, cluster 13.

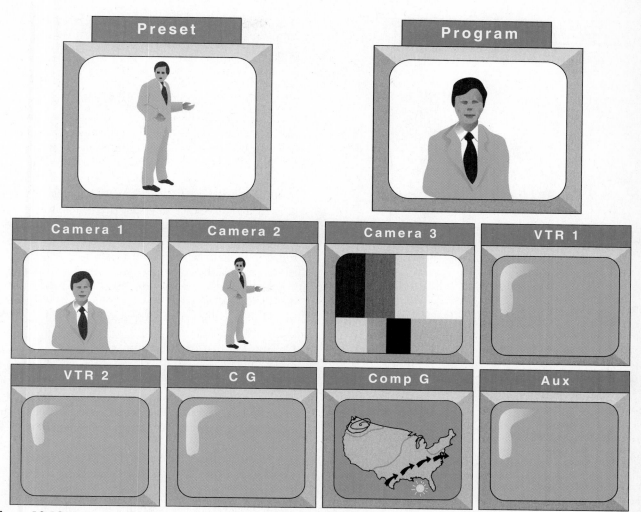

Figure 10.12   The monitor bank. Below the preset and program monitors are several smaller monitors that show the source images for our "newsbreak." At this point, camera 1 is selected on the program bus and camera 2 is selected on the preset bus.

switcher on the program monitor, and the image that will replace it in the next transition on the preset monitor (Figure 10.12).

Planning the Shots

As you begin to set up for the taping, you plan your shots and your initial switcher setup. Our first shot will be a take of the anchor on camera 1. Our second shot will be a composite image of the weathercaster in front of a keyed map. One solution is to set up camera 1 on the program background bus (cluster 1) and create the composite image on the preset background bus (cluster 3).

To prepare to open on the anchor, select camera 1 on the program background bus in cluster 1. The anchor will appear on the program monitor.

Creating a Composite Image

The meteorologist standing in front of the map is created from two sources: camera 2 and the computerized map, which will be keyed into the background (Figure 10.13).

We will create this image in four steps:

1. *Select the foreground.* We will use the weathercaster in front of the blue wall as the foreground, so punch up camera 2 on the key bus in cluster 2. Press KEY in cluster 4: then press CUT in cluster 6. The image will appear on the preset monitor.

2. *Create the key.* The key is the hole cut out of the background. We will cut out the blue wall, so select CHROMA KEY as the source in cluster 12. In cluster 11 adjust the chroma key knob to match the blue of

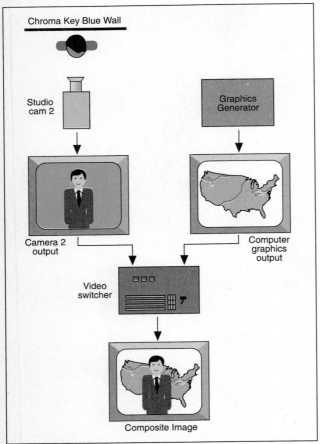

Figure 10.13 Creating a composite image. Using the output of camera 2 as background, we cut a blue chroma key (removing the image of the blue wall) and fill (replace) it with the output of the computer-graphics generator. The weathercaster stands before the map.

the wall. The blue wall on the preset monitor will vanish.

3. *Select the fill.* We will fill the key with the weather map. The map is available on the preset background bus. The map, which is routed through the preset background bus, becomes the fill for the chroma key blue wall. On the preset monitor, the map appears behind the weathercaster.

4. *Adjust the key.* Use the gain and clip controls in cluster 11 to make sure the key is sharp and does not tear.

Preparing the Downstream Key

For our newsbreak, the downstream key comes from an external character generator. Select DSK EXT in cluster 7. Then press DOWNSTREAM KEY CUT in cluster 8, and the character generation will appear.

You may adjust the image using the fill controls in cluster 7. You might add a drop shadow or border, or change the color and brightness of the matte. When the

image is satisfactory, press DOWNSTREAM KEY CUT in cluster 8 again. The image vanishes. You are prepared to bring it back by pressing that button again.

Preparing to Tape

Before you begin the program, double check your settings.

Fader Bar Position (Control 1A). Because we want to begin with camera 1 on the program background bus, the fader bar should be either entirely up or entirely down.

Auto Transition Rate (Cluster 9). A half-second transition (15 frames) is about right for this newsbreak.

Fade to Black (Cluster 8). Also double check the program monitor to be sure that the switcher is in black. Toggle the fade to black button in cluster 8, if needed.

Prepare to Tape a Leader. When the tape begins to roll, the director will create a leader to synchronize the equipment, calibrate output, and identify the program. You will roll the record tape for about 15 seconds until the tape "locks up" with house sync. You may also be required to add slate, color bars, and/or audio tone.

Calling and Taping the Shots

Often, the director calls the shots and the TD operates the switcher to create the appropriate output. The director and crew will rehearse the take first, using abbreviated names for each shot. In this case *chroma key* refers to the weathercaster and keyed map; CG refers to the downstream key or character generator.

Here are the calls and the TD's actions to create our newsbreak. Figure 10.14 shows the shots we are creating.

1. "We're in black." The director will notify the crew after the leader has been created. Tape is rolling.

2. "Ready to fade up. Fade up to camera 1." Hit the fade to black button in cluster 8. You will automatically fade

Figure 10.14 The shot sequence. The newsbreak opens on the anchor (1), switches to the weathercaster (2), inserts and then removes the weather logo (3 and 4), and ends on the anchor (5).

up on the source (camera 1) selected in the activated bus (program background).

Karen Collins, the anchor, appears on the program monitor and introduces meterologist Bob Harper. Bob is still on the preset monitor in front of the keyed map.

3. "Ready on chroma key. Take chroma key." Press the cut button in cluster 6. The image on the preset monitor is exchanged with the image on the program monitor.

Bob Harper begins explaining the massive winter storm headed our way.

4. "Ready on CG. Take CG." Press DSK EXT in cluster 7 and the CG (weather logo) appears on the preset monitor. Press the cut button in cluster 8 and the CG appears on the program monitor.

5. "Lose the CG." Press the cut button in cluster 6; then press the background button in cluster 4 to remove the logo.

Bob Harper wraps up the forecast and turns the program back to Karen Collins.

6. "Ready on camera 1. Take 1." Press the cut button in cluster 6. The anchor appears on the program monitor (and the composite weather image moves to the preset monitor).

The anchor wraps up, "Good afternoon. We'll see you at six."

7. "Ready to fade to black. Take black." Press FADE TO BLACK in cluster 8.

Stop tape after a few seconds of black, and your newsbreak is complete.

Don't forget that this illustration was accomplished on the hypothetical switcher that we "built" using an amalgamation of various switcher features—features that you will not find combined in one unit. We did this to illustrate as many different switcher features as possible in a brief example.

By combining your knowledge of "matrix" switchers (as described in Chapter 7) with the operational techniques of "multilevel" switchers (described here), you'll be able to *figure out* virtually any switcher.

Your ability to use the switcher will allow you to quickly "punch up" the right source on air or tape. In many broadcast, cable, and institutional facilities, the director operates his or her own switcher, so it's particularly important that you master the basic switcher operations through practice.

A program can be saved or lost by the quick wits and action of the director. The powerful impact of many programs produced by live switching has hinged on the ability of the director to capture a **reaction shot** (a shot of a performer reacting to what another performer is saying or to an action happening on screen; see Box 10.2), or a shot of someone making a magnificent catch, or a detail of a program that we might miss if taken only in wide shot.

ADVANCED SWITCHER OPERATIONS

Switcher design is growing "smarter" virtually by the day, and although you may not use some of the smart features now, it's helpful to have a passing acquaintance with them.

"Key Memory" and Digital Graphics

The microprocessor has had a profound effect on the technology of high-end switchers. Some switchers, for example, can maintain a series of shots in their memory. Suppose you open a talk show with the exact series of shots each time; some high-end switchers can be programmed to remember those shots and execute them at the command of a single keystroke. Sometimes called **key memory**,

---

BOX 10.2   THE WORLD'S MOST FAMOUS REACTION SHOT

Don Hewitt, the executive producer of *60 Minutes*, began his career working, among other jobs, as a director. He was in charge of the switcher on one of TV's most famous events: a 1960 Kennedy-Nixon debate.

Hewitt took reaction shots of Nixon as Kennedy spoke. Hewitt reported that Nixon's aides complained about the shots and insisted that there had been an agreement that no reaction shots would be used; Hewitt denied that any such agreement had been made.

In any event, the reaction shots showed an uncomfort-able-appearing Nixon sweating, licking his lips, and shifting his eyes back and forth. Much of Nixon's appearance had to do with the fact that he was ill and did not have the proper clothing or makeup for TV. The "reaction shots" were certainly not flattering to this candidate, and many observers feel that his appearance during the debate (the first of a series) contributed to his defeat. As a point of interest, most TV viewers surveyed thought Nixon lost the debate, whereas radio listeners polled felt that Nixon was the victor.

this feature saves time and mental energy, and helps prevent mistakes.

Another advantage of modern switchers is their ability to handle inputs from sophisticated graphics units. Digital capability allows the director to take advantage of the full range of the graphics equipment that will be described in Chapter 14.

Linking the Switcher and the Edit Control Unit

A final point of interest is the interrelationship between the switcher and the edit control unit. Certain complex editing operations, such as A-B rolling or insertion of special video effects, must be accomplished using a switcher. After all, an edit control unit has no capability to dissolve or create a key to insert a graphic from a computer.

The switcher and the edit control unit need some way to talk to each other. This method of communication is called a **protocol**. If you've ever done even the most rudimentary form of computer operation, you know that a protocol is a standard set of commands recognized by the machine. In the case of video editing, the protocol for

exchange of information is often accomplished by what's called, on some units, a serial interface. An edit control unit, for example, could be attached to the switcher through the serial interface and—via computer instructions—tell the switcher to dissolve, wipe, or perform numerous other functions during the editing process.

The relationship between the switcher and the edit control unit seems more complex than it really is. Although the terminology and computer commands might seem intimidating, they are nothing more than a code to instruct the switcher to perform a certain function in order for the edit control unit to create the desired series of cuts, dissolves, and effects. (Chapter 11 will briefly explore computer-based time code editing, as well as the much more simple process of cuts-only control track editing.)

Irrespective of the number of buttons or levers, always bear in mind that the switcher is simply a *tool*. Even the most high-tech model cannot compensate for lack of directorial skill or a poor understanding of the principles of visual communication.

We'll address the visual meaning of various shots in Chapter 15, "Fundamentals of Directing."

SUMMARY

1. Many modern switchers allow you to layer several video sources. They also have capabilities that let you exchange images at the push of a single button.

2. Sophisticated switchers are gaining in popularity even in relatively low-end environments.

3. One particularly useful feature found in many modern switchers is the *preset* function, which allows you to see the next shot that will go over the air when you hit the transition button.

4. The hypothetical switcher shown in this chapter has three buses: the program background bus, the key bus, and the preset background bus. The key bus is used to summon up the images to cut into the main video picture. The program background and preset background can function just like regular mix buses.

5. If your fader bar has activated the program background bus, the source chosen on preset background will be the next to go on the air. Some switchers give you the capability of seeing each shot "preset" on a

separate monitor that indicates exactly what will go over the air as soon as the transition button is pushed.

6. Many modern switchers have an upstream and downstream key. The advantages of having two key sources are flexibility in picture creation and the fact that the downstream key is a very high-quality image.

7. A key is a hole cut into the existing picture. You use the various controls on the switcher to determine what image will cut that hole, and what will fill it.

8. One of the more common uses of the key in video is called *chroma key*, where a certain color is removed from the picture (creating the "hole") and another video source is used to fill that hole.

9. Switcher design grows "smarter" every day. Some units are able to memorize preprogrammed lists of commands so that the TD does not have to repeat complex procedures. Other switchers interface with computers and computer-controlled edit control units.

TECHNICAL TERMS

auto transition	clip	editor enable key	key mask
auto transition rate	downstream	hue	key memory
chroma	drop shadow	key bus	look ahead

luminance   preset background bus   reaction shot   upstream

matte   program background   self key

pattern control   protocol   tear (key tear)

EXERCISES

1. Produce a diagram of your facility's switcher. The diagram need not go into extreme detail, but attempt to make it a broad, functional diagram similar to the one presented in this chapter. Using numbers to indicate controls or clusters of controls, describe what each does. If this is a class project, experiment with your switcher to be sure that the diagram is accurate.

2. Create three labels on cardboard: Camera 1, Camera 2, Camera 3. Make sure they are bold enough to be seen by the camera.

   Put the cardboard sheets on easels or prop them on chairs and focus your studio cameras on the respective card. In other words, camera 1 should have a close-up of "Camera 1," and so forth. If you have a character generator, type in "Character Generator" so that the letters appear in the lower third of the image. (The exercise is being conducted in this manner because it's easy to become confused about which image belongs to which source when calling and changing shots, but this method leaves no doubt.)

   Here is the thrust of this exercise. Assuming that you have diagramed the switcher and have now become reasonably familiar with its controls, you get to be the TD for a short segment.

   As you may remember from previous chapters, the director typically calls the shots while the TD executes the shots on the switcher. We're going to provide you with a script to be read by the director. You, as TD, are responsible for accurately putting the pictures the director requests over the air.

   So, take your seat, put the board in black, and get ready to fade up on camera 1. The director will now issue these commands. (Slowly, director. Remember, if this is a rotating class exercise, you'll have your turn in the TD chair soon.)

   - "We're in black, 10 seconds to air, ready to fade up on camera 1. Ready to fade up on 1 . . . Fade up on camera 1.

   - Ready camera 2 . . . Take 2.

   - Ready to dissolve to camera 3 . . . Dissolve to camera 3.

   - TD, we're going to be on camera 3 for about 30 seconds. I want you to set up a key from the character generator and key it into camera 3. Tell me when you're ready to key the graphic. Preset CG over camera 3. Good. Key the graphic over camera 3.

   - OK, we're going to keep the graphic up for about 5 seconds. Stand by to lose graphic. Ready . . . lose it.

   - Ready to cut to camera 1. Cut to 1.

   - I want to set up a split screen wipe between camera 2 and camera 3. Let's set it up on preview and see how it looks. [Note: If you have preset capabilities, use preset instead.] OK, that looks good. Get ready to take the split screen. Ready . . . take it.

   - Stand by to cut back to camera 1. Ready 1 . . . take 1.

   - Stand by to fade to black. Ready black . . . fade to black.

   If you've been able to accomplish this scenario with no mistakes, you're ready to work as a TD for regular productions.

operating
the edit
control unit

OBJECTIVES

After completing Chapter 11, you will be able to:

1. Plan the appropriate edit structure you will use to create your program.
2. Utilize on-line and off-line edit strategies.
3. Use various approaches to actually create a program.

As you remember from the brief introduction in Chapter 7, the purpose of editing is to take previously recorded material and rearrange it, and sometimes manipulate it in various other ways, to produce logical and expressive video. In this chapter, we'll bridge the gap between operating the editing control unit and using it as a device to produce a cohesive program.

PLANNING THE EDIT STRATEGY

There are a number of questions you'll have to ask yourself before beginning the editing session, including questions relating to the physical method of editing, what shots from the original source tapes are best, and how your editing process can reinforce the overall thrust of the program.

Those questions aren't always easily answered, but the options—and the reasons for choosing those options—will become more clear as we progress through this chapter. We'll provide a definition of *assemble editing* and *insert editing*, and then discuss the role of planning edit strategies for either type of editing—specifically, logging shots and shooting for the edit.

Assemble Editing

One initial question is whether you will use assemble or insert editing. Assemble editing allows you to lay down segments in sequence (Figure 11.1), adding control track as you go along.

The problem with assemble editing is that you must always start at the beginning and move to the end. Also, it is usually impractical to record audio and video separately, thus limiting your editing choices. Neither is necessarily a difficulty if you have a very simple program that you can visualize in advance and in which you do not need to copy audio and video separately.

Insert Editing

Insert editing requires that you lay down a control track by either having assemble edited a portion of your program already or prerecorded a continuous signal on the final record tape before beginning the editing process. Admittedly, laying down control track on the whole tape (or at least as much of the tape as you plan to use for the program) is an extra step, but insert editing provides you with some significant advantages over assemble editing.

- Your edits are less likely to "break up." When creating an assemble edit, you are asking the machines to back themselves up and create a perfectly matched sync track. That's a tall order, and although most machines can handle it most of the time, occasionally there will be a slight variation in the distance between sync pulses when the new track is created. But when a track already exists, as is the case with insert editing, no new track is added, so control track errors are eliminated.

- You can edit out of sequence with insert editing. In other words, you don't have to lay down the beginning, middle, and end in that order. This frees you from the constraints of having to think and execute your editing in a linear fashion. For example, you may want to create the *end* of the piece before the *beginning*—not an uncommon practice in some news editing. Unless you have a control track already laid down, that option is not available.

- And, of course, insert editing allows you to insert only *part* of the signal from a source tape. You may, for example, want to insert only video or only audio. You may use other audio sources, as

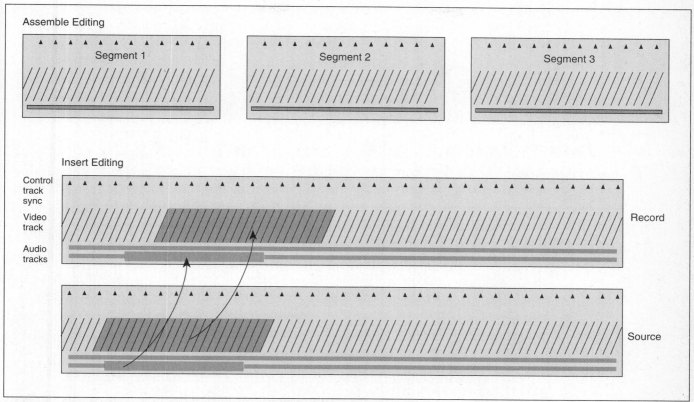

Figure 11.1   Assemble versus insert editing. In assemble editing, tape segments must be dubbed (copied) in sequence, including all the original control, video, and audio tracks. Insert editing allows you to dub any portion of an audio or video track without disturbing the control track.

well. That's impossible with assemble editing; in the assemble mode, you must take *everything* on the source tape and dub it to the control tape—video, audio, and sync.

Logging Shots

A **log** is a listing of shots taken. Logging shots accurately is extraordinarily important to the editing process. When you return to the editing suite, you'll generally be under pressure to find the appropriate shot quickly. Playing through an entire reel of videotape trying to find the shot is time-consuming and frustrating. Forgetting which tape has the correct shot on it is even more maddening.

All of this sounds obvious, but it is surprising how easy it is to lose track of what's on the source tapes. We all have rationalized, at one time or another, that we'll remember what's on the tape and there's no need to encumber ourselves with a clipboard and log sheet.

Two hours, two days, or two weeks later, though, our memories are a bit fuzzy: "The cover shot of the building . . . was that on cassette 2 or 3?" "The talent only had one really good closing—but we've got nine takes. Which was the best one?"

Those are the types of questions that quite literally come back to haunt you when you sit down to edit the program (Figure 11.2). That's why a simple listing of shots, such as the one illustrated in Figure 11.3, can literally save hours of editing time.

The **editing log**, also called a **spot sheet** or **shot sheet** lists shots by hours, minutes, and seconds, along with the

Figure 11.2   Get organized. Without notes, an editing log, and carefully labeled tapes, editing under a deadline is a nightmare.

BY DESIGN IN MOTION
PRODUCTION LOG

Production CIVIL WAR ENACTMENT   **Shoot Date** 2/14/9X

Producer/Director : PHILIP PALOMBO

Scene	Take	IN	OUT	NOTES	OK	NG
1A	1	01:03:22:23	01:03:29:24	FALSE START		X
1A	2	01:04:08:00	01:04:22:12	WALKING - GOOD ACTION	X	
1A	③	01:04:23:00	01:04:29:26	WALKING - REAL GOOD - BEST	X	
2	1	01:05:01:00	01:08:07:21	ENTERING CAMP - OK LIGHT.		X
2	2	01:08:08:00	01:11:13:21	ENTERING CAMP - SHAKY CAMERA		X
2	3	01:11:14:00	01:18:14:03	ENTERING CAMP - TOO LONG		X
2	④	01:18:15:00	01:21:20:25	ENTERING CAMP - GOOD ACTION - BEST	X	
6	1	01:21:21:00	01:21:29:00	MAIL CALL - DROPPED LINE		X
6	2	01:21:30:00	01:21:38:00	MAIL CALL - GOOD ACTION	X	
6	3	01:21:38:15	01:21:47:19	MAIL CALL - LETTERS DROPPED		X
6	④	01:21:48:15	01:21:57:29	MAIL CALL - THAT WAS IT	X	
7	1	01:21:58:05	01:22:07:15	MAN TAKES PACKAGE	X	
7	2	01:22:08:00	01:22:10:12	FALSE START - DROPPED LINE		X
7	3	01:22:11:00	01:22:14:01	BAD PAN -		X
7	4	01:22:25:01	01:22:36:15	MAN TAKES PACKAGE - SMOOTH	X	
7	5	01:22:37:01	01:22:59:02	MAN - PACKAGE - LONG	X	
7	⑥	01:23:01:10	01:23:11:15	MAN TAKES PACKAGE - GOOD	X	
4	1	01:23:13:01	01:23:29:10	CHAPLIN SCENE -	X	
4	2	01:24:00:00	01:24:58:01	VTR PROBLEM -		
4	3	01:24:59:00	01:25:15:01	CHAPLIN LAUGHS		X
4	4	01:26:12:01	01:26:59:13	CHAPLIN SCENE - GOOD ACTION	X	
4	⑤	01:27:00:10	01:27:05:10	CHAPLIN SCENE - BEST	X	
5	1	01:27:06:01	01:27:36:10	FLAG SHOT - SHAKY		X
5	②	01:27:37:01	01:28:38:05	FLAG SHOT - GOOD	X	

Figure 11.3 Editing log. The editing log (or short sheet) identifies tape segments by scene, take, and "in" and "out" points given as beginning and ending times. The director notes the flaws or merits of every shot as it is made. Shots are immediately classified as OK or NG (no good), and the best takes are circled. With such a list, an editor's time will be well focused.

title of each shot and notes for editing. Logging is a simple matter. Write down, on whatever form you use, the in and out times of the cut, and your comments ("Talent blew a word . . . don't use this cut").

Logging Shots on Older VCRs

Some older VCRs have counter numbers or **wheel numbers** that are produced by a device that counts the number of revolutions made by the spinning hub of the VCR. Counter numbers won't be of much help when you put the tape into the edit source unit, because the edit source unit will be reading sync pulses and giving you a readout in *time*, not wheel numbers.

Two options are available to help solve the problem of logging shots on older VCRs. First, log the shots in wheel numbers and keep the original machine with you in the edit suite. Fast forward and rewind on the portable VCR you used in the field, finding your entry and exit points. (Remember, you must rewind and reset the counter to zero and start the record cassette from the beginning in order for the counter numbers to be reproducible. Also, keep in mind that counter numbers are not especially accurate.)

The second option is to ignore the wheel numbers altogether and log your shots with a stopwatch. You can keep a surprisingly accurate running log of material this way. Just time the segments and add them cumulatively. For example, the first taped segment may run 45 seconds. Log it this way:

Cover shot of railroad tracks: 00:00:00–00:00:45

If your next shot runs 30 seconds, do the math in your head and continue the log:

Cover shot of railroad tracks: 00:00:00–00:00:45

Take 1: signal light flashing: 00:00:45–00:01:15

You can also keep a cumulative listing of the ending times, like this:

Cover shot of railroad tracks: 00:00:45

Take 1: signal light flashing: 00:01:15

The cumulative listing involves less writing and is generally just as simple to figure out as the shot listing.

Granted, it won't be a perfect log, but with practice you can become reasonably accurate in constructing an "imitation time code" log.

Shooting for the Edit

Although not, strictly speaking, an editing function, shooting in such a way that the material can be easily edited makes the task much simpler and improves the quality of the final product.

"Shooting for the edit" is sometimes called previsualization: You are conjuring up a mental image of how what you shoot will integrate with other shots in the sequence. This requires you to accommodate factors including leading and trailing space, graphics, continuity, video to cover jump cuts, consistency of time and location, and consistency of point of view.

A brief explanation of these terms will not only help in shooting for the edit, but it will also give you some insight into the overall editing process.

Leading and Trailing Space. You must ensure that you have properly shot for the edit and allowed sufficient lockup time on your camera shots. This is an important point that we chose to mention after the initial explanation of the editing unit because the necessity for lockup time on the raw tape is more easily understandable once you realize that most edit control units must back up the tapes 5 seconds (usually) in order to preroll them and force the sync pulses into exact lock step. But if you have not allowed at least 5 seconds of introductory video before the edit point when you originally shot the tape, you will often jumble the control track and make it difficult to obtain a clean edit.

Along the same lines, remember that you must allow at least 5 seconds of black or nonessential video—and in practical terms, you should allow at least 15 seconds—at the beginning of any tape. If you don't leave yourself this cushion, you won't be able to perform the first edit. Always remember to record the necessary preroll time for all your shots.

Graphics. Will the edited program involve the insertion of, let's say, printed graphics in the lower third of the screen? If so, you'll want to compose the shot in such a way that the lower third of the picture is not exceptionally bright or busy. A good example to illustrate this point is a training tape in which you are showing some sort of machinery and intend to add CG graphics to identify the unit; if the lower third is excessively cluttered, you'll have a hard time producing an acceptable graphic.

Continuity. **Continuity** is the overall trueness of scene-to-scene progression. Suppose one scene must be shot over a two-day period—and your performer wears a different necktie on day two. It will be impossible to edit the shots together because, when the sequence is edited, the tie will repeatedly change color.

Continuity problems aren't always easy to anticipate. Clothing, location of props, even performers' fresh haircuts, all pose difficulties unless you plan in advance and warn others in your production about possible continuity dilemmas.

Video to Cover Jump Cuts. A **jump cut** will be produced if, for example, you have a 5-minute interview taped while the interviewee was held in a consistent close-up. Should you want to edit 30 seconds from the beginning of the interview with 30 seconds from a point near the end, the shots obviously won't match perfectly. The interviewee's image will disconcertingly "jump" an inch or so on the screen. That's why producers who shoot for the edit always gather some sort of cover video to disguise the jump cut. It may, for example, be a reaction shot of the person conducting the interview. By doing a video-only edit, inserting a shot of the interviewer nodding or taking notes, you can edit the interview at will and cover the jump cut. The viewer won't even know the edit was made. (In news there are certain ethical implications involved in this technique, and they will be discussed in Chapter 19.)

Consistency of Time and Location. Consistency is a problem closely related to continuity; but it involves a slightly different dilemma because it deals more with time than with the elements pictured.

Here's an illustration of a discontinuity in time and location that occurs when the producer forgets to shoot for the edit. The scenario is this: We are shooting a real estate commercial. The script calls for a woman to begin talking as she descends a staircase, and then a close-up of her opening the front door while she continues to deliver her lines.

One approach is to shoot the two scenes so that it appears that the woman walks down the stairs and opens the door in one motion, continually delivering her script, in about a 10-second time interval. But if we forget the dictates of consistency of time and location, we're going to have problems in the editing suite.

Why? Assume the actress started her descent from the very top of a long staircase. She talks for 5 seconds as she takes three steps. The next shot clearly shows her at the door, 15 feet away from the 20-foot staircase. If her dialogue is supposed to give the impression of being spoken in one sentence, we've jarred the viewer. The woman has, while talking to the viewer, somehow vaulted 30 feet.

Should you be confronted with such a dislocation in space and time, you might be able to cover the awkward edit by doing a dissolve because a dissolve can suggest a change in location or duration of the shot. But it's best not to have to cover your tracks after the fact.

The best approach is to plan the scene correctly. Consider a cover shot (Figure 11.4). Alternatively, coordinate the duration of the spoken lines with the real time needed to reach the door.

Consistency of Point of View. What's wrong with this scene?

A basketball player runs toward the camera, leaps in the air, dunks a basket, and returns to the ground. Our second shot is a close-up of the basketball player, with the ball bouncing behind him for effect. He has a lavaliere mic clipped to his uniform as he delivers a public service announcement urging . . .

Wait a minute! Where did the mic come from? He certainly wasn't wearing it when he ran the full length of

the court. The wire is plainly visible and, aside from that, basketball players don't wear mics during a game. What we've inadvertently done is to mix points of view. In the first scene, the camera was an observer. In the second scene, the camera is a conduit of information, and the basketball player speaks directly to it just as a television newscaster would.

Neither approach is wrong in and of itself. If you want a straight shot, with no action, of the basketball player talking to the camera, delivering a public service announcement, the mic is not out of character. But combining the two points of view into what is supposed to be one continual action confuses the viewer. Use an off-camera miking arrangement for both shots.

Be aware that viewers have become much more media-literate in recent years, and mistakes in any of the areas just mentioned may be quite noticeable and can detract from the credibility of your program. Box 11.1 on page 158 summarizes some of the more common mistakes that typically haunt producers during the editing process.

The moral: Before you edit, be sure you know where your material is (its location on tape), and know whether it is usable in an edit situation (that you've shot it for the edit).

EXECUTING THE EDIT STRATEGY

Now, it's time to get down to the nuts and bolts of making edits and constructing a program. First we'll conduct an introductory tour of the hardware and explore some of the basic functions of edit control units. Then, to conclude the chapter, we'll walk through, step-by-step, three sample editing sessions.

Before we begin, we should review two terms that relate to video editing: off-line and on-line editing. Usually—although the exact use of the terminology may vary—*off-line* editing refers to cuts-only edits, usually executed through two VCRs and one edit control unit (Figure 11.5, page 158). Generally, the off-line edit is a **workprint**, a preliminary editing job made for off-the-air planning. In cuts-only, off-line editing, the edit control unit can be a simple control track (sync pulse) model.

On-line editing generally refers to editing done with an integrated switcher and a sophisticated computer controlled edit-control unit. On-line editing usually allows use of multiple VTRs, dissolves, A-B rolling, and the introduction of sophisticated special effects. (In some cases, *on-line* is used to refer to any editing done for on-air purposes, regardless of the equipment used.)

At one time on-line equipment was available only at networks, large TV stations, and high-tech production houses—but that is no longer the case. Today many ed-

(a) "We wanted more than a good house and a sound investment."

(c) "Smith Realty found us a home."

(b) (music)

Figure 11.4   Continuity of time and location. Cutting from the long shot (a) to the close-up (c) will jar the audience, as the speaker appears to vault through time and space. The cover shot of the living room (b) and a musical interlude can account for the time the speaker needs to cross from the stairs to the door.

ucational institutions and smaller production organizations are utilizing on-line editing equipment.

Although off-line editing can be executed with a control track or time code system, on-line editing is usually accomplished with a switcher and an edit control unit that reads time code. The time code "in" points and "out" points are programmed into the computerized edit control unit.

An Off-Line Editing Control Unit

Figure 11.6 on page 159 shows a hypothetical off-line editing control unit that we have "built" by mixing and matching several features of the most popular equipment. It includes five clusters of controls.

Cluster 1: Mode Control. Mode control allows you to choose the assemble edit mode. It's default is the insert mode, which means that it will assume you want to insert edit unless you instruct the machine otherwise. If you stay in insert, you can select which elements you want to copy from the source VTR to the record VTR. In this case, you

can choose any combination of video (V), audio 1 (A1), or audio 2 (A2). In many cases, you will push all the buttons. Sometimes, in the case of a video-only edit (the kind we'd use to cover a jump cut, for example) you would press INSERT and VIDEO.

Cluster 2: Source and Record Counters. There are counters on both sides of the edit control unit. The left-hand readout counts the hours, minutes, seconds, and frames on the source tape, whereas the right-hand counter keeps track of the record unit tape. (Readouts on control track and time code units look the same.)

Note that on a control track edit controller the counters are giving an arbitrary readout of how much time has elapsed on the tape according to the number of sync pulses that have passed through the sensor. *This is an arbitrary measurement and will not provide you with useful information unless you rewind the tape and then reset the counters to zero.*

Unlike SMPTE (Society of Motion Picture and Television Engineers) time code editing, control track editing devices do not read any specific time from the tape; they

BOX 11.1 EDITING TIPS

Editing can be a complex process—much more so if you fall victim to some of the more common booby traps. Here are some brief suggestions for avoiding trouble.

1. Log your shots. It's been said before, but it can't be said enough.

2. Label your tapes. The most careful logging won't help if you don't know which tape is "tape 3."

3. Slate all takes.

4. Make sure your logging system can be decoded by others with whom you work. You may have to turn over a job to someone else.

5. If at all possible, check for continuity problems before the scene is wrapped up during the shoot. If you are responsible for editing, try to appear on set or on remote. You can help the director avoid continuity lapses; the editor is the person probably best equipped to sniff out problems with continuity.

6. Direct talent to keep looking at the camera for a couple of seconds after a shot. Tape these extra seconds to get some leeway in editing.

7. Above all, *leave yourself enough lead-in for adequate preroll*. Roll your tape before you cue your talent. You need *at least* 5 seconds of preroll; 10 is more realistic, and 15 is just about right.

---

simply count pulses. There is a reset button that puts the readout back at zero, and you must reset in order for your shot sheets and edit control unit readouts to match.

Cluster 3: Transport Controls. The transport controls allow you to view the tape as you search forward and backward for an appropriate edit point. The farther you turn the dial from center, the faster the tape moves. You can "jog" the tape slowly, or speed through scenes at 40 times the normal speed on some models.

Above the control are the rewind, play, and fast forward controls. For operator convenience, these controls duplicate the controls on the VTR. REWIND and FAST FORWARD will move the tape very quickly but will not allow you to see the speeded-up images.

Cluster 4: Entry and Exit Set Point Controls. The process of copying a tape segment from the source VTR to

the record VTR is called an **edit**. Set point controls allow you to choose where the edit will start and stop. There are controls for both tape decks; on our diagram they are located above the word *entry* on the left-hand and right-hand sides of cluster 4.

Sometimes, newcomers to editing are confused by the mirrored controls. They may not know which entry and exit set point controls to use or how many points to set. Remember that you are copying one segment from the source unit VTR to the record unit VTR. That means you must set an **"in" point** for each tape machine. The edit control unit has to know where the part you want to copy from begins and where you want that part to begin on the final product. So, you need to set two "in" points to control where each segment of the tape starts.

Generally, you will set only one **"out" point**—the point at which you want the edit to end. You can make an edit without an "out" point by stopping the machines manually. This allows you a little more flexibility in finding the next edit point. But if you need to end the edit before recording over some essential material on the record unit's tape, you must set an out-point. Should the "out" point be set on the source unit control or the record unit control? In this case, you already have material that should not be erased on the record unit tape, you would set the "out" point on the record unit side. In other circumstances, you would set the out-point on the source unit machine.

The controls in cluster 4 allow you to choose the beginning and end of the tape segment that you want to copy from one unit to the other. You set the points by using the jog dial in cluster 3 to find the appropriate points of the tape and then press the entry buttons in cluster 4. The **trim** controls in cluster 4 allow you finer control of the editing process. With trim buttons you can fine-tune the

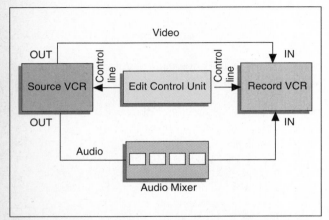

Figure 11.5 Off-line edit schematic. An off-line, or "cuts-only," system consists of one source VCR and one record VCR linked by an edit control unit.

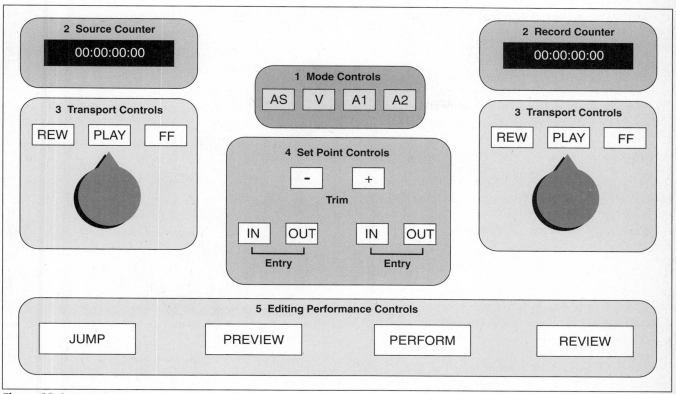

Figure 11.6   Hypothetical off-line edit control unit. Our edit control unit includes (1) mode controls, (2) source/record counters, (3) transport controls, (4) set point controls, and (5) editing performance controls.

position of the edit points without having to go through the whole process of setting an "in" point and "out" point. Pressing the "+" control adds a frame (to make the edit longer), whereas pressing the "−" control subtracts a frame. In addition to allowing you finer control than you could accomplish using the dials, the trim buttons eliminate the need to reset the edit points.

The trim buttons are particularly handy for pulse-counting edit control units because they allow you to make quick adjustments without having to continually replay the tapes to reset edit points. As a general rule, the more often you replay a certain segment of tape, the more difficult it becomes for the machines to perform the edit with precision. Why? Because each time the machines are backed up to "preroll" for the edit, the braking mechanism on the machines may gain or lose a frame. The timer on the edit deck is counting frames (sync pulses), so these cumulative errors can add up significantly after many replays of the edit.[1]

Here is an example of how you might use these controls to set "in" points and "out" points.

• Using the dial in cluster 3, locate the beginning of the segment to edit on the source tape.

• Press IN on the source (left-hand) entry control in cluster 4.

• Repeat the procedure for the "in" point on the record tape. (Use the right-hand entry control for the record tape).

• Repeat the procedure for the "out" point on *either* the source tape or the record tape. Setting the "out" point on the record tape will copy the segment from the source until the "out" point is reached on the record tape. This will protect any material on the record tape beyond that "out" point. Setting the "out" point on the source tape will copy the entire source segment—from "in" point to "out" point—onto the record tape.

• Review the edit. If necessary when setting or reviewing the edit point, use the trim controls in cluster 4 to make adjustments if you only need to change the edit by a few frames.

Cluster 5: Editing Performance Controls. The editing performance controls allow you to preview the edit, reposition the tapes at the original edit point, actually perform the edit, and review your work.

Let's examine the controls as they appear from left to right in cluster 5. JUMP automatically returns both the tapes to the edit points selected. (Sometimes this control is labeled "GO TO"; **go to** is also an edit control unit command that returns both tapes to the selected edit points.) With JUMP you could go back to the original points if you were dissatisfied with your original "in" and "out" point selections and wanted to readjust them.

PREVIEW makes the machines rehearse the edit. The machines will roll back a few seconds from the edit points, automatically roll the tapes so that they get up to speed, and show what the edit will look like. But the preview control won't record the edit. It's purely for checking your "in" and "out" points.

PERFORM makes the edit. Using the preselected "in" and "out" points, the perform control copies the selected portion of the source VTR to the record VTR.

REVIEW lets you admire your work. It backs up the tapes and lets you see the last edit to confirm that the edit was in the right place—properly timed. The review function also lets you determine whether the edit is technically perfect.

That is the basic mechanism by which the off-line editing unit operates. It is a simple process, really: You select the "in" and "out" points you would like to copy from one tape to another and the machine does the rest.

Off-line editing will always have a place in many aspects of television production. For one thing, off-line units are much less expensive than on-line configurations, and for many purposes off-line units perform adequately. News pieces, for example, are typically cuts-only production, and editing suites in news operations (Figure 11.7) very often utilize an off-line unit.

Off-line editing is also used as a "rehearsal" for the on-line process. Often, producers will edit the show, using only cuts, in the off-line suite and then do the final edit in the on-line facility. Although this may seem like doing the same job twice, it's not. Off-line suites are much less expensive to rent or operate on a per-hour basis than on-line suites, and having all the edit decisions made and logged in advance can result in considerable savings.

Many producers, who work on all different sorts of videotapes, are computerizing their postproduction process. This enables an off-line edit session using their personal computer and consumer-level video equipment in their own office. Using the computer provides them with a standardized Edit Decision List on disk or paper, enabling the producers to be very prepared for their on-line edit session.

An On-Line Editing System

The best way to begin an explanation of an on-line system is to show how the on-line edit control unit is integrated

Figure 11.7 A news editing bay. Much news editing is performed on a "cuts-only" (off-line) system. The edit controller (1) links the source VTRs (2 and 3) and the record VTR (4). A time base corrector/frame synchronizer (5) provides simple effects, like freeze frame.

with the switcher and the electronic "brains" that govern the unit. The bank of machines to the far left of the schematic in Figure 11.8 shows the various sources that might be used as inputs for the on-line suite. Virtually any video source can be used, but here we've shown a setup that includes two ¾-inch VCRs, a Hi8 VTR, and two auxiliary inputs, one of which is a computer for generating graphics. Moving along the video signal path, you'll note that a sync generator keeps all the units in synchronization.

Signals are controlled by the **central processing unit (CPU)** of the computer that controls the switcher and the edit control unit. There is also, in this particular configuration, a personal computer included in the system. The PC creates graphics and sound effects.

You'll notice that the on-line edit control unit has a monitor attached. This is not a video monitor (we haven't shown the video monitors in Figure 11.8 in order to keep the illustration relatively uncluttered); it's a monitor for displaying the graphic commands (the menu) entered through the edit control unit.

Farther downstream is an audio console and, at the very end of the chain, a record VTR. Figure 11.8 shows a 1-inch reel-to-reel machine, a common type of record unit in high-end suites.

The point of this conglomeration of equipment is to allow us to use many sources and—thanks to the inclusion of the switcher in the signal flow—to use dissolves, wipes, and other special effects.

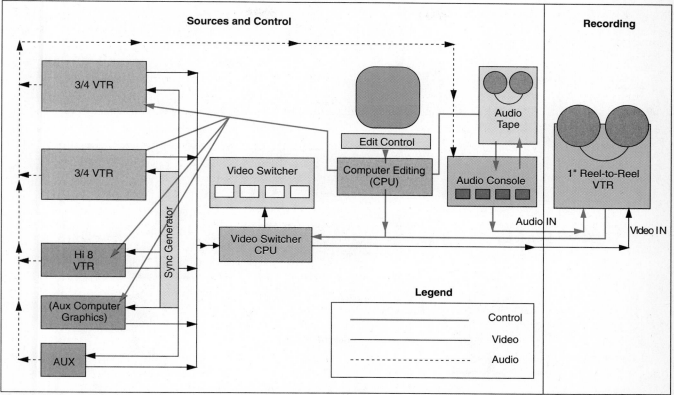

Figure 11.8 On-line system. The on-line edit configuration typically consists of several video and audio sources, a graphics generator, a sync generator, a video switcher, an audio console, and a recording VTR.

An On-Line Editing Control Unit

Now, a close-up look at the edit control unit itself. Figure 11.9 shows a hypothetical edit control unit designed to handle on-line editing. Here's a tour of the edit control unit. We won't mention or illustrate all the controls, but will refer to many of them in clusters.

Cluster 1: Transport Controls. The first cluster contains the transport drives. Whatever source is punched up on the top row will be controlled by the twist dial. The buttons are marked R VTR, P1, P2, for player 1, player 2, and so forth; they correspond to the units wired into the system. (Remember from Figure 11.8 that we have two ¾-inch VTRs, a Hi8 machine, and so forth. Some auxiliary inputs are also accessible via cluster 1.) Notice that on this unit you can select SHUTTLE, JOG, or CRAWL; each indicates a relative rate of speed, with shuttle being the fastest. (The three terms refer to the movement of tape from one speed to another.) These three controls allow you to scan the tape at a very rapid or very leisurely and precise pace.

Cluster 2: Function Controls. The function controls allow you to choose the assemble edit mode (this unit defaults on insert, meaning it starts in the insert mode and

will stay there unless instructed otherwise) as well as to choose which sources you want to use to make the edit (video, audio 1, audio 2, or any combination of the three.) The final button in this row, labeled "FIRST EDIT," is used to instruct the computer control that the edit to be listed next is the first in the entire sequence of events to be executed.

Cluster 3: Effects Selection Bank. The controls in the effects selection bank allow you to choose what sort of transition you want to use for each edit. You can select a cut, dissolve, wipe, and so forth. Your choice is translated into computer language and stored in memory.

Cluster 4: Edit Decision Point Bank. The edit decision point bank is similar in function to the off-line editor's "in" point and "out" point bank. The **mark in** control chooses the start of the edit point, and the **mark out** control selects the end. The mark split control allows you to split the audio and video signals and edit them separately. The all stop control does just what you would expect; it's useful when you have completed an edit on the fly and want everything to come to a halt.

Cluster 5: Edit Function Controls. There are too many edit function controls to illustrate individually, and

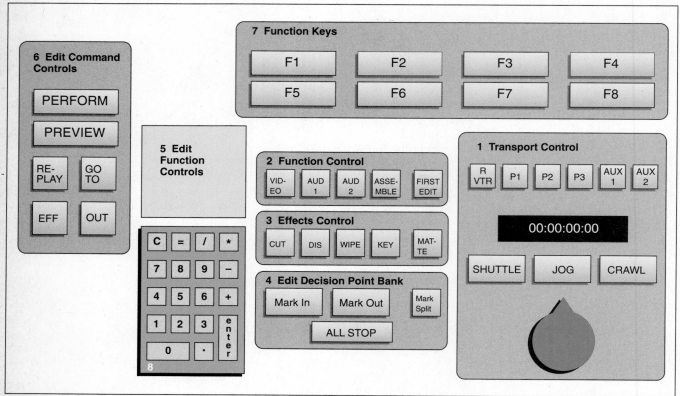

Figure 11.9 Hypothetical on-line edit control unit. The on-line edit control unit provides precise command over numerous video and audio sources. Time code provides accuracy to the frame.

they vary from unit to unit. Essentially, this bank of controls allows you to instruct the switcher about things such as the duration of dissolves or an automatic fade to black. On some machines it allows you to erase the last edit from the computer memory.

Cluster 6: Edit Command Controls. The controls in cluster 6 are reasonably similar to those in the off-line control track unit, but with some additional capabilities. For instance, EFF takes you back to the point of your last special effect. OUT shuttles everything to the point of the last edit.

Cluster 7: Function Keys. The function keys control a series of preprogrammed effects. You might, for example, preprogram a particular function key to interact with your switcher to create, automatically, a 30-frame wipe.

Cluster 8: Numeric Keypad. The numeric keypad allows you to enter the entry and exit points for various shots. If you know your SMPTE time code edit points already, you can enter the numbers into the computer memory without shuttling through the tape and manually setting "in" and "out" points.[2]

SAMPLE BASIC EDITING STRATEGIES

Following are three examples of how editing equipment can be utilized to create various short programs. First, however, here are two useful points to keep in mind:

- When you edit, think in **task-oriented sequence**; that is, remember that just because the program starts with scene A and moves to scene B and then to scene C, you don't have to edit in that order. Rather, execute your edit according to the most convenient method for performing the physical editing process. Likewise, you may want to edit several programs at once in task-oriented sequence.

    Suppose, for example, that all involve voice overs which will be recorded as the first step of the editing process, with video added later. Instead of doing program 1 and the voice over, and then program 2 and the voice over, and then program 3 and the voice over, it may be easier to do *all voice overs on the same day.* You won't have to continually reset the equipment to record the voice overs, and perhaps you'll even be using the same announcer and you can keep him or her on mic and save the announcer several trips.

Break free from old thought habits! Don't work according to the sequence of the eventual program. Work in the sequence that is most convenient for you.

- Lay down audio and video in the sequence that will make editing easier. Editing often involves a "chicken and egg" dilemma: which comes first, audio or video? In other words, do you record audio first and then put video over it, or do you work the other way?

The simple answer is that both methods can work and that you are free to use whichever seems more convenient and appropriate. Most news stories, for example, typically are constructed by recording the audio voice over first (in the segments that involve voice over—we're not talking about the interviews) and then laying video down over the voice. This helps to appropriately match audio and video, as discussed in Chapter 10.

But narrations for instructional tapes often have the audio recorded as the last step. It is frequently necessary for the narrator to *see* the picture as he or she reads the script so that the narration can be more precisely matched to the action. It is much easier for a skilled announcer to match a series of precise instructions ("Now, remove the control panel and insert the testing probe into the . . .") than to attempt to match many video shots to a previously recorded narration. On occasion, you may wish to add one audio source, such as voice, to one channel, and another audio source (music, perhaps) to another channel). Many editors, especially if a rhythm is desired, record their music and edit to that.

With those points in mind, let's follow three editing processes: a basic news package, a simple commercial, and a complex promotional announcement featuring an A-B roll and special effects. The strategy for the news package involves standard cuts-only editing with a video-only edit. The commercial is structured as an edited voice over. And the promotional announcement is created as an A-B roll piece. After you have reviewed the sample edits, you may also want to read Box 11.1, which spells out some tips relevant to all types of editing.

Cuts-Only Editing with a Video-Only Edit

A reporter returns from the scene of a fire with these shots on tape:

- A stand-up close in which the reporter briefly states that investigation is continuing into the fire, and signs off, "This is Joe Johnson reporting for WXXX News." Johnson made three takes of the close. Take 3 is best. Note that the close was done *before the opening.* This is not an uncommon practice. In this case, the reporter did the close first because he was waiting to find out the name of the heroic fire fighter that he wants to use in the open. The closing lines did not require the name of the fire fighter.

- A stand-up open in which the reporter speaks to the camera, telling viewers that a heroic fire fighter single-handedly dragged two unconscious victims from a burning building. The reporter made three takes. The editing log indicates that take 1 is the best.

- A 2-minute interview with the fire fighter.

- Some general cover video of the fire scene.

The reporter wants to produce a **package**—a news segment containing several scenes and some narration either on or off camera by the reporter.

On the way back to the station, the reporter/producer reviews his shots and makes notes of the best takes, the segment of the interview he plans to use, and the most dramatic cover footage. He writes down the "in" and "out" points of each take on his editing log.

When he returns to the station, the reporter is under pressure to edit the piece in time for air. Because of careful logging, however, the construction of the package will be relatively easy. (See Figure 11.10, which shows a cuts-only edit with a video segment superimposed.)

1. *Lay down black.* The first step is to lay down black on the record unit tape. (Many stations do this in advance and keep a stock of tapes with black already laid down.) Now, in the insert edit mode, the reporter instructs the editing control unit that this will be a video and audio edit.

2. *Edit the opening.* The reporter finds the opening segment he wants, cues it up on the source unit, places the black tape in the record unit, and sets the "in" and "out" points on the source tape. The "in" point on the source tape is the start of the best opening. The "in" point of the record unit tape is generally at the beginning; it doesn't really matter as long as the final tape can be rewound to the beginning.

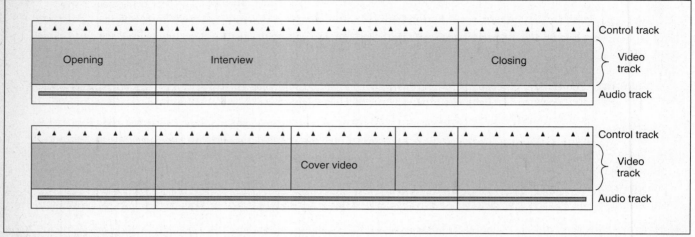

Figure 11.10 Inserting a video-only cover shot. In insert mode, the editor cuts together both the audio and video portions of the opening, interview, and closing (upper tape). Then, to cover the discussion of the fire during the interview, a video-only segment is inserted (lower tape). Note that the audio track of the interview segment is not disturbed.

The reporter previews the edit, decides he likes it, and makes the edit.

3. *Edit the interview.* The reporter uses 15 seconds of the 2-minute interview with the fire fighter. He sets the "in" point at the segment where he wants the interview to begin, and the "out" point at what he deems to be the appropriate place to close the interview. The reporter then cues up the record unit tape to the *end of the opening segment* and marks the "in" point. He previews the edit, likes what he sees, and performs the edit. Now, the fire fighter interview segment is joined to the opening on the record unit tape.

4. *Edit the close.* The reporter cues up the record unit tape to the end of the interview, marks the new "in" point, finds the best-looking close on the source tape, and marks the source "in" point. He then forwards the source tape to the end of the stand-up close, allowing several seconds of cushion at the end. He marks the source "out" point and performs the edit.

5. *Edit video-only cover of the fire.* Finally, the reporter executes a video-only edit to cover some of the fire fighter's interview segment. Specifically, he wants to illustrate references to the fire. He sets the "in" and "out" points on the record unit tape, sets the "in" point on the source unit tape deck (which contains the tape that is cued up to the fire footage) and does a video-only edit. The video-only edit is accomplished by de-selecting the audio edit buttons in cluster 3) (see Figure 11-9.)

Note that we have assumed that the edit was done on a record unit tape that had black laid down, and therefore was made entirely in the insert mode. But you could make

the first three edits in the assemble mode, with the fourth insert being accomplished in the insert mode.

An Edited Voice-Over

The producer wants to show the following scene as part of a tape produced to demonstrate to computer novices how to insert a floppy disk and start the software. The sequence is three shots:

- The computer user sits down at the terminal.
- She inserts the floppy disk into the side opening of the computer.
- She presses ENTER on the computer keyboard.

Using a cuts-only system (see Figure 11.11), the editor constructs the piece by editing video first, making sure that the first shot is relatively wide, showing the computer operator and the computer. The second shot is a medium close-up of the slot into which the disk will slide; it is taken from a slightly different angle, and the camera operator zooms in tightly to show the disk being inserted into the slot. The final shot is a direct view of the keyboard in close-up, showing the operator pressing the enter key.

Note that the shots are planned to first show the overall perspective. Details are shown in close-up, but before we see the close-ups—the slot and the keyboard—we are first shown overall perspective and scale.

Now the narration is added. A narrator, watching the video, reads the script. The portion of the script that covers the three shots is: "You start the program by inserting the disk and pressing the enter key. Here, the operator sits at the terminal and inserts the disk into the slot . . . pushing it in until it clicks. Now, by pressing the enter key, the software is loaded."

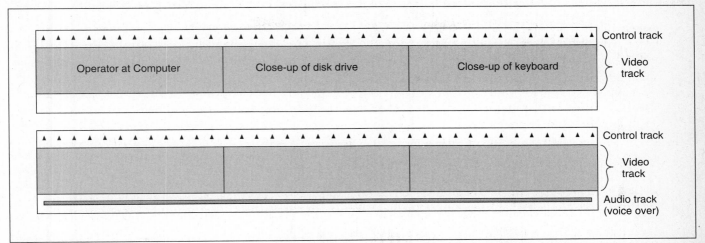

Figure 11.11 Inserting a voice over. The video sequences are cut together first as video-only edits (upper tape). Then the narration is laid over in the audio insert mode (lower tape).

The narrator is recorded on a multitrack audio console. Music from an LP record specifically designed for industrial soundtrack background is mixed on another track. The multitrack console allows the producer to play back each track—the announcer's voice and the music—separately. Each source comes up on a different pot (volume control) so that the proper balance can be maintained. After determining that balance, the editor cues the audio tape to its beginning, the record unit videotape to its beginning, and does an audio-only edit. Thus, the new audio track is dubbed onto the existing tape. This audio track is known as a voice over.

Note that it was convenient, in this case, for the narration to be recorded after the video was edited. There were many cases where the narrator needed to directly refer to the action, a much easier chore when the tape is playing as the narrator reads the script.

A Sample A-B Roll Edit

The producer wants to create the following: A fade up from black to a computer graphic, a tumbling "6". The "6" tumbles into its final position, and the computer graphic shows the words: "Coming Attractions: Tonight's Major Movie."

The shot then dissolves to a prerecorded tape of an announcer, who talks for 20 seconds about tonight's movie. Then, we dissolve to 25 seconds of edited clips from the movie. Finally, the spot finishes by dissolving back to 5 seconds of graphics, and then fades to black.

This complex series of events is accomplished by programming all transitions in advance through the SMPTE-controlled edit control unit. The unit will engineer dissolves between the computer and the two videotapes (the tape of the announcer and the tape of the clips from the movie).

The following describes the sequence of events you might use if you were creating this promo with the system sketched out in Figure 11.9. On-line editing is a fairly advanced function that requires specific instruction and experience at the controls of the particular machine. But if you have access to the equipment, your instructor can lead you through this or a similar sequence to demonstrate the concepts hands-on.

The ability to program a decision list lets the computer do most of the work and allows you greater flexibility in the editing process. For example, by issuing the proper command to the computer, you can insert a segment in the middle of a program. The updated computer list would then drive the editing process.

Such a "nonlinear" capability frees you to make extensive revisions without having to repeat the whole program from the point of the new edit until the end.

Programming a Transition. You'll repeat this step for each edit, but we won't bother listing the action in the following description.

1. *Set the effects type.* Select DISSOLVE from the buttons in cluster 2. The computer will prompt you for the source of the first edit: "From = ?"

2. *Set the source of the first edit.* Enter AUX, the control into which we've wired our graphics-producing computer. The computer will prompt you for the next shot: "To = ?"

3. *Set the source of the next edit.* You want to dissolve to the first ¾-inch VTR (see Figure 11.8), which is wired into P2 in cluster 1 (Figure 11.9). You would press that

source button and the command would be entered into memory. Now, the computer wants to know how long the transition will be. It prompts you: "Transition = ?"

4. *Set the transition rate.* Using the numeric keypad in cluster 8, enter the number of frames. Let's make it 15. Type "15" and press the enter key.

Programming "In" and "Out" Points. Now, you'll mark the "in" and "out" points of your sources.

1. *Mark the start point of the record VTR.* Position the record tape to two seconds past the countdown and press MARK IN from cluster 4.

2. *Indicate the source and duration of the first edit.* Select AUX (the computer) as a source in cluster 1. A computer source must be set by a control called "SET DURATION," which is located in cluster 5. Because there are no SMPTE time code numbers associated with the computer, you enter in the actual time, 5 seconds, on the numeric keypad in cluster 8. In this case, you would key it in as "05:00."

3. *Program the "in" and "out" points for the remaining shots; then program transitions before each shot.* Let's assume

that we know all the time codes for the tapes. Set their "in" and "out" cues on the numeric keypad. (You can also accomplish this by shuttling the tapes and using the MARK IN and MARK OUT commands in cluster 4.)

Remember, you can determine the duration of the tape segments by entering the time codes. But when you use a computer, you are dealing with a "live" source and you must set the durations in real time.

Modifying the Program. Suppose there's something we forgot: We want the tape to fade in and fade out to black. We can go back in the edit decision list and add a fade up from black command at the beginning.

Setting Function Controls, Previewing, and Performing the Edits. Keys in cluster 3 allow you to indicate that this will be a video and audio edit. You're now ready to see the edit. Press the preview button in cluster 6 and the entire sequence will play out before you. If you'd like to fine-tune, you can readjust the "in" and "out" points. But if the preview looks OK, press the perform button in cluster 6.

SUMMARY

1. Assemble editing allows you to lay down edits in linear sequence. That is, you must lay down segment one, segment two, segment three, and so on in that order. You are also copying everything, including all audio and video and the control track.

2. Insert editing allows you to include segments out of linear order and insert any portion of the signal you want—video, audio 1, audio 2, or any combination of the three.

3. One way to make your editing much easier is to log shots carefully. What may seem easy to remember at the time is sometimes difficult to remember hours or days after, and you can waste a lot of time trying to find the shot you want if you haven't kept accurate records.

4. Your editing also will be simpler if you keep the process in mind and shoot for the edit. This involves paying special attention to the graphics, continuity,

the video needed to cover jump cuts, consistency of time and location, and consistency of the point of view.

5. *Off-line editing* is a term usually taken to mean cuts-only editing done as a workprint. *On-line editing* usually means editing done through an edit control unit *and* a switcher; the final product is edited on-line.

6. Cuts-only, off-line edit control units are fairly straightforward. They allow you to enter "in" points and "out" points and copy selected portions of the source unit tape to the record unit tape.

7. On-line units, which allow you to do dissolves, are driven by a series of commands entered into the CPU of the unit's computer. On-line systems typically utilize more than two VTRs, making A/B rolls possible. The operator programs the type of transition and source for each shot.

NOTES

1. For a comprehensive discussion of cuts-only editing, see Ronald J. Compesi and Ronald E. Sheffirrs, *Small Format Television Production* (Needham Heights, MA: Allyn and Bacon, 1990), 303–327.

2. An interesting way to find your time code "in" and "out" points is to make what's called a "window dub" of your tape: a copy of the raw footage that also displays the time code in

a rectangular "window" when the tape is played back on a standard VCR. (Your facility's engineer will let you know if window dubs are possible and if so, how to make them.) The window dub can be edited on a cuts-only machine (off-line) so that you can see an approximation of the final tape *and* read the time code numbers.

TECHNICAL TERMS

central processing unit (CPU)	"in" point	"out" point	task-oriented sequence
continuity	jump cut	package	trim
edit	log	shot sheet	wheel numbers
editing log	mark in	shuttle	workprint
go to	mark out	spot sheet	

EXERCISES

1. Describe a series of at least five shots showing the operation of some item with which you are relatively familiar. Some suggestions:

   • How to start a lawn mower

   • How to change lenses on a 35mm SLR camera

   • How to program a home VCR

   Your goal is to invent a series of scenes that are instructive and show the overall perspective of the device as well as the details.

2. Now, using your description of the scenes from exercise 1, draw, to the best of your artistic ability, the scene as you visualize it on the video monitor. This exercise in visualization will help you determine whether your edits are graceful and appropriate. What you are doing, in actuality, is a technique known as storyboarding, a common practice in TV scripting. We're not concerned with the niceties of storyboarding here; all we want are rough sketches for the purposes of instruction in editing. We will, though, examine storyboarding in Chapter 12.

audio operations

OBJECTIVES

After completing Chapter 12, you will be able to:

1. Select and use the appropriate mics, and make audio operations an integral part of the overall thrust of your program.
2. Operate the console during a complex live show or taping.
3. Ensure "quality control" over the audio signal and troubleshoot problems.

Audio can make or break a production, and the audio director bears a heavy responsibility before and during the program. The stress level is high because mics must be opened and closed precisely on time, and theme music, sound effects, and other audio elements must run precisely when scheduled.

Having said that, it's worth noting that the audio director's job is an exciting one. He or she is squarely in the middle of the program, coordinating inputs, balancing outputs, and making sure everything goes well. In addition, a good audio director will be highly valued by the director and the rest of the crew. Not many people take the time to learn the audio job fully. Those who do are welcome on any video crew.

This chapter will build on the audio tools discussion presented in Chapter 5. It will examine mic selection and placement, console operation, and audio quality control.

MIC SELECTION AND PLACEMENT

Before the show begins, the audio director will have overseen the entire process of placing mics, wiring them up, and checking the proper levels before airtime. Avoiding audio meltdowns during a program or taping is really more a matter of preparation than execution.

Choosing the Correct Mic

Your choice will frequently be limited by what's available, but you'll usually have a variety of mics from which to choose—and it's up to you to make the right selection.

Lavaliere versus Hand-Held and Mounted Mics. Generally, a lavaliere will give you excellent audio quality and control, but there are certain circumstances that make lav use impractical. One is continuity. For example, if you were shooting a scene of a woman riding toward you on a horse, it would be illogical to edit together shots of her (a) riding through two miles of open range, (b) approaching the camera, and (c) talking to the camera—with a lavaliere suddenly stuck to her shirt. (The problem is obviously compounded if the scene was supposed to be taking place in the 1890s.) Likewise, you can't use lavalieres when guests are walking on and off a set. Sometimes there are too many people on the set and you won't have enough lavalieres or enough pots to wire them into; in that case, you'll have to use mics to cover several speakers at a time.

Wireless lavalieres (Figure 12.1) can alleviate many of the problems associated with a trailing wire. You may

Figure 12.1 The wireless microphone. The wireless microphone frees talent from the restrictions of cable length and its unsightly appearance. (Courtesy of Telex Communications, Inc.)

not have access to wireless lavalieres; they are expensive and are relatively scarce in small video operations. Also, remember that wireless mics can pick up stray transmissions from other sources. Even if you have wireless mics, be sure to pack hard-wired gear in case you encounter this problem.

In any event, don't assume that lavalieres are only for indoor, in-studio work. Many performers doing outdoor stand-ups and interviews now prefer to use lavalieres instead of a hand-held mic. Lavalieres are less conspicuous and distracting and also can be shaded from the wind by the performer's body.

The Right Mic to Avoid Noise Interference. You need to invest some thought in mic selection when you're working on remote. In noisy situations—and most remotes are surprisingly noisy—a directional mic is a good choice. Working outdoors often requires a **wind filter** (Figure 12.2) to keep the air current from producing a constant rumble as it blows across the diaphragm.

Figure 12.2 Wind filter. The rubber wind filter protects the microphone from the wind, which would produce a constant rumble blowing across the diaphragm. (Courtesy of Shure Brothers, Inc.)

Mic Placement

As any golfer or tennis player knows all too well, a fine piece of equipment does not guarantee good results. After you have chosen the right mic, you need to keep the mic (and its shadow) out of camera range, make sure that the mic will not be subject to bumping or friction noise, and ensure that the mic is placed close enough to the source to produce an adequate signal-to-noise ratio.

Keep the Mic Out of Camera Range. If you are using a boom or fishpole, be sure you don't cause a shadow or—worse—drop the mic into the frame of the camera. **Boom shadows**, which result when a mic boom gets between the lighting instruments and the part of the set that is shown on camera, are deceptively troublesome. That's one reason why lavalieres have come into such common use. It is difficult to find a spot in which you can position a boom or pole without casting a shadow *somewhere* that might be picked up at *some time* during the program.

When you set up a boom, ask the director to check the shots in all the cameras. If there's a shadow problem, you can either move the boom or move the lighting instrument, but don't try to blast the background with extra light to eliminate the shadow. That just doesn't work.

You need to know what the camera shots will be in order to keep the boom out of those shots. That sounds simple enough, but often a lack of communication between the director and the audio director fails to clear this up at the start of the program. If that's the case, the problem usually persists throughout the whole production.

With news coverage, you don't really care if the boom/pole/mic dips into the picture or casts a shadow. In fact, some news organizations go out of their way to thrust their mic (which of course carries the station's logo on its **flag**) into the frame. But studio work is another matter. If you're moving the mic on a controllable boom, especially when people on set are moving, there's a good chance that it will be seen by the camera unless logistics are worked out beforehand.

Even then, problems remain. When the director says, "I'm not going to be shooting any higher than the top of the railing," that may not be of much help to the person running the boom because he or she doesn't have the right perspective to judge how the geometry of the camera shot works out. The boom may be 15 feet closer to the camera than the railing, throwing off the operator's perspective.

One method of keeping the mic out of the camera is to have a monitor clearly visible to the boom operator. Of course, that only solves the problem after it's occurred, but with practice a boom operator can learn to spot just the tiniest infringement of the mic into the picture and can quickly adjust before the viewer can see the mic.

One frustrated audio director went so far as to hang a tennis ball from the lighting grid and announce that the ball represented the lowest level of the mic; that served as a realiable reference for the boom operator and the director. Although not typical industry practice, you might give this a try.

Avoid Bumping and Friction Noise. Try not to place lavs under clothing. It muffles the sound. Also, don't clip a mic where it is likely to come into contact with dangling jewelry.

Desktop mics are handy under certain conditions, but be careful when you are dealing with amateur performers, such as guests on a community panel discussion. It's not unusual for amateurs to tap the table, or the mic, or both. Tapping is greatly magnified by vibrations through the table and the desk stand. Some inexperienced performers may even grab the mic and slide it, which generally creates an incredibly distracting rumble.

Produce Adequate Signal. As already discussed in Chapter 5, audio must have an adequate signal-to-noise ratio. The signal is the sound you want; noise is unwanted sound.

Signal-to-noise ratio is most commonly used as a measure of the efficiency of audio recording and processing equipment, but it is equally appropriate to consider the signal-to-noise ratio when using a mic.

An obvious (but sometimes overlooked) principle of placing a mic is this: *The greater the distance between the person or other sound source you are miking and the mic, the more ambient (random) noise that will be picked up by the mic.*

How far away should a mic be? That depends partly on the mic, of course. Shotgun mics are meant to be used from a distance, and the only answer in the case of a shotgun is, "as close as you can get without being in the picture." Hand-held mics work well if they're held about 6 inches from the mouth, but in noisy or windy conditions performers may need to put the mic an inch or two from their mouths. Lavalieres are usually placed 3½ to 5 inches below the chin, although there's no hard-and-fast rule (Figure 12.3). Just don't put the lav so far from the speaker's mouth that it produces a muffled sound. Also, a lav that is placed too low on a performer's body is more likely to be struck by a hand or arm.

When miking any scene from a distance with any type of mic, you'll need to use your ears as well as your eyes. How the mic sounds is the final criterion of placement. If the sound is too hollow and weak, you'll have to come up with an alternative that allows you to move the mic closer.

CONSOLE OPERATION

When you take the controls of the audio console during studio operations, you'll be primarily responsible for:

- Bringing up audio sources when they're supposed to be on the air (or going to tape) and making sure they are *not* up on the board when they're not supposed to be.

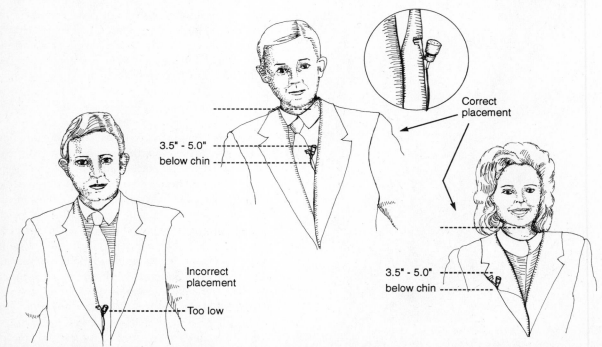

Figure 12.3 Positioning the lavaliere mic. Although the lavaliere mic is compact, it is very sensitive and fairly directional. The proper position for the lavaliere is 3½ to 5 inches from the chin. (Courtesy of Shure Brothers, Inc.)

• Making sure that the sound quality is acceptable and at the proper level on the VU meter.

Although this section primarily deals with console operations during studio work, it does have some application to remote operations. Note that in some cases you will be mixing sources in the field with a **portable mixer** (Figure 12.4), which is a miniature console.

Most console operations are centered around the studio audio area, where the console and other audio equipment, such as cartridge machines, CD players, reel-to-reel tape decks, and audiocassettes are located. Sometimes the audio area is physically separated from the rest of the control room—with noise barriers in place—and sometimes not. In any event, your most fundamental duties at the console involve setting levels, opening and closing audio sources, and riding levels during the program.

Setting Levels

As described in Chapter 5, a console operator is responsible for making sure that sources are mixed properly and that they do not overmodulate.

In order to start the program without any unpleasant surprises (such as a booming, overmodulated mic level), you must take levels before the show. (You will also take a level on remote, even if it is only one person speaking into a mic; you must know, in advance, the approximate setting to be used for mic level.)

Getting a mic level is sometimes difficult. Setting levels for other audio sources, such as theme music from an audiotape, is easier, but remember that you must be prepared to drop the introductory music when a mic opens. Mixing full music (0 dB) and full mic (0 dB) will not work; the performer's voice will be drowned out. Getting the level means gauging how loudly the performer will be speaking—you need to know the approximate position of the pot so that you can begin the show at close to the right level. You'll make adjustments from time to time, but it's important to set levels in order to avoid having the performer's first remark sound like a shout or a whisper.

Usually, the audio director will ask the floor director

to have each person on mic "give a level." The floor director will then ask the performer to "say something." That works well with experienced professionals, who will usually read from their script in a normal tone of voice or take the opportunity to rehearse their opening lines. But an inexperienced performer will invariably ask, "What am I supposed to say?" He or she might then say "hello" a couple of times, which will be useless to you since it won't be in a normal tone of voice and you probably won't have found the pot yet, anyway.

A reasonable alternative is to ask each miked performer (except the professionals) to count to twenty. This guarantees you enough time to find the pot and get a rough level. You can also use pretaping rehearsals, if there are any, to take levels.

Opening and Closing Audio Sources

The most common action an audio console operator performs during a video program involves the opening and closing of mics. In general, you want to keep as many unused mics closed as possible. But during a talk show you cannot be expected to shut off and turn on the mics of each individual as the conversation evolves. That's just impossible, and you'll inevitably wind up cutting people off.

But you will want to turn the mic off on the board when a performer won't be on air for an extended period of time. For example, if you are the audio director during a newscast, you won't want the sports announcer's mic up on the board until immediately before he or she goes on the air. For one thing, if the sports announcer won't be saying anything, you'll simply be putting extra room noise over the air. Secondly, the sports announcer usually leaves the set during the newscast to check on late-breaking scores. You *certainly* don't want the mic up when the sports announcer is clipping it to his or her lapel. So use common sense when determining whether to close a mic or keep it open.

Here are two suggestions for making mic pots easier to identify:

1. Number mics logically, perhaps in the order of their use.

2. Label a mic pot with the name of the person speaking into it.

Running an audio console is something like playing pool: You must think several shots ahead. The director is supposed to give you ready cues ("stand by to bring up theme"), but in the real world, that doesn't always happen. You must be prepared to have the right cart or turntable ready to go, and have your hand on the right pot, when the director suddenly commands: "Theme!" without giving you a ready cue.

Figure 12.4 Portable audio mixer. Portable microphone and audio mixers typically allow only four to eight inputs but are small enough for field production. (Courtesy of Shure Brothers, Inc.)

Riding Levels

Keep your eye on the VU during the program. People's voice levels change as the show progresses. An obvious example is when a shouting match breaks out during a talk show. **Riding levels** means making frequent adjustments so that audio levels do not go too high or too low.

One particularly difficult aspect of riding levels involves the mix of voice and music (Figure 12.5). This most commonly occurs during the opening and closing of a program—times when many concurrent events are occurring, which means a higher likelihood of error.

It's a good idea to rehearse the opening so that you don't add to the general confusion. Consider this common scenario:

• Theme music starts on the director's cue.

Figure 12.5 A studio audio mixer. Monitoring each of the audio channels is necessary to achieve a well-balanced mix.

BOX 12.1 AUDIO TROUBLESHOOTING

PROBLEM: *Weak, buzzing, or otherwise strangely distorted sound from the mic*

You may have what's called an "impedance mismatch." Most high-quality mics are low **impedance**, meaning they offer low electrical resistance to the current. But if you have a high impedance mic, it won't function correctly when plugged into the console. Change the mics or seek engineering help to match the impedance.

PROBLEM: *"Buzzing" audio*

If impedance is not the problem, you may be overmodulating. Check the VU meter.

PROBLEM: *"Humming" audio*

There is probably interference from a lighting fixture or some other electrical installation. Move the mics and wires until the hum goes away. (Audio cables should only cross AC lines at right angles, 90°, to minimize interference. Don't run audio cables parallel to other wiring.)

PROBLEM: *"Crackling" audio*

You may have a broken wire in the mic itself or a bad cable. Switch the cable and/or mic. If you're in a hurry, switch both immediately and do the detective work later.

PROBLEM: *No audio from one component*

If a piece of equipment fails to put out any sound, it may be "patched out" (disconnected) on the patch bay. Check to see whether there are any patch cords rerouting the signal. Sometimes, a lavaliere mic will go dead because

its battery has discharged. Replace the battery; make sure you keep an adequate supply on hand.

PROBLEM: *Some mics don't seem to put out adequate volume in multiple-mic setups*

You've probably encountered what's called a **phasing problem** (**phase** is the motion of a wave—here, a sound wave). When microphones pick up sound signals at slightly different times, they can, under certain circumstances, cancel out each others' signals. What happens is that the positive and negative portions of the sound cycles are being picked up out of phase with each other and are being added; when you add a positive and a negative signal, your output is reduced. The solution usually involves moving the mics around a bit; even a couple of inches can solve phasing problems. Experiment until you get equal-quality signals from all mics. (Some audio boards have phase reversing switches to correct phasing problems.) If that doesn't work, the mic may be defective. In that case, replace it.

PROBLEM: *No audio at all*

Check the board power. Sometimes the power supply to the board is cut off by a circuit breaker, a separate switch, or the power switch on the board. Many people, even some who should know better, aren't aware that audio consoles have power switches, probably because those power switches are hidden in out-of-the way spots that are further hidden, or sometimes made almost inaccessible, when the board and other equipment is installed.

- Theme music is brought down and the talent is cued.
- Talent speaks over theme music for several seconds, until theme is dropped out completely.

How far do you bring down the theme music in order to achieve a proper mix of voice and music? Unfortunately, there's no standard formula. It's almost entirely a matter of judgment. The only realistic advice we can offer is to rehearse the mix in advance and prepare to move to those settings quickly. (You can mark the level of the music and voice pots on vertical faders with a piece of masking tape.)

When setting levels for a voice-music mix, you'll want to have the music level high enough so that it can be heard, but not so high that it drowns out the talent. Again, this is a matter of judgment and practice, but there is one constant: *Under all circumstances, be sure that you have lowered the music pot to whatever level you deem proper before talent starts speaking.* Drowning out talent's first words gives an amateurish cast to the opening of a show. And a fouled-up opening sets a terrible tone for the rest of the show.

A related point: Music is an intrinsic part of many video programs, and production personnel frequently invest a great deal of time in choosing and sometimes comparing music that reinforces the theme of the program.

Controlling Audio Quality

The most immediate concern in audio quality control is to avoid careless mistakes. Make sure pots are completely closed. Be sure you know who is on which mic. And don't put off mic checks until the last minute; 30 seconds before tape roll is the wrong time to discover that you "can't find" mic 1.

Beyond that, there are some typical problems that are not the result of simple carelessness. *Weak audio* and *improper levels* can arise because of technical problems peculiar to your particular situation or because of the actions of talent.

Overcoming a Weak Audio Signal. There are occasions when you *must* move a mic closer. Don't sacrifice sound quality for an easy shot. Feeble, hollow audio is the hallmark of cheaply produced, poor-quality video.

But frequently distance is not the problem; sometimes you need *more* mics. Although you can use two strategically placed mics to cover a panel discussion among six people, this may not work under less than ideal conditions. One of the conditions is when people on the same mic speak at drastically different volumes. Here, you have no choice but to reposition mics and pots and then "get a level" on the performer(s).

Troubleshooting. Sometimes you apparently will do everything right, but the audio will come out wrong—or not at all. When that happens, don't panic. By adopting a logical and orderly mindset, you can often play detective and track down the cause of your difficulty. Box 12.1 contains a troubleshooting chart, should you encounter a mysterious problem.

SUMMARY

1. The audio director is responsible for choosing the correct mic for the job and placing mics correctly. Although there are a variety of factors to be considered when choosing which mic to use and where to place it, the most important is how good the sound quality is. Don't let arbitrary rules as to mic placement divert you from your essential task: to produce a good-quality audio signal.

2. When using a boom or fishpole, be sure you don't cause a shadow or let the mic dip into the picture. Keeping good lines of communication open with the director can usually solve this problem.

3. When you run the console, your primary responsibilities are to bring the proper sound sources up at the right time and eliminate them when they are no longer needed. You also must keep an eye on the riding levels—also called ride gain—to make sure you're not "in the red" (too high, in the red part of the volume-unit meter) or too low, "in the mud."

4. There are a number of problems that can surprise the unsuspecting audio director. Among them are buzzing, humming, and crackling audio—most of which can be traced back to specific problems with the equipment. Be particularly aware of mysterious phasing problems, when mics suddenly become "weak" for no apparent reason in multiple-mic setups. Phasing problems, caused by sound interference and cancellation, can often be cured by changing the positions of the mics.

TECHNICAL TERMS

boom shadows
flag

impedance
phase, phasing problem

portable mixer
riding levels

wind filter
wireless

EXERCISES

1. Catalog the mics you have available in your studio and remote kit. Make a list of their physical types, pickup patterns, and pickup elements. Also, *try* each mic and list what you subjectively and objectively believe to be its particular quality. Does it produce audio that seems "thin" or "rich"? Does it hiss? Does it seem muffled?

   Compiling this list will be instructive, *and* the list itself will be quite useful in future audio operations.

2. Take control of the audio console and start a program. Follow this scenario precisely:

   • Begin with 5 seconds of music up full.

   • Drop the music and bring up the announcer on the director's cue.

   • The announcer reads: "Good afternoon, I'm _____ and this is Money Matters. This week, we'll look at the problem of student aid . . . how do you get it, how [*have music dropped completely out by now*] much can you get, and what strings are attached. Our guest is Tom Morrison, director of . . .

Everyone should run through this exercise, and if possible *record* the opening. Then listen to each other's openings and critique the "sound."

scripting for video

OBJECTIVES

After completing Chapter 13, you will be able to:

1. Use standard script formats.
2. Coordinate audio (including narration) and video into your script.
3. Write a comprehensive script for video that expresses a cohesive theme.

Putting words on paper is one of the most important facets of video production. All the high-tech hardware in the world cannot compensate for clumsy expression on the part of the scriptwriter.

This chapter, which offers an introduction to writing for video, will help you

- Gain a basic understanding of script formats
- Learn the fundamental mechanical strategies of writing for video
- Explore some of the aesthetics of scripting, the way words and pictures interact to express an idea coherently and evocatively

SCRIPT FORMATS

First, be aware that no two people or organizations use exactly the same formula for putting a script on paper. Details will vary significantly. But in general, you will encounter two primary structures: the two-column video script and the film-style script. A third type of script, which includes drawings to represent the pictures on screen, is called a storyboard and is often used to prepare short pieces, such as commercials.

The Two-Column Video Script

The **two-column script** format is used for most nondramatic video programs. The left-hand column contains technical instructions, primarily camera shots and movements, along with descriptions of the motion of talent. The right-hand column contains audio, such as dialogue and description of music or other sounds.

A page from a two-column script used in a news presentation is shown in Figure 13.1.

Some abbreviations in the script in Figure 13.1 may be familiar to you: **CU** is close-up, and **LS** is long shot. The abbreviation **VO** means voice-over. *VO* is used to show whenever anyone is speaking over an image other than his or her on-camera picture. **SOT** means **sound on tape**, a term which indicates that the actual audio on the videotape is what will go over the air. Using the abbreviation *SOT* is often helpful to the director because it lets him or her know that the audio from the videotape is that the viewer is supposed to hear. In one scene from Figure 13.1, for example, the viewer is watching pictures of the fire, but hears—*in the voice-over*—the anchor talking. The next scene shows an interview with the fire fighter and includes the audio from that interview too, meaning it is an SOT segment.

VO and SOT are common abbreviations, especially in news scripts. Abbreviations often used in all types of video scripts include those listed in Table 13.1.

Camera movements, which were first discussed in Chapter 2, are sometimes indicated on the left-hand side of the two-column script. But often, they are not because camera movements are typically left to the discretion of the director. Generally, camera movements are spelled out: zoom, dolly, pedestal, truck, or tilt, are examples. Occasionally, the transitions are spelled out too: fade, cut, dissolve.

External sources of audio and video are also frequently abbreviated, as shown in Table 13.1. None of the abbreviations in Table 13.1 apply specifically to news. Any type of video presentation can use these abbreviations and the spelled-out instructions. Figure 13.2, for example, shows part of an industrial script, a script prepared for a steak restaurant's training videotape, that uses many of the terms and abbreviations shown in Table 13.1.

Don't assume that a script that does not look like the examples shown here is somehow defective. There are many different methods to scripting. Some writers like to

VIDEO	AUDIO
CU ANCHOR TED	TED: City fire fighters call it a miracle . . . they report no injuries in a fire that consumed a ten-story office building this afternoon.
LS TILDEN BUILDING	TED (VO): The Tilden building, a landmark on the corner of Main and Delaware, erupted in flames shortly after two o'clock.
LS WORKERS EVACUATING	But all four hundred workers inside were able to safely evacuate . . . thanks, according to Fire Chief Tom O'Brien, to the fact that smoke detectors and sprinklers operated perfectly and gave the occupants of the building plenty of warning.
VTR O'BRIEN	O'BRIEN (SOT): It took about 20 minutes for what was a small garbage fire in the basement to start climbing up inside the walls. Nobody would have seen the flames until it was too late. But the smoke detectors went off right away, giving everyone plenty of time to clear the building. When the fire finally spread, it was like an explosion. If people had been in that building when the flames erupted, they never would have gotten out. No way.
CU ANCHOR TED	O'Brien says the cause of the fire has not yet been determined, but arson has not been ruled out.

Figure 13.1 A two-column news presentation script.

include every technical detail, including which camera will take the shot. (In most cases that's not really necessary, because a director can call shots.) On occasion, the script will also list various running times, either the times of inserted tapes or an overall chronological listing of when each event in the program is supposed to happen.

Table 13.1
Common Video Script Abbreviations

Abbreviation	Explanation
XLS	extreme long shot
LS	long shot
MS	medium shot
CU	close-up
XCU	extreme close-up
2S	two shot (a shot that includes two people, usually side-by-side)
OC	on camera (an old-fashioned term was MOC, "man on camera," which is now sometimes abbreviated AOC, "anchor on camera," or simply written out with the talent's name, "Bob OC")
OS	over-the-shoulder shot
SOT	sound on tape (a videotape played back with picture and sound)
VTR	videotape recorder or videotape recording
SFX	sound effects
VO	voice-over

But other scripts contain few technical instructions, and their authors may simply choose to write everything out in plain English. Instead of "LS fire screen zoom to CU," they might write, "wide shot of the fire, then zoom in closer."

Simple, plain-English scripts have decided advantages because they don't require a director, editor, or other crewperson to figure out an abbreviation that may be idiosyncratic to your style of writing or your department's script formatting guidelines.

The abbreviations used to indicate technical components of the script can be bewildering, which is why we have introduced them at gradual stages in the explanation of scripting.

The Film-Style Script

The **film-style script**, also known as the dramatic script or **Hollywood script**, follows the format common for screenplays. It does not contain highly detailed audio or video cues, but it does describe the actors' movements and gives the director some indication as to camera shots and movements. Such a script often has extensive description of the mood that the director should attempt to convey. The actors' names and dialog are centered on the page. Figure 13.3 shows part of a film-style script.

Although a film-style format is obviously not practical for a newscast, it allows for much greater flexibility in terms of establishing mood and providing actors and the director

VIDEO

. . .

AUDIO

. . .

CU of clipboards above manager's desk, pulling back to show manager in conversation with kitchen manager

NARRATOR: Scheduling and ordering involves knitting together the entire inventory and the complete roster of 135 employees.

MANAGER: Two things I noticed about the inventory and schedule . . . First, we've got a three-day weekend coming up—Monday's a holiday—so we've got to order more meat on Friday. Friday's going to be a really busy day because of the holiday, and I see that Frank is scheduled to work his station alone. He's still pretty new, and I think he needs some backup Friday.

LS of inventory room, with employee taking inventory of silverware

NARRATOR: Here are some of the facets involved in preparing for a meal. For example, the kitchen manager is taking an inventory of the steak knives. Steak knives get thrown away and stolen. Think about what would happen if a customer ordered an open steak sandwich and there was no knife to cut it.

MCU manager, who is wearing sweater and heavy sports coat, examining and tasting exotic frozen drink

MANAGER TO BAR MANAGER: It's pretty sweet even for a summer drink . . . I think a little less sugar would improve it.

NARRATOR: Even in December, we're preparing the summer menu. Why? Because it takes months to develop, test, and price items for the menu, which is changed twice a year.

Cut to XCU tilt down menu

CU of the adding machine; PULL BACK to show comptroller working at ledger

Long-range financial planning is critical to a restaurant's continued growth.

Comptroller picks up phone, punches intercom connection, talks into phone

COMPTROLLER: Tom? I've costed out adding stir fry to the menu next year. The biggest expense is going to be a tilting skillet, and that item runs about $4,000. Now, the projected return on that is . . .

. . .

. . .

Figure 13.2 An industrial video script.

with hints as to the thoughts and motivations of the characters.

Directors often won't shoot *directly* from a film-style script. They may opt to make an editing log, which is a numbered list of scenes. Remember, you don't necessarily have to—nor do you always want to—shoot a script in sequence. That's why the director might rearrange shots and number them:

22. Molly swings can.
23. Man brandishes knife.
24. Molly asks where the car is.

It may be more convenient to take the shots in this order as an accommodation to time or space, or to actors' or crewpeoples' schedules.

The Storyboard

A **storyboard** (Figure 13.4) is a series of drawings that gives the producer, director, and crew a visual approximation of what will be on screen. Storyboarding is usually used for short presentations, such as commercials. Complex dramatic sequences are often storyboarded too. It's cumbersome to attempt to storyboard longer works, although advances in computer technology have made it possible to illustrate, using storyboarding software, entire feature films in advance of the actual shooting.

The storyboard has the advantage of letting everyone know what you, the scriptwriter, intend the shot to look like. That does not mean the conception is cast in stone, or that anyone will necessarily try to reproduce it literally.

CUT TO:
THE KNIFE, CLOSE UP. THE MAN *unfolds the knife, and inspects it; it is a huge blade, an extra-long hunting knife with a wickedly honed edge.*

CUT TO:
MOLLY, *as she yanks open the green door to the back entrance. She is mumbling, and although we cannot hear what she is saying, it is obviously not a polite conversation she is holding with herself.*

CUT TO:
THE STAIRS, *an extremely long flight—several stories—and we see* MOLLY *descend the stairs as we hold a* FOLLOW SHOT *from below.*

CUT TO:
JERRY and MAX.

                                   MAX
I live in this neighborhood, and I don't remember any alley in back of this building.

                                  JERRY
It's only accessed through the parking garage next door. Super-secret. We don't want our stars elbowing their way through the panhandlers. You *live* around here? This is the worst neighborhood in Manhattan. Cheap studio space, though.

CUT TO:
The ALLEY, *where the* MAN *waits with knife in hand.*

CUT TO:
The STAIRS . . . *the seemingly endless flight of stairs, as an angry* MOLLY *stomps her way down.*

CUT TO:
MAX and JERRY

                                   MAX
I'm—how do you bigwigs say it?—cash poor at the moment. I wrote the book on a small advance. Nobody thought it would take off like it did. I'm a millionaire, but not for three months, when the first royalty payment comes due. So until then I'm just a starving writer.

                                  JERRY
Funny, you think I'm a bigwig and our charm school dropout thinks I'm a tinhorn.

Jerry's face tightens. He wouldn't admit it, but the remark clearly bothered him, and now he's going to try to exact a little revenge through Max.

                                   MAX
You mean what I think you mean?

                                  JERRY
You figure it out. You're the one with . . . (*He pantomimes a snort*) The nose for news.

Figure 13.3 A film-style script. Following the screenplay format, this script includes descriptions of the actors' movements and indicates camera shots and movements.

CUT TO:
MOLLY *as she opens the door to the back entrance, leading into the alley. She sees the*
MAN and shows her impatience. She spreads her hands in frustration . . .

MOLLY
Where's the *car?* I'm supposed to be cross-town five minutes ago.

She sees the KNIFE, and backs away in horror. She turns toward the door, but we . . .

CUT TO:
EXTREME CLOSE-UP of THE MAN's hand slamming the door shut.

Figure 13.3 (continued)

But at least everyone will have the same initial frame of reference.

A second advantage of the storyboard is that it is a terrific "sales tool" when you are trying to convince someone else of the value of your script. That's why advertising agencies almost always use storyboards when presenting commercial concepts to clients. A good artist, experienced at the work, can make up an impressive and highly professional-appearing storyboard in relatively short order. Showing a client a storyboard communicates more and is much more persuasive than handing him or her a script that begins "ECU MOC, ZOOM OUT TO REVEAL . . ."

Few clients can look at a script and visualize the final product; that takes experience. A storyboard may be necesary to "pitch" an idea.

THE MECHANICS OF SCRIPTWRITING

No matter what form you use—two-column or film-style—it's imperative that you pay attention to matching the audio with the video and planning your script in terms of complete scenes.

Coordinating Audio and Video

When you sit down to write a script, much of what you'll be doing is integrating audio with video. That seems beguilingly easy, but it's not. Coordinating voice with visuals, if done poorly, truly calls attention to itself.

Actually, you'll usually be grappling with two basic problems: writing voice-overs and writing sound-on-tape segments.

Voice-overs combined with SOTs comprise the majority of scripted nondramatic video material. Although you will occasionally write a speech or presentation that will be delivered straight to the camera, most shows requiring a script are combination VO/SOT, such as the script shown in Figure 13.2. (Remember that many programs, by their nature, *can't* be scripted; you can't write out questions *and answers* for a talk show, for example.)

We can sum up the thrust of "writing to video" in a few simple points:

1. In a program utilizing VO/SOT, such as a documentary or demonstration, you must not be too obvious in your voice-over. By this we mean that it's awkward and somewhat insulting to show video of an artist painting a picture and write voice-over copy that duplicates what the viewer can plainly see. Here's an example: Video shows a woman painting a beautiful picture. Audio reads: "This is a picture being painted. You can see that the artist is quite competent and that her hand moves steadily. You might be interested to know that she's recovering from a stroke."

2. At the same time, VO/SOT copy must not stray too far from the video. Showing an artist painting a picture and using a voice-over line such as, "A stroke is one of the most devastating medical conditions a person can face" leaves the viewer bewildered.

3. Ideally, voice-over copy should *complement, add to,* the video without restating the obvious. "Five years ago, doctors had grave doubts that artist Mary Macnamara would be able to walk, much less continue to paint her famous landscapes. But she's recovered from one of the most devastating medical emergencies a person can face."

4. When you are leading into an SOT segment, it is important not to have the lead-in repeat the SOT.

Bad Example
NARRATOR: . . . and Mrs. Macnamara feels she's the luckiest woman alive.

MACNAMARA: I'm the luckiest woman alive . . .

Better Example
NARRATOR: . . . but those problems haven't dimmed her outlook on life.

MACNAMARA: I'm the luckiest woman alive . . .

VIDEO		AUDIO

MR. KOLAR CONFRONTS BOB WITH DISCREPENCIES IN THE COMPANY'S BOOKS.

KOLAR: I expect a full explanation in the morning.

BOB: You'll have it, Mr. Kolar, sir.

MUSIC: *Theme begins as an undercurrent.*

BOB WALKS SLOWLY DOWN THE STEPS, OPENS THE DOOR, RECOILS FROM THE STORM, TURNS UP HIS COLLAR, AND TRUDGES OUT INTO THE RAIN.

SOUND EFFECT: *Storm.*

MUSIC: *Theme builds.*

BOB, SLICK WITH RAIN, ENTERS HIS APARTMENT, OPENS HIS CLOSET, AND REMOVES A SUITCASE FROM THE TOP SHELF.

MUSIC: *Theme builds.*

BOB PLACES THE SUITCASE ON THE DESK AND OPENS IT, REVEALING STACKS OF HUNDRED-DOLLAR BILLS.

MUSIC: *Theme climaxes as money is revealed.*

Figure 13.4 A storyboard. Storyboards are pictoral aids for the producer, director, and crew, and are usually associated with commercials or short presentations.

Visual Scenes

Try an experiment. Record a commercial on a standard home VCR and replay it on fast forward *without sound.* You'll notice that somehow, the content and context of the commercial are still communicated. The rapidity of the scenes flashing by will probably augment this effect.

Perhaps the fast-moving images portray a man waiting in line for a bank teller, having the "Next Window" sign slammed in his face, walking across the street to the advertiser's bank, and being served by a smiling teller. The message is understandable even without the dialogue because it has been clearly communicated in terms of scenes.

Scene structure of scriptwriting is an important aspect of the semantics—those aspects of scripting that convey meaning.

THE TECHNIQUES OF SCRIPTWRITING

Throughout the chapters we've covered so far, *communication* has been consistently stressed, and repeated examples have been included to help demonstrate how all aspects of the program, including lighting and camera work, have an impact on the message.

Now we'll see how the orchestrator of the program brings all these elements into a cohesive whole at the beginning of the production: the time when the scriptwriter sits down at the keyboard.

How a Script Communicates an Idea

The central idea, of course, is the acorn from which the tree grows. The entire script germinates from the central idea, and in large part it cannot significantly *depart* from it. A video production must stick to a central theme because scattered ideas and approaches weaken the thrust of the piece and leave the viewer wondering what, exactly, is going on.

Keeping viewer attention is a serious problem in video scripting. If your central idea, the theme, wanders or the scenes progress too quickly or too slowly—or have no easily grasped relationship to one another—you already have script trouble.

You can successfully avoid script trouble if you clearly focus on one central idea, and write for the eye; write for the ear; construct your piece with a clear, narrative flow; and keep the ideas simple and consistent.

Writing for the Eye. A scene is a bite of the action, a small part of the program in which some distinct, clearly articulated action occurs. For example, you might describe a scene as, "Bob walks slowly down the steps, opens the door, recoils from the howling wind, turns up his collar, and trudges out into the rain."

Something has happened in this scene, and you can visualize it easily as a series of actions that communicate one "snapshot" of the plot. You can also visualize how it may interact with other scenes in the production. Perhaps, in the previous scene, Bob's boss inquires pointedly about a growing pattern of errors in the company's books. In the following scene, we might see Bob, slick with rain, enter his apartment, open his closet, and rummage through a suitcase—a suitcase filled with cash.

The important element here is that distinct, self-contained *actions* move the story forward. In other words, *something happened.* Our viewers want to see action unfold and tell a story. That action does not have to involve car chases, fistfights, or gun battles. However, in any video

things must unfold visually, and we must generally be able to understand *by sight* most of what has happened, and how that action interrelates with previous scenes. A good video script is more than just a radio script with pictures added.

Writing for the Ear. Although television is predominantly a visual medium, words are vitally important. Suppose, for instance, you are writing a news script about a spate of accidents that followed an ice storm. Which of the following three examples do you think represents the best example of writing that will be *heard by the viewer?*

1. Something worse happened. The truck slipped on the ice-covered road, and it broke open. Chemicals spilled all over the highway.

2. The worst was yet to come. The truck skidded on the icy roadway and ruptured. Chemicals spewed onto Highway 101.

3. The situation was made worse when a truck skidded on the highway and broke open, observers noted. Chemicals, exiting the cracked containment vessel at a high rate of flow, soon covered Highway 101.

Example 2 is written for the ear. It has powerful words—*ruptured, spewed*—and is written in a conversational style. Example 1 is reasonably conversational, but it lacks punch. The words are limp, weak, and ineffectual. Example 3 reads more like a newspaper article. It makes sense, but it sounds stilted when read aloud.

Keep your scriptwriting conversational. Remember, you are not committing words to paper when you are writing a script; *you are committing speech to paper.* Your script must recreate the spoken word as it naturally flows in normal speech patterns. You are writing words to be spoken out loud—not a term paper.

Keep your sentences clear and short. A long sentence often confuses and loses the listener/viewer. You might even toss in an occasional incomplete sentence. Broadcast journalists do this all the time: "A demolition derby on Highway 101 today. State police say it's the worst ice storm they've ever seen. And more slippery conditions are on the way."

Creating a Narrative Flow

The **narrative** of a script is simply the story line, and telling a story is the point of a video production. Your story may be a relatively mundane one, such as how to use a new computer, but it still has to have a beginning, a middle, and a conclusion.

The Beginning. A beginning must orient viewers, and let them know what the program is about. Beginnings must show the overall environment and cue viewers to the point of the show and what is going to follow. Don't be afraid of your beginning's being too direct. Some of the most famous beginnings in commercial television are explicit in orienting and cuing the viewer.

"This is the city..."   Theme music

Figure 13.5   The beginning. The beginning of a video script establishes setting, characters, and conflict. It invites the audience to anticipate the story to come.

You have certainly seen reruns of the TV series *Dragnet,* or the film parody of the same name. And chances are, the thrust of the opening is indelibly etched into your mind. The shows usually opened with a panoramic shot, and the deadpan voice of Jack Webb saying something to the effect of, "This is the city . . . Los Angeles, California. It's a city where people from all over the world come to take a chance at success. Sometimes they take too much . . . and they take it from innocent victims. That's when I go to work. I carry a badge."

A bit hokey? Maybe; that's probably why parodists had such fun with it. But the opening set the stage and let viewers know exactly what was coming.

Try this experiment: Tonight, watch the first two or three minutes of any show on network television. Chances are you'll find that in those few minutes:

• The characters have been introduced.

• The basic problem or conflict has been demonstrated or stated.

• The writers have cued us as to what will happen in the next half hour or hour.

If you follow the same guidelines, your own writing will improve immeasurably.

The Middle. The middle of the show is where the action is carried out, whether it involves hunting down an armed robber or instructing the novice computer user on the intricacies of a new software package. The most important aspect of intelligently constructing the middle of your show is to keep scenes coming and have them follow a logical progression.

When scripting the middle, think about scenes first. Don't immediately move into putting words on paper; clarify in your own mind what *series of actions* will communicate the point you want to make.

The Conclusion. The conclusion of a show must wrap things up and leave viewers with no uncertainty that the show has finished. Notice that there's a difference between a *conclusion* and an *end.* A show can end just by stopping the tape—and that's exactly the impression you'll

sometimes get when watching a carelessly scripted show in which the writer has made no effort to reach a conclusion.

Engineering a conclusion in your script is reasonably simple. First, *show* the outcome. If you have written a script demonstrating the use of computer software, use some combination of visual and audio to indicate that the person on screen now has mastered the process. Show him or her examining (with obvious satisfaction) a printout, or whatever plot device you think communicates the message.

Second, use the directorial devices used for more than a half-century now to cue audiences that the end is near: Speed up the pace of transitions (cuts and/or dissolves) as you near the end, and bring up the theme music. Audiences, in general, *like* to be cued and "pulled" through a program, especially at the end.

Using Scenes and Reference Points

Finally (doesn't the word *finally* give you a welcome clue that the chapter is moving to a close?), keep in mind that scripting for video lets you think outside of the traditional boundaries imposed by print communication.

For example, you don't need endless words of dialog to show that a job interviewer is a tall, scowling, intimidating person. Just use creative camera technique: Script the scene to be shot from a very low point of view. This gives the impression that the interviewer is intimidating without *saying* a word.

You also can shoot out of sequence. If a shot is not convenient, go back and get it later. For instance, assume you are shooting a three-camera comedy taped before a studio audience. A scene calls for one character to fix a pipe that continues to drip directly into his face. Given the position of your cameras, you may not be able to get a close-up even though a delicious full-frame shot of the character catching the drips right in the eyes would add enormous impact to the scene.

But this is *video.* You can mark a reference point in the script where you want to insert a close-up. You can

BOX 13.1   WHEN SCRIPTWRITING BECOMES TOO CONVINCING

On October 30, 1938, Orson Welles and his colleagues performed for the radio program "Mercury Theatre of the Air" an adaptation of H. G. Wells's science fiction novel *War of the Worlds*. The radio play was presented as an imitation of breaking news, complete with a breathless announcer interrupting the "program" to report on the invasion of Earth by Martians.

The program produced chaos. Many listeners believed that Martians had indeed invaded, even though periodic announcements during the program plainly characterized it as a work of fiction.

What made people believe the story? There are many reasons, but broadcast historians Christopher Sterling and John Kittross note that the verisimilitude of the script deserved much of the credit.

Reports of casualties, traffic jams, transmissions from hapless military pilots, ominous breaking off of on-the-spot reports, the later report of the "death" of the field reporter, and the use of familiar names and places—all gave it reality. As the Martian war machines headed toward New York to discharge their poison gas over the city—to the sounds of fleeing ocean liners, the last gasps of a newsman atop the broadcasting studio, and the cracked voice of a solitary ham radio operator calling "Isn't anybody there? Isn't anybody?"—many listeners did not wait to hear the mid-program announcement that it was a hoax. By 8:30, thousands of people were praying, preparing for the end, and fleeing the Martians.

These reactions were not silly, although it may look that way today. The pacing of the program undermined critical faculties. It convinced the listeners that a reporter had traveled the miles from Groveners Mill "in ten minutes," when less than three minutes actually had elapsed. Already sure that mobs were fleeing, listeners who looked out their windows and saw lots of people going about normal pursuits assumed that everyone was trying to get away from Martians, just as the radio said.

Source: Stay Tuned: A Concise History of American Broadcasting (Belmont, CA; Wadsworth, 1978), 166–167.

shoot the close-up after the show is taped and the audience has gone; you can even shoot it the next day or the next week, for that matter, as long as you maintain continuity.

This is exactly the way many taped shows are produced. The close-ups are shot last, after the wider action has been taped on the stage and edited into the final version of the program. Thinking out of the boundaries of linear, written communication when composing your script allows you to exploit these opportunities, as well as produce a piece that amounts to more than people reading words, words, and more words to a camera.

You also do not need to have your scripts confined to the strict boundaries of reality. A dramatization of a 10-minute meeting need not take 10 minutes. Dramatic dialog and plot lines can create all sorts of unreal images

as long as the dialog and plot are *consistent with themselves*. For example, a common mistake made by beginning science fiction writers is to clumsily handle exposition of their space vehicles—explaining the controls and workings to passengers. Think about it: Do you explain the workings of your car to your passengers?

The point is that the appearance of truthfulness and reality, called *verisimilitude*, does not have to jibe with reality in a dramatic script or invented dialog for, let's say, a corporate script. Remember: Good writing gives the appearance of reality even when compressing a long event into a short period of time. Box 13.1 provides a graphic example. It is not presented with the intent of glorifying hoaxes, but only to illustrate how clever writing can suspend reality.

SUMMARY

1. The two-column video script is probably the most commonly used format in production. It shows video cues on the left side and contains audio cues and content on the right side.

2. The dramatic or "film-style" script more or less mimics a typical screenplay format, and is used for

dramatic presentations such as soap operas. It is becoming increasingly popular, though, in some aspects of production, such as corporate videos that include many acted scenes.

3. Storyboards use drawings to depict scenes. They are particularly helpful when you are describing an

idea to someone not familiar with the conventions of video scripting.

4. A good deal of typical scriptwriting involves writing voice-over (VO) copy and integrating it with sound-on-tape (SOT) segments. The most important things to remember when writing VO/SOT copy is to have the script relate to the video (though it shouldn't continually refer to the obvious) and to integrate the SOT segments gracefully.

5. Think in terms of scenes when you write video scripts. Scenes are what moves a program forward.

6. Never depart too widely from the central theme of the program.

7. Write for the eye and the ear in a video script, keep up the narrative flow, and make sure your script has a beginning, a middle, and a conclusion.

8. Break out of old "paper" writing habits. You're not writing an article, short story, or term paper—you're writing for video. Think visually. And remember that when you script a show, the show does not have to be shot in sequence.

TECHNICAL TERMS

CU	MOC	OS	two-column script
film-style script	MS	SFX	VO
Hollywood script	narrative	sound on tape (SOT)	XLS
LS	OC	storyboard	

EXERCISES

1. Storyboard a 60-second commercial for a product. Use a print advertisement to supply the facts you'll need to make the commercial believable. But don't ape the print commercial's approach. You are free to use whatever approach seems reasonable given the constraints of a realistic commercial.

   Pay particular attention to the timing factor. Read your script aloud and approximate the running time of segments where there is no talking to make sure that you are not over- or underestimating the amount of material that will fit into the commercial.

   If possible, try to produce a storyboard with at least 10 panels.

2. Take a newspaper article and recreate a two-column video script simulating a television news report. Don't invent any quotes or facts; use only the facts that are in the story. All you need conjure up are the video images you'll use with the voice-over—and those will be reasonably apparent from the article.

Have the reporter do a stand-up open and close. If you have any doubt as to what a "typical" news package looks like, watch a local or network newscast. You'll be able to see at least four or five in most shows.

3. Find a newspaper article that depicts a dramatic incident, such as a hostage taking or a violent confrontation between two gangs. (Hint: If you want to make your job easier, look for the article with the most dialog.)

   Now, write up the action in dramatic fashion, as though you were scripting a police drama. Use the film-style script format. Aim for about three minutes of script. (You'll find that a page of script usually equals about a minute of airtime.) Be sure to include more than one scene in the script; that is, change the locale or change the essential thrust of the series of shots at least once.

graphics

OBJECTIVES

After completing Chapter 14, you will be able to:

1. Identify the basic kinds of equipment used to create graphics.
2. Demonstrate basic skills in using that equipment.
3. Create graphics that are not only technically correct but pleasing to the eye.

Modern video equipment makes production of graphics easy, but the technological advances in graphics do not guarantee good graphic design. The most slickly designed computer-generated effect may fall flat if it does not communicate a message, reinforce the thrust of the program, or appear pleasing to the eye.

Let's use an analogy that is probably familiar and is also appropriate because it reflects the evolution of the merging media: desktop publishing. Just a few years ago, publishing a magazine or newsletter required the services of a graphic artist and a professional printer. The whole process was expensive and required technical skills and equipment beyond the reach of many individuals.

Today's personal computer and laser printer, however, make the technical aspects of publishing well within most people's budgetary and technical capabilities. After a relatively small monetary investment and a few days' time spent learning the rudiments of the software, anyone can create columns, insert photos and boxes, and choose from a wide variety of type styles and sizes.

But the resulting publication can still look horrible. Perhaps the designer became infatuated with the variety of type styles available and produced something that has so many different styles and sizes of print that it resembles a ransom note. Or perhaps the text columns are so wide that reading all the way across the page and returning to the beginning of the next line becomes a tedious chore.

The examples are endless. You *know* what a badly laid-out publication looks like because you have certainly seen many, most of which have been churned out from desktop units capable of technical sophistication but *incapable* of giving their owners a sense of graphic good taste.

That is a rather roundabout way of introducing the thrust of this chapter, but it is nevertheless a highly relevant example of what some graphic designers call the "mountain climbing syndrome"—the temptation to climb a mountain or use a graphic effect "just because it's there."

In this chapter, we will meld technical considerations with aesthetic guidelines. First, we'll explain the technical hardware available to the producer and then discuss the fundamentals of using that hardware as a tool for good graphic composition—in other words, as a tool to communicate, rather than a gimmick to be used because it's available.

EQUIPMENT FOR VIDEO GRAPHICS

One early method of placing written words or drawings on the video screen involved an **art card**, a piece of cardboard, usually black, onto which white letters were pasted or impressed. The white of the letters enabled the first generations of video equipment to electronically cut the white letters into the image. In some circumstances, the fader bar was brought halfway between the buses and a camera shot of the main scene was superimposed with a shot of the graphic card. (This "superimposition" produced a weak, thin-looking signal, so it was not the method of choice and is rarely, if ever, used today. Be aware that the word *superimposition* or *super*, is commonly used colloquially to indicate the presence of a keyed graphic. This usage is really incorrect and should be avoided, but the occasional misuse is worth noting because you'll definitely hear it from time to time.)

In the early and mid-1970s, it became apparent that new technologies, which printed characters right onto the screen via a typewriter-style keyboard, were much more convenient than art cards. This new generation of equipment was referred to as a **character generator (CG)**.

But the evolution did not stop there. Video directors, for many years, had longed for some method of displaying

as software libraries. The term *clip art* is derived from books of copyright-free artwork sold to graphic designers

Figure 14.5 Graphics tablet. This ultra-slim graphics tablet is pictured with a stylus and digitizer. (Photo courtesy of Wacom, Inc.)

Figure 14.6 The Quantel Paint Box. The earliest of the video paint systems remains popular in the industry. (Photo courtesy of Quantel Corp.)

Roughly the same effect is accomplished by creating a scene with a computer program and then recording one or two frames; that is, **frame-by-frame animation** (Figure 14.8). What happens is that the computer calls up the

Figure 14.8 Animation. Animation is made up of individual frames of drawings that are combined to create the illusion of movement.

appropriate image from memory, takes control of the VTR, prerolls the machine, and makes a very brief video edit.

Frame-by-frame animation typically uses colors drawn from a *palette*, a term relating to the piece of wood on which painters mix their colors.

Real-Time Animation. With **real-time animation**, the computer creates the entire sequence and plays it back *in sequence*. Instead of recording just a few frames at a time, stopping tape, recreating a few new frames, and starting the tape again, the entire movement is recorded "live." Real-time animation requires a highly sophisticated computer system that can move massive amounts of data very quickly. In general, simple animation systems are surprisingly inexpensive; sophisticated ones are shockingly costly.

Figure 14.7 Graphics menu. The "menu" is where the tools of the system are selected.

Figure 14.9 Digital video effect in titles. The title, "Rogue's Island" and following credits are "supered" over vertical lines and a graphic of Mount Rushmore. The effect is "moved" and "zoomed" across the screen from right to left. Its perspective is expanded and stretched to fill the screen to make the transition more dynamic.

Image Manipulation

The most common form of image manipulation is known as a **digital video effects (DVE)** system. DVEs do not really *create* images, as paint effect systems do. Instead, they take an image and rotate it, or shrink it, or flip it (Figure 14.9). You have probably seen newscasts in which transitions are made from scene to scene by what looks like flipping a page; that is the result of image manipulation.

DVEs can also shrink (compress) or enlarge (expand) a picture. The shrinkage capability allows you, for example, to insert an image over the newscaster's shoulder and then expand it to fill the screen. Expansion lets you fill the screen with only a portion of the original picture (your picture, however, will degrade to the point where it will not be airable after it's magnified three or four times).

You can also "stretch" a picture, lengthening one dimension more than another. This creates interesting special effects, but it also allows for some last-minute "correction." If your graphics don't fit on the screen, you can (within limits) change their dimensions.

All four graphic effects—character generation, paint effects, animation, and image manipulation—rely on the *digital* capabilities of the computer. Computer operations will be explained in some depth in later chapters, but if you'd like a better understanding of what is actually happening, Box 14.1 provides an introduction.

FUNDAMENTALS OF GRAPHIC DESIGN FOR VIDEO

Whether you are using art cards, slides, or a $200,000 computer workstation, there are some basic principles that apply to any visual presentation. In general, the graphic must be technically correct and should be pleasing to the eye.

A Technically Correct Graphic

By "technically correct," we mean that the graphic must be in:

- Correct dimension and size
- Correct contrast

Dimension and Size

The most important facet of a graphic with correct dimension is the aspect ratio.

Aspect Ratio. **Aspect ratio** is the relationship of height to width. A video screen is 4 units wide by 3 units high, meaning that it has an aspect ratio of 4:3. (Irrespective of whether the measurement is in feet, millimeters, or

---

BOX 14.1 DIGITAL IMAGES NEED LOTS OF MEMORY

The type of signal produced by a standard tube-type TV camera is an analog signal. **Analog** means "a representation of." The scanning pattern explained in Chapter 5 is an analog process, which tranduces electrical signals into a form representative of a video picture.

A digital image is one that has been translated into computer language. **Digital** images are those that are represented in computer talk—and the computer knows only two words, *on* and *off*. All computing is done with a series of on and off pulses; an on-or-off pulse is a bit of information. In a computer word processor, for example, each letter represents a different series of on-and-off pulses.

Naturally, it takes an enormous number of bits to reproduce sophisticated information, which is why computer graphics require large amounts of computer memory that can be manipulated at high speed.

Without delving too deeply into the technicalities, consider the amount of information represented by a black-and-white image. A 13-inch screen may consist of an array of 640 lines with 480 picture elements (pixels) displayed on each of those lines. Each pixel is controlled by one bit of information. That is to say, the pixel can be "on" or "off."

A screen of black-and-white video, then, requires over 300,000 bits of information. To produce the illusion of motion, that screen needs to be changed 30 times each second, requiring over 9 million bits of information.

To represent color we need significantly more information. The human eye can finely discriminate colors within the visible spectrum, and "true color" requires a mixture of one of 256 gradations of each of the three primary colors (red, green, and blue) for each pixel. Fortunately, this information plus screen control information can be represented in a string of 32 bits—and processed as a single "byte" of video. Still, a screen or frame of true-color video can require about one megabyte of information, nearly enough to fill a floppy disk. Pumping 30 screens of information per second out to a monitor requires a lot of internal memory and processing power too.

And that is why computer hardware for video typically has been fairly expensive. Decreasing costs, rapidly increasing memory and processing speed, and compression methods, however, are contributing to the growth of digital processing in video.

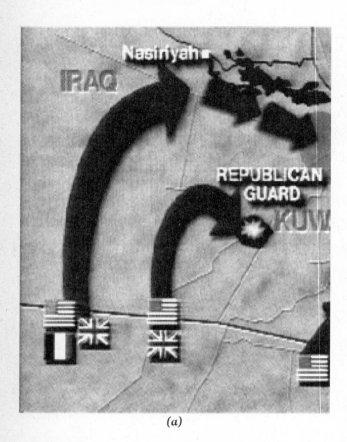

(a)

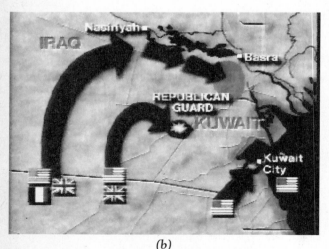

(b)

Figure 14.10 Wrong aspect ratio. If we try to fill the screen with map (a), part of the image will be lost. The map was the wrong shape—higher than wide. Map (b) maintains the correct 4:3 aspect ratio that fits the video screen. (Used with permission, CNN.)

furlongs, the ratio will always be the same.) It stands to reason, then, that a graphic designed to be shown on the air be roughly in the same proportion. For example, a map that is higher than it is wide (Figure 14.10) just won't be acceptable for video if you want so show the entire map. This may seem self-evident, but you would be surprised to find how frequently producers—even experienced producers—forget about this most basic of all graphic rules.

The only realistic exceptions to this aspect ratio are graphic cards to be used when the camera is in motion. Should you wish to tilt down a long list of credits or pan across a picture of a vista, you will obviously want to have a graphic that is not in the standard 4:3 aspect ratio for static shots.

Essential Area. Because almost all video graphics are produced by electronic generation, you usually will not be shooting graphic titles off cards, but there will be occasions when it is necessary to shoot pictures, diagrams, logos, or maps, so the essential area computation will be handy.

An oddity of television broadcasting is that the area scanned by the camera in the studio will not match what is seen by the home receiver. To further confuse matters, the exact part of the image that home TVs will show varies from set to set.

With standard video images, this is usually not a problem. If there's slightly less (or more) image than expected when showing two people seated side-by-side, the distortion won't be too distracting. But if the graphic "News 5 County Conference" doesn't fit into the screen, it may appear as "ws 5 County Conferen," and that *will* be unsettling to the viewer.

You can avoid this problem by making sure that any lettering you shoot off a card fits into what's called the **critical area**, **essential area**, or "safe area." All three terms mean the same: They refer to the part of the picture that will definitely be picked up by all home sets, regardless of how badly out of kilter those sets may be.

The essential area is within a larger area called the scanning area. The **scanning area** is the part of the graphic that will be picked up by a typical studio camera. In turn, there is usually a border left around the scanning area just for safety's sake—an especially welcome option should the camera drift slightly while on air.

Figure 14.11 shows an approximation of the **border area** (the entire area of a card or graphic that is to appear on camera), the scanning area, and the essential area.

Here is a simplified way to determine the approximate border, scanning, and essential areas of a graphics card: Start with the total border dimensions and multiply both the height and the width by 0.66 to find the dimensions of the scanning area. Center this smaller rectangle within the border area. Now take the scanning area rectangle you've created and multiply the height and width by 0.75

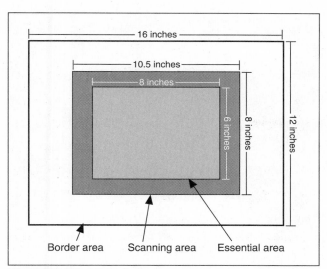

Border area   Scanning area   Essential area

Figure 14.11 Calculating the essential area. The dimensions of the scanning area are ⅔ (.66) of the border dimensions. The dimensions of the essential area are ¾ (.75) of the scanning dimensions. (And therefore, the essential area's dimensions are ½ the dimensions of the border area: ⅔ × ¾ = ½.) *Example*: The border area of this graphics card is 16″ × 12″ (note the proper 4:3 aspect ratio). The scanning area would be 10.5″ × 8″ (16 × .66 = 10.5; 12 × .66 = 8). The essential area would be 8″ × 6″ (10.5 × .75 = 8; 8 × .75 = 6).

to find the dimensions of the essential area. Center that rectangle within the scanning area. (See Figure 14.11.)

Size. Any graphic, particularly lettering, has to be big enough to be seen. Remember that when you create electronic lettering, you generally are sitting only a couple of feet away from the monitor—but the viewer may have an entirely different perspective.

A personal experience serves as a good illustration: One of the authors once worked for a news service that provided teletext—typed words on a screen that briefly summarized the day's news. To all seven staff members of the operation, the seven-line display was perfectly readable. (Remember, we sat about 2 feet away from the screen while making up the graphics.)

After viewing the screen for 8 hours per working day, none of us felt compelled to watch the service at home. When we did, it was usually a quick scan just to make sure the service was operating correctly.

But during a Christmas party we (out of a sense of obligation) turned the teletext service on the television set in the host's living room—and found that from an average seating position the text was very difficult to read. From 8 feet the display on the 12-inch TV required good eyesight and a squint, and from the couch across the room the display was almost impossible to read.

That story has both a broad and a specific moral. First, it is vitally important to approach your graphics from the

viewer's standpoint. It is surprisingly easy to lose your perspective when working up close with equipment. Second, it is generally a wise idea not to use more than six lines of type when you fill the screen with text.

When you are using only single lines of type, you still need type large enough so that it's readable. A good rule of thumb is to never make the text smaller than one-fifteenth of the total screen height.

Contrast

A light graphic keyed over a light background (Figure 14.12) just won't do. There is not enough contrast for the graphic to be readable.

Actually, the contrast problem is two-fold. First, you need to consider color contrast and, second, you need to translate the graphic to black and white.

Color Contrast. It's important to make sure that the colors have an adequate contrast. Although color contrast is largely a subjective judgment, you instinctively know that a pastel blue on a pale gray background is not going to produce a particularly clear contrast.

Remember, too, that there are three components of color: hue, saturation, and luminance. To review, hue is the shade of the color, saturation is the richness of the color, and luminance is the brightness. (Sometimes *chroma* is used synonymously with *saturation*, but there are some technical differences between the two, differences beyond the scope of this chapter; just remember that the terms are roughly equivalent.) Hue and saturation can adequately distinguish one *color* from another, but luminance creates a special problem when a color image is translated into black and white.

Translation to Black and White. You can accommodate black-and-white receivers through luminance con-

Figure 14.12 Poor contrast. A light graphic title keyed over a light background becomes visually "lost."

trast. Color receivers are common, but there are still plenty of black-and-white sets in use. A graphic key that may look perfectly acceptable when viewed in color (where you are comparing hue and chroma) may be barely distinguishable when viewed in black and white because there is not enough luminance contrast with the background.

To determine whether the contrast is sufficient, view the graphic on a black-and-white monitor. Do this often enough and you will develop a reliable instinct as to whether the foreground and background colors will mate in black and white. A hint: Be particularly careful about combining highly saturated primary colors such as red and green. They may show a distinct variation in color, but they'll melt into each other in monochrome. (A second suggestion is to be careful when using red under any circumstances; for technical reasons, it is a difficult color for television equipment to handle.)

How a Graphic "Pleases the Eye"

A video graphic should be visually appealing, lending a sense of order to the screen. In essence, a graphic should impart balance and simplified detail.

Balance. Proper balance is a function of both the graphic itself and its relationship to other elements of the picture when it is inserted into a frame. Note how the video graphic displayed in Figure 14.13 seems out of balance, but when the main elements are rearranged according to the rule of thirds, the image seems more "centered."

A graphic that appears over a newscaster's shoulder requires that the newscaster be moved over to accommodate the insert (Figure 14.14). And, of course, a title, in order to preserve the balance of the shot, must appear in the lower third of the screen (Figure 14.15).

Figure 14.14 Appropriate size graphic. The newscaster is positioned to the right of the frame for graphic insert in the upper left.

Simplified Detail. You can only hope to communicate a *small* amount of information in a single graphic. Graphs, charts, and maps for video must be much more simple than those prepared for a print medium. Video graphics only appear for a short time and are compressed into a small area. A map that might be perfectly readable in an encyclopedia will be incomprehensible if reproduced in full detail on the video screen.

Remember the maps used by all three networks to illustrate the Persian Gulf war? They were extremely simple, in some cases showing nothing more than boundaries of nations and just one or two city names. The producers felt it was necessary to utilize map graphics for those viewers who were not intimately familiar with Middle East geography. Moreover, they realized that detailed maps would

Figure 14.13 Poor balance. The elements of this image seem out of balance.

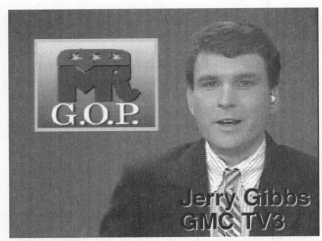

Figure 14.15 Balancing three elements. The newscaster's name is "supered" in the lower third of the frame, maintaining the balance of this frame.

cause more confusion than they would eliminate, so the displays were kept extraordinarily simple.

Figure 14.10, our example of an out of scale map, was a portion of a CNN map created for the Persian Gulf War coverage.

WHAT AND HOW GRAPHICS COMMUNICATE

To restate the opening theme of this chapter, the ability to create graphics does not guarantee that those effects will be meaningful. Although the addition of computer-generated graphics can impart a modern look to a presentation, tumbling, flipping, compressed, and brightly colored lettering can easily be overdone. Therefore, it's important to establish some ground rules for using graphics. It is advisable to use a graphic when it *communicates something difficult to impart by other means*, or when it *creates a specific image or mood*.

Graphics to Communicate or Demonstrate

Some information is best communicated via a graphic. A pie chart, for example, imparts more information succinctly than does a listing of percentages. Many producers also believe that information presented in a well-done graphic will be much better retained by the viewer than information communicated aurally.

During national election news coverage, a map of the United States with the states that have gone Democratic in one color and the states that have gone Republican in another color is just about the *only* way to quickly convey that information.

Graphics, particularly animated graphics, are useful for demonstrating functions or items that simply cannot be pictured by standard video. For example, when institutional video specialists Tanya Weinberg and Stephen Wershing were assigned the task of explaining, via video, a process normally not observable, they relied on animation.

A recent assignment required us to map gas and liquid flow patterns through a fuel injection system. Sawing the fuel pump in half and pointing a camera inside would, in all likelihood, not have produced satisfactory results. The client would not have appreciated getting his injectors back in pieces, either. Our solution was to reproduce engineering drawings in the computer and cycle colors along the paths of fuel and air. The viewers saw an accurate representation of the system they could not have seen in person, with memorable and easily distinguished pathways of brightly colored fuel and air.[2]

Graphics to Create an Image or Mood

Graphics can—indeed, they *must*—reinforce the basic thrust of the program. Perhaps the concept of "reinforcing" an idea is best illustrated by showing bad examples, where graphics send mixed messages.

Your graphics would send mixed messages if:

- You were producing a program where the goal was to produce a "warm," comfortable feeling—and you used severe, steely blue graphics.

- In an institutional video presentation explaining the need for layoffs you utilized flashy, expensive-looking graphics to document the need for cutbacks.

- As part of a tape extolling the high-tech benefits of new computer technology, you utilize old-style lettering in your graphics display.

Projecting moods and concepts is something that will come with practice, but you can intuitively see that contradictory messages detract rather than add to the program. You also can deduce that the best use of a graphic is when there is a compelling need for use of a graphic, such as:

- To communicate an idea not easily put across by words or pictures.

- To display material that is best shown in the "dense" format of graphics. Credits (listing producer, director, and so forth) are one such instance. It takes much less time to display the credits than to read them aloud.

- To reinforce another element. A lower-third graphic identifies the speaker pictured on the screen without having the announcer or other performer make repeated references to the identity of the person pictured.

- To create a particular "feel" for the program.

You certainly know, from your own observations, how graphics change the feel of a program. News programming is an excellent example; remember that only a few years ago news programs were much more "static" than today, lacking the graphic effects that add movement and drive. This is not to be interpreted as a blanket endorsement of graphic glitz for the sake of glitz. It simply reflects the fact that when producers of some news programs wanted to modernize their approaches, graphics were among their most useful tools (see Box 14.2).

In any event, remember that although graphics are powerful tools for communication, *communication* is the key concept. Be certain that the graphic has some meaning, either a *direct* meaning, such as a graph illustrating stock prices, or an *indirect meaning*, such as a typeface that creates a modern mood. Don't use a graphic effect just because it's available. When in doubt, leave it out.

BOX 14.2 GRAPHICS AND NEWS COVERAGE

When Roone Arledge took over ABC News, he invoked some of the same graphics techniques used to enliven his football coverage. (Arledge was originally in charge of sports for the network.)

Although many journalists resented Arledge's "dancing graphics," even some of the most ardent critics of the intrusion of show business into news admit that it was about time that graphics could be more than pure glitz. Barbara Matusow, who has worked as a producer and writer for CBS and ABC, recalls the impact of Arledge's introduction of advanced graphics technology into TV sports and news:

> Although the techniques Arledge introduced were probably overused in the beginning, he did at least succeed in making ABC's presentation look different from other newscasts. A machine called a Chyron IV generated charts, graphs and symbols in dozens of shapes and colors, eliminating the need for laboriously hand-painted artwork. Something called a Quantel [a digital video effects unit] could suck the images in, widen them out, or move them around the screen. Using the latest video technology, it became possible to illustrate almost anything in a correspondent's script, eliminating the need for forty-five-second standuppers in front of the Treasury Department or Pentagon.

Arledge had always been interested in finding ways to allow the viewer to "see" more. With "Monday Night Football" he realized that the guy watching in a bar probably couldn't hear much, so Arledge started plastering the screen with graphics telling the score, identifying the players, and so on. "Roone plays the viewer very well," says producer Dorrance Smith. "Say I have the Israeli defense minister being interviewed on the Sunday show. Roone will call me in the control room and say, 'People don't know this guy. Make sure you keep [visually identifying him with graphics].' "[1]

The changes were initially controversial, but many in the business, including Matusow, concede that television news was behind the times in production values, and it took some prodding from an innovator like Arledge to bring it up to speed.

1. Barbara Matusow, *The Evening Stars* (New York: Ballantine, 1983), 285.

SUMMARY

1. Just because graphic equipment is available, that does not guarantee good graphic design. A producer must pay attention to balance and clarity when using a graphic.

2. Early TV graphics involved pasting letters on art cards. Art cards aren't used much today, but some printed graphics are shot by the video camera for use in certain effects.

3. Election coverage was one of the driving forces in the evolution of TV graphics. Producers needed a simple way to illustrate numbers and states that had voted for respective candidates. Later, graphics used in coverage of sporting events also had a major impact on TV news coverage.

4. For our purposes, we have classified graphics functions into character generation, paint effects, animation systems, and image manipulation systems. There is obviously some overlap in the functions of the hardware.

5. Modern graphics are created digitally, meaning that they use the on-off circuitry of the computer's "brain." One important part of the hardware of graphics is the equipment that translates a digitally produced signal on the computer screen to a video signal. Even though a video screen and a computer terminal screen may look the same, the way the image is produced is not identical.

6. A graphic should be technically correct. This means it should have the proper aspect ratio, contrast, and size.

7. Of particular importance is ensuring that the graphic is within the essential area of the video screen.

8. In general, you want a graphic to have proper balance—in other words, not overweighting one side of the screen. However, an out-of-balance graphic is sometimes acceptable and useful for special effect.

9. Graphics are especially useful when they are utilized to communicate a concept that is difficult or impossible to express through words or pictures.

10. Graphics are also powerful tools for projecting a mood or image.

TECHNICAL TERMS

analog	character generator (CG)	essential area	paint effect system
animation	crawl	frame-by-frame animation	real-time animation
art card	critical area	lower-third graphics	roll
aspect ratio	digital	menu	scanning area
border area	digital video effects (DVE)		

NOTES

1. George Gilder, *Life after Television* (Tyringham, MA: Whittle, 1990), 23.

2. Tanya Weinberg and Stephen Wershing, "Corporate Communications Come to Life with Animation," *Educational and Industrial Television* (March 1986): 41–44.

EXERCISES

1. Assume that you are preparing to tape a lecture on First Amendment rights. The lecture will be conducted using a chalkboard. The assignment is to clearly focus on the board and the text as your classmate writes the following:

   Congress shall make no law respecting an establishment of religion or prohibiting the free exercise

   thereof; or abridging the freedom of speech, or of the press; or the right of the people peaceably to assemble, and to petition the government for a redress of grievances.

   It is up to you to decide how you will plan in advance to fit the text within the proper aspect ratio and essential area. Also, you may have to give some

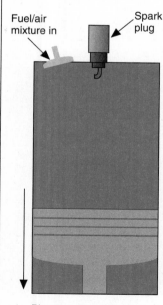
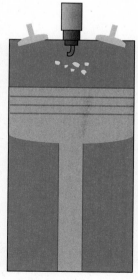

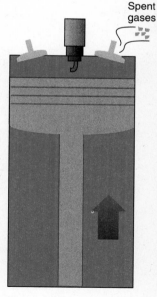

Fuel/air mixture in — Spark plug — Spent gases

Piston creates vacuum, draws fuel/air mixture in through intake valve.

Piston compressed fuel/air mixture.

Spark plug fires, exploding fuel/air mixture and creating power stroke.

Piston rises, and spent gasses are expelled through exhaust valve.

Figure 14.16 *Exercise 2 (on p. 196).* Put these four graphics in the proper aspect ratio to illustrate the workings of a four-stroke internal combustion engine.

thought as to whether the text will fit onto one screen of if you will have to make arrangements to divide it up and change cameras or camera angles. Your goal is to have *one smooth take* of your classmate writing the text on the chalkboard and to have the text *readable*.

If you have access to a character generator, prepare the same text to be displayed electronically. Pay particular attention to the typeface and the number of screens you will need in order for the text to be readable. Be sure to make a test recording and view the text from a normal viewing perspective.

2. Figure 14.16 shows an oversimplified diagram of how a cylinder works in an internal combustion engine.

Your job is to produce four separate graphics *in the proper aspect ratio* to illustrate the workings of a four-stroke engine. In addition to drawing the graphics (which does not take much artistic talent), you should put the captions on CG and insert them. (If you are storyboarding, find an aesthetically pleasing location for the captions.) Also, prepare a narration to read over the graphics. Any encyclopedia will tell you all you need to know in order to write a simple narration.

If possible, produce the whole segment on video. Or, depending on your instructor's wishes, you may simply storyboard the sequence.

PART 3

the applications

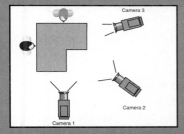

fundamentals of directing

OBJECTIVES

After completing Chapter 15, you will be able to:

1. Manage the fundamental details of studio and remote directing.
2. Work with talent to coax the best possible performance from them.
3. Direct a show from start to finish.

Directing a program is the acid test of your skills as both a video practitioner and as a manager of people and events. It could be argued that no task in modern mass media requires you to keep track of so many mental threads.

This chapter is fairly brief. After all, if you have been reading the chapters in sequence, there is little, technically, that you still need to master in order to direct a straightforward program. You have become familiar with the equipment, the flow of a typical program, and how the director and the technical director team up to call the shots.

In Chapter 15 we will put aside many of the technical considerations and focus on what, exactly, you must do when you take charge of a program. Specifically, we'll look at your role as a manager, an interpreter, and, of course, the person who calls the shots.

THE DIRECTOR AS MANAGER

When a video production falls apart, its pieces collapse faster than falling dominoes. To cite another analogy, no chain is stronger than its weakest link. All video production involves teamwork, and video is, in fact, a *series* of links in a chain. Once one link breaks, it causes a chain reaction of sorts—the links just keep popping.

The breakup can come before or during a program. Because the director is in charge of both the preplanning and actual production-time aspects of the show, your responsibilities don't end until the lenses are capped, the tape is in the box, and the studio lights are shut off.

No one, of course, can physically handle all the duties associated with a production, which is why the duties of studio or remote production are typically distributed along a chain of command.

Managing in the Studio

During a studio shoot, the director reports to the producer. As mentioned in Chapter 2, the producer may be an actual hands-on coworker or may be a distant executive in overall charge of the program but not directly involved in its execution. In either event, the director is responsible to the producer for ensuring that:

- The program is technically acceptable
- The program fulfills its promises—that is, the final product bears a resemblance to what was proposed and expected
- The overall operations go smoothly, on schedule, and within budget

For all intents and purposes, it is the director who is in charge once the cameras are uncapped. Even if the producer is a hands-on type, it is likely that he or she will not countermand orders of the director. The director's chair is something akin to the chair of a ship's captain; the captain may have an admiral on board as a passenger, but the captain still gives the orders.

Sometimes directors feel uncomfortable with being at the top of the chain of command. Indeed, it is a heavy responsibility and there are occasions when the director must firmly instruct the crew as to who, exactly, is in charge.

Remember, though, that crew members typically *welcome* a firm (but not unfriendly) hand. It is disconcerting for a camera operator, for example, to be unsure as to what, specifically, he or she is expected to do. A technical director given incomplete instructions will often be under unneeded and unwanted tension, because he or she has enough to worry about (pushing the right buttons and setting up the right shots) without having to guess at what the director wants.

So keep in mind that authority does and should flow from the director to the crew and talent through a clear chain of command. In most cases you have three primary links: the assistant director, who helps you keep track of time cues and other details; the floor director, who is your link to the studio and passes along your instructions to the talent; and the technical director, who operates the switcher and in some cases assumes additional leadership responsibilities. (Note that many directors do their own button pushing; you won't always have a TD in all cases.)

The camerapeople, lighting director, and audio director usually take their cues directly from you too. They typically do not have people below them in the chain of command, so an order given to one of them—"open the host's mic"—will be carried out directly. But those key people who serve as your links in the chain of command will pass along your orders and make sure they are executed. For example, you may say to the floor director, "Bob is slouching in his chair . . . when we go to the break please tell him to sit up straight." Or you may ask the assistant director to supervise studio setup. The possibilities are manifold, but remember that a director cannot handle each and every detail, so some authority must be delegated.

Managing at Remote Shoots

Handling detail becomes vastly more complex on location, where many factors are out of your control. We'll detail those factors in Chapter 17. At this point, suffice it to say that you'll be worried about variables such as location clearances (permission to shoot in a certain area), power availability, and even weather.

When remote directing is done multicamera through a switcher, it differs little from standard studio directing, except that setup and logistics are more difficult. But when remote directing involves single-camera video, which is probably the most typical scenario, the director must be in charge of setting up scenes and keeping track of the continuity and coherence of the program.

One major function of the director in such a scenario is to brief performers on what will be happening in the shot (Figure 15.1). Although the public generally is not aware of it, the remote site is where a director really earns his or her salary. Many who observe directors coaching talent think that the director's prompting—"Now remember, you've just been told that the major order has been canceled, and you're angry but still . . ."—is self-indulgent acting commentary. But nothing could be further from the truth, and here's why.

The director is the one person who has a complete sketch of the program in his or her head, and because the pieces of a single-camera video program are almost always shot out of sequence, it is the director who must preserve the continuity. That's why directors spend so much time

Figure 15.1   Coaching talent. The director is the one person with the "big picture" in mind who guides how the program will look and feel.

coaching talent. The director may not be concerned so much with wringing a good performance out of them as much as simply letting the performers *know what the scene involves*. The performers may have completely forgotten the context of their lines if, for example, the day's shooting schedule calls for the ending of the tape to be shot first, the beginning next, and the middle scenes after that.

Another underappreciated aspect of the remote-site director's duties is leading the small army of crewpeople and performers from shot to shot. Here, you usually won't be involved in an elaborate chain of command. You will simply be informing the crew as to what the next shot will be and where it will be taken.

This is extremely important! Don't forget that although you know the "big picture," the crew may not, and they'll look to you for *specific* advice. Heed the advice of producer Fred Ginsburg: "The crew must be told what the upcoming shot is supposed to be," he says. "Not the history and planned future of the entire six-day shoot, but merely the next shot. It sounds simplistic, I know, but describing just the single shot for the crew usually stumps a lot of the new directors."[1]

THE DIRECTOR AS COMMUNICATOR

In addition to calling the shots and leading the crew, the director is responsible for making the production communicate the proper message. This means creating the best possible visual image during production and inspiring talent to give their best performance.

The Professional-Quality Video Image

We take it for granted that a director will be able to guide his or her crew to produce properly framed and focused shots, and ensure that the audio quality is decent. (Those

wants. Novice directors have been known to shout, "Get it! Get it!" without giving crew members a clue as to what they are supposed to get.

Let's examine the basic structure of directing commands. To begin the discussion, let's define ready cues, take cues, adjustment cues, and time cues.

Ready Cues. **Ready cues**, sometimes known as "standby cues," are instructions telling crew members to get ready to perform a certain act. You will most commonly use ready cues when communicating with your TD, for example, "Ready to fade up on camera two." (Note: On switchers with preset monitors, the dialog is often "preset two.") "Ready to take graphic . . . Ready to lose graphic."

Ready cues are vitally important for two reasons: They let crew members prepare for the upcoming shot, and they *force you* to think ahead. Ideally, you should give a ready cue almost immediately after putting the current shot on the air. For example, if you are directing a newscast and have just gone to a videotape, *now* is the time to start thinking about which camera you will return to when the tape ends. Even if the tape is a minute and a half long, you should give ready cues and repeat them several times.

Here's an example. When you roll a taped insert, the assistant director will usually keep track of time remaining for you. If you don't have an AD, you must do it yourself. After you've "taken" the videotape (put it on air) your control room dialog may go something like this.

DIRECTOR: OK, we're in videotape. We'll come back to a close-up on camera 3. Camera 3, could you tighten up a bit and check your focus? Thank you.

ASSISTANT DIRECTOR: Sixty seconds to studio. [*meaning that you will return to the live shot in the studio after 60 seconds. There is no standard terminology for this; some ADs will simply say, "60 seconds left in tape" or something similar.*]

DIRECTOR: Ready to come back on camera 3. Ready 3. Ready to mic and cue talent.

ASSISTANT DIRECTOR: Thirty seconds to studio.

DIRECTOR: Thirty seconds to studio. [*You are repeating this command because generally the AD is not on headsets and cannot communicate with the rest of the crew.*] Ready camera 3. Ready to mic and cue talent.

ASSISTANT DIRECTOR: Ten seconds.

DIRECTOR: Ten seconds to studio. Ready to take 3, ready to mic and cue talent. Five seconds . . . four . . . three . . . two . . . take 3, mic and cue talent. [*Note: Some directors prefer to mic and cue talent an instant* before *they take the camera; this can prevent*

---

talent from appearing to have "egg on face" while waiting to start.]

It may seem redundant to throw so many "ready" cues, but by doing so you've accomplished several things: You have kept the audio operator alert, ready to open up the mic; you have kept camera 3's operator alert; and you have kept yourself on track too. Forcing yourself to issue frequent ready cues is a fine antidote for daydreaming.

Taking Cues. You can "take" any output of the switcher—camera, graphic, whatever. **Taking** means to put it on the air.

Some directors have their own idiosyncratic methods of issuing a taking cue, including saying, "take it," or sometimes snapping their fingers. However, it is advisable to issue a full command, such as "Take camera 3," or "Take the news logo."

For example, here's how you might instruct the TD to take the Eyewitness News Weather Watch logo over the shot of the weathercaster.

DIRECTOR: TD, get ready to take the Eyewitness News Weather Watch logo. [*Be very careful about just saying "logo" or "graphic" on first reference because you may have several logos and graphics.*] Let's see it on preview. It's tearing a little in the corner . . . can you adjust the clip? Good . . . ready to take logo in about five seconds. Ready logo . . . take logo.

In an ideal world, you would always give ready cues before taking a shot, but sometimes you'll have no choice but to take an emergency shot without warning. That's acceptable; it happens. But it is unprofessional to sit before the monitors without giving a ready cue and then suddenly announce, "Take one" when you had plenty of time to set up the shot. Camera 1 may be unfocused or otherwise unready for air.

Adjustment Cues. Remember the example given earlier where the director asked the camera operator to tighten up and check focus? That's a common adjustment cue. **Adjustment cues** are instructions to make some change in focus, framing, and so on. You'll frequently find yourself asking camera operators to change shots and check focus, essentially because you are looking at an air monitor that gives a more accurate representation of the shot than the viewfinder in the camera.

The key to giving an adjustment cue is to *always speak the name of the camera (or other piece of equipment) first.* Say, "Camera 3, tighten up please, you're too loose." Don't say, "Tighten up, you're too loose, Camera 3," because cameras 1 and 2 may initially think you're talking to them and start making that adjustment—and one of those cameras will be on air. We are assuming that camera 3 is off air, a safe assumption because you hardly ever want to make adjustments on air unless there's no choice.

You may want to make basic camera movements on air, though. For example, it is often effective to zoom in on air when the host opens the show. Assuming you have rehearsed this in advance, or at the least have confidence in an experienced camera operator, you can instruct him or her to make the move on air. But be *certain* to let the camera operator know that it's an on-air move. Camera operators sometimes lose track of whether they are on the air, and if you say, "Camera 1, zoom in on talent," you may get an abrupt adjustment; worse yet, the camera may go all the way in and focus and then pull back.

So whenever you want an on-air move, say so, and be specific as to what you want. Here is a good example:

DIRECTOR: Camera 1, you're hot [*on air*]. I want to do a slow on-air zoom into talent in about ten seconds. Go to a fairly tight close-up, maybe to the mic clipped on his tie. OK, camera 1, stand by to do an on-air zoom. Ready, do it.

Time Cues. One of the more difficult aspects of the director's job is closing the show and/or the segments on time. In most cases, a show must be closed *exactly* on time—meaning to the second—because you may be butting up against a network ID or network program. This is clearly the case in a local newscast that precedes the national news.

Although the AD may help you with timing of segments, it is your ultimate responsibility to make sure talent begins and ends on time. In that role, you will generally relay your instructions through the floor director. Figure 15.6 shows a comprehensive table of the actions the floor director uses to communicate with talent.

In general, the more time cues you can throw talent the better. **Time cues** indicate how much time is remaining. Talent usually appreciate knowing how many minutes are left in a program or segment, and need a countdown so that they can hit the close exactly. Talent also appreciate crisp, clear starting cues in which the floor director points to the lens of the taking camera.

Get your floor director in the habit of throwing clear cues because an unsure or lazy floor director can sabotage your entire program. For example, if you say, "Cue talent two minutes remaining," it is the floor director's responsibility to make sure he or she is *seen* by talent. Lazily holding up two fingers in a perfunctory gesture that may or may not be caught by the performer is counterproductive but, unfortunately, common. If the floor director is not working up to standards, it is your prerogative and duty to straighten that person out. Virtually all your control room–to–studio operations depend on the floor director.

The Critical Zones

Mistakes seem to happen with alarming regularity in openings, transitions to tape, and closings. The primary reason is that so many things are happening at once that the chances for a foul-up are multiplied.

Openings. Program openings are probably the most difficult sections to direct. Everything happens at once—you're starting the talent's delivery, coming up on the first camera, opening the audio channel, and possibly even flashing a graphic. A flubbed open can set a negative tone for the entire program.

When one of the authors taught a directing class, he did a thoroughly unscientific but nevertheless enlightening sampling, and found that out of 60 programs directed during the semester, of the ones that had serious mistakes almost 90 percent of those mistakes occurred during the first 30 seconds of the show.

Openings are traumatic for everyone, including the most experienced directors. So it is highly advisable to rehearse the opening in advance and to get your opening "patter" down cold. If necessary, write out some notes on what you are going to say. Take no chances, because if you forget to instruct the audio operator to open a mic, he or she may not do it.

According to some schools of thought, the audio operator is not supposed to perform an action on individual initiative, even if he or she is quite confident that it's supposed to happen. There is some merit to this argument, because on occasion there is a good reason for the director to instruct a crewperson to act counterintuitively. For example, a camera operator may know, or *think* he or she knows, that the director will desperately need a close-up in a split second. But perhaps there is a reason why the camera is not being put on close-up: Suppose, for example, the close-up of the book is actually on slide and being fed through the telecine, or being fed from computer memory storage? If the camera operator makes a move, he or she may leave the director stranded without a shot. So for the time being, it is probably best to operate on the assumption that crewpeople should not make any moves unless they are specifically instructed to do so. (This is also good training for the director, who is forced to think through the series of shots and cannot rely on crewpeople to save the show.)

In any event, you must clearly announce every command and brief the crew in advance of taking shots. Here, for instance, is how you might open up a news program.

DIRECTOR: OK, two minutes to air. Audio, are the mics checked? Good. Floor director, has the prompter operator straightened out that script problem? OK. We're going to open up on camera 2 with a wide shot of the set and then cut to a close-up of Cindy on camera 1. Floor, make sure Cindy

CUE

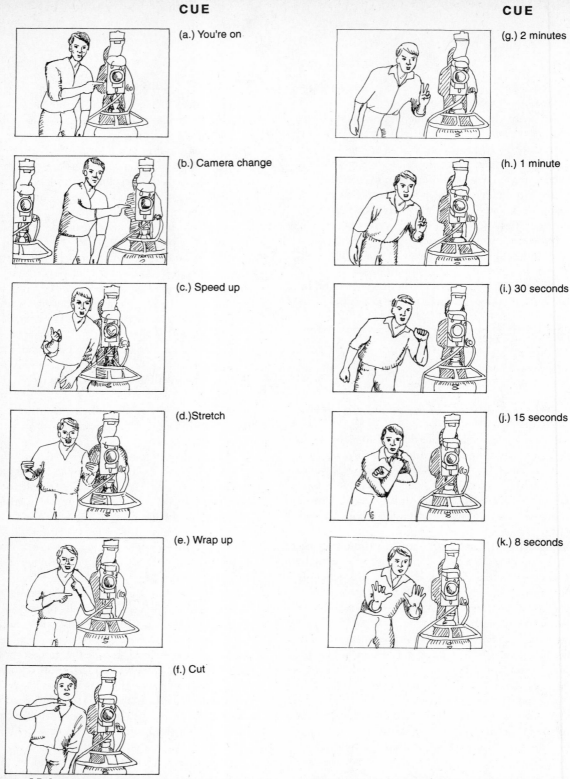

(a.) You're on

(b.) Camera change

(c.) Speed up

(d.) Stretch

(e.) Wrap up

(f.) Cut

CUE

(g.) 2 minutes

(h.) 1 minute

(i.) 30 seconds

(j.) 15 seconds

(k.) 8 seconds

Figure 15.6 Table of floor director cues. These are some of the cues more frequently used by the floor director. Commonly used signals vary from facility to facility so always review with the floor director and talent before taping or going on the air live. A pointed finger (A) means "You're on!" A sweeping and pointing motion (B) indicates a camera change (see also Figures 15.3 and 15.4). One finger twirled (C) means "speed up." A motion imitating stretching a rubber band (D) means "stretch" or "slow down." Two-handed twirling motion (E) means "wrap up." Finger drawn across throat (F) means "cut."

When using hand signals to indicate time, minute cues are given with the fingers of one hand: (G) 2 minutes, (H) 1 minute. A clenched fist (I) means 30 seconds remaining, and crossed arms (J) mean 15 seconds; but these two signals are often used to indicate exactly the opposite timings, so determine the appropriate use for your operation. Counting down on fingers (K) is used to help talent on an exact time: 8 seconds is indicated.

knows she's going to open on camera 1. Tell her now, and be sure to cue her to the camera when I tell you. After Cindy reads the first story we'll go to a close-up of Mark on camera 3. Audio, make sure you don't open Mark's mic until I cue you because he's got a cold and he keeps clearing his throat.

One minute to air. We're in black. Ready to fade up on camera 2's wide shot. Audio, ready to roll theme. TD, get ready to super the logo over the wide shot, then lose it when I cue you.

Thirty seconds to air. Ready to fade up on camera 2, ready to roll theme, ready graphic, ready to mic and cue Cindy.

Ten seconds to air. Five . . . four . . . three . . . two . . .

Fade up on camera 2. Bring up theme. Ready graphic . . . take graphic. Ready to lose graphic . . . lose it. Audio, start bringing down theme.

Ready to take camera 1 . . . ready to mic and cue Cindy.

Lose theme.

Take 1. Mic and cue Cindy. [*Remember, some directors like to cue talent and then take the shot, on the premise that TDs react quickly but talent do not. This is something you'll have to determine for yourself. Do what works best for you and your crew.*] Ready camera 3.

Notice that the dialog left little room for ambiguity and that it clearly led the crew through the opening.

Transition to Tape. Now, let's "listen in" as the director pulls the program through the other critical zone, the introduction of a taped segment.

DIRECTOR: Ready to roll VTR 1 in about fifteen seconds.

The purpose for this dialog is that the director has back-timed a five-second roll, meaning that you have marked in your script the word the talent will be saying five seconds before the tape rolls. There's no secret to this; simply read at a rate approximating the talent's pace and find out how many words he or she reads in five seconds, then back up that number of words from the intro to the tape. That's when you want the tape to roll. Count back *another*

five seconds' worth of words and you've got a five-second countdown to the preroll.

DIRECTOR: AD, give me a countdown to the preroll.

This direction means that you want the assistant director to count down to the time when the tape will start, *which, remember, is five seconds before it airs.*

AD: OK, five, four, three . . .

DIRECTOR: Ready to roll VTR 1

AD: two, one . . .

DIRECTOR: Roll it!

Closings. Here's one way a director can handle this critical zone.

DIRECTOR: Floor, give talent one-minute cue.

We're going to close on the wide shot on camera 2. Camera 2, could you widen out a little more? Thanks. Hold it there.

Audio, ready to bring up theme. Ready to roll credits.

Floor, ready to give talent thirty-second cue. Cue her.

Ready camera 2, ready theme, ready credits.

Floor, ready to give talent fifteen. Cue her. OK, start counting her down from ten.

Ready camera 2; take 2. Ready theme; bring up theme. Ready credits; roll credits.

[*After credits finish rolling from the* CG] OK, ready to fade to black, ready to lose theme. Lose theme; fade to black.

The dialog varies, of course, but we recommend that you study these examples as illustrations of how a director handles some of the more troublesome portions of a studio presentation. And because directing is so closely related to the production of many types of video, you may wish to scan relevant sections in the chapter on editing, remote operations, and, in particular, the talk show. Chapter 18 provides a sample directing strategy for an on-set interview, and is, of all the remaining chapters in Part 3, most directly relevant to the material discussed so far.

SUMMARY

1. A video director is a manager of people and equipment, an interpreter of ideas, and the person who eventually "calls the shots" when the program is taped or aired.

2. Directing can be a studio-based function, where the director essentially calls the shots from the control room, or it can be a function performed in the field. When directing in the field, the task often involves

single-camera video, shot film-style. This particular type of directing is covered in greater detail in Chapter 16. But it is important to note at this point that a critical function of the director's duties is to maintain continuity in single-camera video shooting.

3. The director must assess whether a project is suitable for video and make sure the translation to video is successful. One important, but often overlooked, function of the director is to determine what "works" and what doesn't. As discussed earlier in this book, video has certain strengths and weaknesses, and it is important that the director not plan a program that is inherently unsuited for video.

4. When working with talent, make an initial assessment of each individual's skills. There's no use in coaching a pro on basics or, conversely, overwhelming a novice with intricate detail.

5. Directors must frequently deal with a talent's performance anxiety. One of the best techniques is to discuss the fact that almost all performers are anxious, regardless of their skill and experience, but that the nervous energy generated by a healthy case of camera fright can be put to good use when translated into energy.

6. Advise talent to look directly into the camera lens and keep their energy level high.

7. Most directors lay down test and tone and a slate at the beginning of their tape.

8. A director is often involved in a project from the planning stage right through completion.

9. The core task of directing, of course, is calling the shots. As mentioned in the text and demonstrated by the examples, some of the more important aspects of calling the shots include always giving ready cues, addressing cameras by giving the camera number first (rather than giving the command and then specifying which camera is supposed to carry out the action), and issuing coherent and concise commands.

10. You will give a variety of instructions, or cues, but the four main categories discussed in this chapter are ready cues, taking cues, adjustment cues, and time cues. Try never to give a taking cue without first giving a ready cue.

NOTE

1. Fred Ginsburg, "What Your Crew Expects," *AV Video* (September 1986): 51. Ginsburg, a well-known producer and director of institutional video, writes regularly on hands-on problems encountered in the studio and in the field.

TECHNICAL TERMS

above-the-line personnel	prompting device	slate	test and tone
adjustment cues	ready cues	taking cues	time cues
below-the-line personnel			

EXERCISES

1. Here is a brief script for a news program with a male and a female anchor. For the sake of simplicity, we have identified them as anchor male and anchor female.

Video	Audio
LS news set	Theme music
Graphic: News at 10	
CU Anchor Female	Good evening, and welcome to the News at 10. I'm _____.
CU Anchor Male	And I'm _____. The top story tonight . . . A cargo plane crashes on takeoff at Municipal Airport. Only

Video	Audio
	seconds after leaving the runway, a Western Star cargo transport nose-dived into the pavement.
CU Anchor Female	None of the five crew members were injured, but the plane burned for more than six hours. Fire fighters had to remove individual containers and extinguish the fire bit by bit. A spokesperson for the airline says the plane was carrying containers of mail bound for England.

Assume that you are recording this script. You will want to include test and tone. *Write down* every command you anticipate making, including ready cues, roll and record commands, and so forth. Completely script your directorial commands. It might be interesting, at this time, to compare your scripted commands with those of your classmates.

2. Now, place a man and a woman at a desk and do the recording. Follow your script as closely as possible. If there are any glaring mistakes or awkward moments, correct them now.

3. Direct this opening *without* the script after you have made some practice runs.

fundamentals of editing

OBJECTIVES

After completing Chapter 16, you will be able to:

1. Use your skills as an editor to guide and shape the *concept* of a program, as well as the mechanics.
2. Use various aesthetic techniques to create moods and convey ideas.
3. Develop a visual "vocabulary" with which you can communicate abstract concepts such as pace, tension, and suspense.

Editing methods might be considered the basic grammar of the visual language of television. Those techniques go beyond the technical operations involved in editing (Chapter 7). In this chapter, we'll explore some of the aesthetic questions faced by the person in charge of editing. For example, how does an editor know when to use cuts or dissolves? Fast transitions between shots or slow? Should the cut be made while action is happening on screen or after the action occurs?

THE OVERALL THRUST OF THE PROGRAM

Because editing is an artistic as well as a technical skill, we will explore how to use editing techniques to reinforce the *message* of the medium and keep the program's theme clear and consistent. These are important roles for the editor, and it should be noted that in the best of circumstances, the editor is part of the production process right from the program's inception. So—in order to begin from the beginning—we'll first discuss the editor's role in coordinating with the writer and director and in planning the editing strategy in order to maintain a consistent flow of the program.

Coordinating with the Writer

Video is, by its very nature, a team effort, so the editor will often be involved in coordinating the efforts of several people. Whereas in years gone by the editor might have been regarded by some as a well-trained button pusher, that is no longer the case. Competent editors, in fact, command very handsome salaries in many production facilities

because their expertise contributes immeasurably to the success of a program.

In practical terms, you (as the editor) will often be the intermediary between people who completely understand the video process, such as the project's director, and those who don't; often, that latter group includes "concept people" such as the writers.

We're not asserting that all writers know absolutely nothing about video, but they often will not have the depth of technical knowledge that a director or editor will have. In many cases, writers assigned to video projects have experience with varying media but do not, on a day-to-day basis, commit words to paper *that must then be translated to video*. Even writers with some experience in audiovisual techniques are often "word people" rather than "picture people" and, therefore, need some guidance from the editor and/or director.

It's advisable for the writer, director, and editor to meet several times during the process of writing the script in order to ensure that the program is on track. For the sake of discussion, we are assuming that the writer, director, and editor are three people. In some cases the director and editor will be one in the same, and sometimes, in a one-person production such as a news report in a small-market TV station, one person will assume all three roles. The points to be discussed, though, are relevant regardless of the division of labor.

Many of your early projects may involve you in both the directing and editing process. Although editors in large operations may not be directly involved in the planning and execution of the program, we will approach this discussion from the standpoint of director/editor. If you do become involved in the editing process strictly as an editor, or strictly as a director, you may have the opportunity to interact with the writer at various times during the production. Even if you do not, a thorough understanding of editing techniques can do nothing but help.

Let's assume you are planning to edit a program and have the opportunity to interact with the writer. Is it worthwhile to touch base? Absolutely! Writers, especially those who are not expert in video production, will probably welcome initial guidance—and even if they don't, you'll be saving yourself and them a great deal of remedial effort if you flag potential problems before too much of the script is conceived and written. In order to ensure that the words written will be translatable to the video medium, it is advisable for the editor to instruct the writer to keep the program narrow in focus, not overly dense in its presentation of information, and in the form of a narrative story that has some sort of forward-moving plot.

Narrowing Focus. Employing a "narrow focus" means that the program must pick one theme and stick to it. Elaborate sidebars and subplots may work in a book or long article, but the linear nature of video requires the writer to stick closely to the central idea. As you read initial and successive versions of the script, you can spot digressions that will confuse the viewer.

For example, you are the editor on the production team creating a 22-minute documentary on the plight of the small family farm in America. The writer wants to include a section dealing with one son of a farming family who moved to New York City—but the section, as it stands, will run 7 minutes and will deal with many examples of the son's duties as a stockbroker. Although this might work in print, an editor familiar with "video language" will immediately recognize that the digression will make the program confusing to the viewer.

A much briefer and less-detailed exploration of the stockbroker's life will make the point but not scatter the theme.

Limiting Density. The guardian of video grammar must also be sure that the writer does not pack too much information into the wording of the script. Writers with more experience in print media than in visual media sometimes have a tendency to write for the eye and not for the ear. If the person responsible for the editing (who may or may not be the editor) can spot this early, "mopping up" later won't be necessary.

For example, you are part of the production team for an instructional videotape demonstrating the use of a new computer to novice users. The script reads like a highly detailed instruction manual, listing the operations point by point and referring back to them ("Then repeat the operation you performed in step 2"). The viewer has no way of referring back to the information, so references to the various steps are meaningless. Your goal is to convince the writer to convey a realistic amount of information and make it comprehensible to the viewer; pare down the verbiage and think in terms of visuals.

Maintaining Narrative Flow. You, as the editor, must be sure that the writer understands that a program must (1) have movement throughout, (2) have a beginning, middle, and conclusion, and (3) be planned around a narrative theme.

For example, you are the editor on a production team that is beginning work on a documentary about a major contest among young pianists. During initial planning, you realize that the writer intends to focus on the history of the competition and the multitude of people involved in the event. As editor, you realize that this just won't work. You'll have a lot of talking heads but no real forward motion. Perhaps you'd recommend that the program focus on one contestant—his or her preparation, battles with exhaustion and nerves, struggles with the piece he or she is preparing for the contest, and the pianist's reaction to victory or defeat.

To reiterate, the most important aspect of the editor's interaction with the writer during the initial planning phase is to ensure that the ideas will work on the small screen. Basically, that means the script must be relatively simple and have a clear flow.

Working with the Director

If you are part of a team where the director and editor are separate crew members, you can be of enormous help to the director by making sure his or her ideas actually materialize in the editing room. In fact, an enlightened director will probably be looking to you for guidance in this area.

What kind of guidance can you offer? For starters, you can be sure that you have enough footage, appropriate collateral video, and an economically sound editing plan.

Ensuring an Adequate Supply of Footage. Isn't having enough footage a rather obvious concept? Not really. Directors who worry about budgets and time often undershoot. Sometimes they become too close to a project, and although they are quite comfortable with the broad view, forget about some of the details. Even directors who do their own editing fall victim to these problems, so be careful. Remember that the raw material must contain enough footage to create a complete, comprehensive scene.

For example, the director is shooting a one-camera, film-style drama. A particularly long scene promises to be unpleasantly static. You might take it upon yourself to *tactfully* remind the director that he or she will need a generous supply of reaction shots from the other actor (both to add variety and to allow editing of the main actor's monologue) and close-ups.

Conversely, remember that a director can make an editor's job easier too. Some clarification of how editors

BOX 16.1   THE EDITOR AND THE DIRECTOR

In cases where the editor and director are not the same person, the editor and director can work together to make their respective jobs easier. However, if the editor and director work at cross-purposes, everyone's job can be made considerably more difficult. Here's a realistic look at how the two positions interact.

We have suggested that an editor be involved in preproduction. In an ideal world, that would happen in every case; in reality, such cooperative effort sometimes does not materialize. Often, the editor is brought into the process only in postproduction. But if you are a director, you can help yourself by involving the editor as early as possible. If you are the editor, you can help the director and everyone associated with the project by becoming involved in the project from its early stages.

Recognize that when the editor and director are separate positions, the editor is subordinate to the director. This means, of course, that an editor's suggestions must be made tactfully.

Tactful suggestions are often quite welcome. Experienced producers know that a good editor can vastly improve a program. News producers at CBS, for example, typically place great value in the suggestions of their editors. The producers know that the editors have a unique perspective and can bring a fresh point of view to a piece. Editors are never regarded as mere button pushers.

So there's a mutual give-and-take, and in some cases a great deal of overlap, between the functions. Here are some suggestions on how editors can help directors and vice-versa.

If you're the director, you can help the editor by ensuring that your camera operator takes adequate footage before and after the shot. By all means, be sure that you have at least 10 seconds of control track (even if it's not a usable shot) so that the editing equipment can lock up properly. In addition, be certain that there is a "pad" of usable footage at the beginning and the end of the shot. This will allow the editor more flexibility in choice of the edit point, and also give some breathing room should the editor decide that a longer shot would be appropriate.

The director can also ensure that there is a variety of shots. "Detail shots" are very useful: wringing hands, coffee cups, the pictures on the wall. They frequently add flexibility, believability, and impact.

If you are the editor, you can help the director by keeping close track of the locations of individual shots. Keeping careful records of shot locations and making sure the stack of tapes is organized logically will speed the process considerably.

Don't be afraid to offer suggestions. Be tactful, but remember that you do have a certain expertise that will be valuable to the director.

---

and directors do, and how they can make each other's lives a little less hectic, is outlined in Box 16.1.

Planning Collateral Video. By **collateral video**, we mean other types of video that may be essential to the success of the program. Graphics, animation, and stock shots are good examples. The wise editor thinks ahead; some of this material must be ordered in advance so that it's on hand during the final editing process.

For example, you and the director are working with a script that calls for a shot of the New York City skyline. Unfortunately, you're in Los Angeles. Flying a crew to New York is not only unfeasible but unnecessary. You can simply contact an agency that deals with stock film and video and order the right scene for a reasonable fee. But you must place the order far enough in advance so that you have the shot on hand.

As another example, you are commencing work on an instructional videotape that demonstrates the workings of a complex piece of scientific equipment. You realize that it will be difficult or impossible for the audience to understand what is going on through standard video shots.

Graphics and computerized animation will be necessary. Pointing this out to the director will allow you to secure the needed graphics in time.

Planning for Continuity. In video production, the role of "continuity director" often falls to the editor. *You* are the one who will be putting the shots together, so you should be thinking—well in advance—of what you and the director need to have in hand at the end of shooting, before the footage is edited.

We have discussed continuity in Chapter 11, but it is worth repeating that you must avoid visual lapses. Having a performer's coat disappear and reappear during one scene (which was edited down from shots taken over several days) is an obvious example. Also, pay close attention to the angle from which shots are taken. If you note that shots are "crossing the axis," bring it up tactfully. (For example, if the cameraperson has indiscriminately taken shots from the front and rear of a car traveling down the street, the two sets of shots cannot be edited together because the car will be headed in opposite directions.)

Guiding the Viewer through Space. Here's a classic

example of how the editor "helps" the viewer through a visual sequence. The plot in a TV comedy calls for someone to sneak into his boss's office to retrieve the letter of resignation he'd written as the result of some dreadful mistake. The boss, of course, hasn't opened the mail yet.

But he returns to the office—while our hero is busy rifling through the mail. The boss makes a quick call, telling an associate that he'll be in the office all evening. Our hero hides in the closet and, sensing that the boss sooner or later will hang up his coat, realizes that it's now or never;

he has to make his escape before the closet door is opened.

A good editor, working closely with the director, can make this a compelling scene. Here, step-by-step, is how the editor might cut the scene for maximum impact.

1. We need an establishing shot to show the overall layout of the room. If the viewer doesn't see that there is a closet, and that it's located behind the boss's desk, closer shots will be in "limbo," and won't cause the viewer to make the right mental connections (Figure 16.1a).

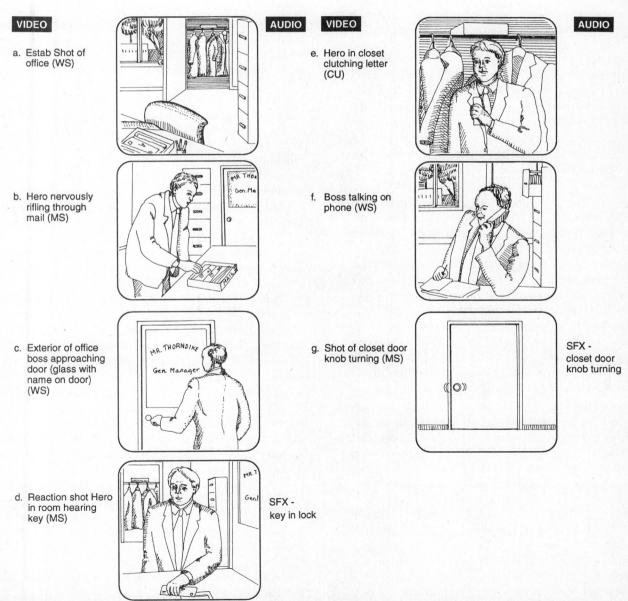

VIDEO

a. Estab Shot of office (WS)

b. Hero nervously rifling through mail (MS)

c. Exterior of office boss approaching door (glass with name on door) (WS)

d. Reaction shot Hero in room hearing key (MS)

AUDIO

SFX - key in lock

VIDEO

e. Hero in closet clutching letter (CU)

f. Boss talking on phone (WS)

g. Shot of closet door knob turning (MS)

AUDIO

SFX - closet door knob turning

Figure 16.1 Guiding the viewer through space. A good director plans a scene so the viewer understands the "geography of the location."

2. To prepare for the moment when the hero hears the boss's key turn in the lock, we need to see him in action, to clearly show his anxiety about rifling through the boss's mail (Figure 16.1b).

3. The suspense will be heightened if we see an exterior shot of the boss approaching his door from the outside (Figure 16.1c).

4. The suspense will largely be lost if the viewer doesn't realize that the door will open right into the room where the hero is rummaging through the desk. (We need to provide what Stephen Spielberg calls a geography of the location.) So the editor might opt for a reaction shot of the hero as he hears the key being turned in the lock, coupled with a quick cut of the interior of the office door *to show the viewer the exact layout of the scene*. It would be particularly helpful to cut from the shot described under point No. 3 to this shot if, for example, the door had one of the old-fashioned translucent windows painted with the legend, "Mr. Thorndike, General Manager." The interior shot, showing the letters in reverse, would clearly set the scene (Figures 16.1c and 16.1d).

5. We need a close-up of the hero hiding in the closet, clutching the precious letter (Figure 16.1e). Note that if we had not already established the scene—desk, office, closet—the viewer might become disoriented.

6. A good editor knows the value of suspense. To have the boss *immediately* look out the window and have the hero *instantly* make his attempt to sneak in back of him to the door would be a horrible waste of good adrenaline. So the editor knows to make this a very long scene. Perhaps the hero pokes his head out at the same time the boss turns to toss a crumpled piece of paper in the trash. Perhaps the boss makes a move toward the closet after hanging up his coat but is summoned back to the desk by the intercom. And as the boss talks on the phone, (Figure 16.1f) back to the closet, we see a cut to the knob on the closet door, the knob slowly turns a bit, (Figure 16.1g) and . . .

You get the idea. Guiding the viewer with good editing is part display of information and part emotional manipulation. Don't be squeamish about the latter point, because at least in our example—the mystery—viewers *want* to be manipulated. They certainly don't want the crime committed and solved in the first minute of the show. Otherwise, what would be the point of *doing* the show?

Making the Best Use of Time. Our previous example showed an editing scenario where it was logical to lengthen a certain section of the scene.[1] But an editor often has to plan the cuts and dissolves to achieve just the opposite effect.

Nowhere is this more evident than in the production of a television commercial. **Stealing seconds** (cutting away unnecessary seconds) is the name of the game, because given the price of broadcast and cable advertising, no one can afford wasted time. Even feature films steal seconds from scenes that do not advance the action. Even though a film director has more than an hour and a half of plot, he or she can't afford to waste time and bore the viewer.

Here's an example that would apply to any scene shot for film, video programming, or a commercial. Assume you are editing a scene in which a woman gets out of a cab, pays the driver, climbs a flight of steps to her lawyer's office, and enters. You would not want to do this in real time unless you want to drag the scene out for suspense value. (**Real time** is the actual time needed to play out an event as it would happen in reality.) Viewers simply won't sit still for mundane scenes played out in real time. So unless there's a compelling reason (the suspense angle) for showing the woman getting out of the taxi, paying the driver, walking up the steps, opening the door, and walking in, don't play the whole sequence as it would appear in reality. (Didn't you get bored just *reading* the sequence of events?)

Instead, take what would be a minute's worth of action and compress it into a few seconds. Use a quick shot of her paying the driver; forget about all the conversation that normally goes along with this ritual ("Thanks, here's five dollars. Keep the change. Can I have a receipt? Have a nice day. Yeah, you too."). Show her taking one or two steps on the staircase, and then cut to a shot of the door opening. Your next cut, after an establishing shot of the lawyer's office, could be a close-up of the receptionist.

There are countless examples of how reality is compressed in television commercials, the medium of the "million dollar minute." If you are showing a couple entering a client's restaurant and being seated by the headwaiter, you certainly don't want to show the 10 seconds of walking that typically accompanies this task. Fill the commercial with shots that show the benefits of the restaurant: the ambience, the clean kitchen staffed with French chefs, the chandeliers—*anything* except meaningless real-time motion.

You're probably now pondering a relevant question: Won't viewers notice your manipulations? No, not if you steal seconds logically. For example, the viewer *will* notice a "jump" if you have someone talking as he takes the first step down a long staircase and continues with the same line when you suddenly cut to a shot of him at the landing near the bottom of the staircase. You've injected another frame of reference (the spoken lines), which will point out that there's been a leap in time. But you can easily fix this by having the actor deliver one line as he descends the *middle* of the staircase and then provide a brief break before he delivers his next line at the landing.

Aside from such obvious breaks in continuity, you can manipulate time quite freely. And if you have remaining doubts about whether viewers will accept compressed reality, take a close look at the way telephone dialogue is handled on TV or film. The next time you see a program or film that shows someone talking on the phone, you'll notice that people rarely say "goodbye," or engage in any of the typical chitchat that accompanies a real-time, real-life phone call. They also absorb much more information listening to the phone than could possibly be communicated in real-life real time.

Why do editors handle telephone scenes this way? Because it's boring to watch what someone at one end of a telephone call really does. So editors take enormous liberties with real time—liberties that you've probably never noticed.

THE EDITOR'S OPTIONS

We'll take some liberties with real time ourselves and fast-forward to the actual production stage—the day when somebody has handed you a pile of tapes and expects you to turn them into a program. What you'll need to do is to choose the proper techniques for editing the particular tapes onto the record unit, all the while keeping in mind the expressive qualities of the various editing methods.

Choosing the Proper Techniques

How you will go about editing all the visual and audio elements involves many decisions, but the first step involves viewing all the footage. What you anticipated after seeing the script may not particularly resemble what is handed to you in the tape packages.

So before you make decisions about cuts versus dissolves, the need for graphics, timing and pace, and other issues, you may first suggest some rewriting or reshooting. Remember, as the person who sees all the footage and who will have to create every inch of the final product, you have a right and a responsibility to express your opinion. If you view initial footage and find, perhaps, that there is not enough cover video, or that the actor misspoke on several important lines, speak up.

Next, you'll put the pieces of the puzzle together, but on paper or on the computer first. The editing suite is really not the place to make initial decisions. Editing is an expensive process, especially when you must rent facilities. When initial shooting is complete, part of your job will be to log the shots to be used so that you can quickly find the proper tape and shot.

For example, let's say you're about to make the first cut of a documentary and have rented time in an editing suite. The cost could be from $160 to $500 per hour. By planning all the edits in advance, viewing the tapes, and constructing an efficient editing plan you can save thousands of dollars. The expensive on-line suite is the wrong place to be spooling through tapes trying to find an elusive shot.

Figure 16.2 Portable video editing. The VideoToolKit™ is a software and cable package that makes it possible to edit a "rough-cut" almost anywhere. Here, powered by batteries, a Macintosh™ Powerbook™, a Sony Hi8 Handycam™, and a VideoWalkman™ are set up to log and assemble a rough edit.

The personal computer can help you make edit decisions. New software allows you to view tape, log shots, and print out an initial "decision list" without having to visit an editing suite. Figures 16.2 through 16.4 show how an editor can plan his or her shot list using one tape deck and a computer running logging editing software.

Expressive Qualities of Various Editing Methods

Now we're approaching the actual hands-on edit. What method—cuts only or A-B roll—is best? If money were not a factor, you would probably always opt for the A-B–capable suite, because that allows you to use dissolves and other effects. But it costs significantly more to book a sophisticated editing suite. Even if your company, school,

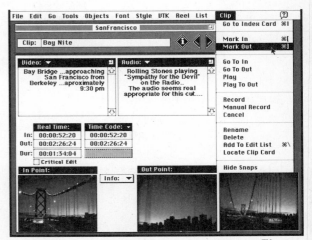

Figure 16.3 Editing and logging. Using the VideoToolKit™ ClipCard commands, you can maintain pertinent audio and video information as you edit a video sequence. The clips you insert in a video sequence are automatically added to an edit decision list.

```
TITLE:    "Bay Bridge"
FCM: NON-DROP FRAME

001  001  A2/V  C  00:00:52:20 00:02:26:24 01:00:00:00 02:20:08:06
SanFrancisco,Bay Nite

002  001  A2/V  C  00:03:00:18 00:03:23:24 01:00:34:11 01:00:57:17
SanFrancisco,Bay Day

003  001  A2/V  C  01:37:46:18 01:42:25:14 01:00:57:17 01:05:36:13
SanFrancisco,drivers

004  002  A2/V  C  01:01:54:02 01:06:00:10 01:05:36:13 01:09:42:21
Bridge,Sky view

005  002  A2/V  C  00:55:02:06 00:56:11:22 01:09:42:21 01:10:52:07
Bridge,Drawings

006  002  A2/V  C  00:50:09:14 00:54:48:18 01:10:52:07 01:15:31:11
Bridge,Planner

007  002  A2/V  C  01:08:48:22 01:26:03:01 01:15:31:11 01:32:45:20
Bridge,Sky view 1

008  001  A2/V  C  00:03:47:16 00:05:31:24 01:32:45:20 01:34:29:28
SanFrancisco,Construction Plans

009  001  A2/V  C  00:07:30:18 00:09:57:11 01:34:29:28 01:36:56:21
SanFrancisco,Demographic Survey

010  002  A2/V  C  00:31:48:20 00:37:55:28 01:36:56:21 01:43:03:29
Bridge,Architect

012  002  A2/V  C  01:01:08:12 01:01:39:14 01:47:10:07 01:47:41:09
Bridge,Community Reports

013  001  A2/V  C  01:37:46:18 01:42:25:14 01:47:41:09 01:52:20:05
SanFrancisco,drivers

014  001  A2/V  C  00:03:00:18 00:03:23:24 01:52:20:05 01:52:43:11
SanFrancisco,Bay Day
```

Figure 16.4 Edit decision list (EDL). As a tool for final editing, the EDL describes each segment (or "clip") in a video sequence, identifying the segment number, the source tape number, the edit type, and the transition (*Cut*, *Dissolve*, or *Wipe*). The time codes represent the source in and out points and the record in and out points.

The second line for each segment is reserved for comments. In this case, source tape 1 is called SanFrancisco, and the first segment is called Bay Nite.

or organization owns the suite, there will be some cost involved, including wear and tear on the equipment and the indirect cost of moving other projects out of the on-line suite.

Your decision, then, primarily centers on whether you need the capability to do dissolves and add sophisticated graphics. Dissolves can change the thrust and focus of your program by offering an additional method of expression. At this point you are ready to make this first-stage decision. You know that dissolves (and in some cases wipes) let you:

- Indicate transitions of time and place
- Make gentler transitions between shots, a virtual necessity if you are editing together a ballet, for example

You also realize that high-end editing suites will typically offer you more options for graphics. High-tech graphics are not always necessary, but enhanced graphics capabilities let you:

- Give the program a slick, high-tech look. Although this is not always needed or desirable, it is a factor to consider if you are editing, let's say, a video annual report for a computer firm.

- Show representations not easily created by standard video.

The choice is not always clear-cut, but remember that it is sometimes more difficult (and in the long run, more expensive) to scramble about for some way to create a necessary effect.

Note, too, that the newest generation of editing gear allows you to work in a nonlinear fashion. Box 16.2 contains some information on what this technology means to directors and editors.

HOW EDITING CAN CHANGE THRUST AND FOCUS: PRACTICAL EXAMPLES

Now we'll draw all the previously presented information together and close on a very practical note, a demonstration of the implied visual grammar of:

- Fast versus slow shot changes
- Cuts versus dissolves and wipes
- Close-ups versus long shots
- On-camera action versus voice over
- Cutting audio before video or vice-versa
- Cutting on action versus cutting on a static scene

These six choices represent fairly typical decisions you'll confront as you edit your piece. We'll present a rationale for each method, because the choices should be made by design and not by happenstance. Why? Because each choice represents not only a technical decision but a decision about the way you are *expressing* your ideas through the editing process.

Fast versus Slow Shot Changes

Do you want to use lingering shots of long duration, short-duration shots, or a combination of the two? You'll probably opt for a combination, but it's important to know what the fast and slow pace communicate.

What Shorter Shots Communicate

- *Action or excitement.*
- *Building energy or tension.* You'll typically speed up your transitions toward the end of the program.
- An *overview of the scene.* Fast transitions can serve to cue viewers that they are seeing a series of "snapshots."
- *Anticipation.* You can use rapid cuts to indicate that something is about to happen. Cutting quickly between the closet door (remember the hero) and the boss sitting at his desk is a sure tension builder.
- *Instantaneous change.* Fast cuts indicate that things are happening quickly.

BOX 16.2 NONLINEAR EDITING

Digital editing technology is now used by many major production firms and has, in effect, made the need for a linear program laid down piece by piece on a record unit tape obsolete. The editor using a digital system can store video in computer memory and select shots in a **nonlinear** fashion, meaning that the editor can decide, after the program has initially been edited, to expand the middle of the show by three minutes: The program material does not have to be edited "in a line."

Normally, this would require re-editing and redubbing all the segments onto the record unit tape, but a digital, computerized editing system stores all the information in computer memory. As a result, adding a segment to the middle is as easy as adding a paragraph to the middle of a term paper using a word processor.

Is this a science-fiction scenario for the distant future? Hardly. A great number of units like this are in use today. A recent PBS retrospective documentary on the 1960s, for example, was produced entirely on such a device. One is called the Avid Media Composer (Figure 16.5), and it is fed digitized video through several disk drives.

Nonlinear video will be a particular convenience for editors of programs that require changes to the internal structure of the show. The historical documentary is an obvious example. When producers found that they wanted to

Figure 16.5 The Avid 2000 Media Composer. The components of this nonlinear editing system from left to right are: high capacity hard disk, Macintosh Quadra 900, high resolution computer screen showing digital video footage, and another high resolution monitor displaying the edited sequences. (Courtesy of Avid Technology, Inc.)

expand coverage of an event in the chronology of the 1960s, they did not have to recut an entire tape. And that was an enormous convenience because a show which essentially is a chronology *must* be shot in a particular order. (In other words, something that happened in 1963 couldn't be tacked on to the end of the show.) Firms that use video to demonstrate new products will find nonlinear video editing systems to be a wonderful convenience when product lines change.

What Longer Duration Shots Communicate

- *An elongation of time.* Does your scene call for one person to endure a long, uncomfortable meeting with his or her boss? Long scenes will reinforce the message.

- *The need for concentration.* Leaving an image on screen for a long time cues the viewer to pay attention. If you have a graphic of "Four Critical Safety Warnings When Operating the Doohickey 5000," leaving it on screen for a reasonably long time will emphasize its importance.

- *Important locations.* Is it necessary for viewers to know that the upcoming scene takes place in the highlands of Scotland? A series of long, loving pans will drive this point home.

Cuts versus Dissolves (and Wipes)

To add to our previous discussion on the duration of shots, here are some additional points to consider.

What Cuts Communicate

- *Changes within the same time reference.* When viewers see a cut, they normally expect to see an

event that occurs immediately after the previous scene. (But don't forget that you can compress real time by stealing seconds and using cuts.)

- *Changes within the same spatial reference.* Viewers typically expect the next scene to be in the same locale if a cut is used.

- *A "news" feel.* If you are aiming for a "realistic" atmosphere, cuts will work best. Viewers always see cuts on news programs, and equate them with harsh reality.

- *Interaction between characters.* If you are taping a conversation between two main characters, you would use cuts. Cuts indicate two people interacting within the same space and time.

What Dissolves (and Wipes) Communicate

- *Changes in time.* A slow dissolve might be used to project the scene days, weeks, or months into the future.

- *Changes in locale.* When the scene changes from the ranch in Texas to the boardroom in New York, a dissolve will serve as a visual cue to guide viewers through space to a new establishing shot.

- A *subdued mood*. A scene of two elderly people enjoying a peaceful boat ride on a pond at sunset will be reinforced by the gentler images created by dissolves.

Close-ups versus Long Shots

As discussed in other sections of this book, video is a detail-oriented, close-up medium, so the use of the long shot is therefore somewhat limited. But it certainly does have a place. Close-ups and long shots each communicate different ideas.

What Close-ups Communicate

- *Significant detail*. A close-up is your way of saying, "This is important."

- *Intimacy*. A love scene shot from a distance would have little impact.

What Long Shots Communicate

- *An overview*. The long shot is your way of saying, "This is where we are."

- *An impersonal atmosphere*. Picture in your mind an uninterested interviewer at an employment agency. Are you seeing a close-up of the interviewer's face? Probably not; you have more than likely conjured up a picture of a huge desk, a long stretch of carpet, and a "keep your distance" shot of a barely visible, distant (physically and emotionally) person.

Don't interpret the fact that TV is a close-up medium to mean that long shots are always inappropriate. That's not true. In fact, long shots are quite necessary to establish locale and, sometimes, atmosphere.

Although long shots convey location and close-ups detail, be careful about cutting from one to the other. You do not want to go from an extreme long shot to an extreme close-up because the frame of reference may be lost and the shot will appear awkward. You also do not want to cut from a long shot to a close-up when the shots are taken from essentially the same angle because you'll be "pumping in" on the scene. (**Pumping in** is an effect that occurs when an edit is made between a long shot and a close-up shot from the same angle.) This is occasionally useful as a special effect (shock value, for example), but you generally want your close-up to be from a different angle or separated from the long shot by a cutaway.

On-Camera versus Voice-Over

Voice-over is a technique used frequently in news and documentaries, and will be addressed in greater detail in Chapter 19. Here, we'll simply note that a voice-over is a narration used in conjunction with cover video.

As an editor, you will sometimes be faced with the decision of whether to let the story tell itself or to have a writer create some narration for an announcer to read over related video. (The decision ideally is made before editing, but in reality the editor may confront this situation quite often.) This is often a matter of practicality, and it is difficult to draw a point-by-point comparison between the two methods.

You should, however, note that the purpose of a voice-over narration is to compress events into a coherent whole. Sometimes, characters or observational footage just cannot tell the whole story in the time available, and a voice-over narration is necessary to tie all the pieces together.

But there are times when you would logically want the characters to tell the story themselves. Having someone describe his feelings as he saw flood waters bearing down on his town is far more effective than having an announcer *describe* what the person felt. In general, scenes that communicate action and emotion play much better when presented as on-camera action as opposed to a voice over.

Cutting Audio Before Video; Video Before Audio

It is sometimes effective to "split" your edit points—to cut to the audio before the video or vice-versa. Cutting so that audio changes before video is sometimes called an **L-cut**, a throwback to the days of film editing when the strip holding the audio track was extended to the left or right. This created the shape of a backward or forward letter *L* (Figure 16.6), but more importantly made either the audio or the picture change first. (In reality, most cuts made on film had an *L* shape, because with film, where the sound is stored on an optical "strip" the audio and video are at different locations, anyway. But changing the shape of the *L* allows the editor to create a lag or a lead between the change audio and video.

Today, videotape editors still sometimes use the phrase *L-cut*, but more often refer to the operation as a "split edit." Modern editing units, such as the Sony BVE 910, graphically display a command titled "Mark Split," which allows you to create precisely this effect. **MARK SPLIT** is a command that allows you to choose which component—audio or video—will change first and how much time difference will be programmed between the audio and video changes.

But why *L-cut* in the first place? Well, you can often use this technique to create a special mood or effect. For example, changing the audio before video would be an interesting way to illustrate a person overhearing a conversation in another room. The person peeps through a door and hears the conversation; then we cut to the scene in the other room.

The effect just described is often called "audio precede video," and is useful in other applications as well. It is a

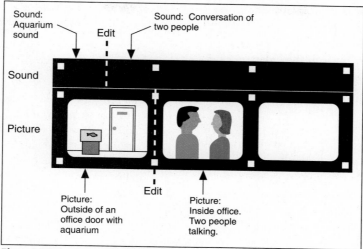

Figure 16.6 "L" cut. This term is a carryover from film editing. In essence it means the same as the "mark split" edit in video, an edit starting with either video or audio followed by the other track.

particularly powerful transition: We hear a scream before cutting to a shot of an accident, or we hear a telephone ring before cutting to an office scene.

Some interesting effects can be achieved by doing the L-cut in the opposite direction: changing the video before the audio. Suppose you are editing a confrontation among a group of lawyers grouped around a conference table. Cutting to the video of the person a second before he or she talks is a very effective way to build anticipation and add drama to the scene. Watch a rerun of *L.A. Law*, and note how this technique is used to add some spice to scenes that could otherwise be quite dull.

Cutting on Action versus Cutting on a Static Shot

When you **cut on action**, you cut (or dissolve) while there is appreciable movement in the scene. For example, if you are editing together two shots, one showing a man turning and storming out the door, you would probably elect to cut during his turn. It makes for a far more dramatic shot

than would letting him complete his turn *and then changing perspectives in the moment that he pauses before charging for the door.*

You will generally cut on action when the action continues in the next shot; that's pretty much a standard of video grammar. By cutting on action, you reinforce the concept of constant motion and keep the momentum strong. You also make the edit easier. You'll have a simpler time avoiding easily perceived changes in motion that will appear as jump cuts.

Sometimes you'll elect to cut on a static shot. Perhaps a woman walks into a room and is frozen by the sight of a dead body on the floor. Remember the two key words used to described this scene: *frozen, dead.*

We want to show the woman frozen in terror; if she moves, we want to start from the frozen position as, for example, she backs out of the room. Dead bodies, of course, tend not to move—and you don't want to impart any motion by moving the camera while it is focused on the body. The stillness of the body is what is important, and that's what cutting on the static shot communicates.

SUMMARY

1. Editors are more than equipment operators. They make important artistic contributions to the work. In fact, their contributions begin right from the planning stage, when they help coordinate the outline of the program with the writer and director and plan for the overall flow of the program.

2. Writers may or may not be familiar with the language of video expression. If they are not, it is your job as editor to help them translate their ideas to video. Although your director will be intimately familiar with video, he or she may not be deeply enough involved in the detail of the editing process to spot

possible problems. Look ahead and anticipate problems in continuity and collateral video.

3. Part of the editor's job is to arrange shots in such a way that they guide viewers through the program. Viewers need to be cued and led.

4. The editor often must compress time by eliminating some of the aspects of real life that are too time-consuming to picture on screen.

5. The editor will often be the first person to view the raw footage in its entirety and, as a result, is in a good position to determine if reshooting is essential.

6. The editor may have to decide whether to edit using cuts only or A-B roll. This can be a major decision

because on-line editing facilities cost considerably more than cuts-only suites.

7. Advanced digital technology allows many editors to break free of the constraints of laying down video in a linear fashion on a record unit tape.

8. You'll need to make some decisions on the actual transitions when you edit. Among those decisions are choosing between fast versus slow scene changes, cuts versus dissolves and wipes, close-ups versus long shots, on-camera action versus voice over, cutting audio before video or vice-versa, and cutting on action versus cutting on a static scene.

NOTE

1. Sometimes, scenes are lengthened in order to pad a program so that the individual segments are long enough to fill the available time, such as the spaces between commercial breaks. This is hardly an artistic consideration, but a realistic one.

TECHNICAL TERMS

collateral video	L-cut	nonlinear	real time
cut on action	mark split	pumping in	stealing seconds

EXERCISES

1. Using a portable camera, shoot these scenes:

   • A long shot of someone getting into a car on the driver's side and saying, "Let's go" to the passenger.

   • A medium close-up of the driver closing the door and starting the engine.

   • A medium shot of the car pulling out of the scene.

   Note: Be *extremely careful* when working around autos, especially moving autos. Don't shoot this scene in traffic, and be sure everyone is clear of the car when it moves.

   Your assignment is to do this edit sequence the right way and the wrong way.

   To do it the right way:

   • Do your first cut just as the car door starts to close.

   • Change your angle slightly when cutting from the long shot to the close-up of the people in the car.

   • Shoot from the same side of the car when you take the third shot (the car driving out of the screen).

   Now, here's how to shoot it the wrong way:

   • Do your first cut *after* the door closes.

   • Keep the same angle when you cut to the second shot; make sure you "pump in."

   • When the car pulls away, shoot from the *passenger side* of the car.

   Compare both edited scenes and decide what makes one look "right" and one look "wrong." Hint: One thing "wrong" with the second effort is that you have crossed the axis of the shot, a problem explained in Chapters 8 and 15.

2. View a dramatic film, a documentary, and a situation comedy. Keep a running record of the kinds of edits used and, in a brief paper, compare the editing strategies. Speculate as to why the particular strategies were chosen.

preparing and coordinating a remote

OBJECTIVES

After completing Chapter 17, you will be able to:

1. Organize a remote shoot.
2. Avoid many of the common problems that occur on remote.
3. Manage a remote shoot from start to finish.

Make a list. Check it twice. That's good advice for anyone contemplating shooting on remote, and it sums up the theme of this very brief but important chapter. Essentially, we will deal with planning, overcoming on-scene problems, and executing a remote shoot. The purpose of this chapter is not to polish your directing and scripting skills—areas covered in other chapters—but to help you circumvent Murphy's Law: Anything that can go wrong on a remote probably will. You are depending on delicate and complex equipment, unpredictable power supplies, and the equally unpredictable human element. Although it's impossible to avoid all on-site problems, planning can avert the more typical difficulties.

Throughout this chapter, we'll operate under the fundamental assumption that a good measure of successful remote planning and execution involves producing tape that will be edited later (except, of course, for live feeds). That's why we have placed this chapter after the chapter on fundamentals of editing. Understanding the editing process is a decided advantage when planning and executing your remote.

PLANNING A REMOTE SHOOT

As silly as it may seem, people have shown up at remote shoots without a camera. To put this in proper perspective, when you have several people loading a truck or van with hundreds of pounds of equipment, it's quite conceivable that each crew member might expect that the other one has loaded a particular piece of equipment. After all, who would forget a camera? But more stinging, from the remote producer's standpoint, is the fact that the lack of a connector or cable can bring the entire operation to a halt just as surely as the misplaced camera.

That's why planning is so critical—and that's why virtually every producer makes a list of items to take along on the shoot. Of course each list will vary according to your own inventory of equipment and particular shooting requirements, but we'll offer some packing guidelines that are adaptable yet still specific enough that you can apply them to your next remote. We'll first discuss the problems encountered with tapes and batteries—typically the biggest troublemakers on remote—and then we will consider other equipment that is frequently a cause of on-site difficulty simply because it is left behind.

Tape

Estimate the amount of tape you'll need to shoot the entire remote and then double it. The number of remotes interrupted because someone had to go back to the studio for more tape is truly dismaying. The situation is, in a way, something of a comedic tragedy, *but the person paying the bill never sees the humor in it.*

Extra tapes take up such a small amount of room that there's really no excuse not to carry double, or even triple, the amount you think you'll need. Remember, a number of circumstances can cause you to drastically increase your need for tape time:

- In news, an unexpected event can occur and prolong the length of your shoot. (And isn't that really the *nature* of news?)

- Tapes can malfunction. They can also be broken or lost.

- Things can go badly, requiring much more shooting time than you anticipated. Perhaps an actor in a commercial keeps turning in a poor performance and you need 25 takes of his or her scene. Suddenly, what you thought would be a generous tape supply will seem awfully skimpy.

One other point: Tapes do not function well when they are cold, so when you arrive on scene on a winter's day, find a warm place to store the tape supply. If the tapes feel cold to the touch, immediately get them to a room-temperature storage area before you start setup; the tapes will usually be back up to operating temperature before you are ready to shoot. (It's a good idea to let your VCR warm up gradually too.)

Heat is no friend to your tapes either. Keep them out of direct sunlight or other excessively warm spots. Be particularly careful of auto or van interiors on hot days.

Prepare your tapes in advance by fast-forwarding and rewinding them before the first use. This "stretches" and "packs" them to the proper tension. (**Pack** means to fast-forward and rewind a videotape to ensure even distribution.) Be sure that the tapes are completely rewound before going out on remote so you don't waste time and battery power rewinding them.

Batteries

"Battery problems" are among the most frequently heard excuses for blown remotes. Although you cannot reduce the chances of battery failure to zero, some careful planning can help keep you out of an unpleasant, embarrassing, and often expensive predicament.

The same caveat for carrying extra tapes applies to batteries: Bring more than double what you think you'll need. All sorts of perils await you when you deal with powering the camera and recorder (and sometimes lights). You may unexpectedly not have access to an electrical outlet into which to plug your camera and VCR or camcorder, and thus may require much more battery supply than you anticipated. Batteries do malfunction; so expect it at an inconvenient time.

Also be aware that batteries wear out. As a battery ages, its chemicals break down and weaken its ability to take and hold a charge, so a box of old batteries may be less useful than a handful of new ones. And although batteries can be expensive, this is the last area where you want to scrimp. If possible, lobby for regular purchases of all new or reconditioned batteries.

A useful option for a producer on an all-day remote shoot is a gang charger (Figure 17.1). A **gang charger** allows you to start recharging exhausted batteries immediately. Many batteries can be recharged in as little as an hour and a half, so your supply of power can be extended considerably if you find a place where there's a plug available. For instance, if you are shooting outdoors, too far from household current to use an extension cord, you still might be able to gain access to an outlet, a five minutes' walk away, where your batteries can be recharging.

Most producers agree that it is best to completely discharge a battery before recharging it. In some cases, a battery can develop a kind of "memory" if the discharge is

Figure 17.1 The battery gang charger. Having the ability to keep as many batteries charged is a necessity when performing field production work.

stopped at the same time each use. In other words, it will act as though it is discharged, even though it theoretically should have more power left.

However, many experienced producers note that it is more difficult to "train" a battery than is commonly thought. We won't take sides in the argument except to note that what is sometimes mistaken as a "battery memory" problem is really the deterioration of an old battery and the resultant lack of charge.

Equipment Checklist

In addition to tapes and batteries, there are some other items you'll need to bring along. Box 17.1 is a checklist of equipment you'll usually want to bring. You may not need each and every piece of equipment on this list, but it's nonetheless a good idea to run down the inventory each time you prepare to leave the studio.

OVERCOMING COMMON PROBLEMS

Many problems on remote are not directly related to production. Frequent foul-ups include power problems, interference, and difficulty gaining clearance and access.

Power

Aside from the battery dilemmas already discussed, video crews typically encounter a vexing predicament when it comes to plugging things in: They blow circuit breakers and fuses.

Lighting instruments use up a great deal of power. Although cameras and VCRs are not so power hungry, they too can put additional drain on a circuit. A **circuit** is an electrical "loop" carrying current.

BOX 17.1   REMOTE EQUIPMENT CHECKLIST

You may use these recommendations as the basis of an equipment checklist to prepare your crew for a remote shoot. Tailor your list to your available equipment, and always check your list and test your equipment before you leave the checkout location.

- Cameras
- Backup camera (An old reliable camera can save the day when your preferred equipment fails.)
- Recorder
- Backup recorder
- Tapes (Take more than you think you will need.)
- Batteries (Take more than you think you will need.)
- Headphones
- White balance and registration cards
- Lighting instruments (Pack versatile instruments that can be used under a variety of conditions for fill, key, or back.)
- Clamps
- Lighting poles
- Script
- Storyboards
- Microphones (It won't hurt to pack a couple of extras.)
- Lavalieres
- Hand-helds (Take these if you are using condenser mics.)
- Backup mic batteries
- Audio cable (Be sure to bring more than you think you'll need, because you'll probably need every inch of it.)
- A portable mixer (Figure 17.2) (What you thought was a simple mic setup may turn out to be complex

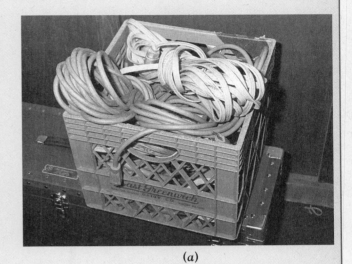

(a)

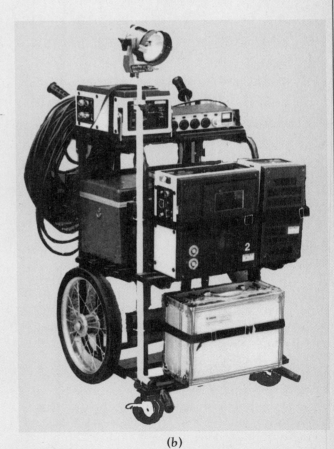

(b)

Figure 17.3 (a) Milk crates provide a durable and inexpensive way to transport cables. (b) The Porta-Brace Grip. The Porta-Brace Grip, is a heavy duty production cart designed to customize for moving production equipment from shot to shot. (Courtesy of Porta-Brace.)

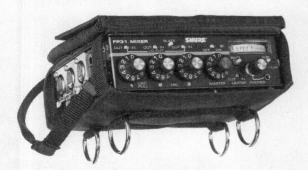

Figure 17.2 The portable audio mixer will enable a good balance with a number of mics and lines in the field. (Courtesy of Shure Brothers Incorporated.)

and require additional inputs and balancing of levels.)

- Video cable (See the audio cable listing.)

- Electrical extension cords (See the audio cable listing. Many producers keep a variety of different-length cords in a milk crate as, for example, in Figure 17.3*a*. That's as good a way as any to carry your cords.)

    A handy unit to have once you get on location is the Porta-Brace "Grip," a heavy-duty production cart manufactured specifically for moving production equipment from shot to shot (Figure 17.3*b*).

- Power strips (You'll often encounter a shortage of outlets.)

- Three-prong to two-prong electrical adapters

- Monitor (Don't rely on your camera viewfinder. You'll need a good monitor to determine the quality of the picture. Remember to bring the appropriate connections for the monitor.)

- Tape (adhesive) (A big roll of duct tape or any strong and wide tape will allow you to tape down cables—see Figure 17.4—and tape anything anywhere you want it.)

- Connectors and adapters. There are few things more disheartening than finding out your shoot will be delayed because you need to mate a male XLR to another male XLR and don't have the connector to do it. Bring along every *conceivable* connector or adapter you might need. It's best to keep these segregated in a box only for remote use; that way, you

Figure 17.4 Taping cables. Duct or "gaffers' tape" is used on-location for a variety of needs. In particular, cables that run across passage ways require taping to prevent anyone from tripping over them.

won't have to hunt them down each time you leave the studio.)

- Waveform monitor (Although not always used on remote, the waveform monitor can be very handy if you master the technique of employing it. Use of this device is explained in Chapter 21.)

You'll probably think of more items to add to your list. But irrespective of the particular makeup of your catalog, be sure you run through the inventory before each departure.

When you end a remote shoot ("strike the location"), be sure equipment is returned to its proper storage place. A little extra effort will prevent major headaches later. Report malfunctioning equipment so that it can be repaired or replaced for the next shoot.

When plugging in your equipment, your goal is a simple one: to receive an adequate supply of power without continually plunging the home or office at which you're shooting into darkness. You do this by plugging your lighting and video instruments into different circuits; that is, different lines emanating from the main power supply. Just plugging into different outlets won't always distribute power drain, because those outlets may all be wired on the same circuit. So, your first question when arriving at an interior location should be, "Where's the circuit breaker (or fuse box; sometimes it's called a "power box")?" Surprisingly, many people, including home owners who have lived in their domicile for many years, won't know. So hunt down the breaker box (Figure 17.5) first.

The **breaker box** is the box located at the point where the main power line enters the building; the box sends the power to several circuits, or loops, through the building. The circuits are equipped with "breakers," which cut off

Figure 17.5 Most buildings now maintain their circuits in a breaker box; in the event of an overload the circuit switches to "off."

current flow if the demand becomes too heavy for the wires to bear.

Finding the breaker box will accomplish two important goals:

1. You can usually find out what plugs are on which circuits.

2. If you do blow the breaker, you'll have an easier time finding the box when the lights go out.

Some breaker boxes will be conveniently labeled for you (Figure 17.6). The label beside the switch, for example, might say, "Living room and south wall of den," or "Conference room and hallway." More often than not, though, they won't be labeled, so you might want to invest some time in discovering for yourself what breaker controls which circuit. The reason for this is that each breaker represents one circuit, and by discovering which outlets correspond to each breaker you can distribute your power load among two or more circuits.

Here is one way to do this. *With the permission of your host,* have a crewperson flip each switch to the off position and have another crew member take note of what lights go off when the switch is turned off. To save yourself the trouble of plugging in lights and appliances to see if the power is out, you can use a power sensor (Figure 17.7), a device that lights up when plugged into the outlet and is specifically designed to safely detect whether power is being routed to the outlet. Power sensors are available at almost all radio supply and electrical goods stores.

Let's assume you've discovered that the living room (where you want to shoot) is on one circuit and the bedroom is on another. Using your extension cord, you can route some of the power from the bedroom circuit to the living room and, it is hoped, avoid overtaxing the circuit.

Estimating Your Power Needs. To gauge power consumption, you need to know the wattage of your instruments. **Wattage** is a measure of power (your engineer or studio supervisor will be able to tell you the wattage of your instruments). You can also check for a label on the back of many lighting instruments.

As a rule of thumb, a 1000 watt (1 K) lighting instrument will draw about 9 amperes (amps). An **ampere** is a

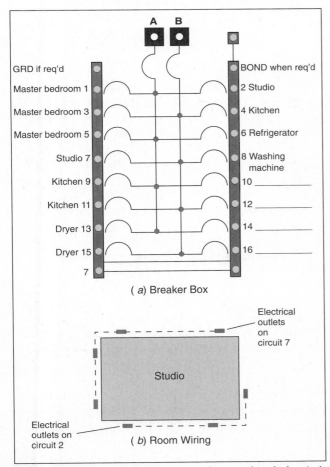

Figure 17.6 Building circuit diagram. To determine how the location's circuits are distributed, study the building's breaker box; sometimes there will be labels. Decide which circuits in the room can support more equipment and especially notice how arbitrary circuits can be wired.

Figure 17.7 Sensing for power. A power sensor will light up if power is present in the plug.

measure of current flow (amperage is part of the calculation used to determine wattage). Because electrical circuitry in most buildings is rated in terms of amps, it's easier to think in terms of amps than watts.

Now, most household circuits are designed to handle 15 or 20 amps. The total electrical capability of a residence is usually in the 100 amp range. So you'll want to distribute your lighting instruments accordingly. If you have a 1000 watt lighting instrument plugged into the bedroom circuit and a 1000 watt lighting instrument plugged into the living room circuit, you're drawing 9 amps from each and are in little danger of overloading the circuit breaker (with exceptions to be noted in a moment.) But if you plug in an additional 500 watt instrument, you're also drawing another 4.5 amps (half of 9 amps); your total drain on the circuit is now 13.5—close to breaker-busting capacity.

Removing Competing Power Draws. What determines whether or not you blow the breaker is also the amount of other power-drawing devices on the same circuit. You can blow a circuit even if it is highly rated when other devices are using electricity. Commercial buildings, for example, usually have generous power supplies, but more than one remote crew has been plunged into darkness when someone decided to run the copy machine—a device which uses an enormous amount of power. So be careful of the other units, such as copy machines and window air conditioners, on the circuit. If necessary, get permission and unplug them. An effective way to make sure that they won't be used during your shoot is to unplug the power-draining copiers and air conditioners and insert *your* plugs into the outlets. Someone will be less likely to pull a plug and reinsert, say, the copier's plug, than to simply plug the copier back in to an empty outlet. Remember to plug everything back in when you leave.

When In Doubt, Test. If you do not have time to check out the circuitry, you may have to engage in some guesswork to determine which outlets are on different circuits. Be forewarned that just because an outlet is in a different room it does *not* mean it's on a different circuit. But using an outlet in another room is still a better bet than using two in the same room. You are well advised to let your equipment run for 10 minutes before beginning the shot, just to test the circuits.

Interference

Electrical units and transmission devices generate power fields that can interfere with the quality of your picture and audio. Because of this:

- Don't place your monitor right next to your VCR, because the monitor emits a strong field that may interfere with your recording of both audio and video. With audio, it often creates a hum; in

video, the monitor may create bands of interference across the picture, sometimes called **hum bars**.

- If at all possible, turn off fluorescent lights. In addition to color temperature problems, fluorescents can also create a hum on your audio line.

- Keep audio cable runs to a minimum. In other words, if you only need 10 feet of cable, use a 10-foot cable. Don't use a 50-foot cable and leave the remaining "spaghetti" loosely coiled on the floor. Long cables act like an antenna, and they tend to pick up interference from lights, monitors, and even nearby radio stations.

- If you are planning to use a wireless mic, always bring a conventional mic and cable setup as a backup. Should you be near an FM radio station, there may be too much interference to use the wireless mic.

- If you have interference problems and can't track down the source, try plugging the camera/VCR into another circuit or running it off batteries. Sometimes, the interference is carried by the household current itself.

Clearances and Access

You should investigate what local laws and ordinances apply to taping on public property. (See Figure 17.8.) Although you can generally tape on public property, some special restrictions do apply in various locales. For example, in Washington, D.C., you need to obtain a permit to tape on the public grounds of the White House. When you tape from a bridge or the side of a highway, you'll often need to clear that activity with the local or state police and sometimes hire a police officer to be on-scene. Any taping that disrupts traffic or involves an imminent threat to your safety or the safety of motorists (for example, staging an accident scene on a public street) will require a police officer on duty.

News camera crews should be aware that access to a crime scene is often an arbitrary decision made by the police officer on the scene. In some cases, you will not be allowed into the confines of a crime scene, even if that scene is a public place. (There is often good reason for this, as evidence can be lost or disturbed by trampling reporters.)

You should also be aware that a "public place" is not the same thing as "public property." The owners of a shopping mall (a public place), for example, may not allow you to tape on the premises. Sometimes access is restricted in publicly owned places too, such as courtrooms and airports. The rules vary by state and locality.

Be careful about whom you shoot, too. In general, any-

LOCATION SURVEY

Production Name: _____

Production/Program Title: _____

Survey Date: _____

Production Date: _____

Contact Person: _____

Contact Phone: _____

Accessibility and entry to site:
Notes should include: Elevator? Loading Dock? Business Hours of Location, Ceiling Height.

_____

_____

Power Consideration:
Adequate Power? Yes No Generator Necessary? Yes No
Location of Circuit Box? Principal Background? Is a seamless necessary? Is there reflectance, such as mirrors?

_____

Lighting Considerations:
Available light? Sun or house light? Are Gel necessary?

Audio Considerations:
Traffic noise? Potential disturbances? Microphone choice?

_____

_____

Figure 17.8 Location survey. A location survey will help you prepare for a remote shoot. It is very difficult to consider all of the details and situations that may occur during a production, so unless you are very familiar with a location, a thorough scouting session is required.

PERFORMANCE RELEASE

In consideration of my appearance on the video program entitled

_____

(PRINT TITLE OF PROGRAM OR PRODUCERS NAME)

and for no subsequent remuneration,

I, _____

on behalf of myself, my heirs, executors, and administrators and assignors authorize to use live or recorded on tape, film, or other media, my name, voice, likeness and performance for television and/or radio broadcast and cablecast throughout the world and for audiovisual and/or educational purposes.

I further agree on behalf of myself and others as above stated that my name, likeness, and biography for promotion uses and other uses.

Further I agree to indemnify, defend, and hold harmless the producer and an associated establishment harmless for any claims, suits, liabilities arising from my appearance and the use of any of my materials, name, or biography.

CONDITIONS: _____

_____

_____

SIGNATURE: _____

IF TALENT IS MINOR, AN ADULT SIGNATURE IS REQUIRED:

SIGNATURE: _____

NAME: _____
                              Print

ADDRESS: _____

CITY, STATE & ZIP CODE: _____

PHONE: (_____) _____

DATE: _____

Figure 17.9 Model release. In many kinds of presentations, a performance release, or model release, form should be signed by anyone whose image you use.

one on a public street is "fair game" if you are shooting a news program—as long as those people are not portrayed in a false light or deliberately portrayed in a way calculated to embarrass them. But for any other type of presentation, *particularly* an advertisement, you should secure a model release (a sample is shown in Figure 17.9). A **model release** is a document signed by a person to grant you permission to use his or her image.

Get releases signed before shooting. Sometimes, a person will change his or her mind after appearing on camera. It is much more difficult to retract written permission.

When shooting at a place of business for, let's say, a commercial or a corporate videotape, confirm in advance that you have access to the facilities you'll need and that the people assigned to you as performers will be allotted an adequate amount of time. Problems sometimes arise when a midlevel employee informs you that there's "no problem" taping on the floor of a factory, but the superintendent—unaware of the taping—suddenly sees a threat to safety, production, or both and orders you out. So be sure that the person giving you clearance has the authority to do so.

In addition, make it clear that an employee who is to appear on camera for five minutes will be needed for more than five minutes. An entire morning or perhaps an entire day would be more realistic, depending on the circumstances. Unfortunate misunderstandings can and do arise when an employee is assigned to you for an unrealistically short period of time and is expected to handle his or her regular duties in addition to the video appearance.

Finally, here's a tip toward gaining *future* clearances and access. Be a good citizen. Be careful of people's offices and homes; show respect for their privacy and property. It's an interesting learning experience to suddenly view the situation from the other perspective. One of the authors, a 20-year veteran of television production and performance, was recently interviewed in his home by a TV news crew who knocked over a lamp; tracked mud on a white rug; immediately, without any mention of what they were doing, starting rummaging through the apartment looking for the circuit breaker; and blew the power three times anyway.

People with no knowledge of the TV production process might not be particularly understanding of the TV crew's boorishness. Remember that you are a guest. Be careful while you are there, and clean up before you leave.

EXECUTING A REMOTE

Some activities unique to the remote production are transmitting your signal if you are shooting live over the air, managing the remote vehicle, and coordinating with the studio.

Transmission Options

It is unlikely that you will be involved with satellite transmission during an introductory video production course, but it is worth noting that many news programs, and some institutional conferences, are transmitted live by ground-based microwave links or satellite dishes.

The **satellite news vehicle (SNV)** (Figure 17.10) has become a common sight in all major, most medium, and some small commercial TV markets. You can also rent satellite dishes that can be pulled on a trailer behind a standard auto or truck, and new developments allow satellite transmitters to be packed into suitcase-size containers (Figure 17.11).

The technology has advanced to the point where live transmission is relatively commonplace and simple to bring about. Because this area lies largely outside the typical framework of remote operations as you'll encounter them in most college-class remotes, we'll address the subject more fully in Chapters 21 and 22.

Managing the Remote Vehicle

Your vehicle may not be an SNV, but you will be using some sort of transportation on remote, whether it be a standard auto, a truck, or a van.

The vehicle may or may not be outfitted for regular use by a video crew, but there are some things you can do to equip it for traveling with equipment and use as part of the production process on-site.

For obvious reasons, it is more convenient to use a van, minivan, truck, or some other large-capacity vehicle to haul around equipment. But the problem with a large-interior vehicle is that equipment tends to move about and break if not properly secured. Some padding—even a few old blankets—on the floor will help alleviate the breakage problem, and a set of plywood shelves will help keep things

Figure 17.10 The satellite vehicle. Satellite vehicles are most commonly used as the uplink connection for transmitting news, but are quickly becoming popular in corporate communication.

Figure 17.11 Satellite cellular telephone. Current satellite technology has become consolidated enough to fit into a small case, making instant communications possible from almost anywhere. (Courtesy of Manhattan Microwave Communications Co.)

in place. You can build the shelves yourself; simply nail together wood in any configuration that can easily be moved in and out of the vehicle and will have several compartments to keep equipment contained.

You'll need to find cable quickly and store it neatly. One option is to use a sheet of pegboard hung vertically in the van or truck and hang loops of cable from the extended pegboard hooks.

The bed of a truck is an excellent spot on which to mount a camera for coverage of many outdoor events. You can move the truck and camera if circumstances dictate. But be careful; if you have a camera and/or camera operator in the back, you must *creep* along. A jolt at even low speed can cause injury or equipment damage.

A van is convenient for remote video operations and is, in fact, the vehicle of choice in most operations. But consider the fact that vans usually have generous window space into which prying eyes can peer, and if they like what they see, can guide prying hands into your expensive cache of equipment. It's best never to leave your van out of sight or unattended. If that's not possible, at least invest in some curtains that can be drawn across the windows when the vehicle is parked.

If the vehicle is used for production work on a permanent basis, you might be tempted to emblazon it with your video organization's logo. It is wise to resist this temptation. Owners of production agencies often believe it encourages theft. Managers of news organizations sometimes contend that a logo incites people to actions they would not normally take if there were not a recognizable video van in the area. Many organizations, including CBS, have opted for removal of identifying logos from their remote vans.

The presence of TV equipment can incite all sorts of bizarre behavior on the part of passersby, and theft is not necessarily the worst of it. Box 17.2 presents details of the sad story.

Remote-Studio Coordination

Should you be working with a satellite or direct microwave link to the station, you will have no problem communicating. You'll have a **private line**—a transmission "line" not intended for broadcast—with the studio and often an additional private line for talent. (Obviously, there is no "line" involved in the transmission, but the word is a carryover from studio terminology.)

But given the fact that you are not likely to encounter satellite or microwave links soon, you'll undoubtedly be grappling with remote-studio communications. Coordinating remote-studio communications may seem trivial, but not being able to contact someone looking for you in the field or vice-versa is a *constant* problem—one that is incredibly frustrating and time wasting for any production crew.

Suppose, for example, you are to meet an actor to do a shoot at 211 Elmgrove Avenue. He's not there. You call from a pay phone and cannot reach him at home. Now, there are a number of events which may have transpired:

- The actor is running a half hour late, but he'll be there.
- Either you or the actor made a mistake, and he is at 211 Elm*wood* Avenue.
- You are waiting at 211 Elmgrove Avenue in the city while your actor is at 211 Elmgrove Avenue in an adjoining suburb.

Although the name of the street is fictitious, all three scenarios are real and occurred recently. None needs to be a major inconvenience, because all can be fixed quickly with a phone call. But if you have no mechanism to exchange messages, you are likely to waste an entire morning or afternoon.

At the very least, give everyone involved in the remote a number where he or she can leave a message. It may be a secretary back at the studio or a telephone recording machine from which messages can be retrieved by remote control. When the message is taken, be sure that the caller is asked for his or her telephone number. That way, the late or lost participant can call in and leave a message. As soon as you suspect something's wrong, you can call and check your messages. Once you make contact, the situation can be sorted out.

BOX 17.2 BULLETPROOF VESTS FOR VIDEOGRAPHERS?

Video equipment can bring out the worst in people, and a distressing symptom of this is the fact that many news photographers now wear protective body armor. John Premack, chief cameraperson at WCVB Television in Boston, discussed this in an article, "Straight from the Shoulder."

It wasn't so long ago that unless you were covering a war, the biggest threat to a photojournalist was a well-thrown rock or bottle or spray of tear gas. No longer. Instead of covering anti-war protests and student demonstrations, we're documenting the violence of a generation raised on drugs and television. The riot helmets and gas masks that were standard issue in years past are useless in the neighborhoods where handguns cost no more than a pair of sneakers and life is cheaper still.

This spring in Oklahoma, a TV news photographer was shot in the chest as he sat behind the wheel of his unmarked news car. Miraculously he was not killed. Bill Merickel normally wears a bulletproof vest when covering drug busts in Oklahoma City, but not when chasing tornadoes in nearby Lindsey. Investigators theorize that the carload of teenagers who have been charged in the incident may have mistaken Merickel, who was talking on a cellular telephone when the drive-by shooting occurred, for a police officer.

But there was no question of mistaken identity in Boston when a news photographer covering the funeral of a member of one of the city's many youth gangs was warned that he will be shot next time gang members find him on their turf. Nor in Dallas, when a reporter and photographer were fired upon as they cruised one of that city's housing projects.

Nowadays news crews from Boston to San Diego, and in dozens of smaller markets in between, are increasingly becoming targets for a generation of street gangs, warring youths who can't seem to decide if they'd rather see themselves on the six o'clock news or assault the photojournalists who put them there.

Source: John Premack, "Straight from the Shoulder," *The Communicator* (June 1990): 20.

Far too often, though, the person who answers the phone at the studio knows only that the crew is "out on a remote" somewhere and has no way to relay messages to them. You can overcome this problem via cellular phone or two-way radio, but giving *everyone* an emergency phone number can keep an inconvenience from turning into a disaster.

SUMMARY

1. Make a list of everything you need to take with you and run an inventory before you depart. When several people are packing many items, it is easy for something to be forgotten.

2. Always take much more tape than you think you'll need. Getting caught short of tape is embarrassing and sometimes expensive.

3. The same warning applies to batteries. In addition to taking along an adequate supply, take advantage of existing power outlets to recharge your batteries if you are going to be on location for several hours. Also, be wary of old batteries; they tend not to hold a charge very well.

4. Don't forget to check off the rest of the equipment you'll need, including cables and connectors. *Always* take along a variety of connectors and adapters.

5. Blowing circuit breakers will always be a possibility when on location. To avoid this, locate the central power box first and check out what outlets are on which circuits. Plug your lighting instruments into different circuits.

6. Various devices can cause interference with your video and audio signal. Your own monitor is one; don't place it too near your VCR. Also be wary of fluorescent lights, and don't use excess cable runs.

7. Check on local laws and ordinances that govern shooting in public areas. Also, seek permission *from someone in a position to give that permission* before planning a shoot on private property. For newspeople, access to a crime scene will be decided on a case-by-case basis, usually by the police officer in charge.

8 Show respect for people's homes and privacy. Don't wander around without permission, don't destroy their possessions, and clean up before you leave. Remember, you are a guest, and your behavior is a

reflection on yourself, your colleagues, and your organization.

9. Most television news organizations have one or more satellite news vehicles (SNVs). Some transmission is done by microwave from fixed points on land.

10. When you take your equipment on remote, try as best you can to pad the interior of the vehicle. Use whatever device you can invent to make compartments for equipment so that it does not move about the vehicle during transit.

11. Keep the van attended if at all possible, and don't display video equipment to passersby. It is probably wise not to have any logo that identifies your van as a video production or news vehicle.

12. One of the most frustrating experiences in a remote producer's career is to have a problem locating talent or crewpeople and not be able to make telephone contact. Always leave a central number with everyone. Check in at that number if there's a problem.

TECHNICAL TERMS

ampere	gang charger	pack	satellite news vehicle (SNV)
breaker box	hum bars	private line	wattage
circuit	model release		

EXERCISES

1. Here's an exercise in making everything go wrong so that you can learn to identify the symptoms.

   a. Place your monitor near your VCR to see if your particular setup will create audio hum or video hum bars. (Clear this with your engineer or instructor first.)

   b. Tape a segment in a room lighted entirely by fluorescents. See if you can balance the camera to compensate. Try using a pink card for balance and observe the results.

   c. In the same room, hook together every mic cable you have and run them along the floor. See if your cables are picking up a hum from the fluorescent lights. Run your audio cable over a power cable and see if you pick up a hum there.

2. Here's an exercise that will help you become more familiar with the layout of your home's electrical system and at the same time will allow you to do something that should be done anyway.

   Produce a drawing of the circuits in your house or apartment. Map out the rooms, and by shutting off each switch on the circuit breaker box, determine which outlets are controlled by each switch—and hence are on each circuit. In addition to drawing the map, label each circuit breaker. Almost all circuit breakers have a paper label expressly for this purpose, and seldom is it filled in by the installing electrician. (Note: We do not recommend you try this if you have a fuse box instead of circuit breakers. Fuse boxes contain glass-tipped plugs rather than switches.)

the talk show

OBJECTIVES

After completing Chapter 18, you will be able to:

1. Identify the strengths of the talk show format and exploit them to their fullest advantage.
2. Plan a talk show, from developing the basic idea to creating sets to booking talent.
3. Direct the talk show from beginning to end, as well as operate in any other capacity as a crewperson in this format.

The talk show has become a staple of broadcast television and, in many cases, institutional and corporate video. What we think of as a talk show (which might, depending on the circumstances, more accurately be called a "talk-interview" format or segment) has a variety of modern incarnations. In addition to *The Tonight Show*–type of blueprint, talk-interview productions are used within broadcast newscasts as a format for locally produced cable access public affairs programming, corporate "meet the manager" productions, and literally dozens of other applications.

Because the talk-interview format is an integral part of so many types of productions, it is essential that anyone involved in television or video production have an understanding of how such programs are structured, planned, and executed. This chapter provides an introductory guide to dealing with any situation where an interviewer and guest appear in studio, and it lays the groundwork for future skills that you may develop in advanced directing or production classes.

Specifically, this chapter covers:

- *The basics of the talk-interview format.* Included will be a discussion of the overall thrust of such programs, the advantages and disadvantages of using the format, and the personnel involved in the production.
- *Planning a talk show.* We will also investigate methods of making preparations for the physical setup of the program and how to prepare on-air performers.
- *Directing the talk show.* Finally, we will examine how the director and production crew put the pieces together and create a smoothly sequenced

show that utilizes a logical progression of shots and scenes. A sample script will illustrate, step by step, the opening, development, and closing of a brief talk-interview program.

Note: Although the term *talk show* might imply a different type of program than a talk-interview format, for the sake of simplicity, we will use the terms *talk show*, and *talk-interview format* more or less synonymously. When there is a major difference between the implication of these terms as they relate to production, that difference will be noted.

THE BASICS OF THE TALK-INTERVIEW FORMAT

The primary difficulty involved in the production of a talk show is the fact that although the show is supposed to appear *natural*, it is produced in a decidedly *unnatural* environment. Viewers may perceive a talk show as a leisurely chat in what looks like a neighbor's living room, but the program really emanates from a brightly lighted studio staffed by a team of scurrying production personnel (Figure 18.1). The host, as well as the director and production staff, are operating under complex and merciless time constraints. In sum, the program has the artificial appearance of unaffected spontaneity because of the practiced skills of the production crew and the host. Only when things go wrong do the seams show—letting viewers in on the secret that the easygoing conversation is stitched together from a conglomeration of sounds and images produced by cameras, mics, and sets.

Why does a well-produced talk-interview segment appear so natural? How does it manage to hold the audience's

Figure 18.1   Preparing to tape. The talk show crew carefully rehearses shots, so the taped show appears natural and spontaneous.

attention? The answer is, essentially, that it follows what have become standardized conventions in video production. That is, the segment communicates in an accepted "TV language," a language with which we have become quite familiar since television's infancy.

Overall Thrust of the Program

That "TV language" did not emerge full-blown. In fact, early television innovators really did not know quite what to do with the new medium. Talk shows, as such, evolved from ground zero; no one knew what a "talk show" was supposed to look like, because before television no one had ever *seen* a talk show.

But the techniques of pleasing an audience would soon be learned through trial and error. In 1949, for example, a television pioneer named Dave Garroway was host of a Chicago-based program called *Garroway at Large*. The program segments were long and low key; some observers of the Chicago program thought, at the time, that television was simply not the right medium on which to conduct interviews and chat with guests. But by 1952, a masterful television executive named Pat Weaver (the father of actress Sigourney Weaver) had found a firm handle on the public's tastes, and in the process reshaped Garroway and his show. The program—now carried by the NBC television network—was revamped to consist of fast-moving segments: snippets of weather forecasts, chatty visits by appealing guests, and visually exciting program elements. And in case you don't know, the program that evolved from *Garroway at Large* was named *The Today*

Show, and it has retained roughly the same format to the present day.

Television continued to evolve new ways of handling on-camera conversation. Some are highlighted in Box 18.1.

Pluses and Minuses of the Talk-Interview Format

The talk show is a relatively inexpensive form of video, in that it usually does not require elaborate pre- or postproduction chores. Although a dramatic program must be scripted virtually in its entirety, only broad outlines of program content are planned in advance for a talk segment. Many television talk shows air live, so there is no postproduction. When taped talk shows are edited, that postproduction work usually involves nothing more than a basic cleaning up of awkward moments or production goofs.

Also, a talk-interview program is an appealing format for viewers. A talk segment provides the impression of spontaneity, giving viewers the impression that they are involved in what is happening right now, participating in an event as it happens. Some media critics, in fact, feel that the variety of "talk show," which is really a program-length commercial, violates the trust of viewers, leading them to believe that the spontaneous-sounding material is really a completely genuine conversation. Box 18.2, reprinted from the April 29, 1991, edition of *People* magazine, points out one perspective on this particular use of the talk-show format.

From a production standpoint, the talk-interview program presents some significant difficulties. It is a talent-intensive format, meaning that it relies heavily on the skill of the performers; all the expert production help in the world cannot "fix" a live show moderated by an inept host. Guests cause their share of headaches too. Even the most talented team of host, producer, and crew cannot salvage a show in which the guest is wooden and uncommunicative.

Production personnel are under a great deal of pressure during a talk-interview program. Because many talk shows air live or are taped and replayed with only minimal editing, there is little opportunity to remedy poor production technique. Editing cannot fix a show where the director was consistently late in taking shots of the guest and hosts. Poor camera work cannot be corrected once the set has been struck and the guests have left the studio.

There are methods to avoid such problems, though, and they will be discussed later in the chapter.

The People Involved in Talk-Show Production

It is not apparent to most viewers, but the talk show is an intensely team-oriented effort. Although a documentary,

BOX 18.1   A LOOK BACK AT THE EVOLUTION OF THE TALK SHOW

After the success of *The Today Show*, another Weaver-inspired program, *The Tonight Show*, brought viewers into what might be described as a regularly scheduled party, peopled by fascinating guests. Again, this is a format (and a program) still very much alive today.

Edward R. Murrow and Fred Friendly developed a pioneering public affairs series, *See it Now*. But the Murrow-hosted program that really captured the hearts, minds, and eyes of the American viewing public was *Person-to-Person*, a conversational show that brought the television camera into the homes of celebrities—a startling feat in the early days of television, and a concept that would set a standard convention for talk programs for years to come. In *Person-to-Person*, the camera became the eyes and ears of the visitor, bringing viewers to the scene and bringing them into the conversation.

More new talk-interview conventions have emerged. The venerable Mike Wallace was instrumental in "inventing" a facet of the talk-interview format in his 1950s program called *Night Beat*. *Night Beat* expanded the scope of the talk-interview format, or, perhaps more accurately, *contracted* it. Instead of the standard medium-range shot of the guest, Wallace and his producers insisted on tight close-ups. They were catching on to the ways in which video production values could reinforce the overall thrust of the program. "Just as interviews never cut too close to the bone in those days" Wallace recalls, "neither did the cameras. They had always kept a decorous distance, a medium close-up, to assure the

guest that he or she would be portrayed in the most flattering way. On *Night Beat* we used searching, tight close-ups to record the tentative glances, the nervous tics, the beads of perspiration—warts and all."[1]

The talk-interview format pioneered by *Night Beat* has, of course, become the basis for many modern programs that seek to probe the guest's psyche. And it is a continuing example of the production values that comprise a talk-interview program—the message we want to communicate to viewers. That message might be, "This is a hard-hitting program where we search the souls of our guests," or alternately, "This is a chatty, friendly show where we invite viewers into our living room."

That type of decision is up to you, the producer. You can use the various standardized techniques of video talk-interview production to create whatever overall thrust you choose. Remember that the pieces of equipment used in video production are merely tools, and video can only illuminate or inspire to the extent that people are willing to use it to those ends. Otherwise, as Edward R. Murrow noted, the medium is "merely lights and wires in a box."[2]

1. Mike Wallace and Gary Paul Gates, *Close Encounters* (New York: Berkeley, 1984), 15.
2. From a 1958 speech to the Radio-Television News Directors Association, quoted in Christopher H. Sterling and John M. Kittross, *Stay Tuned: A Concise History of American Broadcasting* (Belmont, CA: Wadsworth, 1978), 371.

for example, can be written, taped, narrated, and edited by one person, a talk show obviously cannot. Everything is happening in real time, so several different cameras must be used. A talk show is not shot with one camera and edited at a later date.

The hierarchy varies from place to place, but the production team is generally headed by a producer, who oversees a director, who in turn supervises the production crew. In talk-show lexicon, a producer may be anyone from the executive in charge of program (someone who might never set foot in the studio) to the person responsible for booking guests, selecting topics, and bringing the doughnuts and coffee. More often than not, the producer has some sort of hands-on role in the planning and execution of the program. The director typically calls the shots—a formidable task in talk-show production—and ensures that the program begins and ends on time. Talk-show production crews are usually fairly large. A full complement of camera

operators, floor director, technical director, lighting director, and audio director are generally necessary to deal with the complex and frequently changing dimensions of the program.

This chapter is written from the perspective of the production personnel, and the information applies to the producer, director, and any member of the crew. Some of what follows relates specifically to directing and is tied in with the basic information presented in Chapter 15. (If you are not reading chapters in order, it would be beneficial to review Chapter 15 before reading further.)

Sometimes, a producer's viewpoint will be assumed when the text relates directly to a producer's typical duties—likewise for directors and crewpeople. An understanding of all roles and duties is essential for *all* members of the production team. Camera operators will certainly perform better if they have an understanding of exactly what the director needs from camerapeople. The reverse

---

BOX 18.2 . . . IT'S AN INFOMERCIAL!

The talk show is a natural vehicle for communicating ideas, but sometimes the line between a real talk show and a sales pitch becomes rather blurry.

Let the viewer beware: Here's an excerpt from an article that takes phony talk shows—infomercials—to task.

On first viewing, an infomercial may seem as strange a beast as, say, a game-show mini-series. But these half hour–long hybrids of advertising and programming, already familiar to late-night insomniacs, are popping up more frequently in daytime hours on cable and broadcast channels, usually as ersatz talk shows or newsmagazines. Everyone has mistaken couch-perched Ali McGraw and Meredith Baxter for standard talk-show guests—until the talk about cosmetics went on and on.

Infomercials were born in 1984, when the government ended its 12-minutes per hour limit on TV ads. . . . Stars are singing hosannas for financial plans, car wax, male-pattern baldness preparations and weight loss

systems. Why? Mostly it's not to boost sagging careers but, as an infomercial might put it, "to maximize hidden earning potential." According to Greg Benker, president of Guthy-Benker Corp, a major producer of infomercials, participating celebrities may be paid as little as $5,000 up front but can earn a big chunk based on sales generated by the spots.

There have been grumblings, both from consumers and the Federal Trade Commission, about unfounded claims made for some products (for instance, a diet-device "show" featuring Michael Reagan was withdrawn after an FTC challenge). And infomercials haven't always been labeled as such. So the National Infomercial Marketing Association—a self-monitoring (but technically powerless) group of producers—has recommended that, at the least, these shows should carry a label. . . .

Source: "Honey, Cover the Kids' Eyes! It's an Infomercial!" *People* (April 29, 1991): 41–44.

---

is also true: Directors who have no understanding of some of the peculiarities of running a camera during a talk show often make unrealistic demands on the camerapeople.

With this perspective in mind, we will now trace some of the steps in the initial planning of a talk-interview segment.

PLANNING THE TALK SHOW

Often, the producer is in charge of creating the overall atmosphere and thrust of the program—a task that includes arranging the physical setup on the studio floor as well as advance planning involving guests and the program host.

The Set

The producer and/or director generally are responsible for determining what the set will look like, how the cameras will be arranged, and how production values related to the set will contribute to the program's overall impact. Here are some points to keep in mind when placing backgrounds, chairs, and cameras for your talk program: Use simple sets, move performers away from the wall or cyc, and carefully plan the location of the host and guests *first*, before planning the cameras, lights, and set. Location of the monitor is also an important consideration. In addition, you'll need to pay special attention to proper base

lighting, a critical aspect of talk-show production. Finally, you should scope out any possible problems with the set, such as the edges of the scenery showing should a guest move.

The Benefits of Simple Sets. Simple sets often appear better on camera than do complex ones. Although it is tempting to raid the studio's storage area for an array of bookcases, potted plastic plants, and imitation bay windows, intricate backgrounds can be, and often are, distracting. Complex sets are also difficult to light because some elements may be highly reflective whereas others soak up illumination like a sponge.

Another problem: If you have many different props on the set, awkward situations can arise when cameras are moved and focal lengths are changed. The potted plant that added such a nice touch when camera angles were first scoped out may now appear to be sprouting from the top of the guest's head if some action on set requires a hasty camera move.

The Need for Space between the Talent and Background. Keep the host and guests away from the set walls or cyc. There is a strong temptation to jam performers up against the background, primarily because we're used to seeing what *appears* to be the host and guest sitting only a couple of feet away from the wall. This is an optical illusion created by the properties of the camera lens, which tends to compress distances under certain circumstances. This illusion becomes even more visually unflattering when performers really *are* up against the wall. Move your talent as far away as practical. Note the difference between the "comfort level" of the set shown in Figure 18.2.

By moving the host and guests away from the wall (or cyc), you will also immediately eliminate two lighting problems. First, the back light can now be placed at a comfortable angle, instead of beating down directly on the top of talents' heads. Second, shadows on the wall will be diffused or eliminated when the talent is moved away from the wall. (Try this experiment using your hand, any lamp, and a wall: Move your hand closer to the wall and watch how distinct the shadow becomes; move your hand away and the shadow disappears. That's exactly what happens when you move talent away from the background.)

Planning the Placement of the Host and Guests. Decide how you want the host and guests placed before planning too many other aspects of the production setup. From a production standpoint, the simplest design is usually to

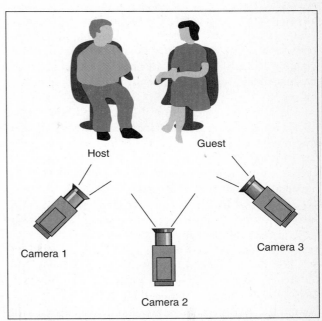

Figure 18.3 Standard talk show layout. A standard talk show setup for three cameras uses Camera 1 for guests and Camera 3 for the host. Camera 2 is available for both wide shots of talent and for close-ups of props.

have the host and guest(s) more or less facing forward, with their chairs "cheated" a few inches toward each other, as shown in Figure 18.3. Such an arrangement requires only one finished background wall and simplifies camera setup. Camera 1, as shown in Figure 18.4, can be used as the

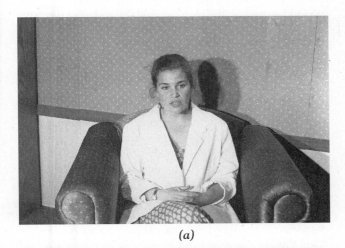

(a)

(b)

Figure 18.2 Separating the set from the background. When the set is too close to the background, the actors seem cramped (*a*), as the video lens foreshortens distance. Proper separation of set from background conveys a level of comfort to the audience (*b*).

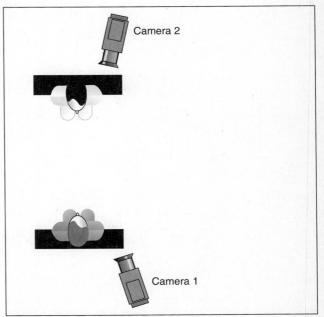

Figure 18.4 Face-to-face talk show layout. Seating the host and guest face-to-face requires over-the-shoulder camera shots that can seem either intimate or confrontational.

close-up camera on a guest, or for a shot showing two more guests. Camera 2 will be focused on a wide shot, useful for opening and closing the show, and camera 3 will hold a close-up of the host. During the program, camera 2 can be broken from its wide shot to be used as a close-up camera for props.

Face-to-face placement of the guest and host (Figure 18.4) creates an appealing and sometimes intriguingly confrontational atmosphere, and allows for compelling over-the-shoulder shots. However, you will have to provide two acceptable backgrounds because your cameras will be aimed at opposite ends of the studio.

One of the most pleasing setups, and one that is not used very often, involves placing the guest(s) and host at a 90-degree angle as they sit at a table or counter, as illustrated in Figure 18.5.

Location of the Monitor. A monitor visible from the set area is often a good idea, but it is also a good idea to place it where the host can see it but the guest(s) cannot. Nonprofessional performers are often distracted by the monitor and will look toward it when on camera. But a professional performer can benefit from having an easily visible monitor, especially when he or she is handling a prop and needs to know, for example, if a book cover is reflecting into the camera lens and causing glare. Also, most performers like to steal a glance at the monitor from time to time in order to determine how tight their shot is. On a tight shot, professionals want to hold their heads very still in order to avoid moving out of the frame, but on a looser shot they want to inject more movement and gestures.

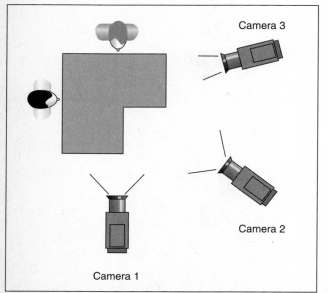

Figure 18.5 Ninety-degree talk show layout. Positioning host and guest at a 90-degree angle around a table or counter draws them together. Camera assignments are similar to the standard layout (Figure 18.3).

Planning Base Light. Be sure that you have a smooth, even base light across all working areas of the set. Owing to the nature of a talk-interview segment, unexpected events do occur; a guest, for example, may walk several feet away from the specified location during a stand-up demonstration segment. Attempt to anticipate these factors and avoid any "black holes" in your lighting.

Avoiding Set Problems. By the same token, anticipate any problems movement may cause in regard to the background. A guest who moves too far to the right during, let's say, a cooking demonstration, might leave you with a shot that shows the edge of the scenery.

Advance Planning with the Host and Guests

The producer, director, or other production specialist will let the host and the guest(s) know what is expected of them during their on-camera appearance, and will help them make the best possible showing. Here, the production specialist must deal with some of the human aspects of video as well as the technical facets. Some points we'll examine here include techniques for starting and stopping on time, infusing energy into the guests (and sometimes the host), calming nervous guests, offering advice on clothing, giving guidance on the topic, and planning the opening and closing.

Talk Show Timing. Timing is the bane of the talk-show producer's working life. In general, segments must begin and end precisely on time—a tall order when dealing with the vagaries of the video talk-interview format. Hitting time cues is not such a difficult task in some other types of productions: The elements of a newscast, for example, can be added or subtracted until the time frames are correct, and if miscalculations are made, an experienced anchor can make smooth adjustments quickly. Things are not so easy when dealing with guests who are not professional performers and who have no true sense of how critical timing really is.

Timing is the host's responsibility, but guests are concerned about timing, and sometimes they have no real conception of how long a minute, or five minutes, or half an hour really is. Remember, guests usually won't see time cues; and they can't really glance at their watches; they only know how long the program *feels*. Guests may drastically underestimate or overestimate how much material can or should be covered within a certain time period. One of the more frequent questions asked by guests, in fact, is "How do I know when to stop talking?"

An adept host often says, simply, "Just watch me and you'll know." Indeed, this tactic usually works well. After all, can't *you* tell, from body language and other nonverbal or verbal indicators, when someone is anxious to conclude a conversation with you? Forewarned that they will instinctively know when to stop talking, many guests are thus placed considerably more at ease and can better concentrate on other aspects of their performance.

Sometimes, the host will work out a cue with a guest who is particularly worried about when to stop talking. When one of the authors was hosting a daily talk show on commercial TV, he would tell guests that they should wind up their remarks when he uncrossed his legs and leaned forward. (This worked perfectly for 700 shows except for the one occasion when he accidentally uncrossed his legs and leaned forward one minute into the program—and the guest refused to speak for the remaining four minutes of the segment.)

The host is worried about timing too—for a number of reasons. You must be certain to make things easy for the host by providing adequate time cues. When directing a talk segment, it is usually advisable to have the floor director give time-remaining cues for every minute of the segment. (Check with the host as to what intervervals he or she favors.) A complete sequence of time cues allows the host to plan the overall flow of the program and to allow enough time to cover all the relevant material.

Note: It is the floor director's responsibility to *be in a position that's easily observable by talent*. If this means crawling across the studio floor beneath camera range in order to flash talent a one-minute cue, so be it. Talent must never be expected to hunt all over the studio for the floor director.

Energy Level. Guests and hosts must be briefed on the amount of energy they need to project. This, of course, is a particularly important point to stress when briefing the nonprofessional performer. Television is an enervating medium; it somehow saps the apparent energy level of the person on camera. People who visit a television studio production for the first time are often astounded by how strongly the performers play to the camera. But what appears to be an overenergetic, "hyped" performance when viewed in the studio often appears just right when filtered through the energy-sapping camera lens. Guests must be made aware of this, and in good operations, they are. When one of the authors was a guest on the *Good Day* program on WCVB Television in Boston, for example, a production aide told him (and every other guest in the "green room," the talk show's holding pen): "Keep your energy up! Be vivacious! Remember, there's something about TV that robs your energy!" That's good advice for anyone who appears on camera—host or guest.

Dealing with Jittery Guests. A member of the production staff, in the process of planning the program, should screen guests and determine whether they are particularly anxious about their upcoming appearance. Stage fright is a common problem, but properly addressed, the problem can virtually be eliminated. Many nonprofessionals—and a good many pros too—are terrified by the thought of appearing in public. What professionals have learned, though, is that nervousness can be translated into *nervous energy*.

The point is that guests, especially those exhibiting obvious anxiety about an upcoming appearance, need to be informed that almost *everyone* is nervous about appearing on the mass media, but that those fears can be put to constructive use. Moreover, it is wise to advise guests that a viewing audience is a very poor perceptor of a performer's nervousness, anyway. Although shaking knees and a jittery stomach are obvious to the owner of the anatomy, audiences simply do not receive those particular signals. Also, inform guests that the reality of their worst fear (usually a fear of freezing on camera) actually occurring is so rare as to be statistically insignificant. As host, producer, or director of thousands of talk or news-interview segments, one of the authors has seen an interviewee "freeze up" or otherwise self-destruct on camera exactly once.

Proper Wardrobe. When planning the talk-interview segment, be sure to offer suggestions to guests about proper clothing. In general, men appear best when wearing solid, dark-colored (but preferably not black) suits. Tight-fitting suits usually look better on camera than loosely fitted ones. It is a good idea to advise guests to wear lightweight suits, for two reasons: First, the TV studio often gets hot, and second, heavyweight fabric tends to bunch up and create an unflattering on-camera appearance.

Women do well to avoid bold patterns and should avoid large jewelry. Bulky necklaces present a particular problem because they can clang against the clipped-on mic.

Herringbone patterns or other patterns featuring tightly placed lines or stripes are not the best choice for video because they sometimes make the camera **strobe** or **moiré**, creating a wavy appearance flashing across the cloth. White shirts are now perfectly acceptable for good quality television equipment. There was a time when video cameras could not handle the contrast problems caused by a white shirt, but modern, high-quality gear can handle the contrast. (If you are working with older or cheaper cameras, check out the appearance of white shirts; in some cases you may have to resort to blue.) Irrespective of the quality of your cameras, it is still advisable not to wear a white shirt or blouse with a black jacket.

The host of the show may wish to change outfits if several days' worth of shows are being taped in one session. However, it is worth noting that viewers really do not seem to remember what clothes a host wore yesterday. If the host wants to wear the same clothes for the entire week of shows, probably no one will notice.

If you doubt this, think back to the long-running TV series *Dragnet*. It's off the air now, but is in syndication in many markets and cable networks. Stars Jack Webb and Harry Morgan wore the same individual wardrobe in *every episode* during the *entire run of the show* except for seven scenes. Webb wore the same blazer and slacks and Morgan wore the same suit. Did *you* notice? (Opinions of Jack Webb's acting ability vary, but he is universally regarded as a consummate production manager. He turned out shows in record time and insisted that he and Morgan never change wardrobe in order to prevent any inconsistencies in the show's continuity when edits were made. The editor would never have to worry about cutting in a certain scene from any given time period because the wardrobe was always the same.)

Offering Guidance about the Topic. Prospective guests often ask production personnel for a list of questions that will be asked during the segment. Although it is perfectly reasonable to provide guests with guidance about the general topic, furnishing them with a list of questions is hardly ever productive. Having such a list often results in the guest's providing flat, rehearsed answers. Giving out a question list also can cause an unexpected glitch: The guest assumes that these questions are the *only* ones to be asked and balks at any discussion of a subject not on the list.

Openings and Closings. Finally, plan the opening and closing with the host. It is advisable, if at all possible, to have opening and closing remarks scripted. This allows the director to know exactly what will be happening during these critical portions of the show, and this practice is also a hedge against the host's flubbing the introduction and closing. It can be very difficult to ad-lib openings and closings, and this is when many of a host's mistakes are typically made.

Incidentally, a factor that relates to many of the production values discussed so far is theme music. Music not only plays a valuable role in setting the emotional tone for the program, it is a terrific problem solver when used to close the show. A **foldback** system, a device that feeds music back into the studio but in such a way that it does not cause feedback through the studio mics (this is an informal definition but is accurate within the parameters of our discussion), cues the host and guest(s) that the show is wrapping up. Theme music piped in over the foldback speaker is a very efficient way of giving a wrap-up cue.

Now that the advance planning has been disposed of, the cameras are uncapped and the segment is ready to roll. The next part of this chapter deals with the production duties of the director and crew immediately before and during the program.

DIRECTING THE TALK SHOW

The director and crew may arrive a couple of hours before the actual taping of the show. Time periods vary, of course, depending on the complexity of the program and whether extensive changes are needed in lighting or scenery.

Your first concern, practically from the instant you unlock the studio door, is whether all the equipment is working properly. Immediately power up the cameras, lighting instruments, the switcher, and the audio console. Also, be absolutely certain that the video and audio signals are being fed to the videotape recorder. Do a test recording (of anything, even a shot of the camera registration charts), not only to make sure that the videotape recorder is working, but also to ensure that it is correctly patched into the system. If someone from the previous shift has patched a different source into the VTR, you need to find out about it posthaste and do the necessary rerouting.

Next, plug in mics, test them, and find the appropriate pots on the audio console. For some reason, mics are often neglected until the last minute, when the crew scrambles to find the mics on the console and the guests wonder why everyone is so disorganized. Make sure the mics are working well in advance of the host's and guests' arriving.

When the performers appear on the set, get an audio level as soon as they are seated. A usually successful method of doing this is to ask the guests to count to twenty. Simply asking them to "say something" usually prompts an absurd dialog in which the guest says, "Hello, hello, is that enough?" while the audio director has not yet even located the pot. The audio director may respond that no, that was not enough, in which case the guest invariably asks, "What am I supposed to say now?" Granted, the level of a guest counting aloud won't precisely match the level of his or her conversation, but the counting to twenty routine is usually a reliable and practical indicator that provides enough time for the audio operator to make a realistic setting on the console.

As air or taping time approaches, crew members are told to take their positions. Experienced directors make the crew take their places earlier than is absolutely necessary, because a last-minute call to battle stations often turns up a missing crewperson who is out in the hall or in the cafeteria. If camera operators grumble about having to "wait around," you can use the time to rehearse shots and camera movements.

In fact, rehearsal is essential if there is a prop involved in the talk-interview segment. Should the prop or its manipulation be complex, much advance thought should be invested in how the segment will be shot. More on that in a moment.

Framing Shots

In general you will be cutting quickly between the host and guest. To avoid jarring viewers, frame both subjects at a similar distance. For instance, cut from a close-up of the host to a close-up of the guest, not from a close-up to a medium shot. You may want to use a two-shot to bridge between a close-up and a medium shot of an individual if a medium shot is useful to accommodate a speaker's gestures, for instance.

Calling Shots

Typically, the director orders the VTR to roll, activates test and tone, and slates the program. (Refer to Chapter 15, "Fundamentals of Directing," for details on this and other general aspects of the directing process.) Video and theme music are brought up, along with the title graphics and any other opening material. Then the opening cue is thrown to the host.

The Opening. The operative theory behind opening a talk show, and most video programming, is that viewers like to be *introduced* to the setting and the participants. Viewers are most comfortable when they see a wide shot of the set and the participants, then a medium close-up of the host, followed by a medium close-up of the guest. Then, if desired, the shots can be further tightened.

You can relate this to your own experience when, for example, you enter an unfamiliar office. You first quickly get your bearings by glancing around the room. (Actually, studies indicate that most people first look at the floor, an instinctive response with which we check to see if the surface is safe to walk on.) Then you glance at the person behind the desk and at others in the room. As introductions are made, you move closer, and physically establish contact by shaking hands.

Viewers are made uncomfortable by heads suddenly appearing in full screen, just as uncomfortable as you would be if the occupant of the office thrust his or her face an inch away from yours as soon as you opened the door. That is why video production generally starts wide and gradually moves in close. There are some standard techniques for accomplishing this effect. Among them:

• Start with the wide shot on camera 2 (as indicated in Figure 18.3). As the host opens the show, zoom in with camera 2 to a medium close-up of the host.

-or-

• Start with the wide shot on camera 2, have the host speak a few words of introduction to camera 2, and then cue the host to change to camera 3, which is taking a medium close-up.

-or-

• Open on the wide shot from camera 2, hold the shot during the opening few seconds of the title and theme, and then cue the host to *start* talking to camera 3 the instant after you take camera 3.

What happens next? Generally, the host introduces the guest. This is the perfect time to take a brief shot of the guest, which would be a close-up on camera 1. A key

of the guest's name and title might also be added. Do not linger too long, though, because you want to cut back to the host before the first question is completed. The next camera change, of course, will be back to the guest when he or she answers the first question.

The opening of the talk-interview segment is by far the most troublesome aspect of the whole program, and it must be done sharply—not only for the sake of producing good video but because the opening sets the tone for the rest of the program. A flubbed beginning is demoralizing for the control room crew and disconcerting to viewers.

The Middle Game. The show then proceeds as the director follows the exchange of ideas between the host and guest(s). Often, some sort of prop, such as a book, is held up or a demonstration is given with a prop. Following verbal exchanges and cutting to shots of the appropriate people on time is difficult, but it is largely a learned skill, and with practice you will be able to stay on top of the conversation. The body of the talk show is also the time when the props are brought out. Dealing with props is often quite perplexing, but some basic techniques can make the task simpler.

Following are some suggestions for smoothly handling these situations.

When following the conversation and cutting back and forth:

• Do not become hypnotized by the air monitor. Keep an eye on the camera monitors because *they* are the source of your next shot. You will be much better prepared to take the appropriate camera when a performer responds because you can see him or her getting ready to speak.

• Along the same lines, *listen* for an intake of breath; this is a good clue that a question is about to be asked or answered, or an interjection will be made, and you can cut to the appropriate camera immediately. Breath intake is hardly noticeable to viewers watching and listening via a standard TV, but if you keep your control room monitors at a fairly high level, breath intakes will be very evident to you.

• In general terms, it is better to make your cuts too early than too late. Viewers quickly catch on to the fact that there is a lag between the time a particular person starts speaking and when he or she appears on camera. Falling behind the rhythm of the show is a very evident directorial failing.

• If you do elect to follow the "better early than late" strategy, though, it is inevitable that you will cut to someone who appears to be ready to speak but winds up not saying anything while another person continues speaking. That happens to *every* director.

When it happens, do *not* frantically attempt to cut back to the person who is still speaking. It will make the mistake *look* like a mistake. Instead, hold the shot for a reasonable time so that it appears as if you are taking a *reaction shot*. If you so choose, you can order the camera to slowly pull back to reveal both participants—the speaker and the listener. Done correctly, you can cover your miscue in such a way that viewers (and maybe even your technical director) will think you planned it that way.

- Speaking of reaction shots, do not be reluctant to use them. They add spice to the program, especially if you can get a shot of a guest when the host or another guest is saying something not particularly flattering about him or her. (But be sure the person is actually *reacting* or the shot won't be appropriate.)

When using a prop:

- Make every effort to convince the host or guest to thoroughly plan the prop sequence with you ahead of time. Guests, and even experienced hosts, often believe that they can simply wave a prop in the air and you will somehow come up with an acceptable shot. Let every performer know that you and the camera operator need several seconds to find and focus on the prop before the shot can be taken.

- If at all possible, try to devise a situation in which the prop is held in a relatively stationary position. Asking the host to keep the prop on the table but tilt it up slightly is a good option (Figure 18.6).

- Because of their experience, hosts will (usually) be better prop handlers than guests. Whenever possible, have the host hold up the book, the compact disc jacket, or whatever.

- When taking a close-up of a prop, *always* leave yourself with a safety shot, meaning a shot you can immediately take should the prop suddenly be moved, dropped, or pulled out of focus.

The End Game. The closing of the program is nearly as hazardous as the opening, primarily because you are dealing with shots and sequences of events that usually must terminate at a precise time. There is also something of a letdown factor involved: The show is almost over, the major crises have passed, and cast and crew now tend to lose a little of their concentration.

Your closing will go much more smoothly if the floor director is feeding the host consistent and regular time cues. Even professional television performers sometimes have trouble gauging how much time has passed during a

Figure 18.6 Proper prop handling. Try to keep the prop stationary by supporting it on a solid surface.

given segment, and their judgment may vary from show to show, from situation to situation.

The most experienced host can become enraptured with a sparkling conversation, or, conversely, bored silly by a lethargic lecture, and thus seriously miscalculate remaining showtime. That is why it is advisable for the floor director to give a complete set of cues, ranging from the standard minute cues to cues for 30 seconds, 15 seconds, and a 10-finger countdown to zero.

Most directors like to close the show on a wide shot, usually a wide shot showing the guest(s) and host chatting amiably, but with no audio (except for theme music). The floor director should always, at this point, advise the guests that there is still video being televised. Otherwise the guests may get up from their chairs or commit some other inappropriate action. The worst case scenario involves the guest who suddenly gets up to leave and forgets about the microphone, which is either torn from its wiring or from the wearer's clothing.

A Sample Talk Show

What follows is an approximation of the sequence of events that might occur during a two-minute talk-interview segment. Although it is written in two columns, it is *not* a script. As noted in Chapter 13, "Scripting for Video," talk shows are not scripted; even if they were, they would not look like what follows. This is merely an approximation of what the segment might look like if it were scripted after the fact and the director's thoughts, plans, and actions were written into a document.

So, with that in mind, Figure 18.7 shows a segment on home security. Note that some of the more difficult aspects of directing the talk show are *not* included in Figure

A Sample Talk Show Segment

Following the Shots

Program opens with a wide shot of the host and guest facing front with chairs slightly cheated toward each other. Floor director points to the camera with the wide shot and throws the host the opening cue.

Cut to CU of HOST

Take a reaction shot of Kinsella and key his title.

Cut back to CU of HOST

Cut to CU of CAPTAIN
The director sees that HOST is about to ask a question, and also notes that the CAPTAIN is going to reach for the prop.

Cut to CU of HOST

Director sees that CAPTAIN is about to speak and is ready to pick up the deadbolt lock on the table, so the director . . .

Cuts to CU of CAPTAIN . . .

The director sees that CAPTAIN is about to reach for the lock, so the director alerts the operator of the close-up camera . . .

CAPTAIN is holding up the lock; the director waits until the close-up camera is in focus and then takes CU of lock . . .

The director sees that HOST is ready to ask a question, so the director gets off CU of deadbolt and takes CU of HOST.
Quickly, the director readies cut to HOST . . . take it!

Cut to CU CAPTAIN . . .
This is going to be a long answer; take a quick reaction shot of HOST nodding, then cut back to CU of CAPTAIN.

Director can tell CAPTAIN's wrapping up, so ready . . .

Audio

HOST: Hello, I'm Paula Mason . . .

and today's topic is how to keep what's in your home in your home and keep burglars out.

My guest is Captain Ned Kinsella of the police department's crime prevention unit. Captain Kinsella is a specialist at preventing burglary, and he has a relatively simple and inexpensive idea that just might save you a lot of money and grief.

What are we talking about, Captain?

CAPTAIN: A deadbolt lock, the kind you can pick up at a hardware store for less than twenty dollars . . . and if you're handy with tools, you can install it yourself.

HOST: But what's different about a deadbolt lock? Why would it stop a burglar when an ordinary lock won't?

CAPTAIN: First of all, it doesn't have the wedge-shaped bolt that closes automatically when you shut the door, the kind of bolt that a thief can just slide back with a credit card.

Now, with a deadbolt, he can't do that. A deadbolt lock has a long bolt that you have to manually turn with a key or with a knob, and it slides into the strikeplate.

As you can see here, this bolt is an inch and a quarter long, and there's no way that you can pry that back with a credit card or even a screwdriver.

HOST: OK, but couldn't a burglar just break down the door, or the door frame?

CAPTAIN: Sure, but all our statistics show that the typical burglar is going to follow the path of least resistance. He's usually not ready to bash down a door, and he's not carrying heavy-duty tools or a pocketful of lock picks. He just wants easy in, easy out. If you make things hard for him, odds are he'll just look for an easier target.

(continued)

Figure 18.7 A sample talk show script.

A Sample Talk Show Segment (*continued*)

Following the Shots	Audio
Cut to CU of HOST	HOST: Well, there you have it, a simple way to turn the odds in your favor.
The show is wrapping up, so the director . . .	
Cuts to two-shot of HOST and CAPTAIN	
Director rolls the theme music for a few seconds, holding the shot of HOST and CAPTAIN, then goes to a commercial break.	

Figure 18.7 (continued)

18.7; giving time cues, adjusting shots, and other aspects are not incorporated. But the sequence of events does provide a general perspective on how you might begin, sustain, and end a short talk-interview sequence.

SUMMARY

1. The talk show, which might also be termed the talk-interview format, is an integral part of video production, and is used on broadcast television, corporate and institutional video, and within other types of programs, such as newscasts.

2. The talk show appears to be part of a spontaneous and natural process, but it is not. Instead, a talk-interview segment is carried out within rigid technical constraints. The resulting program appears natural because it is in the video language we have come to accept as the standard convention of video communication.

3. Talk-show segments have the advantage of being relatively inexpensive to produce, but they do require a full crew, and the success of the program depends to a great extent on the abilities of the host.

4. Simple talk-show sets often work better than more complex sets. An important point in planning the set is to move guests away from walls or the cyc.

5. Even base lighting is essential for a talk show because this type of program is often less static than other shows; no movement should fall into a poorly lighted "black hole."

6. Some member of the production crew should brief on-camera performers in advance about such items as dress and energy level.

7. Audio and lighting are two of the major culprits that cause problems during the minutes before the talk show starts. Check lighting and mics as early in the production process as possible.

8. The basic visual theory of a talk show is that viewers like to be oriented with a wide shot, and then move into the scene via tighter shots.

9. Props are difficult to handle and photograph. Work out the details of prop handling well in advance of the program's air date or taping.

10. Keep an eye on the camera monitors. They are the source of your upcoming shots. If you become mesmerized by what is going over the air, you may find yourself falling behind and taking shots too late.

TECHNICAL TERMS

cheat	moiré	reaction shot	strobe
foldback			

EXERCISES

1. Watch two shows that feature the talk-interview format. Write a two- or three-page paper comparing the contrasting production elements in the programs. Pay particular attention to:

   - Rapidity of cuts

   - Tightness of close-ups

   - Amount of zooming (if any)

- Position of guests on the set
- Atmosphere of the set

Analyze the differences between the production elements in the two shows, and explain why you think those particular production elements were used. (Note: Be sure you watch shows that have a true contrast in style and substance; don't try to contrast programs that are virtual clones of each other.)

2. Using classmates or co-workers as on-camera performers, produce and direct a five-minute interview program. There are two requirements:

    a. It must be a legitimate interview, meaning that the guest must actually speak about a topic with which he or she is familiar.

    b. A prop must be used. Some possible topics include demonstrating the operation of a 35mm film camera, using chopsticks, how to play Solitaire, and how to use a particular program on a laptop computer. The secret here is to carefully plan who will be holding the prop and how it will be manipulated. The entire class can rotate through this exercise, assuming various production and on-camera duties.

3. Stage a brief talk segment without props, but tape the segment twice, altering the set between tapings. Stage the first show with an "open" set: having guests face mainly forward against a brightly lighted background and utilizing medium close-ups. Now, stage the same segment using harsher lights, have the host and guest face each other, and shoot over-the-shoulder shots using tight close-ups. Play back the tape for the class and discuss the differences in the overall thrust of the programs.

producing news and documen- taries

OBJECTIVES

After completing Chapter 19, you will be able to:

1. Identify all the typical elements in a news report.
2. Write some basic news copy.
3. Construct a basic news package and a simple documentary.

As mushrooming audiences rely on commercial and institutional video for news and information, it becomes increasingly important for the producer to understand the basic structure of news production.

This chapter is a basic introduction to producing short news reports, longer documentary-style news programs, and a studio-based newscast. Although news reporting and news judgment are clearly beyond the scope of this chapter and this book, we can offer some suggestions for further locating information, and other sources are listed in the Recommended Readings section in the Appendix.

THE NEWS FIELD REPORT

When TV reporters are assigned to cover a story, they generally return to the studio with raw footage that is edited into a form which, in turn, can be inserted into the newscast.

The Structures of News Reports

Although terminology varies from market to market, we'll term the formats of the material gathered in the field and edited back at the station (or simply inserted into a newscast) as sound bites, voice overs, and packages.

The Sound Bite. A **sound bite** is a segment of video and audio, usually an interview, that is inserted into a news program. It is often called an SOT (sound-on-tape) segment. The sound bite can be incorporated in other formats too. Rather than running it as a part of a newscast introduced by the anchor, it can be used in a package or a documentary (two forms we'll define presently).

The sound bite is inserted into the news show and introduced by an anchor's lead-in and often followed by an anchor's close. A **lead-in** is a spoken line that sets the scene and introduces the piece. For example, let's assume that you have covered a major fire and that you have a

sound bite of the fire chief commenting on the cause of the blaze. It might look like this:

Video	Audio
Fire chief OC	We'll have to let the arson investigators take a closer look, but right now I'd definitely classify this as a possible arson. The fire started in the middle of two rooms at the same time. That just doesn't happen unless somebody piles up flammable material and lights it.

If you were to use this sound bite during a newscast, you would probably write an introduction for the anchor to read, an introduction that gives a brief description of the situation and introduces the tape. The introduction would state the most important and newsworthy facts. For example:

Video	Audio
Anchor OC	No injuries but heavy damage in a fire this morning at the Smith Furniture Warehouse on Clinton Avenue. Fire officials don't have an official verdict on the cause yet, but Chief Tom McDougal says he's suspicious . . .
Fire chief OC	We'll have to let the arson investigators take a closer look, but right now I'd definitely classify this as a possible arson. The fire started in the middle of two rooms at the same time. That just doesn't happen unless somebody piles up flammable material and lights it.
Anchor OC	Chief McDougal says the building is a total loss, and estimates the damage at more than three hundred thousand dollars.

You'll notice that the anchor's lead-in did not introduce word for word what was to come; that's a standard technique of newswriting. Notice how awkward the lead-in appears if you ignore this scripting principle:

Video	Audio
Anchor OC	. . . and Chief Tom McDougal says that although the arson investigators still must make an official ruling, he'd classify the fire as a possible arson because the fire started in the center of two rooms.
Fire chief OC	We'll have to let the arson investigators take a closer look, but right now I'd definitely classify this as a possible arson. The fire started in the middle of two rooms at the same time. That just doesn't happen unless somebody piles up flammable material and lights it.

The Voice-Over. A **voice-over** is a segment where an announcer speaks over the video. The sound of the video is not used, except for the purpose of providing meaningful background noise, such as the sounds of flames crackling for a video about a fire.

Why would you elect to use a voice-over? Well, if you had dramatic shots of the fire, you might choose to show them on screen while the anchor reads the script rather than use the fire chief sound bite.

Video	Audio
Anchor OC	No injuries but heavy damage in a fire this morning at the Smith Furniture Warehouse on Clinton Avenue.
Cut to LS burning building	Fire officials don't have an official verdict on the cause yet, but Chief Tom McDougal says he'd call it a possible arson because the fire apparently started in two rooms at the same time.
Cut to Anchor OC	Chief McDougal says the building is a total loss, and estimates the damage at more than three hundred thousand dollars.

The voice-over is an effective technique for showing the subject to which your script refers. It's important, though, that you don't make the script too obvious. Don't write, "Here you see a burning building." Viewers can figure that much out for themselves.

The Package. A **package** is usually a mixture of voice overs, sound bites, and tape of a reporter delivering lines

Figure 19.1 A typical stand-up. Dave Dent, shown here working as a general assignment reporter for WKRN-TV in Nashville, addresses the camera. We've photographed this stand-up off the screen to show the monitor edges and to illustrate the typical framing for a stand-up.

to the camera. When a reporter delivers lines straight to the camera, it is often called a **stand-up** (Figure 19.1). Stand-ups can occur at the open of a package, at the close, or in the middle. When a reporter does a stand-up in the middle of a package, it is often called a **bridge**, and is generally inserted to help the viewer navigate a change in time or location.

Using material we've gathered at the fire, we can put together a package that includes an opening voice over, a sound bite, and a stand-up close. This is a fairly typical pattern, by the way; reporters almost always appear at the end of their packages. The stand-up open is still sometimes used, but it is much less common today than it was in years past. Usually, a stand-up bridge is used only to indicate a change in time or place.

Our package, which would be introduced by an anchor, might look like this if it were scripted:

Video	Audio
Anchor OC	No injuries but a lot of damage at a well-known downtown furniture warehouse. WXXX reporter Barbara Olson is on the scene with this report.
[Now, the package . . .]	
LS burning building	You could see the smoke for miles as a four-alarm fire tore through the Smith Furniture

Video	Audio
	Warehouse on Clinton Avenue. Fire officials don't know the cause yet, but Chief Tom McDougal says he thinks arson is a strong possibility.
Fire chief OC	We'll have to let the arson investigators take a closer look, but right now I'd definitely classify this as a possible arson. The fire started in the middle of two rooms at the same time. That just doesn't happen unless somebody piles up flammable material and lights it.
Barbara Olson OC	McDougal says the building is a total loss, and estimates the damage at more than three hundred thousand dollars. This is Barbara Olson, WXXX News at Ten.

Most packages are not fully scripted. They are pieced together from sound bites and cover video and some script written for the voice over; then, cover video is added. (**Cover video** is any video without sound or with simple background noises.) Sometimes, when deadlines are very tight, the voice over is ad-libbed. So remember that scripted packages are primarily for the sake of illustration. Some stations script entire packages; most don't.

Also keep in mind that this is a very simplified package. Most packages include multiple sound bites and several interwoven sequences of voice overs and cover video.

Choosing and Using Sound Bites and Cover Video

Irrespective of the number of sound bites and cover shots, the logic of the package is always the same. In essence, we want all elements of the package to have meaning and to advance the story. Notice that even a very long, very complex story is relatively simple in concept once you appreciate how the segments are integrated into a narrative flow.

For example, a CBS News report on a Milwaukee job training program contains what might initially seem to be an overwhelming number of segments. They're listed in Figure 19.2. A total of 19 separate elements in this news package will run 3 minutes and 18 seconds—a long story by broadcast news standards.

If the sequence in Figure 19.2 seems extremely complicated, read through the actual story written by CBS News correspondent Bob Faw and producer Carl Ginsburg. Note that the elements tell a logical narrative (Figure 19.3).

1. An opening scene with natural sound.
2. Narration voiced over cover video. The cover video might be a continuation of the opening scene.
3. A change of scene with natural sound, leading to the next narration.
4. Brief narration that leads into an SOT interview (a sound bite, in other words).
5. The first interview segment.
6. Narration over cover video, with an occasional piece of cover video shown without narration, just with natural sound.
7. The narration leads into the next interview segment.
8. Interview segment 2.
9. Narration that advances the story, relating interview segment 2 to interview segment 3.
10. Interview segment 3.
11. Narration that continues to move the story forward to another interview segment, segment 4, which reinforces the basic idea of the piece while showing another angle of the story.
12. Interview segment 4.
13. A bridge. (A bridge is a reporter's on-camera appearance in the middle of the segment. It is generally used only when location or time is changed and the reporter's appearance is necessary to help make that clear. Let's assume, for the sake of argument, that the reporter, off camera, had been talking about a training center but now wants to shift location, discussing a neighborhood down the street—change in location—that also serves to train workers.)
14. Narration over cover video of the new scene.
15. For variety, an interview segment of a person previously introduced over some cover video relating to what he's talking about.
16. Reporter's narration again, beginning to wrap up the story.
17. A quick SOT from one of the people interviewed; she offers a concluding remark.
18. A quick SOT from another person interviewed. The pace is being quickened, the remarks are obviously of a concluding nature, and it becomes apparent that the piece is about to wrap up.
19. A concluding statement by the narrator and the narrator's standard outcue: name, news organization, location.

Figure 19.2 Elements of a news package. A total of 19 separate elements in a news package that will run 3 minutes and 18 seconds—a long story by broadcast news standards.

There are probably a few more cuts in this story than most, and also notice that there is a bridge, a somewhat unusual technique. Finally, one segment uses the voice of a newsmaker as a voice-over for the cover video to communicate directly with the audience.

MILWAUKEE'S SMALL HOPE
FAW/GINSBURG/MIKLAUS
EVE NEWS

NAT SOUND – DEMOLITION

NARR: AS AMERICA'S RUST BUCKET CRUM-BLES . . . NEIGHBORHOODS GUTTED, JOBS MOVED AWAY AND PEOPLE FORGOTTEN . . . A PROGRAM IN ONE SMALL BUILDING NO ONE WANTED ON MILWAUKEE'S SOUTH SIDE, IS NOT ONLY HELPING SALVAGE A POOR COM-MUNITY . . . IT'S ALSO SERVING AS A MODEL FOR THE REST OF THE COUNTRY.

NAT SOUND – REPAIR SHOP

NARR: ESPERANZA UNIDA IS A COMMUNITY ORGANIZATION WHICH PRODUCES JOBS – SKILLED JOBS – AND, AS ITS SPANISH NAME SUGGESTS, HOPE.

SOT: (RICHARD OULAHAN, DIRECTOR, ESPER-ANZA UNIDA) "YOU CAN PUT ANYBODY INTO A MINIMUM WAGE JOB . . . I'LL PUT EVERYBODY INTO MINIMUM WAGE JOBS TOMORROW, BUT THAT'S NOT WHAT WE'RE ABOUT: HOW DO YOU PUT HIM INTO A JOB THAT SUPPORTS HIS FAMILY. THAT'S WHAT WE'RE ABOUT."

NARR: HERE, TRAINEES LIKE DUANE VAN-LOAN, LEARNING FRONT-END ALIGNMENT . . . OR STEVE DEAN WORKING ON BRAKES . . . RE-PAIR CARS IN THIS ONCE ABANDONED CAR DEALERSHIP . . . THE MONEY MADE FROM THE REPAIR WORK GOES TO HIRE OTHER TRAINEES.

NAT SOUND – RICARDO. HAMMERING AWAY ON DOOR.

NARR: RICARDO RAMIREZ CAME TO MILWAU-KEE. HE WAS UNEMPLOYED AND ON WELFARE . . . NOW HE'S IN LINE FOR A $30,000 A YEAR JOB WITH A CAR DEALER.

SOT: (OULAHAN) "WE GET DISLOCATED WORKERS WHO WENT FROM $16 AN HOUR TO $6 . . . WE GET PEOPLE WHO NEVER WORKED IN GENERATIONS, AND WE'RE SAYING: WE WANT TO MOVE THOSE PEOPLE INTO OUR ECONOMY BECAUSE IF THEY'RE NOT, WE'RE NOT GOING TO MAKE IT AS A COUNTRY."

NARR: ESPERANZA UNIDA'S SUCCESS IS ITS FORMULA – GOVERNMENT AND PRIVATE GRANTS, BUT MOSTLY THE MONEY IT MAKES, AND THAT MEANS COMPETING SUCCESS-FULLY, FOR CUSTOMERS LIKE RAOUL MAYAN.

SOT: (RAOUL) "GOOD LOCATION, GOOD

PLACE, AND THEY DO A GOOD JOB.
Q: AND THE PRICE? A: IT'S GOOD."

NARR: AND IT'S NOT JUST RUNNING AN AUTO REPAIR SHOP . . . THE SHOP'S PROFITS ARE PLOUGHED INTO A WOODWORKING SHOP TO TRAIN CABINETMAKERS . . . AN AUTO BODY SHOP WHICH REBUILDS THEN SELLS DO-NATED JUNK HEAPS . . . AND A TRAINING PRO-GRAM WHICH TEACHES NEIGHBORHOOD MOTHERS HOW TO SET UP AND RUN DAY CARE CENTERS . . . ALL UNDER ONE ROOF.

SOT: (JEANETTE BARQUET, DAY CARE TRAINER) "THIS IS ANOTHER WAY TO STAY HOME WITH THEIR KIDS. TAKE CARE OF THEIR KIDS. PLUS GET SOME INCOME FROM THE OUTSIDE."

O/C: (BOB FAW) WHAT STARTED IN THE AUTO REPAIR SHOP DIDN'T END THERE . . . JUST DOWN THE STREET AND AROUND THE COR-NER WERE ABANDONED HOMES . . . OPPORTU-NITIES TO TRAIN NEW CARPENTERS AND HELP REBUILD THE COMMUNITY.

NARR: ESPERANZA UNIDA IS NOW TURNING DILAPIDATED EYESORES LIKE THIS . . . INTO HANDSOME DUPLEXES LIKE THIS . . . BY TEACH-ING AND TRAINING UNEMPLOYED RESIDENTS IN THE COMMUNITY.

SOT: (VOICE OF OULAHAN OVER WORKING IN HOUSE) "WE REHAB HOUSES EVERYONE ELSE GIVES UP ON – DEVELOPERS. THE CITY WAS READY TO TEAR THESE DOWN. WE SAY GIVE THEM TO US. WE'LL TRAIN PEOPLE. WE'LL REN-OVATE, WE'LL GIVE THEM SKILLS. WE DO IT AND SELL THEM AT A PRICE PEOPLE CAN AF-FORD . . . THAT'S HOW YOU STABILIZE A NEIGHBORHOOD. GIVE A PERSON A JOB, AND A CHANCE AT A DECENT HOUSE, AND YOU'LL SEE SOCIAL PROBLEMS REDUCED . . . "

NARR: FRANK MARTINEZ – WHO'S OVERSEEN EIGHT REHAB PROJECTS – KNOWS WHAT A SHOT IN THE ARM THEY'VE BEEN IN RUN-DOWN AREAS.

SOT: (MARTINEZ) "AFTER I FINISHED THIS HOUSE, MORE THAN 90 PERCENT OF THE NEIGHBORS HERE, THEY FIXED THEIR HOUSES. TOO."

SOT: (OULAHAN) "IF WE EMPHASIZE OUR PEO-PLE, AND THEIR STRENGTHS, THEN WE'LL GET OUT OF OUR PROBLEMS. OTHERWISE, WE'RE JUST MARKING TIME."

(CONTINUED)

Figure 19.3 A news script. Script formats vary. This is the way it's done at CBS. (Courtesy of CBS News)

Figure 19.5 shows the rundown format that CBS uses as the skeleton for its newscast. The first column of the rundown, "correspondent/story," lists the components of the newscast in the order to be presented. The second column lists the time of the copy the anchor Dan Rather will read. Column three is the "Vtime," the video time of the inserts. Column four shows the origin or dateline of the video report. Your rundown can take any form decipherable to you and your crew (and rundowns do appear in widely differing forms).

Once all the stories that will comprise the newscast are known, the producer/director's next logical question is: How do I arrange the stories I have available for insertion into the rundown?

Choosing Story Order

The most immediate consideration when ordering news material is putting important stories first. In most cases, the lead story will be the one that affects the most people and/or involves the most unusual set of circumstances on the day's news menu.

Choosing the lead is generally not as much a problem as you might assume. Important stories stand out *because* they are important, and in many cases the choice of the lead is self-evident. But the rest of the newscast is waiting to be filled, and there are several strategies for grouping stories.

First of all, if your newscast follows the pattern of local newscasts—news, weather, and sports, along with regular segments dealing with such topics as entertainment or medicine—the stories fall into fairly self-evident categories. However, there are exceptions. A sports story can become the lead story of a newscast if it has great importance and broad general interest. For example, if a university's athletic department is put on probation for recruiting violations, it will become a general-interest story and will probably lead the local newscast.

Some methods of choosing story order includes grouping them by theme, by geographic segment, and by the technical aspects of the individual stories.

Grouping by Theme. If you have three stories dealing with employment, it makes sense to place them back to back. Not only will it seem more logical to viewers, the thematic grouping will enable your writers to make graceful transitions between the stories (for example, ". . . although national trends show more Americans out of work, Centerville University can't recruit enough faculty members. Dean Robert Smith says . . .").

Grouping by Location. Whether you have three stories about Great Britain or the New York Stock Exchange or the campus placement office, the stories will usually flow better if placed back to back. To be frank, this is sometimes considered an old-fashioned way of grouping stories—

probably because stories from "far away" are no longer unusual owing to technical capabilities that make gathering news from afar relatively easy—but the practice still remains common.

Grouping by Technical Content. Whether or not a story includes tape in part determines where it will be placed in proximity to other stories with tape. More precisely, we generally aim to *separate* stories with tape because we don't want all the taped segments to run back to back. This would inevitably leave us with a consecutive string of "tell" stories. Aim for a peak-and-valley mixture of taped and tell stories whenever possible.

Timing and Backtiming

Your final collection of products before airtime will generally consist of taped segments, either packages, standups, sound bites, or voice-over tape; several tell stories; and copies of the script and rundown distributed to the anchors and crew.

The process of putting all this on the air is really not so complex. After all, you know what a newscast looks like, and this chapter has filled in many of the technical details. But making all the pieces fit within the rigid time structure of a typical newscast is where directors earn their salary—and sometimes their gray hairs.

Timing of the show involves two primary functions:

1. Making sure the segments begin and end on time. They mustn't run over into commercial breaks, and the whole program must end precisely on time.

2. Coordinating the leads-ins and exits from taped segments.

Timing of Segments. A newscast is typically not, strictly speaking, an hour- or half-hour program. Rather, it is a series of program segments that have a running time of only a few minutes each. The news segments between commercials must be timed precisely, as must the sports and weather. And, of course, the entire show must end on time if it is on air and abuts another program.

Your rundown will give you a second-by-second breakdown of the show and let you know how much time is allotted for each segment. For example, let's assume a segment of your program (between the first and second commercial break, perhaps) runs 4 minutes. If you want to include:

- A 2-minute tape package on a campus demonstration

- A 30-second tell story about similar demonstrations on other campuses

- A one-minute, twenty-second anchor SOT story (anchor lead-in and come-out with a sound bite sandwiched in between) about local student aid reductions

```
lineup              17:33:47                      display  1
the cbs evening news with dan rather            11-27-90
          correspondent/story        copy    vtime    orig/city
--------------------------------------------------------------------
aa         LEADER                    *0:00
bb       Headline                     0:20
cc         ANIMATION                 *0:00
1.       Good Evening                 0:10
2.       Hearing                      0:25
3.          SCHIEFFER/HEARINGS                 2:00     WASH
4.       Uninations                   0:15
5.          PLANTE/UNIATIONS                   1:45     WASH/LIVE SANDWICH
6.          MUHAMMAD  vo              0:20              AMMAN
8.       Troops                       0:15
8a.      Vols                         0:20
9.          THRELKELD/VOLUNTEER ARMY           3:25     NY
10.      Tease: FENTON-PETERSEN  vo   0:20              LONDON-MOSCOW
--------------------------------------------------------------------
11.        1st  cml:KEL/THERA/KMART*/SUN       1:35
--------------------------------------------------------------------
12.      Major                        0:15
13.         FENTON/MAJOR                       1:45     LON
14.      Soviet                       0:20
15.         PETERSEN/SOVSHORTAGES              2:20     MOSCOW
16.         ISRAEL vo                 0:20              LON
16z.     Stay:  BRAVER vo             0:10              WASH
--------------------------------------------------------------------
17.        2nd cml:OLDS/NABISCO*/NESTLE        1:50
--------------------------------------------------------------------
18.         TORNADO vo                0:25              COLUMBIA
18a      Fatty                        0:25
19.         BRAVER/FATTY                       1:45     WASH
20.      Discrim                      0:25
--------------------------------------------------------------------
           STOX BUMPER
21.        3rd cml:MET/ROB/SALAD/RL-PET        1:40
--------------------------------------------------------------------
20a.     Trade                        0:20
22.      Retrain                      0:20
23.         FAW/RETRAINING                     3:18     NY
24.      Goodnight                    0:15
--------------------------------------------------------------------
25.        4th cml:SINE/KMART*/DAIRY/DP        1:35
--------------------------------------------------------------------
26.         CREDITS: THRELKELD        0:20              NY
27.         CTN:  MORNING             0:15
--------------------------------------------------------------------

                                   6:15   22:58
      lee's clock 00:06:15        cx+copy+vtr 00:29:13
         +00:00:18   OVER
```

Figure 19.5 Sample news "rundown." This rundown lays out the exact timing of each segment of a 22 minute, 58 second newscast. The program begins with the headline and opening animation, followed by the anchor's "Good Evening," welcoming the audience. The first news segment is a hearing in Washington reported by Schieffer and introduced for 25 seconds by the anchor. It is followed by actions at the United Nations as reported by Plante with an anchor introduction of 15 seconds. (Courtesy CBS News.)

- A twenty-second tell story about where students can find out more about financial aid on campus . . .

. . . you're in trouble. The segment is 10 seconds too long. Granted, many newscasts don't have to hit the breaks on the nose (although many do, for various reasons including local commercial insertions on network newscasts), but the breaks are mileposts for the whole program. If you hit a break 5 seconds late, it means that 5 seconds must be made up somewhere in the newscast because almost all commercial and most noncommercial TV newscasts must end on time. It's better to hit each break to the second and not have to scramble at the end.

So from this rundown you'll need to trim 10 seconds from the segment. You might choose to lose the time from the tell story about similar demonstrations on other campuses. Because you have 30 seconds with which to work, there's a little flexibility in which to edit. The packages and SOT segments are a bit more difficult to alter because you'd have to physically re-edit the tape in order to alter the time.

Assuming that you want to cut the 30-second story to a 20-second story, how do you know how many words must be cut? Simply read the story out loud, make the changes, and read it out loud again, timing it on each try. Don't feel awkward, because "talking to the keyboard" is a standard practice in newsrooms across the nation. It's usually the best way to get an accurate indication of story length.

There are two other methods. Some writers rely on word and line count to calculate reading time. Note, though, that line count, as related to time, varies according to type size and script format. And although you might determine that an anchor reads a certain number of words per minute, remember that all words are not the same. A story with many long words, or a story that by its nature is read slowly (an obituary, perhaps) will foul up your word count formula. Better to read the copy at a rate that approximates the anchor's speed, and make your calculations using a stopwatch.

Important: Read the story out loud in full voice. Some production people tend to mutter the story to themselves and, as a result, finish reading in far less time than would the anchor reading in a normal conversational rate. If you're lucky enough to work in a computerized newsroom, each anchor's reading rate will be programmed into the software, and you'll get an automatic readout on the estimated time of the copy. However, don't fall into the habit of believing numbers just because they have the "authenticity" of a scientific formula. When in doubt, grab the stopwatch and read aloud.

Coordinating Lead-ins and Exits. Hitting a sound bite is a difficult task, both for the anchor and the producer/director. In order to hit the sound bite correctly, you must:

1. Calculate how much **preroll** your tape machine needs in order to get up to speed and cue the tape up to that point. For example, if you need 5 seconds for the tape to lock up and stabilize, you must back the tape up 5 seconds from the beginning of the sound bite. This is easiest if you have a time code or sync pulse reader on your VTR, of course, but you also have the option of slating the sound bite when you edit it from your raw tape.

2. Next, find the point 5 seconds into the anchor's lead-in copy. For instance, here's some sample copy leading up to a tape segment.

> Rumors of a new wave of blue flu are spreading around police headquarters. Today, almost half the patrol officers scheduled for duty called in sick. Although police union president Stan LaLond won't come right out and call this a job action, he does hint that there's widespread dissatisfaction with the current contract.

TAKE TAPE OF LALOND

As a *general rule*, 10 words will usually equal 5 seconds. However, two fairly long words in the sample copy you just read—*dissatisfaction* and *widespread*—make the last 10 words read a bit over 5 seconds for most readers. Try it for yourself, reading out loud and using a stopwatch. You'll probably find the best spot to mark the roll tape cue is before the ninth word leading into the tape, *hint*. Actually, you'll be closer to 4½ seconds, which is what you want; there's no reason to hit the opening statement of the sound bite so tightly that it "leaps" on the screen right after the anchor's intro. Keep lead-ins tight, but allow some breaking space.

If you've marked the anchor lead-in "roll tape cue" correctly, usually like this:

> Rumors of a new wave of blue flu are spreading around police headquarters. Today, almost half the patrol officers scheduled for duty called in sick. Although police union president Stan LaLond won't come right out and call this a job action,

ROLL TAPE

> he does hint that there's widespread dissatisfaction with the current contract.

and if you've cued the tape backward 5 seconds, you'll hit the sound bite or package cleanly.

One more problem: You now need to keep track of how long the tape runs so that you can cue the anchor. Anchors need adequate warning, preferably a countdown by the floor director, if they are to gracefully pick up the cue and start reading again. For example, the director would note that the tape is coming to an end and tell the floor director to stand by to cue the anchor.

("Ready to cue anchor")

TAPE: . . . dissatisfaction with the current contract.

("Cue anchor, take Camera 2")

ANCHOR: . . . Actually, the agreement expired three months ago and the patrol officers are working without a contract. Police Chief Bob Hanna says he may call for federal mediation if the issue isn't settled soon.

In order to make that transition fluid, the producer/director must know the *exact* running time of all sound bites and packages. That's really a simple matter; just play it and time it. But putting that knowledge to use usually involves having a cooperative assistant director (Figure 19.6) who will feed you constant time cues and help you

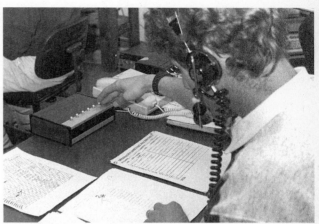

Figure 19.6   Timing the news. Feeding constant timing cues to the director of a newscast is the responsibility of the assistant director.

BOX 19.2   THE VIEWER AS ANCHOR

The nature of news will undoubtedly change once video becomes more interactive—that is, controlled in various ways by the viewer. Journalist and commentator Linda Ellerbee speculates about what news will be like when viewers get to pick and choose what they want.

Will Dan, Tom, Peter and Bernie be our anchors in the year 2000? No. They'll have burned themselves out globe-trotting to where the big story is, as they began doing in 1989.

They'll have stood in front of so many walls coming down, guns being fired, treaties being signed, countries being formed, that finally, one by one, they'll collapse from exhaustion, allowing us to see, at last, the picture they blocked with their own bodies. Imagine. Americans will be confronted with the very news from which the anchors protected them for 10 years.

Most people won't miss the anchors because interactive television will have killed off the need for an anchor anymore. Interactive television will have changed everything. It will be possible to sit at home and participate in a game show or vote in a national election; however, as the Federal Election Commission and the A.C. Nielsen company will surely verify, more people will play games than vote.

As for news, you'll sit at home, check your screen and, on any given number of channels, be able to dial up the news you want. If all you want is news of the Mideast, then you'll dial up those stories. "Give me everything from the Mideast in the last 24 hours, please," you'll say.

If all you want are stories about women who kill

their mothers with ashtrays, then you'll dial up those; and, as with the Mideast, there will always be enough of those stories to go around.

And if all you still want is the sight of Tom's cute little smile or a glimpse of Peter's manly chin, you'll have to dial up one of the zillion nostalgia shows that will be available, including the one for 13-year-olds: *nostalgia for next week*.

The choice will be entirely yours. What this means, in effect, is that you will become your own anchor. You will select and connect the news. Probably, after a while, you'll walk around your own house saying things like, "Stay with us," and "Coming up . . ."

Pretty soon your family will start to rate you. One of them will want you to change your hair, to dress or sit differently. "Can you lean more to the left, Dad? Your sincerity isn't showing enough for me." You'll begin putting on makeup before you sit down in front of the television set, in hopes your family won't cancel you after dinner.

Worst of all, you'll get very, very tired of sorting through all the events available to pick the right ones to show. Framing a newscast is hard work. Finally, you'll find yourself searching for some all-purpose sign-off, something that sums up the news of the day and your feelings about it, and then one day, instead of telling your family goodnight, you'll find yourself saying something like, "And so it goes."

And so it does.

Source: Linda Ellerbee, "The Viewer as Anchor," *Newsday Magazine* (December 9, 1990): 11.

count down to the anchor's cue. It is also important that the anchor's script includes the *outcue* (the last words spoken on the tape).

The role of the studio crew in news is somewhat diminished today (automated cameras and tape-roll units are becoming increasingly common), but the director's role is enhanced. He or she must coordinate a vast array of production elements and assemble a show *fresh every day* that will inform, entertain, and motivate. In fact, as the nature of television news changes, the role of the producer will probably be enhanced. Author and producer Linda Ellerbee offers her opinion in Box 19.2.

But let's close on a thought directly related to the thrust of this book: Production personnel are every bit as integral to the creation of a newscast as the people we see on air. Producers, who generally have equally balanced backgrounds in news and production, are often the driving force in the newscast. News videographers do more than point and shoot; they are journalists in their own right and contribute to the success of the story in equal proportion to the reporter and producer.

SUMMARY

1. The three basic categories of pieces for insertion into a television newscast are sound bites, voice overs, and packages.

2. All elements of a TV news package must advance the story. In other words, there must be a logical reason for including each scene. In essence, always be aware that you are *telling a story*.

3. Although the word has no universally accepted meaning, *documentary* is used to describe a program that is generally longer than a news package, investigative (meaning that it uncovers new information), and a complete program having an underlying theme.

4. A documentary always starts with a central theme. Some documentaries involve writing the script first and then shooting to accommodate the script. Sometimes the video is shot first and the script is written next, with a final cut made after the fine points are honed. Sometimes documentaries are made with no script at all.

5. Irrespective of how your documentary is made, remember that it should feature a central character, have dramatic values, and in some way involve a conflict.

6. The newscast is a challenging task, requiring the producer and director (or producer/director) to assemble the news packages, sound bites, and voice overs, along with straight "tell stories" (which are read to the camera), into a cohesive whole.

7. A rundown is used in almost all newscast productions because it is essential that everyone know the story order and the timing.

8. Story order is, in part, determined by the relative importance of the stories. Your most important story will lead the newscast. After that, stories may be grouped according to a number of criteria, including theme and geographic location.

9. A key role of production personnel in the newscast is to time and backtime the inserts and the copy. You need to know when to preroll the tape and how long the tape runs.

NOTE

1. List adapted from Carl Hausman, *Crafting the News* (Belmont, CA: Wadsworth, 1992).

TECHNICAL TERMS

bridge	lead-in	rough cut	stand-up
cover video	package	rundown	tell story
docudrama	preroll	sound bite	voice-over
documentary			

EXERCISES

1. Produce a news package using:
   a. A sound bite opening
   b. A voice-over script relating the opening sound bite to the cover video
   c. An interview
   d. A stand-up reporter close

   Use whatever topic you like, but try to stick to this format. Also, be sure your segments are cohesive.

For example, if you are doing a story on student aid, you might open with:

a. A sound bite of a student saying how she's going to have to drop out of college because she has no more money.

b. A voice-over script briefly discussing problems with student aid; the cover video might be generic shots of students walking across campus.

c. An interview with the campus student aid director, in which he or she might say that student aid isn't really shrinking, it's just available from different sources—and then describe a few.

d. A stand-up close with the reporter summarizing the current situation and mentioning other sources where viewers can obtain information about financial aid.

2. Using the package you prepared, produce a short newscast segment utilizing:

a. A tell story
b. A story with a brief voice over
c. The package
d. A tell story and a brief "good-bye."

Aim for a segment approximately 4 minutes long. But whatever time you choose, be sure to prepare a rundown *first* and make the pieces fit later. (You don't have to recut the package. It can be whatever length you want as long as you can group the rest of the stories around it.)

dramatic programs, sports, and other formats

OBJECTIVES

After completing Chapter 20, you will be able to:

1. Structure, block, and rehearse a video drama.
2. Produce and direct several types of sports programs.
3. Demonstrate the basics of producing other formats, including commercials and music videos.

This chapter takes a very brief look at some popular video program structures, giving a basic introduction into the strategies used to produce them. We hope that the sketches presented here will serve as starting points for further exploration of dramatic programs, sports programs, and other formats including commercials, music videos, and video art.

DRAMATIC PROGRAMS

The early years of television brought what had been a theatrical medium to the tube—and they also gave producers some insight into what makes a television program different from a stage play or a radio drama.

Shows such as *Playhouse 90* (Figure 20.1) were laboratories where writers and producers could experiment with the emerging medium. Some experiments were harrowing because the early programs aired live and were often accompanied by music from a live, in-studio orchestra.

Whereas modern technology allows us to reshoot, edit, and mix audio tracks, many of the basic principles for producing the program remain much the same as in the early days. When producing a drama, the producer/director must block and rehearse the scenes, interpret the drama for video, and understand the principles of dramatic structure.

Blocking and Rehearsing

Blocking is a term borrowed from the theater. It refers to planning where props and actors will be located, when they will move, and how they will move.

Careful blocking is enormously important in video because talent can ruin a scene by walking out of the lighted area or into a soft-focus area in your depth of field. Also, blocking gives the crew a chance to move through each stage of motion, thereby allowing them to make sure they

can get all the shots without getting another camera in the frame or even physically bumping into someone else.

Rehearsals let actors try out their lines—from the positions you have supplied in the blocking process—and they let the director help the actors deliver their lines with more authority and authenticity.

Your exact blocking and rehearsal routine will vary with the show at hand. But here are a few suggestions relating to the positioning of actors, the blocking of movement, and the planning of breaks and reaction shots.

Figure 20.1 *Playhouse 90.* This early dramatic TV program was a live-on-air laboratory where much was learned by writers and producers. Shown here is a still from *Requiem for a Heavyweight.*

Positioning Actors. In drama, you *must* keep other cameras out of the shot unless you are using the camera as a prop. Check everybody's position, and keep an eye on intrusion from other cameras, shadows, and the edges of cycloramas. If necessary, put an X on the floor (masking tape works well for this) to mark the position of the actors.

Blocking the Moving Shots. Our use of the word *blocking* involves both the positioning and *movement* of the actors. When you block, you determine what will happen when the actor (or sometimes the camera) moves from place to place. You are blocking the scene in order to see the action through the camera(s).

We've already covered most of the obvious pitfalls, such as the actor's moving out of the focal range or into a dimly lighted area. But blocking also uncovers some unexpected problems (which is precisely why it's done). For example, during blocking you can uncover that as your actor walks toward the door, whirls around, and pulls a gun viewers never see the gun because the shot is too long.

Blocking involves more than ferreting out mistakes. It also allows you to maximize the effectiveness of your camera shots. In the preceding example, you would want a close-up of the person with the gun, perhaps even a close-up of the gun itself.

Remember that you want your opening, establishing shots on wide shot and your dramatic shots (and those that show necessary detail) on close-up. When you are working out the long shots, medium shots, and close-ups during blocking, remember that you want to avoid whenever possible cutting or dissolving from a very wide shot to a close-up. That's simply too disturbing visually and is only useful for certain special effects.

Breaks. There's a secret to handling the execution of a show that has several breaks or is divided into several installments: End on a suspenseful note. If your character is going to shoot someone, it's usually best to show the gun and ready the scene *before* the break; that way, you'll most likely keep viewers from tuning out.

Reactions. In planning your shots, you should also specifically blueprint your reaction shots. Reaction shots are extremely important to good drama, so choose them with care. During blocking and rehearsal, don't be afraid to practice the reaction shots with the actors. A believable reaction shot takes some planning and skill; don't leave it to chance.

The Director as Interpreter of Drama

Now that we've defined the mechanics, it's worthwhile to back up a bit and examine more closely how those mechanics of shot planning are applied to the basic structure of the program. That basic structure, of course, is determined by the script.

We introduced the concept of the dramatic script in Chapter 13. The important consideration, from the director's standpoint, is to turn the script into *drama*.

How is that done? Well, video has its own requirements; what makes for a good novel or short story, or even a good feature film, may not play well on the small screen. As the director, you're partly responsible for "red-flagging" problems with a script. You know what will play well on the small screen and what won't.

Here is a suggestion for avoiding possible problems: Look for drama that has a simple plot and small cast, that is practical for video, and that can be organized logically and economically during the shooting process.

Plot. An experienced television director knows that the drama must have a series of crises *and* that it must fit into the time available.

If you have taken a "creative writing" course geared toward writing the great American novel, you have certainly been introduced to the importance of multiple plots, subplots, subtext, and complexity of characters. Now that you're directing for video, you can forget most of that. Video requires a very simple and *absolutely clear* plot line. Too many subplots serve only to confuse—something that constantly confounds novel and short story writers who do not understand why their intricate plots must be pared for video or film.

A director often works with writers who are not experienced in the video medium, and must serve as sort of a "gatekeeper" to ensure that inappropriate plotting and characterization does not end up on the small screen. The too-intricate plot is the first red-flag item you'll need to spot.

Cast and Characters. Next comes an examination of characters. Characters in video cannot be too introspective. As screenwriter Alan Armer notes, thoughts and internal struggles just do not play well on video.[1] It's too difficult to convey such subtleties.

Too many characters cause trouble. You'll notice that when your favorite book is translated to film or video many of your favorite characters are eliminated. The reason? A linear video or screen production is not the medium in which to present a vast array of characters; although minor characters may add richness to a book, they can hopelessly muddle the plot of a television drama.

One other point: When you start your planning, be sure that all the characters are introduced early. In general, main characters should be introduced in the first five minutes of the show; a major character appearing late in the plot can confound viewers and sabotage your plot.

Timing of the Script. Some obvious factors are sometimes overlooked before the rehearsal begins; it's surprising how often the cast and crew discover that there's too much script for too little time. If your script looks something like the one in Figure 13.3, you can usually count on an *average* of one page of script per one minute of tape.

Don't forget, too, that you are limited by pure physical restrictions. If you have several car chases and a scene in which a building is blown to cinders, you'll need either an enormous budget or a good source of stock footage.

Organizing around the Central Theme. Organizing around the central theme is where the director earns his or her paycheck. You must keep the big picture in your head and direct the actors accordingly.

We've been through the intricacies of shooting single-camera video (film-style with one camera), but it's worth mentioning here that in your capacity as an interpreter of drama, you must ensure that the actors perform in continuity—that is, perform properly within the context of the scene.

You have probably seen clips of directors coaching talent, and the dialogue usually goes something like, "You're really angry, and this has been building for a long time, but you can't tell him directly because . . ." However self-indulgent and obvious these directors may appear to the casual observer, they are anything but. Film and TV actors often—in fact, usually—are called to perform scenes completely out of sequence in relation to the actual script. They need and welcome the director's reminders of what exactly has preceded the current scene and what factors are motivating them for the scene they are now taping. Setting the scene is your responsibility. It is a very important—and exceedingly difficult—task.

You'll also need to keep track of what's been taken care of in principal photography and what remains to be finished later. **Principal photography** consists of the basic scenes, the major chunks of the presentation. Details, special effects, and close-ups will be added later.

Principal photography is done in the sequence most expedient to the cast and crew, even if it sometimes produces an awkward sequence of events. During single-camera shooting, principal photography might involve having one actor do his lines (Figure 20.2a) with a script assistant filling in the actress's lines (Figure 20.2b). Sometimes, the scenery is erected only behind the actor. Then, principal photography continues when the actress does *her* lines, with the appropriate scenery located behind her. The actor and actress may never actually be on the same set during some scenes in which they apparently have an extended dialog.

Even live-on-tape production involves principal photography. It is often impossible to take all the close-ups you'll need, but that can wait. For example, the principal photography might involve having a man trying to back out of a room but getting his tie caught in the door. That's a tricky scene—but there's no reason why you must try and tape it all at once. Have the actor mimic the tie-catching maneuver *and shoot the close-up with the tie caught in the door later.*

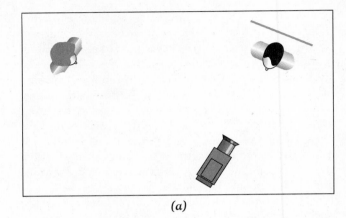

(a)

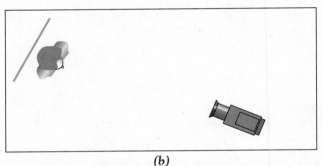

(b)

Figure 20.2 Single camera principal photography. With one camera, the actor can deliver his lines (a). Then, the set can be moved and the actress can deliver her lines (b). Then the tape can be edited together. Taping this way can save a great deal of setup time and effort.

That's the essence of thinking like a director. It's a difficult skill but one that can be learned with practice.

Principles of Dramatic Structure

A final point relates to the nature of drama or, for that matter, comedy. Now that we've covered the mechanics and some of the basics of directing a dramatic program, it's important to consider the very nature of an entertainment program: It is a series of crises.

The crises may not be major. In fact, they may be entertaining, but they still must represent some obstacle, some confrontation. Even the most ludicrous series of events qualify, in dramatic terms, as "crises." You certainly have seen one of the all-time classic comedy shows, Jackie Gleason's *The Honeymooners.* (We're using this as an example because it is in continual syndication throughout the country and will be an example with which almost everyone is familiar.) In one particular episode, Ralph is hired to do a candy commercial, but . . .

Crisis 1: He can't learn his lines.

Ralph diligently tries to learn his lines, and we're left wondering whether he's going to be able to perform the

BOX 20.1 WHAT'S MISSING? TROUBLESHOOTING A DRAMATIC SCRIPT

Sometimes, when a program doesn't hold the viewers' attention, there's something fundamentally wrong with the script. And usually this means that something's missing. For example:

- *There's no conflict.* Unless someone is in friction with someone or something else, or some concept, there's no spark.
- *There's no crisis.* The conflict never becomes critical.
- *There's no deadline.* Crisis and conflict can be heaped on by the pound, but unless there is some time element involved—some reason why the situation must be resolved in a reasonable time—the viewer just might not care.
- *There's no "sympathetic" hero.* That is, there is no central character with whom we can share feelings, care about. Our hero could face crises, deadlines,

and conflict by the truckload, but if he or she is a boorish clod, nobody will *care* whether a solution is reached.

- *The plot is too complex.* There's no way for the audience to figure out what's going on. If you get too close to a script, the plot and subplots may make sense to you *but you won't realize* they are incomprehensible to viewers. Remember, you've been working on the program night and day for months. But viewers are trying to follow the plot in between trips to the refrigerator. Keep it simple.

A script must give the audience reason to care what's going on. Whether it's because of a threat to a sympathetic character, a compelling locale, hand-wringing suspense, or whatever, *some* combination of people and events must keep viewers tuned in.

(live) commercial, when . . .

Crisis 2: He develops a throbbing toothache.

Faced with the dual problem of the toothache and his bad memory—but still lusting for the money and fame associated with doing the commercial—Ralph goes on the air. He delivers his lines (not well, but manages to stumble through) and concludes the commercial by . . .

Crisis 3: Taking a bite out of the candy bar, which sends him into such a paroxysm of agony that he crashes through the set and into the orchestra.

Neither drama nor comedy ends on a crisis—at least, it almost never does. So in the end, Ralph, contrite over his grandiose dreams of becoming a star from the candy commercial and the way in which he fouled up the whole affair, is forgiven by his long-suffering wife Alice. The resolution, sometimes called a **denouement**, is an essential conclusion to the story and provides the necessary closure.

Remember that crises and suspense are the twin axles of drama and comedy. There must be peaks and valleys, and viewers must be given a reason to, as the saying goes, stay tuned. A program without crises is a program without interest for viewers.

If you have something "missing" in your show, it may be the lack of crises or some of the other troubleshooting items in Box 20.1. The list expands on some earlier points and summarizes what you might look for when facing something known as "script trouble," a condition genuinely dreaded in the entertainment industry.

PRODUCING AND DIRECTING SPORTS PROGRAMS

There are three major problems associated with covering sports on video. They are, in descending order of importance, logistics, logistics, and logistics.

With a sports program, you are always at the mercy of circumstances and location. Typically, you are working at someone else's facility and may fall victim to the vagaries of power, accessibility of camera location sites, security clearances, and so on. Sporting events, by their very nature, are also unpredictable. Baseball games can run into extra innings. Football usually begins and ends on time, but the game requires many cameras and sophisticated camerawork in order for coverage to be effective.

Here are brief thumbnail sketches of some primary considerations in covering football, baseball, basketball, and other field and arena sports.

Football

Camera height is important when covering football. Obviously, camera placements will be dictated by availability of suitable locations, but remember that in many cases the plays are incomprehensible when viewed from ground level. However, a sideline camera is useful for picking up reaction shots and occasional details of plays viewable from ground level.

Camera Placement. Regardless of how many cameras you have, you cannot cross the axis. That is, the cameras

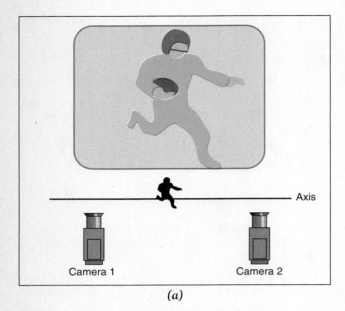

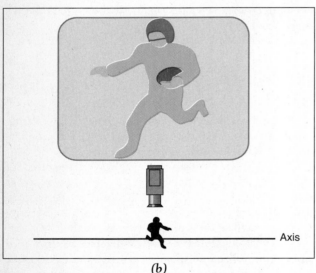

Figure 20.3 Camera placement and the "axis of action." Cameras cannot be at opposite sides of the field, or players will appear to switch directions when you cut between cameras.

cannot be on opposite sides of the field. Otherwise, the runner shown on camera 1 (Figure 20.3) will change direction when the director cuts to camera 2.

At a minimum, you will want two cameras, well elevated, on each side of the field (near the end zone). A sideline camera is also useful. A luxury is a camera placed to get a view from each end zone. Such a setup is shown in Figure 20.4.

Mic Placement. Parabolics or shotgun mics along the sidelines are useful for picking up the sounds of the contact noise and the audibles called by the quarterback. Parabolics have always been a particular favorite of football directors.

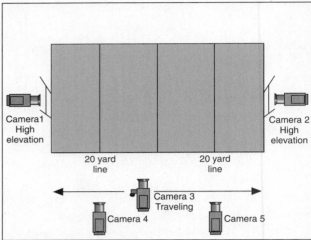

Figure 20.4 Suggested camera placement for football. Cameras 1 and 2 are positioned high on either end of the field, a traveling camera (3) will assist with coverage of ground details. Cameras 4 and 5 are positioned above the field at the 20-yard lines.

Special Problems. It's often hard to follow the play. Good quarterbacks are masters at tricking skilled defensemen into following the wrong player, and the director can fall victim as well. Also remember that football fans are impatient with long shots. They like close-ups. But close-ups can be dangerous if you lose sight of the ball and wind up losing the shot.

Note that football has some particular problems, one of which is that the games are played in all sorts of weather. You'll need to make special provisions for covering cameras in the event of rain or snow (Figure 20.5).

Baseball

Baseball allows the director some flexibility in camera and mic placement. The game is typically viewed from a variety of angles—fans sit in the outfield, behind the plate, or from behind either the first- or third-base lines, so about any angle is recognizable. Also, the game progresses in a counterclockwise motion, providing viewers a constant reference. There are few "wrongs." Watch any game and you'll see a variety of camera placements.

Camera Placement. One aspect of camera placement should concern you: You need some elevation of the cameras in order to produce a decent shot. Many a novice director has been surprised to find that baseball fields are sloped for drainage, and a camera set up at eye level will make the outfielders appear to be wading in the grass. The primary exception is the camera that takes the shot of the pitcher and the catcher (Figure 20.6). It can be modestly elevated.

Because the baseball diamond provides a frame of reference, you do not need to be overly concerned about

Figure 20.5 Cameras covered because of inclement weather. Because football is a sport played in all weather conditions, it is important to cover the cameras for protection.

Figure 20.7 The scoreboard shot. This long-shot from center field of the pitcher, batter, and catcher appears to be very compressed. Notice that there is very little distance between the players.

crossing the axis. With a camera on the first base side and the third base side, viewers can easily follow the action. The camera on the third base side is especially effective for capturing plays at home plate.

A staple of baseball coverage is the scoreboard camera, which shows the field from the scoreboard perspective and, on close-up, shows the pitcher, batter, and catcher (Figure 20.7). The problems with overuse of this camera are that viewers quickly become bored with the long shot, and the distorting compression of pitcher, batter, and catcher when the camera is used on close-up.

A possible setup for baseball coverage is shown in Figure 20.8.

Mic Placement. Parabolics and shotgun mics are used to cover baseball games even though there is much less emphasis on field noise in baseball than in many other sports. Crowd noise is integral to baseball, though, and you

can often get a good crowd-noise source by lowering a mic out of the press box. Be careful, though; one foulmouthed spectator near your crowd-noise mic can considerably complicate your audio.

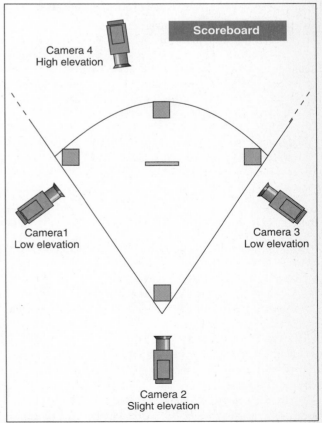

Figure 20.8 Suggested camera placement for baseball coverage. Cameras 1 and 3 are set-up low for coverage at first and third bases. Camera 2 can have slight elevation and camera 4 should be elevated high over center field.

Figure 20.6 The incoming pitch. Most baseball cameras must be elevated above the slope of the field. The camera positioned for the pitcher and catcher shot, however, needs to be only modestly elevated to give a ground-level effect.

BOX 20.2 SPORTS PROBLEMS: DON'T SAY YOU HAVEN'T BEEN WARNED

Here are some problems you're likely to encounter in televised sports other than those discussed in the text.

Hockey

The main problem with shooting a hockey game is that it's extremely difficult to see the puck on video. All sorts of solutions have been tried, including using brightly colored pucks, but hockey still remains an enormously difficult sport to televise. Your only real solution is to use camera operators who know the game well. They can take the action close-ups and, it's hoped, follow the puck. Don't forget to keep one camera on a wide shot, however, in case everybody loses the puck (which happens).

Boxing

The main complication with boxing is the referee. The third person in the ring is supposed to be unobtrusive, but the referee somehow always seems to be between the camera and the boxers. This was more of a problem when directors were concerned with keeping all cameras out of the picture. If you watch boxing today, though, you'll see that directors are not at all shy about taking a shot that shows a camera operator on the ring apron. So don't be afraid to have handheld cameras in the corners and the aprons; they'll get into each others' shots, but at least you'll have a better shot than the back of the referee.

(Ahem . . . a word about words. If you're using a mic in the boxers' corners to pick up the manager's instructions, be forewarned that some of the language will probably be less than suitable for airplay.)

Golf

You'd be surprised at how much golf is broadcast in local markets, either on broadcast TV or cable. Virtually every city has some sort of golf tournament that is of local interest.

One problem with golf is self-evident: Unless you have a remote van and dozens of cameras, you can't be everywhere on the course. One possible solution for small video operations is to delay-broadcast the event, and make the delay as long as practical so that you can edit the footage together. It helps to have two or three "anchor" spots from which you provide most of the coverage. Two interesting holes and the final hole will work well.

Tennis

The tennis match lends itself well to video and is reasonably easy to capture on the small screen, but there's one aspect of coverage you need to know before taking your cameras to the court: Tennis *cannot be shot very well from the side*, except for occasional close-ups. Although a sideline seat is desirable for a spectator, panning back and forth with the camera produces an awkward—not to mention nausea-inducing—effect.

One other problem with shooting from the sides of the court involves the sun. Good tennis courts are designed so that the setting sun does not shine in the eyes of either player. If your cameras are shooting from the wrong side, the setting sun may shine directly into their lenses. So if you do elect to use a side-shooting camera for some close-up shots, remember to position it so that the sun sets to the back of the camera. Your main coverage cameras, however, should be located at both ends of the court.

Basketball

Basketball is a relatively easy sport to televise because it is inside and the distances of the playing field—in this case, the court—are usually quite manageable.

Camera Placement. In a pinch, you can get away with three cameras—one in the middle and one shooting from each end (Figure 20.9). A portable sideline camera is a help if one is available.

Don't cross the axis, or you'll wind up with the motion-reversal problem pointed out in the section discussing football coverage.

Mic Placement. Commentary for basketball is often done right at floor level, so there will be an enormous amount of noise. Noise-canceling headset mics (Figure 20.10) are useful for almost any sports announcer, but they are virtually essential for basketball coverage.

Other Field and Arena Sports

Any sport played indoors will often cause you problems with lighting. Gym lighting can be uneven both in terms of strength and color temperature. Indoor sports also involve running a great deal of cable, which is a potential safety hazard. You'll want to string cables out of the way or safely tape them to the floor when there is any possibility that someone could trip over them.

Whether you are indoors or out, you'll probably have considerable cable runs to your truck or switching unit. Very long cable runs can cause the signal to degrade and not synchronize well with other video.

You may have occasion to cover sports other than those just discussed. Box 20.2 provides a brief rundown of the problems peculiar to several sporting events.

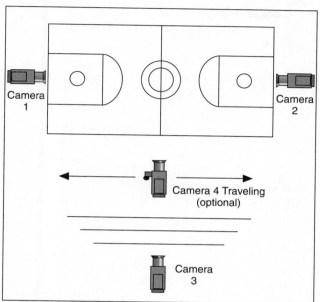

Figure 20.9 Suggested camera placement for basketball coverage. Basketball is one of the easier sports to cover. In tight conditions, three cameras (one positioned in the middle and one at each end) will provide adequate coverage. A fourth portable camera would be extremely helpful traveling along the sidelines.

OTHER FORMATS

As we wrap up this quick look at some specific types of video production, let's do a snapshot summary of commercials, music videos, and video art.

Commercials

Commercials are generally little dramas played out on a little screen. They are designed as the first step in the process of selling a product.

Reconsider that last sentence: *They are the first step in the process of selling a product.* If you become involved in commercial production, you'll do well to remember that concept because you will frequently find yourself in a tug-of-war between the expectations of the client (the person who pays for production and airtime for the commercial) and the viewing and buying public.

Commercials alone are rarely the *entire* motivation for a purchase; there are many other links in the chain, including the quality of the product, the desirability of the product, the effectiveness of the sales force, and so on. Unfortunately, many clients hold unrealistic expectations of the power of video advertising. They frequently hold the producer responsible for what may be a break in the chain at any level.

Worse, you may find yourself in the dilemma of weighing whether you should produce a good commercial or produce what the sponsor wants. What's a good commercial? Something that motivates, that appeals to an inner need.

Figure 20.10 Insulating the announcer from noise. When basketball is announced from the floor level, noise-canceling headset mics are necessary. (Courtesy of Shure Brothers, Inc.)

What's a bad commercial? Well, here's an example: Some merchants like to follow the same strategy in video commercials that they use in large newspaper display ads—namely, cramming lists of merchandise into their commercials. A shoe store owner once insisted that his commercial list virtually every brand of shoe carried in his store. But the ad agency producer balked; after all, what on earth is the point of airing a commercial that simply tells people that this store carries shoes? Don't most people *assume* that a shoe store will carry a variety of shoes?

The ad agency owner took a gamble and persuaded the shoe store owner to air a spot that focused on the nostalgia aspect of buying shoes for the new school year. The "back to school" nostalgia angle proved effective, and although it cannot be definitively proven that the imaginative little nostalgic drama increased sales, it is almost certain that *anything* would have been more effective than a 30-second spot featuring an announcer reading shoe brands at top speed.

Commercial production has no hard-and-fast rules. Every time a "rule" does get handed down, someone breaks it with enormous success. At one time, conventional wisdom told us that humor does not sell—but in the last 10 years, a variety of very funny commercials have spurred very heavy sales for clients.

There are only two rules that apply in almost every case, and they are quite rudimentary.

- A commercial must have a crystal-clear theme. "This coffee has a richer taste than other brands" will do. "Our telephone system is big enough to handle all your problems" works well too. Basically, if you cannot sum it up quickly, it probably won't work.

- A video commercial must be visual. That may sound obvious, but some producers wind up with a product that is essentially radio with pictures. TV commercials without strong visual elements probably won't be a total waste, but why overlook the possibilities of integrating sight, sound, and motion?

Remember that commercials are what provide the payroll on commercial stations. Although some may be lighthearted in tone, the process of commercial production is serious. Never take commercial production lightly; not only is it important, but it's highly competitive. If you produce one weak effort, there are many skilled professionals ready to replace you.

In fact, many in the communications industry contend, publicly and privately, that the people involved in commercial production are the best in the business.

Music Videos

Music videos are largely experimental. Because the genre is still young, there are no real rules, other than the general notion that the cuts and dissolves are generally quickly paced and they keep time, more or less, with the music.

You can create a music video simply by exploring various options on bringing the theme of the song to tape. Often, this is accomplished through lip sync; in other cases, elaborate and sometimes surreal dramas are played out without the artist's mouthing the words.

Videos often tell a story. Figure 20.11 shows a sequence of shots from a student-produced video, along with some commentary about how the images communicate a message.

There is probably little point in belaboring a description of a format with which you are probably already familiar, but it is worth noting that the roots of today's music videos began to grow in the 1970s in early experimental works, which we'll discuss in the next section.

Video Art

In the 1970s, artists interested in experimenting with video had to be creative because the technology did not

Figure 20.11 *Julie Jetson. Julie Jetson* is an all student-produced rock video show which airs on RIC-TV (Rhode Island College, Providence RI). *Julie Jetson* conveys a sense of spontaniety by keying featured music videos around the host. Produced by: Barry Allbright, James Bannon, Julie Bertrand, and James Kosinski.

Figure 20.12   A video art installation. *Video Garbage* displays images of garbage on the monitor in a trash can, with a sound track of garbage trucks approaching for a pickup.

lend itself to particularly sophisticated special effects. Many artists used video as a tool for personal expression, with occasional odd and interesting results. One of the authors, for example, placed television in a sculptural context in a 1979 exhibit: The work, entitled, "Video Garbage," is self-explanatory (Figure 20.12).

Some video art involves the use of multiple screens to produce an image, a process that has recently come back into common practice with the advent of modern computer technology.

Video is an evolving medium, so what is experimental today may be common practice tomorrow. But irrespective of how much of an experimental tack you take when producing or directing a video, your goal is never simply to astound or amuse—your goal is to communicate.

SUMMARY

1. Early television drama paved the way for modern small-screen drama. The emerging medium taught aspiring television writers and producers how to create for the small screen.

2. A video director handling drama must be able to block and rehearse the scenes, interpret the drama for the small screen, and understand and apply the principles of dramatic structure.

3. Video drama needs a relatively small cast and a simple plot line. Plot devices that work for books or films won't necessarily be successful on video.

4. Above all, the director must keep the plot organized in his or her head. Actors are frequently called on to pick up in the middle of a scene, and they need to be reminded of the context of that scene.

5. Drama is always a series of crises. There must be crises—and of course an eventual resolution—in order for the piece to be effective.

6. Sports coverage is unpredictable by its very nature, and the logistics of coverage in a remote site compounds the problems. Each sport has its own requirements. Football and basketball, for example, require that you not usually cross the axis in camera placement. You can cross the axis in baseball, but baseball is a sport that requires steady camerawork over long distances.

7. Commercials are essentially small dramas designed to persuade viewers to take the first step toward buying a product. You, as producer, are responsible for creating a commercial that meets this criterion—while remaining aware that your client may not share your understanding of the medium.

8. The music video is a relatively young genre, one in which you are limited only by your imagination.

9. Don't forget that music video is only a part of what we're loosely calling *video art*, a method of expression using the video medium in new or unexpected ways.

NOTE

1. Alan A. Armer, *Writing the Screenplay: TV and Film* (Belmont, CA: Wadsworth, 1988), 81.

TECHNICAL TERMS

blocking   denouement   principal photography

EXERCISES

1. Write a one-minute commercial for a product of your choice. Just make sure the product is demonstrable in a standard TV studio. Also, be sure that you include dialog from at least two actors, and that there is an exchange of dialog (meaning that actor A makes a statement, actor B responds, and actor A responds to what actor B just said).

2. Now, if you have access to editing equipment, shoot the commercial film-style using single-camera video. Be sure to shoot as economically as possible: Have the actor do all his lines and *then* have the actress do all her lines. Don't be tied to the chronology of the script.

3. Select a song to which you would like to set a montage of pictures. Now, clip pictures from magazines, pictures that you expect will convey a message related to the music. Mount the pictures on cardboard and place them on easels; focus one camera on each. Sit at the switcher, roll tape, roll music, and have an assistant change the cards as you dissolve or cut from one to another. See how clearly expressive you can be directing this simplified version of a "music video."

PART 4

specialized operations

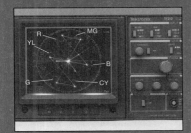

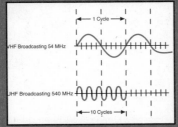

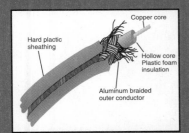

technical aspects of video: engineering for the non-technical operator

OBJECTIVES

After completing Chapter 21, you will be able to:

1. Use the waveform monitor and vectorscope as indicators of adjustments needed in your picture.
2. Explain the principles of many pieces of equipment that technically process the signal.
3. Explain the basics of how a signal is transmitted.

J ust a few years ago, the "technical" side of video was the domain of the engineer, a specialist with extensive training and, usually, a federal license granted after he or she passed a rigorous written examination.

But the increasing user-friendliness of video equipment has resulted in the *user* performing some functions that were previously regarded as "engineering" duties. In this chapter, we'll examine the use of typical engineering displays, the composition of a typical video signal, and the way in which a signal is transmitted.

ENGINEERING DISPLAYS AND CONTROLS

You can't always judge the quality of a video signal by looking at the monitor. If, for instance, the monitor is adjusted so that it produces a very dark picture (in other words, someone fiddled with the brightness control and cranked it down too far), a perfectly acceptable signal will *seem* dim—even if it is technically perfect. If you boost the lighting or the intensity of the signal to compensate for what you see on the out-of-whack monitor, you will distort the signal as you attempt to correct it.

Some other problems are not so obvious. When combining several sources of video, such as two portable cameras used for taping different parts of a program, the color shade and intensity may not match exactly. Or perhaps the contrast range of the pictures won't jibe with precision. Sometimes this won't be perceptible as you tape, but when you attempt to edit the footage together, the differences in color will be dishearteningly apparent.

You need some method of objectively judging the picture strength, contrast, and color. Two types of oscilloscopes (devices that display electrical patterns) are useful

for precisely evaluating the quality of the signal: the waveform monitor and the vectorscope.

The Waveform Monitor

A **waveform monitor** (Figure 21.1) measures the luminance (intensity) of the signal. It also graphically displays the "hidden" commands that govern the transmission of the signal. (The hidden commands will be explained in the section titled "The Video Signal.")

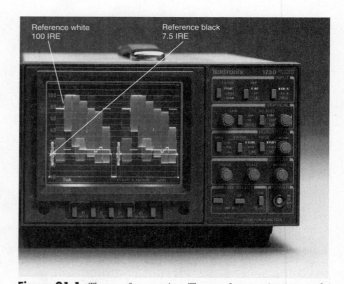

Reference white
100 IRE

Reference black
7.5 IRE

Figure 21.1 The waveform monitor. The waveform monitor accurately measures the luminance of the video signal. Reference white is measured at 100 IRE and reference black; also known as "pedestal," at 7.5 IRE. Notice that on the waveform monitor we see a line dipping below 7.5 IRE down to −40 IRE, which is where we measure the horizontal and vertical synchronization information or sync portion of the signal.

The screen of the waveform monitor shows an electronic display on a scale ranging from −40 at the bottom to 100 at the top. The scale is in increments called IREs, developed by the Institute of Radio Engineers. The most basic use of the waveform monitor is to measure the high and low luminance points, known as reference white and reference black respectively; those two components of the wave are labeled on Figure 21.1.

Reading the scale is quite simple: The brightest white—known as **reference white**—should read 100 IRE. In other words, if you were to aim the camera at a pure white card in a properly lighted studio, the peak should reach 100 IRE—no more, and no less. Should the signal exceed 100 IRE, the picture will be too "hot." As a graphic example, Figure 21.2 shows a hot picture and the corresponding reading. (Remember that the waveform monitor *measures*. It does not *adjust*. Adjustment of the signal will be explained shortly.)

A reading below 100 IRE indicates that the picture is not carrying a full range of white, and the image will be dim. Although you may wish to produce a picture such as Figure 21.3 (which shows a dim picture and the corresponding waveform reading) for a special effect, you generally will want the reference white peaking at 100.

Reference black is a representation of the darkest possible black that can be produced by the system. Reference black is also known as **pedestal**. (Not to be confused with the physical device that holds the camera.) Reference black usually is set at 7.5 IRE because other parts of the signal—signal components that control the scanning process—are located below the lowest black; therefore, it's important to have some separation between reference black and the other signal information.

Another reason for proper attention to setting reference black is the contrast between black and white. If reference black is too low, the darks in the picture will be too dark and produce a stark image with too much contrast (Figure 21.4). If reference black is too high, there won't be adequate contrast between the highs and lows, and the

(a)

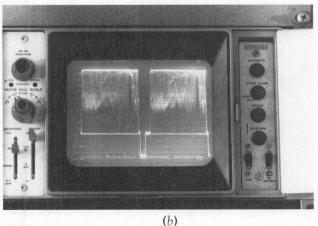

(b)

Figure 21.2 Overly "hot" video signal. The result of lighting that was set too high, causing a "hot" video signal is shown in (a). The corresponding waveform reading is shown in (b).

(a)

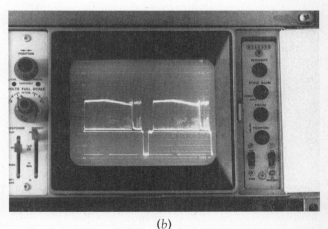

(b)

Figure 21.3 Dull or "crushed" video signal. Inadequate lighting results in a dim image (a) and its corresponding waveform reading (b).

(a)

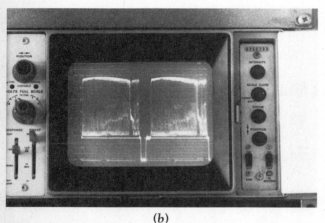

(b)

Figure 21.4   Black level set too low. This photograph represents the effect of setting the black level too low, thereby preventing a full tonal range of grays. Notice how stark the image appears.

picture will appear washed out. Details will be "crushed" and dull (Figure 21.5).

Adjusting Reference White and Black

As already mentioned, the waveform monitor only measures. There are four ways to *adjust* reference white and reference black.

Adjusting the Camera Control Unit. The camera control unit (CCU) contains mechanisms that adjust white and black levels as well as the hue and intensity of colors transmitted by the camera. A typical CCU, with its controls labeled, is shown in Figure 21.6.

The CCU is sometimes located in master control, but more often is found in the control room. The CCU can be adjusted during the program to compensate for varied lighting conditions. Some cameras have the CCU built into the camera itself. Although you cannot, strictly speaking, make CCU adjustments on such a camera, it is still

Figure 21.5   Black level set too high. A distinct lack of detail is evident in this photograph. It occurs with too high a pedestal setting.

worthwhile to visualize the output through the waveform monitor to ensure that the camera is functioning properly.

Adjusting the Lighting. Sometimes the problem is not related to the camera or CCU. If the lighting is too bright, or a highly reflective object is causing glare, the reference white can be brought down to 100 IRE by making adjustments in the lighting. Reference black cannot be adjusted by lighting; adjustment of reference black is an engineering function. However, you *can* increase the aes-

Figure 21.6   The camera control unit (CCU). Adjustments on the camera control unit optimize the camera's output. The CCU maintains a number of settings remotely such as white balance, iris, color temp or "painting," and phase to optimize the camera's output.

The labeled controls are: **A** Intercom- Share/Private **B** Blue Gun Vertical Center **C** Blue Gun Horizontal Center **D** Blue Gun Pedestal **E** Blue Gun Gain **F** Horizontal Phase **G** Subcarrier Fine **H** Subcarrier Coarse **I** Camera Bar or Camera Signal Toggle **J** Cable Length (coarse) Compensation & Fine Adjust **K** Manual/Auto Iris **L** Gain Settings **M** Manual/Auto White Balance **N** White Balance Indicator **O** White Balance Button **P** Power Switch

thetic quality of the picture by including dark and light objects in the picture. (Doing this, of course, amounts to adjusting the reflected lighting.) If you construct a set that is all medium beige, and your host has light brown hair and wears a beige dress, the picture is going to appear washed out, irrespective of what reference levels you set at the CCU.

Adjusting the Camera. Changing the iris setting can compensate for an incorrect lighting level. Cameras also have internal controls that adjust luminance output, but those settings should be accessed only by bona fide engineers.

Adjusting the Time Base Corrector/Frame Synchronizer. The preceeding three solutions are based on prerecorded scenerios but here is what you do if you have a videotape that needs correction in reference white or black. A time base corrector provides controls that adjust pedestal as well as other aspects of the video signal.

The Vectorscope

The **vectorscope** (Figure 21.7) measures attributes of color. Each primary additive color—red, blue, and green—is represented by a dot on the vectorscope screen. Also represented are the complementary colors—magenta, cyan, and yellow. (Refer to the color plates in Chapter 3 for reference and explanation of the primary and complementary additive colors.) The rotational location (their position around the clockface of the vectorscope) of the bright dots measures the shade or tint of colors—the *hue*.

A vectorscope gives you the information to adjust the balance of hues of colors coming from various cameras. A number of factors, including the length of the camera cables, can alter the respective hues.

By adjusting the proper control on the CCU the video operator can put all hues in proper balance; the readout on the vectorscope provides an objective measurement of the colors.

As the CCU is adjusted, the display (not the scale printed on the screen) will rotate until each dot is aligned with the proper 360-degree position. Note that on the vectorscope, the 0-degree mark is at the extreme left of the circle, not at the top.

Here is where you will find the locations of rectangles indicating the proper rotational position of the color dot.

Red = 61 degrees
Blue = 168 degrees
Green = 284 degrees

Magenta = 104 degrees
Cyan = 241 degrees
Yellow = 348 degrees

The distance of the dots from the center of the display indicates the intensity of the color, the **saturation**. The further from the center of the circle, the greater the saturation. When dots are closer to the center, the vectorscope indicates that saturation is low.

Squares on the vectorscope face indicate the proper position of the dots. The ideal situation is to have the dots positioned within the squares, and indeed that is typically accomplished with a simple twist of the dial on the CCU. But it's worthwhile to understand exactly what is happening when the adjustment is made—and now, you do.

These adjustments are part of what is typically called camera setup.

THE VIDEO SIGNAL

Intensity and color are only two of the components that make up the total video signal. The signal also contains synchronization information.

Sync information, such as the length of the blanking intervals, can be measured graphically on the waveform. Although adjustment of sync is often regarded as a pure engineering function, there is an adjustment known as "timing" that can occasionally fall into the producer's domain.

As you remember from Chapter 3, video is composed of 525 lines scanned onto the screen in two frames (odd lines and even lines). Various impulses hidden in the signal control the vertical and horizontal scanning patterns (blanking and horizontal sync), as well as control the way color itself is inserted into the signal.

The parts of the signal are melded together in a composite. A composite signal—a video signal carrying the sync and video—must be within certain technical specifications so that all standardized transmission, recording, and receiving units can properly process the information.

The standards for an acceptable and universally usable video signal were originally set by the National Television

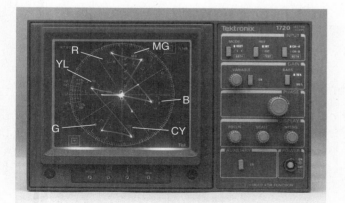

Figure 21.7 The vectorscope. The vectorscope provides measurement for color attributes. Here the dots are reading color bars starting at: red (R), magenta (MG), Blue (B), cyan (CY), green (G), and yellow (YL). Also note that black is measured at 9 o'clock or the 0-degree line.

System Committee (NTSC), a group of engineers convened by the FCC in 1940 to formulate a scanning process that would become the United States' standard. The NTSC standard is utilized throughout all of North and Central America, as well as certain parts of Asia.

There are other standards: SECAM (an acronym for Systeme Electronique Pour Couleur Avec Memoire) is used in France and portions of Eastern Europe and Asia; PAL (Phase Alteration by Line) is the method of encoding video and signal utilized in Great Britain and Western Europe, as well as certain African nations. Signals created under all the different systems are incompatible, but some video recording units have the capability of switching between systems, and commercial laboratories routinely transfer programs from one standard to another when tapes are shipped overseas.

In any event, keeping the signal within NTSC standards generally means maintaining broadcast quality. **Broadcast quality** is a rather loose term that applies to the programming as well as the technical standards, but in a discussion of engineering we can assume that it translates to video that meets NTSC standards: proper sync intervals, appropriate color saturation, adequate contrast, and so forth.

The vectorscope and waveform monitor are tools for gauging (but not adjusting) the quality of the signal via an objective, quantified readout—thereby keeping the signal within NTSC broadcast standards.

Processing the Video Signal

Whereas the waveform monitor and vectorscope measure the video signal, other pieces of equipment *effect* the video signal. You're already familiar with much of the equipment pictured in the video chain (Figure 21.8): The cameras, the CCUs, the sync generator, and the time base corrector

have already been introduced. But to review:

- The CCU governs the output of the camera, allowing the engineer or operator to adjust the technical parameters.
- The sync generator imposes a standard signal or sync on all equipment, keeping the scanning patterns in lockstep.
- The time base corrector (TBC) stabilizes the output of a videotape playback unit, compensating for the sync timing errors caused in various ways including the inevitable shrinkage or stretching of the tape as it passes through the VTR mechanism.

Other engineering equipment pictured in the diagram of the video chain includes the frame synchronizer, the processing amplifier, various distribution amplifiers, and the transmitter.

The Frame Synchronizer. The **frame synchronizer** is primarily used to lock the sync of incoming sources, such as satellite feeds, with the studio's in-house sync. The frame synchronizer accomplishes this by converting the video into a digital (computerized) signal. (We'll explain the difference between a standard video signal and a digital signal more fully in Chapter 22.) Extremely precise computerized timing mechanisms then release the stored frames in a rhythm that exactly matches the house sync.

In addition to its original purpose, the frame synchronizer has also become a popular tool for producing special effects. For example, the frame synchronizer's capability of storing and releasing the picture enables the operator to create a "strobe" effect in which the image changes position in a choppy motion, producing a distortion in the normal sense of timing. The strobing effect is produced by adjusting the frame synchronizer to display fewer frames per second than the normal scanning pattern.

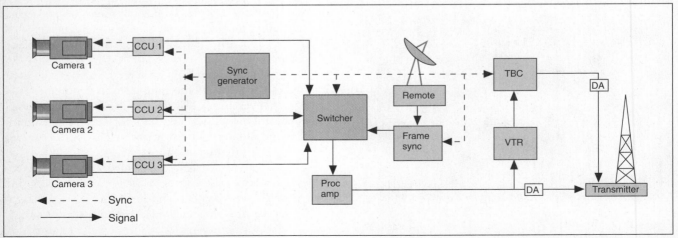

Figure 21.8 The video chain.

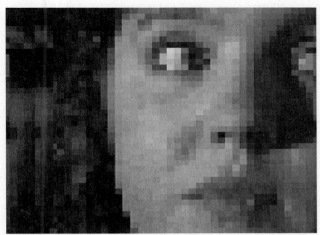

Figure 21.9 Pixelation. Frame synchronizers commonly offer a pixelation feature that magnifies individual groups of square pixels, resulting in a mosaic effect.

Pixelation (Figure 21.9) is produced by the frame synchronizer's capability of magnifying individual square groups of pixels. Still frame can also be created by the frame synchronizer: as the name implies, **still frame** is a single frame that is captured digitally and held in suspension.

The Processing Amplifier. The **processing amplifier** stabilizes the sync information and allows a final adjustment of color hue and saturation. Some units provide "drop-out" compensation to remove any video noise or loss of parts of the picture caused by erosion of the videotape.

Distribution Amplifiers. Video signals tend to degrade—lose quality—when they travel over long cable runs. **Distribution amplifiers** boost the signal and prevent "noisy" video. *Noisy* is a colloquial term meaning video that has a low ratio between the video signal and the random electronic noise in the system. Distribution amplifiers are generally used when a cable carrying composite video and audio exceeds 50 feet.

The Transmitter. The transmitter allows broadcast video signals to be imprinted on a carrier wave. In technical terms, the carrier wave is *modulated* by the video and audio. Modulation is the process of imprinting signals on a carrier wave. The transmitter sends the wave to an antenna that then puts the signal over the air.

TRANSMITTING THE VIDEO SIGNAL

Broadcast waves are electromagnetic signals. To oversimplify, electromagnetic waves are a type of radiation that includes radio, light, and gamma rays. An electromagnetic wave is not the same as a sound wave. Sound is a pattern produced by compression and expansion of molecules in the air or other medium. Electromagnetic waves exist independently of any medium. For example, light and radio (both electromagnetic waves) can travel through the vacuum of space.

The Electromagnetic Wave

Electromagnetic waves are called "waves" because they travel in cycles. A wave completes a cycle when it travels from its starting point to its high point to its low point and back to the starting point again. The sine wave is a representation of measurement of the electronic wave. (Remember, a signal doesn't *look* like a sine wave; a sine wave is only a visual representation of the measurement of the signal.)

Radio waves are measured in cycles per second. The term *hertz* (Hz) is used to represent cycles per second; the term was coined to commemorate the achievement of scientist Heinrich Hertz, who is credited with first generating and detecting electromagnetic energy and measuring its wavelengths. The number of cycles per second, or the hertz, is the measure of the frequency of the electromagnetic wave. Frequency indicates how many times the signal completes a cycle per second.

Most electromagnetic applications in broadcasting involve very high frequencies, so engineers have developed standardized terms to indicate large measures of cycles per second.

1 cycle per second = 1 **hertz** (Hz)

1000 Hz = 1 **kilohertz** (kHz)

1000 kHz = 1 **megahertz** (MHz), a million hertz

1000 MHz = 1 **gigahertz** (GHz), a billion hertz

AM radio is broadcast in the United States on frequencies ranging from 535 to 1705 kHz. FM radio transmits on frequencies ranging from 88 to 108 MHz. TV channels 2 to 6[1] are transmitted on frequencies ranging from 54 to 88 MHz; TV channels 7 to 13 are transmitted on frequencies ranging from 174 to 216 MHz. The entire FM radio band is located between channels 6 and 7 of the VHF (very-high frequency) TV band. UHF (ultra-high frequency) television channels, channels 14 to 69, are allocated a frequency range of 470 to 806 MHz (Figure 21.10).

Television audio is transmitted by frequency modulation. Frequency modulation (FM) is a method whereby the imprint of the signal on the carrier wave is created by modifying the frequency. The video portion of the picture is carried by an AM wave. Amplitude modulation (AM) is a system in which the carrier wave is modulated by changing the power of the carrier wave.

As you are probably aware, some video information is

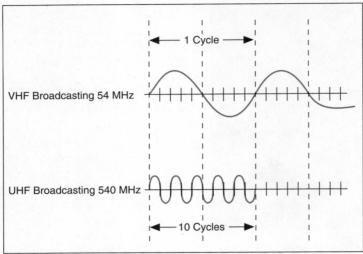

Figure 21.10 UHF and VHF broadcast frequencies. Ultra-high frequency television stations (UHF channels 14 to 69) broadcast in a frequency range that is up to 10 times higher than very-high frequency stations (VHF channels 2 to 13).

transmitted by microwave. Microwaves cover a spectrum of about 1 to approximately 300 GHz.

So what's the point of this recitation? A basic vocabulary of the electromagnetic spectrum is essential so that you can now appreciate these two basic points:

1. High-frequency waves travel in a more concentrated pattern. That's why microwaves are used to transmit up to and down from orbiting satellites—satellites used to relay broadcast and other information across the planet. Lower frequencies would scatter and dissipate; high frequencies (namely, microwaves) tend to stay focused and therefore retain a more concentrated power level.

2. Now that you've been introduced to the concept of frequencies, it's easier to understand that the more information you are trying to transmit, the greater the size or slice of the electromagnetic spectrum needed to transmit a signal—the **bandwidth**. Broadcast television's complex composite of audio, video, and sync signals requires a bandwidth of 6 MHz—600 times the width of an AM radio signal![2]

New Transmission Options

The problem with signal width and the limited availability of the broadcast spectrum is a prime factor in the search for new technologies with which to transmit a signal. Cable television was one solution to the lack of available channels.[3] However, the standard coaxial cable (Figure

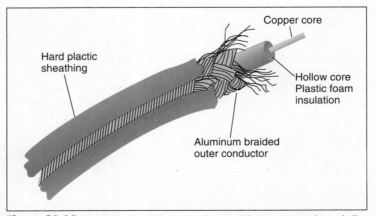

Figure 21.11 Coaxial cable. This two-conductor cable is constructed as a hollow tube with a wire core running down the middle and wrapped in multiple layers of insulation.

21.11) is limited in the number of channels it can carry, and running additional coaxial cables is expensive.

Also, long cable runs require frequent amplification; most cable companies must reamplify the signal every third of a mile. This, too, is expensive.

But *fiber-optic* cable may solve many of these problems. A **fiber-optic** cable (Figure 21.12) is a bundle of hair-thin glass that carries a laser signal. Fiber-optic cable can carry a much wider range of frequencies than coaxial cable, and signal attenuation (weakening over distance) is far less pronounced.

The promise of superefficient fiber-optic cable, combined with the new technologies of digital compression and transmission which allow a huge amount of information to be compressed into a computer-language signal, will radically change the complexion of video mechanics.

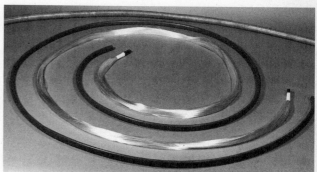

Figure 21.12 Fiber-optic cable. A bundle of hair-thin glass wires transmits concentrated laser signals carrying millions of bits per second; a pound of fiber can carry more information than a ton of copper wire. In addition to weight, fiber-optic's advantages over coaxial cable include less signal attenuation, less needed amplification, and imperviousness to electrical interference and extreme weather conditions. (Courtesy of Galileo Electro-Optics Corporation.)

SUMMARY

1. Many "engineering" duties are now within the domain of the producer. Among those duties are monitoring the properties of the signal using the waveform monitor and the vectorscope.

2. The waveform monitor and vectorscope only measure signals. Actual adjustments are usually made through the CCU, by adjusting the light level on the set, or by adjusting the camera iris.

3. The National Television System Committee (NTSC) set up standards for video. In general terms, video that meets those standards is considered "broadcast quality."

4. The video chain includes cameras, CCUs, sync generators, and time base correctors (TBCs). Other parts of the video chain are the frame synchronizer, the process amplifier, distribution amplifiers, and the transmitter.

5. 1 cycle per second = 1 hertz (Hz)
   1000 Hz = 1 kilohertz (kHz)
   1000 kHz = 1 megahertz (MHz), a million hertz
   1000 MHz = 1 gigahertz (GHz), a billion hertz

6. A composite video signal requires an enormous bandwidth. That's why new transmission technologies, such as fiber-optic cable and digital compression, are intriguing.

NOTES

1. There used to be a channel 1, but the FCC took that frequency away from commercial television in 1948 and reassigned the frequency for other uses. To avoid confusion, the existing channel assignments were retained.

2. Sydney Head and Christopher Sterling, *Broadcasting in America*, Brief Edition (Boston: Houghton-Mifflin, 1991), 114.

3. It would appear that there are plenty of channels on the television, but remember that a local area's television channels must be assigned in such a way as not to interfere with channels from nearby localities, so very few cities would be able to use all 12 VHF channels; UHF does not travel well enough to produce a quality signal under a wide range of conditions.

TECHNICAL TERMS

bandwidth	frame synchronizer	pedestal	saturation
broadcast quality	gigahertz (GHz)	processing amplifier	still frame
distribution amplifiers	kilohertz (kHz)	reference black	vectorscope
fiber-optic	megahertz (MHz)	reference white	waveform monitor

EXERCISES

1. Set reference white at about 90 IRE and record a scene where the talent demonstrates (as an example) the use of a telephone answering machine. Does the picture communicate adequately? Are all details clear?

2. Map your video facility. Follow the signal flow and label each signal and control device.

the new video

OBJECTIVES

After completing Chapter 22, you will be able to:

1. Use simple digital processing equipment with a fundamental understanding of what is happening behind the knobs and dials.
2. Identify the primary tools in desktop video graphics and animation.
3. Depending on the availability of equipment in your facility, create some computer-generated graphics or animation.

The computer has changed the way we balance our checkbooks, listen to music, and—as you read this—computer technology is relentlessly changing the video screen.

We're familiar with the basic functions of the computer, its ability to add, subtract, and multiply with blinding speed. As you probably know, the compact disc is a direct outgrowth of computer technology: It is recorded and played back using "digital" technology, a concept to be explained momentarily.

And with the computer shrinking—both in terms of physical size and price—the device is bringing about a profound change in the way the producer generates graphics and animation. New technologies even allow the melding of computer and video into a hybrid technology, a sort of "new video" that mixes a variety of media.

This chapter will examine the role of digital processing in video, the advances in "desktop video," and the ways in which various media are melding to produce a futuristic video that combines various media, reinforcing the old notion that today's science fiction is tomorrow's science.

THE DIGITAL REVOLUTION

What you see on a computer screen and what you see on a standard video receiver are two different entities. Video, in most cases, is the NTSC signal described in Chapter 21. This is analog video—created as an electronic "analogy" of the original light image. The transduced electrical signal is analogous to the light it represents.

However, digital video uses a computer "brain" to construct a picture using a series of on-and-off pulses.

These pulses turn a pixel on or off, and can do so much more quickly than the NTSC scanning beam. Another major difference between analog and digital video is that digital images can be manipulated by the computer. Because the digital image is nothing more than a series of stored numbers, the computer can recalculate these numbers in order to change the image.

Given the right software, the computer allows the operator to recalculate the image and enlarge it. Or shrink it. Or rotate it. Or change its color. The possibilities are intriguing and growing exponentially.

Analog to Digital

Analog video is transformed into a digital signal by a process known as *sampling*. During a sample, the computer takes a representative portion of the analog signal and stores it in memory. The faster the sampling speed, the greater the fidelity (literally, "faithful" reproduction of the original). These samples are then encoded—meaning that they are put into computer on-off pulse language. Scanning can be accomplished on a "moving" signal, such as the output of a camera, or from a static image. The flatbed scanner (Figure 22.1), for example, can take an illustration or drawing and convert it into digital code.

Pluses and Minuses of a Digital Signal

A digital signal is attractive to the producer because it is "clean," it can be manipulated by the computer, and it can be reproduced many times without degradation. A copy of an analog signal is like a photocopy of a photocopy; the integrity of the reproduction degrades. But digital signals are either on or off, and there's no degradation of the signal

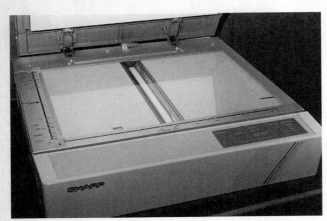

Figure 22.1 The flatbed scanner. The scanner transforms two-dimensional images such as flat art into a digital format that the computer understands.

when you copy a mathematical pattern of on-and-off pulses.

One disadvantage of a digital signal, though, is that it takes space in computer memory and in any cable or broadcast channel through which it is transmitted. A frame of video can require as much as one megabyte of storage; this means that you can fill up the hard disk of a very large personal computer with only a few seconds' worth of full-motion video. Even the enormous storage capability of **CD-ROM** (compact disc read-only memory, the same type of laser-read media used in standard CDs) can't keep up with full-motion video; only about 30 seconds of uncompressed full-frame video can be stored via CD-ROM.

Digital signals need a large transmission bandwidth—in some cases, 10 times the bandwidth as an analog signal. Compression of digital signals appears to be the most feasible answer to problems associated with handling bandwidth- and memory-hungry video. **Compression** is physically making the amount of information in a signal more compact. Researchers are looking for efficient ways to delete picture information the eye won't miss. Also, compression technology is honing methods of filtering out redundant information—parts of the picture that have not changed and do not need to be retransmitted in the next frame.

A point of interest worth adding here: Various methods of compression are being perfected, though at the time of this writing there is no universally agreed-upon standard. However, some computer hardware firms are working on methods of compressing and decompressing digital video irrespective of the format in which it was compressed. One such firm is a Santa Clara company called Integrated Information Technologies, which is marketing a $150 computer chip that the company claims can handle any of the three major compression/decompression standards.[1]

Although prognostication is risky, most experts agree that the combination of ever-increasing computer memory and new compression technologies will make digital video—rather than analog video—the new standard for production.

DESKTOP VIDEO

Desktop video is computer-generated or enhanced video created on a personal computer. The computer's ability to interact with video is opening a new horizon for the producer. Computer-generated images are nothing new; they've been in common use for graphics since the 1970s and achieved significant sophistication in the early 1980s. The real news is the availability of interactive video programs for the personal computer.

The PC

Advances in computer storage and processing speed have been nothing less than astounding. In the early 1950s, the Univac computer was more than 10 feet long, by 7 feet high, by 6 feet wide and used about as much electricity as 20 electric stoves with all four burners operating. But this "monster" had just a fraction of the computing power available to the owner of today's department-store-bought laptop.

Even a 10-year-old computer seems hopelessly primitive by today's standards, and if current trends continue, we probably will be sniffing at the capabilities of 2-year-old computers.

The point is that computer storage and speed has increased so quickly that we hardly can keep up with the capabilities of modern units and the software they run. But we're trying. In particular, video professionals are using the power of the personal computer to draw and paint images, to animate, and even to drive the editing system.

Before demonstrating some of these applications, let's more closely define what we mean by a "personal computer." The term *PC* is generally applied to anything that can fit on a desktop. Some people use *PC* only to refer to an IBM-compatible unit, but for our purposes we'll employ the term as a reference to the three popular brands of desktop computers used in video: the IBM, the Commodore Amiga, and the Apple Macintosh.

IBM. IBM (Figure 22.2) and IBM-compatible machines have lagged behind their counterparts in adapting to media production demands. However, IBM's basic structure has great processing power, and it appears that IBM may be poised to make significant inroads into the video market via new processing and compression equipment.

Commodore Amiga. Amiga has targeted the video market and, as a result, has made significant inroads into

Figure 22.2 Multimedia PC. The IBM personal computer configured for multimedia applications consists of a CD-ROM drive and an internal card for displaying PC-TV. In the lower right of the screen, a video display enlivens a spreadsheet presentation. (Courtesy of IBM Corporation.)

video production. Unlike IBM and Apple, Amiga produces an NTSC signal; in other words, it feeds a standard video signal that can be wired directly into a standard television set. IBM and Apple's outputs must first be processed through a separate unit in order to be translated into NTSC.

Apple Macintosh. Apple (Figure 22.3) was the unchallenged leader in desktop publishing, and the user-friendly graphic approach has translated well to video. Macintosh's graphic orientation makes "cutting and pasting" video a natural extension of the computer's existing capabilities.

Figure 22.3 The Apple Macintosh. Apple's Macintosh popularized a standardized graphical user interface (GUI) that offers a universal "look and feel" between programs. This universality and graphic orientation lowers the learning time from program to program and provides easier integration into the video studio.

Figure 22.4 QuickTime. Apple Computer's system for handling dynamic media on the desktop, *QuickTime*, provides the means to standardize the handling of video, audio, MIDI, SMPTE time code, animation, graphics, and text. *QuickTime* also provides on-the-fly compression and decompression.

Apple's system software for handling the mixture of video, audio, and graphics (in Apple terminology, "dynamic media") is known as *QuickTime*, and it promises to vastly simplify the process of melding the computer and video. *QuickTime* offers a simple, icon-driven menu (Figure 22.4), allowing the producer to easily access various dynamic sources (compress/decompress on-the-fly) and mix them together.

QuickTime promises to become the standard for interplatform computer/video interaction, much the way NTSC is the standard for video. In fact, *Quicktime* is the major thrust of Kalieda, the joint multimedia company between Apple and IBM.

All PCs, assuming they are equipped with large enough memory and the appropriate software, can handle intricate programs for video character generation, painting and drawing, importing and assembling, animation, and editing.

Character Generation

A typical character generation (CG) program gives the user a choice of style and **font** (typeface). Figure 22.5 shows how we've selected a font to write the word *Tornado*. (Note that character generation is often a part of a program that includes other graphics capabilities as well.)

Tornado

Figure 22.5 Character generation. The word *Tornado* was created with *VideoQuill*, an example of the high-resolution character generation programs available on the PC. *VideoQuill*, a product of Data Translation.

Painting and Drawing

Paint and draw programs let the user create free-form images. The user usually has a "palette" of drawing and painting instruments from which to choose (Figure 22.6). Programs typically allow you to choose a "tool" that simulates a pencil, a paintbrush, a spray can, and so on.

Programs that create images on-screen are referred to as bit-mapped and vector-based. A **bit-mapped** drawing or painting is created by activating pixels that, when melded together, create a visual image. The pixels are activated by the movement of some sort of tool, such as a stylus that has been programmed to act as a paint brush or pencil (Figure 22.7). **Vector-based** programs use a mathematical

Figure 22.7 The stylus. The stylus, an input device, operates like a PC's mouse. Together with the graphics tablet, it has the "look and feel" of a traditional drawing or painting implement.

formula to store the images. The artist usually uses the stylus to enter points that the computer memorizes and stores; lines and other patterns are then computed from point to point.

The advantage of a vector-based program is that because the images exist as mathematical equations, they can quickly be adjusted—enlarged, downsized, or even rotated in three dimensions without distortion.

Figure 22.8 shows how the user of a paint program selects an airbrush tool to draw the swirling image of a tornado.

Importing and Assembling

Many programs have "scrapbook," "clipboard," or "glue" utilities that allow the user to take one image and move it

Figure 22.6 Paint tools. Tools available in Adobe's *Photoshop*, a paint software program.

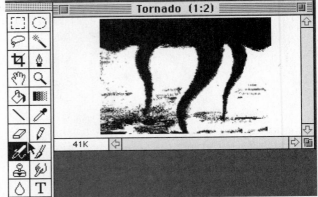

Figure 22.8 The airbrush. One tool available in most paint packages is the airbrush. It simulates an airbrush by creating a spray effect, with many variables for the density and the width of spray.

Figure 22.9 Combining images. The word *Tornado* has been combined with the drawing of swirling wind to more effectively illustrate a news story.

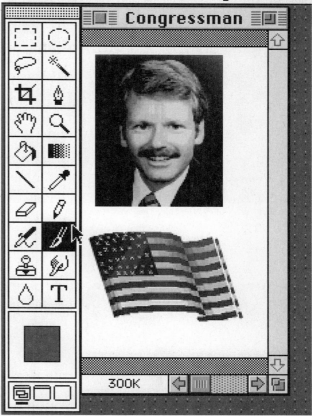

Figure 22.10 Combining photos and graphics. The photo of the Congressman is digitized and imported into a graphics package like Adobe *Photoshop* where the flag can be added and both images retouched.

into another image. Figure 22.9 shows how we've taken the word *Tornado* and imported it into the swirling image. Now, we've got an illustration suitable for use in a news program.

The capability to import and assemble makes the use of existing images quick and easy. For instance, let's assume you want to create a news graphic showing the newly elected congressman's portrait superimposed over an American flag. You have:

1. An 8-×-10-inch publicity photo of the congressman
2. A flag graphic stored in an electronic "clip-art" program

First, you'd scan the image of the congressman into digital form. Next, you would import it into the program in which the flag graphic has been pasted (Figure 22.10). Then you would clean up the images and superimpose them into a box (Figure 22.11). Finally you would import the completed image into an animation program so that you could fit the elements together nicely to key over the left shoulder of the newscaster (Figure 22.12).

Animation

Traditional **cel** animation involved an artist drawing an image on a piece of celluloid; the images were then individually photographed onto a frame of film.

Modern computer-generated animation systems can operate in much the same fashion. An image is created and transferred to a frame of video; the image is altered to create motion and another frame of video is recorded.

Such systems are relatively inexpensive but painfully

Figure 22.11 Creating a composited image. The retouched images from the graphics program are imported into an animation program like MacroMind-Paracomp's *Director* software. The images are composited into a box and output to a tape or to a video switcher.

Figure 22.12 Using the graphic. The complete graphic is keyed over the newscaster's shoulder.

slow. More modern "real-time" animation systems are replacing frame-by-frame systems. Real-time animation can involve movement of a great deal of computer information very quickly, so it requires a high-end personal computer.

The series of photos in Figure 22.13 shows how a simple animation program is used to create an opening for a video show. Using a program that creates the image of rotating an object in three dimensions, we've brought a camera (taken from a computer-video clip-art file) and "turned" it so that the lens points toward the camera.

Software and hardware that create computer-generated art offer a producer the option of using an image or a series of images and making a product that, according to NBC News Editorial and Production Services General Manager David Schmerler, allows you to have motion pictures "even when there's nothing to point a camera at."

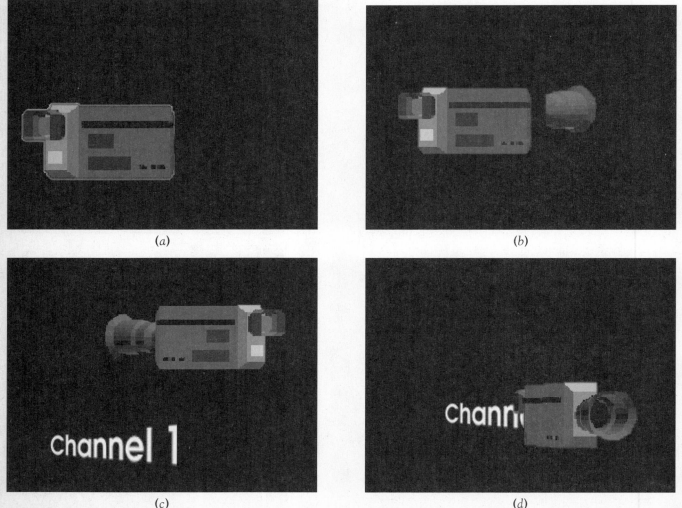

Figure 22.13 Real-time animation. Here, a camera is "assembled" and turned toward the viewer as an animated introductory segment.

Schmerler offers some insight into paint and animation systems in Box 22.1.

Editing

High-end editing systems utilize computer decision-lists to keep track of edit points. But innovative software for the personal computer permits editing to be brought to the desktop (See Figures 16.2 to 16.4.) Following Apple Computer's direction with QuickTime enables VideoToolkit™ editing software to compile an Edit Decision List directly into a QuickTime Movie. This innovation in a low-cost program empowers the user with digital nonlinear "rough-cuts" once available only on the highest end editing systems.

VIDEO OF THE FUTURE

Computer technology has done more than create new methods of animation; it has begun the process of completely changing the way we view—physically and intellectually—the media. We're now moving toward true multimedia interactivity, high-definition television, ISDN, and even a way of recreating the visual environment known as virtual reality.

BOX 22.1 ELECTRONIC PAINT SYSTEMS TELL THE STORY PICTORIALLY

What *are* television graphics? Television graphics are still or animated pictures created by a designer which can help an anchor, reporter, or producer to tell a story. A graphic is literally "created video."

The bread and butter work of most television graphics departments is the "box" or video insert graphics which appear on the screen alongside the anchor to reinforce his or her words.

When the anchor tells you that a hurricane is coming, chances are that story will be accompanied by a graphic: perhaps a hurricane shape superimposed on a map showing where the storm is supposed to strike, or there might be a satellite photo animation showing the storm's track. Perhaps the graphic will simply be a picture of black clouds with the word, "STORM!", angled across the picture in big type. The quantity and complexity of a graphic is a function of the artist's skill, the amount of time the artist has to make the graphic, and the quality of the electronic gear the artist has available.

The graphics department of NBC News creates more than 100 insert graphics every weekday for our network. That wouldn't be possible without electronic paint systems which allow designers to cut and paste pieces of video pictures and to "stencil" and "airbrush" video ten times faster than an artist using conventional tools.

Electronic paint systems also allow video artists to save "cutouts" of picture elements in electronic memory. A cutout (a portion of a video picture) of the President is available in a few keystrokes. An American flag background comes up with a swipe of an electronic pen. A few more strokes of the electronic pen and the picture of the President is composited over the background. Several more keystrokes and there is a "slug" or headline across the graphic. It hardly seems possible that only seven years ago, it took an artist all day to create the same effect with scissors, paste and paint.

An electronic paint system used to be a six-figure investment. Now the technology is working its way downmarket. Quite respectable electronic paint systems are appearing for smaller stations and cable systems which will run on $15,000 worth of personal computer equipment. The same personal computer can handle sales and billing information, and schedule the technical crew.

But it's still expensive to create graphics from scratch. First-rate video artists are hard to find and salaries are rising in line with the demand for their skills. The paint system is just one of the tools the artist needs for the most basic graphics suite. There must be a camera to capture hard copy photographs, a still store to hold and play back the graphics. For a moderately sophisticated system, add a switcher, character generator and a digital effects device. Animation requires even more equipment: videotape machines, cel recorders and animation workstations. It is no wonder the network syndication feeds of news graphics are very popular with affiliate news directors.

Entrepreneurs who supply stations with generic or customized news graphics have been around for some time, but, until recently, there has been a distribution problem. Next-day courier service can't get a station a set of animated weather graphics for today's broadcast.

Help is on the way. There's at least one weather graphics service which has begun to create animated, localized weather maps at small station prices and feed them on a telephone line as data to the station's personal computer. The data feed takes about 15 minutes. No expensive satellite time and gear are required. All you

(a) Is this what SDI technology will look like?

(b) Animation shows how powerful laser guns might work.

need is a modem and that same personal computer with the paint system. The PC weather graphics can have moving hot or cold fronts and transition effects that look like they came from a high-end system. You even can buy a customized voiceover from "our own meteorologist" on the same phone line.

A weather map probably was the first story-telling graphic ever used on a television news program. Weather graphics have evolved from an acetate-covered map and grease pencil on the "weather set" to computer-enhanced animation from satellite photographers, weather radar with moving thunderstorms and animated five-day forecasts with full-color animated rain clouds and shining suns.

There's a reason why stations want animated weather graphics. Animated graphics are "story-telling" graphics. You can have motion pictures on the screen even when there is nothing to point a camera at. There may be no other pictures because the story is in the future: you can't shoot pictures of tomorrow's storm because it hasn't happened yet. The story may be abstract: business and financial news. The "animation" can be as simple as a full screen panel with the main points of the President's speech, revealed as a reporter talks about them.

Animated graphics allow you to tell a story pictorially which you couldn't tell very well in any other way. For example, we wanted to tell the story of the "Star Wars" defense program. The Defense Department wanted to build a lot of new, high technology weapons to detect and destroy enemy missiles heading for the United States. The plan included powerful laser guns and space platforms loaded with anti-missile missiles. The story was complicated and took a long time to

explain. The new weapons didn't exist yet, and even if they did, the Pentagon would never let us take pictures of them.

We turned the problem over to Steven Giangrasso, a highly skilled animator in our network graphics department. Using publicly available information and some shrewd guesses, he created three-dimensional computer models. The sequence he created allowed our Pentagon correspondents to explain what the proposed weapon system was all about. The animation elements were reused constantly in different combinations by NBC News and by affiliate news programs. Even now, years later, our producers still call for them. Steve's shrewd guesses were so good that we didn't have to change his graphics very much as more information became public.

It's no coincidence that science and business reports became a popular and successful element of network news broadcasts at the same time that stations and network news divisions were acquiring sophisticated graphics equipment.

Many business reporters came to TV from print. They had to learn that they couldn't write about "small investors sitting on the sidelines on Wall Street" for TV news unless there was a way to get a picture of an undersized investor sitting on a sideline on Wall Street. The successful business and science reporters have learned to work with graphics producers and designers and to write scripts which work with graphic animations.

Electronic graphics have not only made television news look better, they have allowed it to become more meaningful as well.

David Schmerler, "Electronic Paint Systems Tell the Story Pictorially," *Communicator* (October 1989): 11.

Multimedia Interactivity

CD-ROM technology has helped make interactivity commonplace. You've probably used an interactive device in a kiosk in a hotel lobby, for example, to find out about local tourist attractions.

The use of interactive multimedia in education is common. The U.S. Army, for example, uses computer workstations to train maintenance technicians. The trainees are offered a choice (*Which panel do you remove next?*). The choice is made by pressing the appropriate square on the video screen. If the choice is correct, the visual lesson continues; if not, the program moves to a remedial lesson.

High-Definition Television

High-definition television (HDTV) is an emerging technology that promises to change the aspect ratio of the standard video screen to 16 units by 9 units (as opposed to the current 3:4 aspect ratio). Also, HDTV would increase the number of scanning lines by a factor of two (approximately) and the number of pixels by a factor of four. This would be accomplished by complete digitization of the signal.

The image produced by an HDTV unit (Figure 22.14) would more closely resemble the aspect ratio and high resolution of feature film as opposed to video. Despite various agencies' current attempts to settle on a standard, HDTV is not compatible with current receivers and channel designations. Another problem is that the massive amount of digital information needed to fuel the high-definition picture cannot (at this time) be squeezed into the existing 6-MHz-wide broadcast channel. Developers are investigating methods of compressing the signal or finding additional spectrum space on which to transmit.

Integrated Services Digital Network

The concept of an **integrated services digital network (ISDN)** promises to combine voice, data, and visual images over one fiber-optic cable. If an ISDN were to evolve, audio (including phone messages), video, and computer transmissions would all be sent on the same carrier. Perhaps the concept of video phones will become popular; perhaps the video screen will become a truly interactive device through which we can call up text, video (including HDTV), even digital representations of artwork.

Virtual Reality and Artificial Reality

You don a headset that projects a landscape through which you "move." Electronic gloves allow you to "handle" objects that don't really exist. That's all part of **virtual reality**.

Such "science fiction" technology currently exists in media laboratories across the nation. Currently, the headset is capable of projecting images that create the illusion of movement in three dimensions; at some point, experimenters predict the headset will be abandoned in favor of a unit that projects images directly onto the retina, the part of the eye that receives images and transmits them through the optic nerve to the brain.

One researcher, Dr. Myron Krueger, is well known for his studies with artificial reality, which he describes as the ultimate form of interaction between human and machine (Figure 22.15). Through the use of projection and powerful graphic workstations, Dr. Krueger develops video environments where participants interact with a "sense of place." The environment is referred to as *videoplace*. "In an arti-

Figure 22.14 High-Definition Television. HDTV produces a high-resolution image and uses a 16:9 aspect ratio that resembles a motion picture. Current standard TV uses an aspect ratio of 3:4.

Figure 22.15 Parachuting into an artificial reality. A participant parachutes into a graphic world. In an artificial reality, ungoverned by physical laws, a participant's image floats freely about the screen. (Photo courtesy of Dr. Myron Krueger of Artificial Reality.)

ficial reality, everything you perceive is generated by a computer that responds to your movements with sights and sounds designed to make you think you are in another world."

Another video system under development is the tactile glove, a device that will interact with the computerized video projection and provide the user with the "feel" of the object he or she has touched.

CONCLUSION

High tech is fascinating, but it's important to remember that technology is only a tool of expression. The newest gizmo can provide glitz, but not the substance of communication.

If anything, that substance has been the focus of this book. Although we're fully aware of the wonders of modern video, we also recognize that the basic, fundamental principle of video endures. What principle is that? Essen-

tially, that video—at any level of sophistication—is designed for the *viewer*.

It's intoxicatingly easy to become swept up in the rush of technology. After all, gizmos *are* fun. But it's a mistake to think that technology is the be-all and end-all of video. If you take nothing else from this text, remember that any time you uncap a camera, you're in the business of communicating, or entertaining, or motivating—or doing all three at the same time. These are the goals of video production; using the hardware is secondary, a means to an end.

As a final thought, balance this notion with the concept that sometimes new ideas *are* better. Although there are conventions in video, production is not a static medium. Sometimes the rules are meant to be broken—when there's a well-thought-out reason and communication is enhanced in the process. So when you pick up a camera, sit down at the word processor to write a script, or begin your editing session, keep an active mind—and an open one.

NOTE

1. Rachel Powell, "Digitizing TV into Obsolescence," *The New York Times* (October 20, 1991): 11.

TECHNICAL TERMS

analog	compression	integrated services digital network (ISDN)	tactile glove
bit-mapped	desktop video	real-time	vector-based
CD-ROM	font	sampling	virtual reality
cel	high-definition television (HDTV)		

"that golden distance"

The following is the script for the opening 5 minutes of the Emmy-Award-winning documentary "That Golden Distance," produced and directed by Frederick Lewis with additional videography by Philip J. Palombo.

Video	Audio
MS RUNNERS LINE-UP AT START	THEME MUSIC UP AND UNDER SFX STARTING GUNSHOT
WS CRANE SHOT; MARATHON START MS RUNNERS BODIES PASS CAM. WS FROM BEHIND: RUNNERS HEADS WS CRANE SHOT: CROWDED STREET OF RUNNERS, TOWN IN BACKGROUND SUPER TITLE: THAT GOLDEN DISTANCE	NARRATOR: Marathon running—there was a time when it wasn't a sport for the masses, overseen by corporate sponsors with staggering amounts of prize money. There was a time when all that didn't matter. All that mattered was That Golden Distance.
	MUSIC FADE UP
DISSOLVE TO B & W FOOTAGE: WS CRANE SHOT: RUNNERS IN ST. PAN RIGHT ABOVE RUNNERS	THEME MUSIC FADE OUT; CROSSOVER TO PIANO MUSIC FADE UP AND UNDER:
DISSOLVE TO CROWD OF RUNNERS	NARRATOR: The Boston Athletic Association Marathon; runners have been plodding along this twisting, turning 26-mile route since 1897.
MS BEHIND RUNNERS ON STREET, CAM MOUNTED IN MOVING CAR WS CRANE SHOT, BEHIND RUNNERS, CAM TRACKING RUNNERS	
DISSOLVE TO AMBER FOOTAGE: 2 RUNNERS SIDE BY SIDE, PAN RIGHT	Every April on Patriot's Day in Massachusetts, they come, and go.
MS FOLLOW RUNNER, PAN RIGHT MS 3 COPS CARRY RUNNER AWAY MS PACK OF RUNNERS, TRACKING SHOT SUPER BOTTOM RIGHT: 1932 MS RUNNERS' FEET, TILT UP TO FULL BODIES	In the early days, they were bricklayers or plumbers or milkmen; working class athletes who trained before and after their day's labor.
MS RUNNER BESIDE CAR, TRACKING SHOT DISSOLVE TO PHOTO: DEMAR CARRIES JACKET DOWN STREET DISSOLVE TO PHOTO: DEMAR SITS AT PRINTER'S TABLE	NARRATOR: Clarence DeMar, a 7 time winner who dominated during the 20's, was a printer at the Boston Herald. He'd run the marathon in the afternoon, then report to work where he'd literally set the type describing his own victory. MUSIC FADE OUT

Video

WS CROWD OF RUNNERS PASS CAM.

DISSOLVE TO PHOTO: BROWN & PAWSON RUNNING
DISSOLVE TO PHOTO: CU KELLEY
DISSOLVE TO PHOTO: CU COTE
DISSOLVE TO PHOTO: ALL 4 ABOVE RUNNING
DISSOLVE TO PHOTO: 3-S RUNNERS POSE
COLOR FOOTAGE: PAWSON WALKS FROM RIVER
    TOWARDS CAM.
DISSOLVE TO MCU PAWSON TALKING HEAD
SUPER: Leslie Pawson
'33–'38–'41

CU NEWSPAPER CLIPPING: "MARATHON WINNER IS
    PATTERN WEAVER"
CU PAWSON TRAINING LOG: "1933. Run 6 miles easy;
    Rest."
CU BOTTOM OF LOG: "Won B.A.A. Marathon"
MCU PAWSON TALKING HEAD

CU BEACH PAINTING, PULLOUT TO MS KELLEY
    BRUSHING CANVAS

DISSOLVE TO MCU JOHN KELLEY TALKING HEAD
SUPER: John A. Kelley
'35 & '45

CU B & W PHOTO: KELLEY RUNNING

MCU WALTER YOUNG TALKING HEAD
SUPER: Walter Young
'37

DISSOLVE TO B & W PHOTO: CU YOUNG RUNNING

Audio

NARRATOR: The marathon's most colorful competitive era was during the 1930's and 40's when a smooth running pair of Rhode Islanders, one a Narrangansett Indian, combined with a plucky Boston Irishman and a flashy French Canadian to win the race eleven times in sixteen years. This was Boston's golden era. But there was little gold in it for the blue collar amateurs who competed. In 1933, Leslie Pawson was a mill weaver in Pawtucket, Rhode Island.

LESLIE PAWSON: Well, I would run mostly at night after I got through work. I would probably come home and have my supper and umm, probably lay down for about an hour or so, and, then I'd go out and run.

PAWSON V.O.: And a lot of times, I was running at 9 o'clock at night and 10 o'clock.
Used to be the idea in the old days, that if you trained too much, you left all your running on the road.
So, it was better just to run three days a week and save your strength for the race, y'know? But it hasn't worked out that way, not the way the runners do now, (CHUCKLES) they train everyday.

NARRATOR: Two-time winner, Johnny Kelley is retired on Cape Cod now, but he remembers the hard times.

JOHN KELLEY: We ran through the Depression years, there were no jobs anyway. But, whatever you could pick up, odd jobs here and there, but ah, I worked in a gas station and I knew the Vice President of the Boston Edison Company and I went to see him and I worked there for 37 years. Plus, before that it was any old thing I could get my hands on.

KELLEY V.O.: There was nothing permanent, nothing steady.

WALTER YOUNG: Oh yes, I had been unemployed working a few days here and there for the past year.
YOUNG FADE OUT UNDER:

NARRATOR: Walter Young came to Boston from Canada, 3 weeks before the 1937 marathon. A week before the race, his money ran out. He took a watch he'd won in a race just a week earlier and pawned it for the $7.00 train fare back to the city of Verdun.

Video	Audio
DISSOLVE TO YOUNG TALKING HEAD	YOUNG: I had all the confidence in the world which I was able to express to the Mayor of Verdun and, due to his belief in my belief, he gave me the funds to return to Boston.
DISSOLVE TO PHOTO: CU YOUNG RUNNING	NARRATOR: The Mayor of Verdun not only gave unemployed Walter Young the money to return to Boston; he made him a promise.
MCU WALTER YOUNG TALKING HEAD	YOUNG: He did tell me that if I made good in winning the Boston Marathon that I would get a position on the Verdun Police Department
DISSOLVE TO TRACKING SHOT BEHIND RUNNERS; OVER CAR HOOD SUPER BOTTOM RIGHT: 1937 REVERSE ANGLE: TRACKING SHOT KELLEY & YOUNG RUNNING MS TRACKING SHOT; YOUNG AHEAD OF KELLEY CU KELLEY'S FACE, TRACKING SHOT WS KELLEY RUNNING ALONE, CARS FOLLOW BEHIND MS 2 RUNNERS, YOUNG PASSES KELLEY CU YOUNG PROFILE, TRACKING WS YOUNG RUNS ALONE, TRACKING	NARRATOR: Young attached himself to the hometown favorite, Johnny Kelley and never let go. The lead changed hands between them 16 times in the last five miles alone. Kelley had apparently made a winning move at 20 miles. But 3 miles later, he faultered. Young's superior strength carried him over the last 3 miles to the finish and to the steady employment he'd been promised.
MS CROWDED FINISH LINE, YOUNG RUNS IN MS YOUNG STANDS SURROUNDED BY SUITS; FREEZE	YOUNG V.O.: I immediately after, that is—within a week after winning the race, I was employed full time and I have had a regular payday from that time for the next 41 years.
FRAME DISSOLVE TO YOUNG TALKING HEAD DISSOLVE TO PHOTO: YOUNG HOLDS UP NEWSPAPER AND CROWN	FADE UP MUSIC
PHOTO ZOOM OUT TO SLATE: THAT GOLDEN DISTANCE FADE TO BLACK	FADE OUT MUSIC

Many reading lists offered at the conclusion of texts are simply collections of every book and periodical written on a particular subject. We would like to avoid that approach by suggesting a smaller number of books and periodicals that can comprise a realistic library for the producer. If a work is omitted it is not intended as an editorial judgment; rather, we have chosen to list another work that covers the subject as well and complements the other readings on the list.

GENERAL VIDEO PRODUCTION

Burrows, Thomas D., and Donald N. Wood and Lynne Schafer Gross. *Television Production Disciplines and Techniques*, 5th ed. Dubuque, IA: William C. Brown, 1992. Good basic text especially appropriate for producer interested in technical details.

Compesi, Ronald J., and Ronald E. Sherriffs. *Small Format Television Production: The Technique of Single-Camera Television Field Production*, 2d ed. Boston: Allyn and Bacon, 1990. Direct and readable text offering cogent explanations of small-format video. Especially clear technical explanations.

Kuney, Jack. *Take One: Television Directors on Directing.* Westport, CT: Greenwood/Praeger, 1990. Worthwhile study, interesting concept.

Mathias, Harry, and Richard Patterson. *Electronic Cinematography*. Belmont, CA: Wadsworth, 1985. An important manual for producers who want to add "cinematic values" to their video productions.

Millerson, Gerald. *The Technique of Television Production*, 12th ed. Stoneham, MA: Focal Press, 1990. Venerable work with generous attention to technical details.

Millerson, Gerald. *TV Lighting Methods*. Stoneham, MA: Focal Press, 1982. Highly detailed guide to solving one of the most nettling production problems.

Rabiger, Michael. *Directing the Documentary*. Stoneham, MA: Focal Press, 1986. Practical book, offering step-by-step instruction.

Schneider, Arthur. *Electronic Post-Production and Videotape Editing*. Boston: Focal Press, 1989. Well-organized book; good explanations demystify some of the more complex aspects of the field.

Utz, Peter. *Video User's Handbook*, 4th ed. White Plains, NY: Knowledge Industry Publications, 1989. Primer for producer and operator; starts from absolute basics.

Yoakam, Richard, and Charles Cremer. *ENG: Television News and the New Technologies*, 2d ed. New York: Random House, 1989. Listed here instead of under the news category because so much of the text is applicable to any sort of production. One of the clearest books of its genre.

Zettl, Herbert. *Sight-Sound-Motion: Applied Media Aesthetics*, 2d ed. Belmont, CA: Wadsworth, 1990. Deep study of the factors which make video a communicative medium.

Zettl, Herbert. *Television Production Handbook*, 5th ed. Belmont, CA: Wadsworth, 1992. Definitive reference on most aspects of TV production; very good and detailed encyclopedic overview.

AUDIO

Alten, Stanley. *Audio in Media*, 3d ed. Belmont, CA: Wadsworth, 1992. Very useful for the video producer who wants high-quality audio.

Nisbet, Alec. *The Use of Microphones*, 2d ed. Stoneham, MA: Focal Press, 1983. Thorough study, good reference.

O'Donnell, Lewis, Philip Benoit, and Carl Hausman. *Modern Radio Production*, 3d ed. Belmont, CA: Wadsworth, 1992. While intended for radio producers, several chapters deal with microphone use and setup.

INSTITUTIONAL VIDEO

Cartwright, Steve R. *Training With Video: Designing and Producing Video Training Programs*. White Plains, NY: Knowledge Industry Publications, 1986. Complete guide, with special attention paid to planning.

Gayeski, Diane. *Corporate and Instructional Video.* Englewood Cliffs, NJ: Prentice-Hall, 1983. Broad treatment of the field; somewhat dated but new edition expected soon. Gayeski's company, Omnicom of Ithaca, NY, also publishes *Interactive Toolkit*, a combination workbook/software collection. *Interactive Toolkit* is distributed through Knowledge Industry Publications, White Plains, NY: 1987.

Hausman, Carl. *Institutional Video: Planning, Budgeting, Production and Evaluation.* Belmont, CA: Wadsworth, 1991. Broad treatment that can be used as quick reference because most chapters can be used on stand-alone basis.

Stokes, Judith Tereno. *The Business of Nonbroadcast Television.* White Plains, NY: Knowledge Industry Publications, 1988. Authoritative guide which provides extensive information about the nation's institutional video industry.

Wershing, Stephen, and Paul Singer. *Computer Graphics and Animation for Corporate Video.* White Plains, NY: Knowledge Industry Publications, 1988. Understandable reference with special attention paid to personal-computer users.

SCRIPTING AND BUDGETING

Hilliard, Robert. *Writing for Television and Radio*, 5th ed. Belmont, CA: Wadsworth, 1990. Comprehensive guide to writing for media, very clear instruction.

Matrazzo, Donna. *The Corporate Scriptwriting Book*, 2d ed. Portland, OR: Communicom Publishing Co., 1985. While basically a book on scripting, this work is valuable for learning techniques of thinking *visually* and putting those thoughts on paper.

Singleton, Ralph S. *Film Scheduling/Film Budgeting Workbook.* Beverly Hills, CA: Lone Eagle Publications, 1984. Some useful hints for producers of films, perfectly translatable to video.

Wiese, Michael. *Film and Video Budgets.* Stoneham, MA: Focal Press, 1984. Very practical guidebook; many workable formulas.

PERFORMANCE

Hyde, Stuart. *Television and Radio Announcing*, 6th ed. Boston: Houghton-Mifflin, 1990. Comprehensive reference; well-written and readable.

O'Donnell, Lewis, Carl Hausman, and Philip Benoit. *Announcing: Broadcast Communicating Today*, 2d ed. Belmont, CA: Wadsworth, 1992. Useful for TV performers, especially nonprofessionals who need a crash course in on-camera performance or directors who need to coach those nonprofessionals.

NEWS

Hausman, Carl. *Crafting the News for Electronic Media: Writing, Reporting and Producing.* Belmont, CA: Wadsworth, 1992. Special emphasis placed on production.

Hausman, Carl. *Crisis of Conscience: Perspectives on Journalism Ethics.* New York: HarperCollins, 1992. Exploration of rights and wrongs on news practice.

Hausman, Carl. *The Decision-Making Process in Journalism.* Chicago: Nelson-Hall, 1990. A study of news judgment, showing how experienced reporters find the core of a story.

Stephens, Mitchell. *Broadcast News*, 3rd Ed. New York: Holt, 1993. Especially good sections on writing.

PERIODICALS

Magazines and journals do go out of print and change publication addresses, so by the time you read this there may be some changes. But even periodicals no longer produced are frequently kept in libraries and often are excellent references when dealing with subjects other than new equipment.

Incidentally, keep an eye on the computer magazines that line the newsracks. Many contain articles of use to video producers.

Audio-Visual Communications. Media Horizons, Inc. 50 W. 23rd St., New York, NY 10010. Strong emphasis on scripting and development.

AV Video. Montage Publishing, 701 Westchester Avenue, White Plains, NY 10604. Hands-on production publication; also good regular features on facility construction, operation, and management.

BM/E (Broadcast Management/Engineering). Intertect Publishing Corp., P.O. Box 12901, Overland Park, KS 66282. A very technical but still comprehensible publication for people involved in engineering management. Most is understandable to the nontechnical professional, and it is a good guide to developing technologies.

Broadcasting. Broadcasting Publications, 1705 DeSales St., NW, Washington, DC 20036. While not geared specifically for video producers, the trade journal of broadcasting and cable contains a wealth of information about the industry.

College Broadcaster. The Magazine of the National Association of College Broadcasters. (NACB). 71 George St. Providence, RI 02912. Serves broadcast and cable radio and TV facilities in education.

EITV (Educational and Industrial Television). Broadband Information Services, Inc., 295 Madison Ave., New York, NY 10017. Updates on equipment and good articles on techniques.

The Independent. The Publication of the Association of Independent Video and Filmmakers, Inc. (AIVF). Particularly geared to and with a wide range of information for the independent film and video producer.

Millimeter. Penton Publishing, 826 Broadway, New York, NY 10003. Publication that does an excellent job in providing a personal look at the producers of motion pictures and television. Equally covers the technology and the user.

New Media. Multimedia Technologies for Desktop Computer Users. Hypermedia Communications, Inc. 901 Mariner's Island Blvd., Suite 365, San Mateo, CA 94494. Focuses on emerging technologies with an emphasis on desktop video.

Post: The Magazine for Post Production Professionals. Testa Communications, 25 Willowdale Ave., Port Washington, NY 11050. Technical but readable guide for postproduction workers; geared toward entertainment industry.

Television Broadcast. P.S.N. Publications, 2 Park Ave., New York, NY 10016. Geared primarily to television station operations, contains very valuable updates on equipment and production trends. Read regularly now: it's a good habit to start if you want to enter the field.

TV Technology. Industrial Marketing Advisory Services, Inc., 5827 Columbia Pike, Suite 310, Falls Church, VA 22041. Wide range of news and information on new trends and products, including computers, high density television, and computer use.

Videography. P.S.N. Publications, 2 Park Avenue, Suite 1820, New York, NY 10016. Offers particularly strong sections on new technologies and their applications.

Video Systems. Intertect Publishing Corp., P.O. Box 12901, Overland Park, KS 66282. For professionals in nonbroadcast video who have purchasing authority. In-depth coverage of new equipment. Official publication of ITUA, International Television Association.

glossary

A-B roll   A term held over from the time when filmmakers would send a reel of film marked "A" and one marked "B" to the lab, and the reels were synchronized so that the processor could make dissolves between the two. In video, A-B rolling is the capability to dissolve between tapes or between a tape and another source.

above the line personnel   A term indicating personnel (and budget matters relating to those personnel) who are nontechnical, including writers, producers, and performers.

additive color mixture   A mixture of light obtained when pure light waves are mixed.

adjustment cues   Communication from the director to the crew to make some change in focus, framing, and so on. For example, "Camera 1, you're a little out of focus. Would you sharpen up, please?"

AM   Amplitude modulation. A way of impressing a signal (modulating) on an electromagnetic wave by varying the amplitude (meaning height or power of the peaks of the wave).

ampere   A measure of current flow. Most household circuits can handle 15 or 20 amperes (amps).

amplitude   The height of a wave. By extension, a term that can usually be used to indicate the volume or strength of a signal.

analog   A signal that is reproduced through mechanical means to resemble the original source. Essentially, a word used to mean any signal not classified as digital.

animation   The illusion of movement.

aspect ratio   The relationship of height to width. A video screen is 4 units wide by 3 units high.

assemble editing   Adding pieces sequentially onto a tape as you edit. Assemble editing copies all information on the tape: audio, video, and control track.

assistant director   Usually, the person who keeps track of time cues and other details.

audio   The electrical signal to which sound is converted. In other words, the electrical signal representing sound.

audio console   The device that governs the loudness of audio signals and allows them to be mixed together.

audio director   The crew member who sets up audio equipment before a taping or broadcast. The audio director usually operates the audio console during the program. Abbreviated *AD*.

audio-only edit   An edit in which you copy only the audio from one unit to another.

audition channel   A separate audio channel for listening to audio sources off-air.

auto transition   A video switcher control that automatically makes a preselected transition.

auto transition rate   A setting on the switcher that allows you to preprogram how quickly the switcher will make a transition between pictures.

automatic gain control (AGC)   A control that adjusts an incoming audio or video signal, thereby limiting its power or boosting the signal as needed.

back   A light that is shined on top of an object or a performer's head and shoulders to visually separate the object or person from the background.

bandwidth   The slice of the electromagnetic frequency spectrum used to transmit a signal.

barn door   A flap on a lighting instrument that gives you reasonably effective safeguards against light spilling into areas where you don't want it.

base light   The overall light spread over your set or shooting area.

batten   An individual beam that is part of a lighting grid.

bayonet connector   See *BNC connector*.

beam splitter   A prism that separates red, green, and blue from the light picked up by the lens. The light is separated so that it may be processed by the parts of the camera that handle red, green, and blue light.

below-the-line personnel   A term indicating personnel (and budget matters relating to those personnel) who are technically oriented, including engineers and production crew members.

Betacam SP   A videotape format utilizing a compact half-inch tape.

bidirectional   A pickup pattern in which the microphone is sensitive to sound in two directions.

birthmark   A permanent marking, emblazoned by the time code generator, that tells you the time and date when a piece of video was shot.

bit-mapped   A bit-mapped painting is created by activating pixels that, when melded together, create a visual image. The pixels are activated by the movement of some sort of tool, such as a stylus that has been programmed to act as a paintbrush.

blocking   **1:** The part of a rehearsal in which the performers' movements are planned. **2:** Putting your performers through their on-stage motions so that camera angles, shadows, and other problems can be worked out in advance.

BNC connector   A type of connector used at the end of a video cable. Also known as a bayonet connector.

boom   A long pole used to hold a mic.

boom shadow   The problem caused when a mic boom gets between the lighting instruments and the part of the set that is shown on camera.

border area   The entire area of a card or graphic that you want to appear on camera. Put another way, the physical dimensions of the map or card.

breaker box   The central junction of power wires that shuts off power when a line becomes overloaded. Some older buildings still use fuses.

bridge   A stand-up in the middle of a package. Used to help viewers navigate a change in time or location.

broad   A type of flood light with several illuminating lamps inside; it is broadly diffused.

broadcast quality   Video that meets standards set by the NTSC in terms of sync intervals, color level, and so forth.

burn   A "scar" produced when a tube camera is pointed toward a bright light. The image of the bright light will be partially imprinted on the imaging device of the camera and will mar the picture.

camcorder   A combination camera-videotape recorder in one unit.

cam head   A type of camera mount that uses lubricated cams to allow the camera head to move smoothly.

camera control unit (CCU)   A device that controls white and black levels as well as hue and intensity transmitted by the camera.

camera light   A tightly focused light that illuminates only the subject and not the background.

cardioid   Literally "heart shaped"—meaning a microphone pickup pattern that is roughly heart shaped and which accepts sounds from the front and slightly to the sides, but which rejects it from the rear. In reality, a cardioid pattern more closely resembles, in three dimensions, a giant apple, if you pretend the microphone is the stem.

cartridge (cart) machine   A machine that plays back an endless loop of tape, which automatically recues itself at the beginning of the segment.

cassette   A closed reel of tape.

CCD   See *charge-coupled device.*

CCU   See *camera control unit.*

CD-ROM   See *compact disc read-only memory.* Typically stores 600 + megabytes of memory.

cel   Traditional, noncomputer animation in which the individual images were painted on celluloid.

central processing unit (CPU)   The "brains" of the computer that controls the switcher and edit control unit.

character generator (CG)   A device that produces on the video screen letters and sometimes other types of graphics and animation.

charge-coupled device (CCD)   An electronic pickup element (a solid-state chip) in which photosensitive elements translate a visual image into a video signal. Used instead of a pickup tube in some cameras.

cheat   To move performers so that they face the camera a little more directly than they would in a real-life situation.

chief engineer   A high trained technician who is in charge of repair and maintenance of the equipment. The chief engineer in larger operations supervises a staff of technicians.

chip camera   A camera using a charge-coupled device.

chroma   When referring to a video switcher, a control that allows you to select a shade of color (for example, a shade of red).

chroma key   An electronic process that cuts out a certain color, actually producing a "hole" in the picture where another video signal can be inserted.

circuit   An electrical "loop" carrying current. Most dwellings have several circuits, and circuits have a limit on how much current they can carry. This is a primary concern of crews who shoot on remote. Most household circuits can carry 15 or 20 amps.

clip   A control that governs the level at which the key will be inserted.

clip art   Term originally applied to printed art that was meant to be clipped from a page and pasted up onto a newsletter, ad, menu, or other publication. Today, the term is also used to refer to computer graphic images stored for use in desktop publishing or desktop video.

close-up A shot where the camera is fairly tight on the subject. When the subject is a person, the close-up usually is from the shoulders up, with the face filling the screen.

collateral video Types of video, such as stock shots, graphics, animation, and titles that are essential for completion of the program.

color temperature A measure of light that, for practical purposes, indicates its relative bluishness or reddishness. Light that burns at a high color temperature appears blue to the video camera; low-color-temperature light appears red.

compact disc read-only memory (CD-ROM) A compact disc that can be played back but not recorded on.

complex waveform Combinations of various sound waves that add up to produce a total and complete sound.

composite signal A video signal carrying sync and video information.

compression Physically making the amount of data more compact so that the information can be more easily stored and manipulated.

compressions Those parts of a sound wave in which the air molecules are packed tightly together. Compare with *rarefaction*.

condenser mic A microphone that uses a capacitor (*condenser* is an old-fashioned term for *capacitor*) to produce an audio signal.

continuity The overall trueness of scene-to-scene progression. If, for example, your performer is wearing a different necktie on day 1 and day 2, and you edit those shots into a scene that is supposed to take place within the space of an hour, you have a continuity problem.

contrast ratio The difference between very light and very dark parts of the picture. *Ratio* means a comparison of numbers. The ideal contrast ratio for video is often thought of as 30:1, but modern cameras can handle both wider and smaller ratios.

control room The area where the director and the director's staff operate and monitor equipment that chooses the sounds and pictures to go over the air.

control track The track on a videotape containing the pulses that act like electronic sprocket holes, keeping the tape playing at a consistent rate.

convertible cameras Cameras that can be used both in the field and in the studio. Parts for studio use, such as a viewfinder, can be replaced with a field-type eyepiece.

cover video Any video without sound or with simple background noises.

cradle head A cradlelike device that holds the camera on its base and rocks the camera head back and forth.

crawl As applied to graphics, a movement where text moves horizontally across the screen.

critical area The part of a graphic that will definitely be picked up by all home sets. Also called *essential area*.

CU Abbreviation for *close-up*.

cue A channel on an audio console that allows you to hear a sound off air so that you may find the proper place in an audio source at which to start—for example, the beginning of a song on a reel-to-reel tape. Cue can also mean a signal given to someone in the production process, usually the on air performer. ("Cue Bob to start talking.")

cut An instantaneous change from one picture to another.

cut on action A fairly standard technique in which the director makes his or her cut when something is happening, usually when that "something" is action that leads into the next shot. Cutting on action reinforces the concept of constant motion and also makes for an easier edit because you will have a simpler time avoiding easily perceived changes of motion that could appear as a jump cut in static video.

cyc (cyclorama) A curtain behind the set.

decibel A measure of sound loudness. It is a complex measurement, but in the most basic terms 1 or 2 decibels (dB) is usually the smallest difference in sound level the human ear can detect, and 6 dB is usually perceived as a doubling of sound.

denouement The conclusion or resolution of the story.

depth of field The range of distance from the camera lens in which all objects are in good focus.

desktop video Computer-created or enhanced video created on a personal computer (PC).

diaphragm A thin piece of metal, part of the microphone, that vibrates in sympathy with sound waves and is part of the chain of events in which sound is transduced into audio.

diffusion filter A type of filter, usually screwed onto the end of a camera, that makes a scene appear very "soft" by lowering contrast.

digital Digital video uses a computer "brain" to construct a picture using a series of on-and-off pulses. These pulses turn a pixel on or off, and can do so much more quickly than the NTSC scanning beam. Moreover, digital images can be manipulated by the computer. Because the digital image is nothing more than a series of stored numbers, the computer can recalculate these numbers in order to change the image.

digital video effects (DVE) Devices that take a video image and, through computer digitization, manipulate it in various ways, such as shrinking it, rolling it, or tumbling it.

dimmer A variable control switch that adjusts power levels to lighting instruments.

director   The person in charge of the video crew. The director chooses what camera and audio sources are used in a live or taped program and also oversees the activity of the performers.

dissolve   The gradual replacement of one picture with another. Compare with *cut*.

distribution amplifier   A device to boost the video signal when it covers a long distance.

docudrama   A video format that mixes drama and fact.

documentary   A video format that is broadly investigative, requiring deep research into an issue, and that is longer than a standard news package.

downstream   An effect that is the last source added to the video signal.

drop shadow   A border, usually along the bottom right edge of a graphic.

edit   The process of copying a tape segment from the source VTR to the record VTR.

edit control unit   A device governing equipment used in editing. See *editing*.

edit decision list (EDL)   A listing of edit points printed out by the computer or displayed on the computer screen.

editing   The process of rearranging portions of tape into a coherent program.

editing equipment   The tools used to rearrange portions of tape into a coherent program.

editing log   The "spot sheet" or "shot sheet" that lists location of shots on tape, usually by hours, minutes, and seconds, along with the title of each shot and notes for editing.

editing suite   The room(s) where equipment for video-tape editing is located.

editor enable key   A control that allows the video switcher to be controlled by an external source.

EFP   See *electronic field production*.

electronic field production (EFP)   Sometimes, video other than news that is shot with one camera in the field and edited back in the studio. Often the term is used to denote multicamera programs produced out of studio.

electronic news gathering (ENG)   Generally, news shot with a single camera and edited back at the studio. Sometimes used to refer to live, on-the-scene coverage.

ellipsoidal spot   A sharply focused spotlight that has internal shutters to shape the light pattern. Also called *leko*.

ENG   See *electronic news gathering*.

essential area   **1:** Part of a scene to be shot on video, usually a flat graphic, in which the important information must be contained. When making up a graphics card, you usually leave about 15 percent extra space around the essential area. **2:** See *critical area*.

establishing shot   A long shot that lets the viewer become acquainted with the surroundings.

exposition mode   A perspective in which people present themselves to a camera, without any pretense that the camera does not exist. In a television newscast, for example, the camera is simply a substitute eye for the viewer.

external reflector   A type of lighting instrument that has no lens; the light is focused by moving the element and reflector forward or backward.

fade   Going to black from a picture (fading to black) or coming into a picture from black (fading up from black). Note that in most cases, this is considered the only correct usage of the term. You do not, for example, fade between pictures—only to and from black.

fiber-optic   A hair-thin glass fiber that carries a laser signal.

field   One-half the video picture. In the United States, video is scanned in fields, which are either all the odd or all the even lines. Two fields add up to one frame. There are 60 fields, and thus 30 frames, in each second of video.

fill   **1:** As used to refer to a lighting instrument, an instrument that produces a broad, diffused light. **2:** A light that "fills in" some of the harsher shadows but does not wipe out the modeling effect created by the key.

film chain   The equipment used to convert standard film and slides to video. Also known as the *telecine*.

film-style script   A script that does not contain video and audio broken out in separate columns. Rather, a film-style script uses extensive description of the scenes, moods, and so forth in centered text. Also known as *Hollywood script*.

filter wheel   A rotating wheel with a variety of built-in filters that helps the camera adapt to varied lighting conditions. It is usually located directly behind the lens of the video camera.

fishpole   A hand-held pole onto which a microphone is attached. Particularly useful for remote and news audio.

flag   **1:** In audio applications, the station's identifying logo attached to a microphone. **2:** With regard to video-tape flagging, a bend at the edge of the picture caused by time base errors.

flags   In lighting, commercially made flanges that can be used to block off the spillage of light.

flat light   Overall lighting with no highlights. Flat lighting creates a one-dimensional look.

flood   A light that produces a broad, diffuse light. Also called a *soft light*.

floor director   The person who is the director's link between the control room and the people in the studio. The floor director is in charge of all operations on the studio floor.

FM Frequency modulation. A way of impressing a signal (modulating) on an electromagnetic wave by varying the frequency (meaning the number of cycles per second made by the wave).

focal length In technical terms, the distance from the theoretical optical center of the lens to the point at which it is focused when the lens is focused at infinity. In practical terms, the "size" of the lens as it relates to the kind of picture it will produce. A lens with a long focal length will produce a magnified picture; a lens with a short focal length will produce a wide-angle picture.

foldback A system in which audio is fed back to the studio in such a way that it does not cause feedback.

font In informal usage, a typeface style.

footcandle A unit of measurement of the intensity of light, abbreviated "ftc."

F-plug A type of connector that typically has a wire protruding from the center of the male unit.

frame One complete video image, composed of two fields. There are 30 complete video images in American television, and they create the illusion of movement.

frame-by-frame animation Recording one or two frames of animation on videotape, recreating the art (usually by computer) and then recording one or two more frames. Compare with *real-time animation*.

frame synchronizer A device to force the sync signals of incoming video signals into lockstep.

French flags In lighting, a term usually used to refer to a flag that is mounted on the camera lens.

frequency The number of times a wave goes through a complete cycle in one second. As an informal definition, the "pitch" of a sound.

Fresnel lens A type of lighting instrument that uses a lens having concentric rings to focus the beam of light.

F-stop A number indicating the amount of light transmitted through a lens. The f-stop is the number to which you "set" the iris. The larger the f-stop, the smaller the amount of light passing through the lens.

gaffer's clamp A clamp that allows you to mount a lighting instrument virtually anywhere. One end attaches to the lighting instrument; the other end is an alligator clamp.

gain A term referring to the level of a signal. The most popular uses are to "increase the gain" (meaning to boost the level) or "ride the gain" (meaning to maintain steady control over levels). Gain can refer to either audio or video.

gang charger A device to recharge several batteries at the same time.

gel A colored transparency usually fitted into a frame that fits in front of a lighting instrument.

genlock A system that locks together the sync patterns from video sources.

gigahertz A measurement of millions of cycles per second, abbreviated "GHz." See *hertz*.

go to A command on an edit control unit that returns both source and record tapes to the selected edit points.

hard light A spot or directional light.

HDTV See *high-definition television*.

headroom The distance from the top of the head of the person pictured to the top of the screen.

helical scan A method of scanning tape whereby the tape is wrapped in a portion of a spiral around a drum. *Helix* is a synonym for spiral.

hertz A measurement, abbreviated Hz, meaning cycles per second.

high-definition television (HDTV) An emerging technology that provides much greater and clearer resolution than standard television.

HMI element A type of lighting element that burns at outdoor color temperature. *HMI* stands for halogen-metal-iodine.

Hollywood script See *film-style script*.

hue When referring to a control on the video switcher, a control that allows you to select a certain part of the color spectrum (say, for example, if you want to choose a color to fill in a graphic).

hum bars Bands of interference sometimes caused by placing the monitor next to the VTR.

imaging device The electronic component that produces the basic video signal. The imaging device is one of the first steps in translating light images into electronic images.

impedance Resistance to current. Generally used to refer to various types of mics. Most are low impedance; a few are high impedance. An impedance mismatch results in a weak, buzzing, or distorted sound.

incident light Light that emanates directly from a lighting instrument. Compare with *reflected light*.

"in" point The place where the edit is to begin, set in the memory of the edit control unit.

insert editing An editing process in which part of the signal on tape—video, either audio track, or video and audio—can be copied from one unit to another.

institutional video Programs made in-house by companies, schools, hospitals, and other institutions for viewing by their employees or as part of a public relations effort.

interactive video Programs that allow a viewer to watch a presentation and choose which "branch" he or she would like to follow. Often used in training to simulate various situations, such as what decisions a pilot should make when flying an airplane.

integrated service digital network (ISDN) A concept that promises to combine voice, data, and visual images over one fiber-optic cable. If an ISDN network were to evolve, audio (including phone messages), video, and computer transmission would all be melded together into the same carrier.

internal reflector A lighting instrument with the reflecting element built inside; generally the internal reflector is focused through a lens.

inverse-square law A formula that tells us that as the distance from the light source is doubled, the intensity of the light is cut to one-quarter.

IRE A measurement of signal level, named after the Institute of Radio Engineers.

iris A variable opening of a camera that governs the amount of light entering the lens.

iron oxide Rust; used as a coating on many kinds of audio tape and videotape.

ISDN See *integrated service digital network.*

jump cut A generally distracting movement caused when tape is edited together and the people or objects on camera move slightly. Usually, cover video is used to disguise a jump cut.

Kelvin scale A scale that is used to measure color temperature. It is like the Celsius scale, except that 0 Kelvin is at absolute zero, the coldest point to which anything can be cooled.

key **1:** As used in reference to lighting, the principal source of illumination; it is a relatively harsh light and casts shadows that add dimension to the subject. **2:** A switch, often a lever, that turns a signal on and off and directs it into the program channel or the audition channel. **3:** The process of cutting out a portion of the video picture and replacing it with another picture.

key bus The bus that lets you select the picture or graphic that will be keyed into the picture.

key level An adjustment that sets the level at which one picture will cut out and be replaced with another picture. This allows for a crisp, distortion-free key.

key mask An advanced function on a switcher that allows you to hide part of an image that you do not want to use in your key.

key memory A control that allows the switcher to remember a series of commands and execute them in the programmed order.

kilohertz A measure of thousands of cycles per second, abbreviated kHz. See *hertz.*

lavaliere A type of microphone originally worn like a necklace, but now generally clipped to the talent's tie, jacket, shirt, or blouse.

L-cut A term that is a throwback to film days, when film was cut and pasted together in either a forward or backward *L* to make sound and picture change at different times. Today, the term is used to denote a transition where audio changes before video or video changes before audio.

lead-in A line spoken by an anchor that sets the scene for a taped piece.

leading space Room in the picture provided for a moving object or performer, showing what the object or performer is moving into. This mimics eye pattern and makes the shot appear natural to viewers.

leko See *ellipsoidal spot.*

lens A device that gathers the light and focuses it. On a video camera, a lens often refers to what is really a number of individual lenses mounted in a tube.

lighting control panel A group of controls that govern the amount of current being fed to a particular lighting instrument or to the entire setup of lighting instruments.

lighting director The crew member who selects, positions, and adjusts the lighting instruments. The lighting director is responsible for a great deal of the overall "look" of the show.

light meter A device for measuring reflected and incident light.

live and live-on-tape switching A method of putting together a program. The director chooses which camera goes on the air as the show unfolds. The director also selects appropriate shots or sequences of shots, and the program either is transmitted live or is recorded on tape as it happens.

log A listing of shots taken. Used for locating items on a videotape. See *editing log.*

long shot A shot in which a great deal of the background is included. When used to refer to a shot of a person, the shot usually shows the whole person and some of his or her surroundings. A long shot is useful to show the scene or setting.

look ahead A capability that allows you to see what image will appear on the air in advance and "swap" it with the preset image.

lower-third graphics Titles used to identify a scene or person.

LS Abbreviation for *long shot.*

luminance The amount of light in a color; the brightness of a color. A luminance control adds brightness to the hue you have selected.

luminance key   A type of key in which the picture processing equipment cuts out a part of the original picture when the second image reaches a certain voltage.

M-II   A type of videocassette format.

mark in   A control on the edit control unit used to mark the point where the edit will begin.

mark out   A control on the edit control unit used to mark the point where the edit will end.

mark split   A command on certain edit control units that allows you to split the video and audio edit points and create an *L-cut*. See *L-cut*.

master control   The place where engineering functions are carried out. Master control usually, though not always, adjoins the studio.

matte   A term with several meanings, but very often used to indicate a color used to fill a hole cut by a key.

medium shot   A fairly close shot. When used to refer to a shot of a person, a medium shot usually shows the subject from about the waist up.

megahertz   A measure of thousands of cycles per second, abbreviated MHz. See *hertz*.

menu   Literally, a list of things offered. Used in video graphics to describe menu-driven systems, where a non-artist can create artistic effects by choosing them from a menu.

miniphone-plug   A small connector commonly used to terminate a line that carries audio.

mix bus   The collection of circuits that allows the person using the video switcher to select the shots that will go over the air.

MOC   Old-fashioned term for *man on camera*, meaning performer on camera. Largely replaced by the abbreviation OC (on camera).

model release   A document signed by a person to grant you permission to use his or her image.

modulation   The electrical imprint of a sound signal on the audio wave.

moire   See *strobe*.

mouse   A sliding table-top device used to move a pointer or other point of reference across a computer screen.

moving coil   A microphone pickup device in which a coil is attached to the diaphragm and audio is produced as the moving coils cut through electronic lines of force.

MS   Abbreviation for *medium shot*.

multichannel console   An audio mixing board that incorporates several channels; especially useful in the production of complex audio programs and music.

narrative   A story line.

nonlinear   Program material that does not have to be edited "in a line" (the literal meaning of *linear*). New digital editing equiment, for example, allows you to shorten material in the middle of a program without having to reconstruct—in a linear fashion—everything that follows. The digitally stored material expands or contracts at your will, meaning that you do not necessarily have to work from beginning to end.

noseroom   The space into which a subject can look when his or her head is turned to the side.

observational mode   A method of shooting in which the camera is an observer—never directly addressed but acting as a surrogate person on the scene.

OC   Abbreviation for *on camera*.

octave   A doubling or halving of an existing frequency.

off-line editing   Cuts-only editing that is done with an edit control unit. The term is usually taken to mean editing done as a "rough cut" before the final edit.

omnidirectional   Describes a microphone that picks up sounds from all directions equally well.

omni light   A type of lighting instrument that can project narrowly or widely focused light.

on-line editing   Editing done with a switcher, usually featuring dissolves, graphics, and other special effects. In general usage, the term means the final edit.

OS   Abbreviation for *over-the-shoulder shot*.

"out" point   The place where the edit is to end, set in the memory of the edit control unit.

pack   running a new videotape fast forward and rewinding it to the beginning to ensure even distribution, or a good "pack," of tape on the reel.

package   A news report that usually is a mixture of sound bites, voice overs, and on-camera reports. It is typically signed off by the reporter.

paint effect system   A system that produces video graphics, usually with the aid of an electronic stylus (pen). Paint systems allow you to create a number of images plus a translucent effect.

pan   A side-to-side sweeping movement of the camera.

pan lock   A device that, when activated, prevents side-to-side sweeping of the camera.

parabolic reflector   A dish-shaped reflector that collects sounds and bounces them back toward a microphone mounted inside.

patch bay   A bank of receptacles, looking something like an old-fashioned telephone switchboard, into which you plug cables connecting the audio console to other equipment. The most common purpose of a patch bay is to break the connection that usually exists between one piece of equipment and the control that governs it. Patching would allow you to use a different control to govern a piece of equipment than the one that is hard-wired.

pattern control   A control on the switcher that allows you to select a pattern to use in a wipe. For example, you may be able to choose among horizontal, vertical, and circular.

pedestal   1: The basic black level; the lowest amount of black that can be reproduced while still maintaining a usable video signal. **2:** When referring to a camera movement, vertically raising or lowering the camera itself—not tilting the lens up or down, but raising or lowering the whole camera.

persistence of vision   The phenomenon whereby images "stored" in the optical processing centers of our brains are perceived as continuous motion if the images are changed at a fairly rapid pace.

perspective   The way a camera—and therefore the viewer—"sees" a scene.

phase/phasing problem   Phase is the motion of a wave; when two mics are "out of phase" it means that they are picking sound up at slightly different times—at different points in the phase of the sound waves—therefore, some sounds are canceling each other out.

phone connector   A connector with a protruding plug that is commonly used to carry audio.

pickup element   A device (either a tube or a charge-coupled device) that transduces light into a video signal.

pickup pattern   A representation of the directions from which a microphone receives sound. The most common pickup patterns are omnidirectional (from all sides equally well), bidirectional (from two sides), and cardioid (a heart-shaped pattern that picks up sound from in front). Pickup patterns are also known as *polar patterns.*

pickup tube   A device that scans a photosensitive target with an electron gun to produce pulses of differing voltage (the video signal) representing the visual image captured by the lens.

pin   To make a light very narrowly focused.

Plumbicon   A trademarked name for a type of camera tube.

point-of-view (POV) shot   A type of shot in the subjective mode, directly imitating what a person would see. A POV shot might, for instance, depict an attack by shooting straight up from the ground as a mugger with a knife slashes down at the camera.

polar pattern   See *pickup pattern.*

portable camera   A camera designed to be used for hand-held work. Also referred to as a *hand-held camera.*

portable mixer   A small audio console, usually used in remote applications.

pot   An abbreviation for *potentiometer.* A device, either a circular knob or a vertical fader, that turns volume up and down. Sometimes the term *pot* is only used to refer to the circular control, with *vertical fader* referring specifically to the vertical control.

potentiometer   A device that offers varying resistance; in video, the device that governs an audio signal. The potentiometer, generally called a "pot," is twisted or raised to adjust the volume of the signal.

preroll   The amount of time allotted for a tape to come up to speed. For example, when editing you usually need about 5 seconds of preroll for the mechanics to get up to speed and stop jiggling the videotape as they pass through the mechanism.

preset   Usually, the monitor that shows the next shot to go over the air or onto the final tape.

preset background bus   The bus that selects the next video to be taken when the next transition is made.

preview   Usually, the monitor that shows any shot punched up for off-air or off-program viewing. Often, the preset and program monitors are the same thing.

primary color   Red, green, and blue—the colors from which all other colors are produced in an additive color mixture.

principal photography   Shooting of the major scenes, often with the large pieces of scenery in the background. After principal photography, close-ups and reaction shots can be added.

private line   A transmission line not intended for broadcast, sometimes not really a line made of wire (but a radio transmission) between talent and studio.

processing amplifier   A device that stabilizes the sync information and allows a final adjustment of color hue and saturation. Some units provide "drop-out" compensation to remove any video noise or loss of parts of the picture caused by erosion of the videotape.

producer   The person in charge of a program, whether the program is a newscast, a talk show, or a documentary. The producer dictates the main theme of the show, handles budgeting, and in general is the final decision maker.

program background bus   The bus that selects the main picture going out to the transmitter or the tape on which the program is being recorded.

program channel   The channel that carries the signal that goes out over the air or to the main recording unit.

prompting device   A mechanism that displays lines to talent so that talent can look at the lens and still deliver the lines. Most prompters used to have cameras trained on sheets of script fed through on a conveyor belt, but modern prompters use text taken off the computer.

protocol A way for electronic devices to "talk" with each other. Often used to refer to the interface between the edit control unit and the switcher.

pulling focus When the camera operator refocuses the lens on a second subject, pulling the initial subject out of focus.

pumping in An effect that comes about when an edit is made between a long shot and a close-up shot from the same angle. The result is that the subject "jumps out" at the viewer. Sometimes, this is useful as a special effect but in most cases is best avoided.

quad Literally, four; in video, refers to a four-head machine.

quartz elements A common type of lamp that uses a quartz tube which may hold a highly reactive and excitable halogen gas. This combination of elements causes the lamp to burn very brightly.

rarefaction That part of the sound wave where air molecules are pulled far apart. Compare with *compressions.*

RCA connector A device used to couple cables to machines or to couple cables together. It consists of a rigid metal prong in a segmented metal sheath.

reaction shot A video shot of a performer reacting to what another performer is saying or to an action happening on screen.

ready cues Reminders by the director to stand by to perform a certain action. For example, "Ready to take camera 1 . . ."

real time **1:** The actual time needed to play out an event as it would happen in reality. Generally, you do not want to shoot scenes in real time, because so much of real-time action is boring (a 30-second shot of someone descending a staircase, for example). Careful editing can shorten events and make them more palatable to viewers. Note, however, that there are occasions where you do want to shoot in real time and perhaps exaggerate time, such as when you are trying to build suspense. **2:** In animation, animation played back in actual time—a 10-second sequence plays back in 10 seconds, for example. Some animation systems must be recorded frame by frame, stopping the tape and/or changing the computer image continually.

real-time animation Animation in which the computer creates the entire sequence and plays it back as it will appear—over a series of several seconds, usually. This requires much more computing power and memory than frame-by-frame animation, where images are recreated and laid down one or two frames of video at a time.

record unit The videotape recorder which, in the editing function, records the final program.

reference When used as in *reference black* and *reference white*, the shades of those colors that will be used to gauge the top of the white scale and bottom of the black scale. Many producers like to have a small black and a small white object in the scene so that they can set a full range of reference white and black.

reference black The darkest part of the properly adjusted video signal. Basically, the same as *pedestal.*

reference white The brightest part of the properly adjusted video signal.

reflected light Light that bounces off an object. It is reflected light that really paints the visual images seen by our eyes and the camera.

reflector Any device that bounces light. Commercial reflectors are available, although many producers simply use cardboard covered with foil.

registration Adjusting the camera so that it accurately reproduces shades of gray and colors.

reverse shot A shot taken of the interviewer, sometimes (when using single-camera video) after the interview segment has been completed. The reverse shot is then added in for visual variety and to simplify editing.

RF connector A connector that terminates a line carrying RF (radio frequency) information, meaning the complete, modulated television signal.

ribbon mic A microphone that uses a thin metal ribbon to sense sound waves.

riding levels Keeping close watch and making frequent adjustments so that audio levels do not go too high or too low. Also known as *riding gain.*

roll An effect where visual information moves up the screen, although it can roll down too. Credits at the end of a program are an example of a roll.

rough cut A first edit of a show that can be changed later.

rule of thirds An informal rule relating to graphics. In most aesthetically balanced shots, the important details usually appear on the lines that trisect the frame.

rundown A listing for stories to be played during a newscast.

sampling During a sample, the computer takes a representative portion of the analog signal and stores it in memory. The faster the sampling speed, the greater the fidelity (literally, "faithful" reproduction of the original sound or video). These samples are then encoded, meaning they are put into computer on-off pulse language.

satellite news vehicle (SNV) A vehicle equipped for transmitting a live signal via satellite or back to the station's antenna.

Saticon A trademarked name for a type of camera tube.

saturation   The intensity of the color, usually as measured by the vectorscope.

scanning area   The part of the graphic that will be picked up by a typical studio camera.

scanning pattern   The method whereby the image is scanned, in alternate odd-and-even fields, by the camera and then, in a reversal of the process, onto the video screen.

scoop   The most common type of flood light, so called because of its scooplike shape.

scrim   A sheet of spun-fiber material, often held by a metal frame, that slides into slots on the front of the scoop. It softens the light and provides some measure of protection should the lighting element implode.

SCV   See *single-camera video*.

self key   An effect where the fill signal is combined with the signal that cuts the hole in the background.

servo   Any device that governs a function by remote control.

SFX   Abbreviation for *sound effects*.

shot box   A device that allows the operator to preset several shots and select them by pressing a button; the camera "remembers" the series of shots.

shot sheet   A listing of in and out video cuts. Usually used in reference to new tapes. Also known as an *editing log* and *spot sheet*.

shotgun   A type of microphone usually suspended from a pole or boom and used to pick up sounds at fairly long distance. So named because of its resemblance to a long-barreled firearm.

shuttle   Movement of tape from one spool to another.

side light   A lighting instrument shining from the side, often used to separate talent from the background.

signal-to-noise ratio   The comparison of how much signal—meaning actual video or audio—to extraneous interference, or "noise." High signal, low noise is best.

sine wave   A wave that represents a complete cycle of sound or electricity from zero to positive peak to zero to negative peak back to zero.

single-camera video (SCV)   A method of production in which one camera is used to take all the shots, and then the order of the program is rearranged using editing equipment. The editor (meaning the person) figuratively "cuts and pastes" the program segments in the order they'll run.

skew   A problem, the symptom of which is flagging (a bend in the picture) caused by time base errors.

skin tone   The shade of the performers' skin. It's important to keep lighting conditions and camera adjustments consistent in order to keep skin tones comparable from one scene to another.

slate   **1:** A visual indicator of what's on the tape. It used to be on an actual slate chalkboard, but today slates are almost always electronically generated with some sort of automatic countdown. **2:** To "slate" something orally, announce to the camera the take number and count down.

SOT   Abbreviation for *sound-on-tape*.

sound bite   A segment of video that includes a shot of a person talking along with that person's voice. In other words, sound and picture on the same segment.

sound-on-tape (SOT)   A videotape played back with picture and sound, as in the case of someone speaking.

source unit   The videotape recorder that is used to play back the raw material during the editing process.

special effects generator (SEG)   A term sometimes used to refer to a switcher capable of producing special effects. More often, a term referring to the part of the switcher that generates effects such as split screens.

spot   A light that throws a highly directional, focused beam. Also called a *directional* or *hard light*.

spot sheet   See *editing log* or *shot sheet*.

stand-up   A term used to describe when a reporter delivers lines straight to the camera.

star filter   Devices that create multipointed "stars" where light is intense.

Steadicam   A device to smooth movements of a camera.

stealing seconds   Cutting away seconds, here and there, that are not necessary. Stealing seconds is a valuable skill, particularly in commercial production. See *real time*.

steering ring   A ring on the camera pedestal that lets you change the direction of the casters and point the camera pedestal, in the direction you want to move before you push or pull it.

still frame   A frame stored digitally and displayed with no motion.

storyboard   A series of drawings used to represent the shots in a program.

strobe   When used to refer to "strobing," or "moire" on clothing, a pulsing effect where a tight pattern produces an apparent movement on the screen. The problem of strobing can often be overcome by not wearing clothing with a herringbone design or other tight pattern.

studio   As commonly used in video production, the room where performers and the camera crew are located.

studio camera   A large camera, usually of very high quality, used exclusively in the studio. It is not suited or used for hand-held work.

studio pedestal The mobile camera base used for high-quality studio cameras.

subjective mode A method of shooting in which the camera is put in the position of a person, simulating his or her vision under a variety of situations.

S-VHS A high-quality version of VHS (video home system). S-VHS provides higher quality than the consumer-grade VHS.

switcher A device that allows the director to choose among several video signals by pressing various buttons and operating levers.

taking cues The director's actual command to perform the action. For example, "Take camera 1 . . ."

talent All-purpose word used to describe any performer who appears on camera or speaks over a mic in a voice-over.

tally light A light that is activated when the camera is on-air.

target The part of the pickup element that receives the image focused by the lens and converts it to an electronic video signal.

task-oriented sequence The method of editing and producing in which you schedule events and tasks in the order most productive and convenient for the producers and crew, rather than adhering to the order of events that occur during the final show. For example, if you have several voice-over segments, you would be operating in task-oriented sequence if you taped them all in one day, when the announcer was available and the equipment set up, rather than recalling the announcer when you reached the points where voice-over was scheduled.

tear (key tear) A raggedness at the edge of a key.

technical director A crewperson who operates the switcher and is in charge of most technical operations in the control room. Abbreviated *TD*.

telecine See *film chain*.

television Generally, the term used to describe programs that are broadcast and transmitted to the home by video. The term *video* is coming into widespread use as a replacement for *television* because it refers to other functions as well.

tell story A TV story read straight to the camera, without any video covering the anchor. Sometimes called a *reader*.

test and tone A test pattern and a test tone laid down at the beginning of many tapes so that the playback engineer can adjust the colors and the volume level on the playback unit.

three-point lighting Illuminating people or objects pictured on video from the points, using a combination of harsh and soft light to provide shape, depth, and detail

and eliminate harsh shadows. Three-point lighting is necessary because the camera does not perceive depth and shapes in the same way as does the human eye.

tilt An up-and-down sweeping motion of the camera.

tilt lock The device that prevents tilting of the camera. The tilt lock is an important control because it prevents the camera from accidentally tilting upward and pointing toward a lighting instrument.

time base The information on the tape that governs the speed of the tape as it is played back by the VTR.

time base corrector (TBC) A device that stores and emits the video image on a regular basis to keep the speed of the frames stable. This prevents jitter and other time base errors.

time cues Indicators of how much time is remaining, usually given by the (floor) director or the assistant director and passed along to talent.

tongue A movement made by a camera mounted on a crane.

touchscreen A device that allows the user to point to an answer on a monitor, rather than accessing a computerized system via a keyboard or mouse.

tracking The path of the tape through the VTR. A tracking adjustment is used when the tape is not tracking correctly and a distorted "band" appears.

transduction The process of changing one form of energy to another.

trim Fine adjustment of an edit point. Trim usually moves a tape forward or backward by one frame.

tube The device inside a camera that converts the image into video.

two-column script The most common format for video: video commands are on the left, audio commands are on the right.

UHF connector A connector used on a video line, larger but similar in shape to an F-plug.

umbrella An umbrella-shaped lighting instrument that reflects light backward; a good source of soft light.

upstream Used to describe an effect that is placed into a picture early in the chain of events, such as an upstream key.

VCR Abbreviation for *videocassette recorder*.

vector-based Vector-based, or drawing, graphics programs are those that use a mathematical formula to store images. The artist usually uses the stylus to enter points that the computer memorizes and stores; lines and other patterns are then computed from point to point. The advantage of a vector-based program is that because the images exist as mathematical equations, they can quickly be adjusted—enlarged, downsized, or even rotated in three dimensions without distortion.

vectorscope   A device that measures attributes of color. Each primary additive color—red, blue, and green—is represented by a dot on the vectorscope screen. Also represented are the complementary colors—magenta, cyan, and yellow. The rotational location (their position around the clockface) of the bright dots measures the shade or tint of colors. A vectorscope allows you to adjust the balance of hues of colors coming from various cameras.

video   In the most basic meaning, the picture portion of a television signal. The word has evolved to mean non-broadcast applications of what we commonly call television. As of late, the word has been broadened to mean almost all applications of moving pictures and sound on the screen, although television is usually used to describe what is sent to home sets by broadcast or cable.

video news release (VNR)   A video piece prepared by a public relations practitioner and sent to TV news organizations in the hope that the information will be aired.

video only edit   An edit where you copy only the picture portion of the tape from one unit to another.

videotape recorder (VTR)   A device used to record and playback video tapes.

vidicon   A particular variety of camera tube with a target and scanning gun.

viewfinder   The device that shows the operator what the camera is "seeing."

virtual reality   An emerging technology in which a headset or other device recreates an entire video-based environment.

VNR   See *video news release.*

VO   Abbreviation for *voice-over.*

voice-over (VO)   A segment where the announcer reads over the video.

volume unit (VU) meter   A meter that gives a visual representation of sound level.

VTR   Abbreviation for *videotape recorder.*

watt   A measurement of total power consumption.

wattage   A measure of power. Amperage is part of the formula used to compute wattage.

waveform monitor   A device that measures the luminance (intensity) of the signal. It also graphically displays the "hidden" commands governing the transmission of the signal. The screen of the waveform monitor shows an electronic display on a scale ranging from -40 at the bottom to 100 at the top. The scale is in increments called IRE (see *IRE*).

wheel number   A readout of the position of a tape produced by a device that counts the number of revolutions made by the spinning hub of the VCR.

white balance   A control that allows you to "tell" the camera what mixtures of light it should perceive as white under the prevailing color conditions so that the camera can see all the other colors accurately.

wind filter   A covering, usually of foam, that muffles the sound of wind striking the mic.

wipe   A type of special effect whereby you take one picture and insert it into another picture using a preselected pattern. The most common type of wipe is a moving split screen, where one image "wipes" across the screen, replacing what's on screen as it moves.

wireless   A term usually used to refer to wireless microphones.

workprint   1: A preliminary editing job done as a rough cut. 2: An experimental edited program designed for viewing and eventual alteration.

XLR connector   A connector used in the transmission of audio.

XLS   Abbreviation for *extreme long shot.*

zoom   A movement in which the camera operator magnifies the shot or makes the shot wider by changing magnification. As a verb, the word is commonly used in phrases such as "zoom in" and "zoom out."

zoom ratio   A numerical representation of how many times you can increase the focal length of the lens. For example, a lens with a wide focal length of 20mm that can be zoomed in to a telescopic photo length of 200mm has a zoom ratio of 10:1.